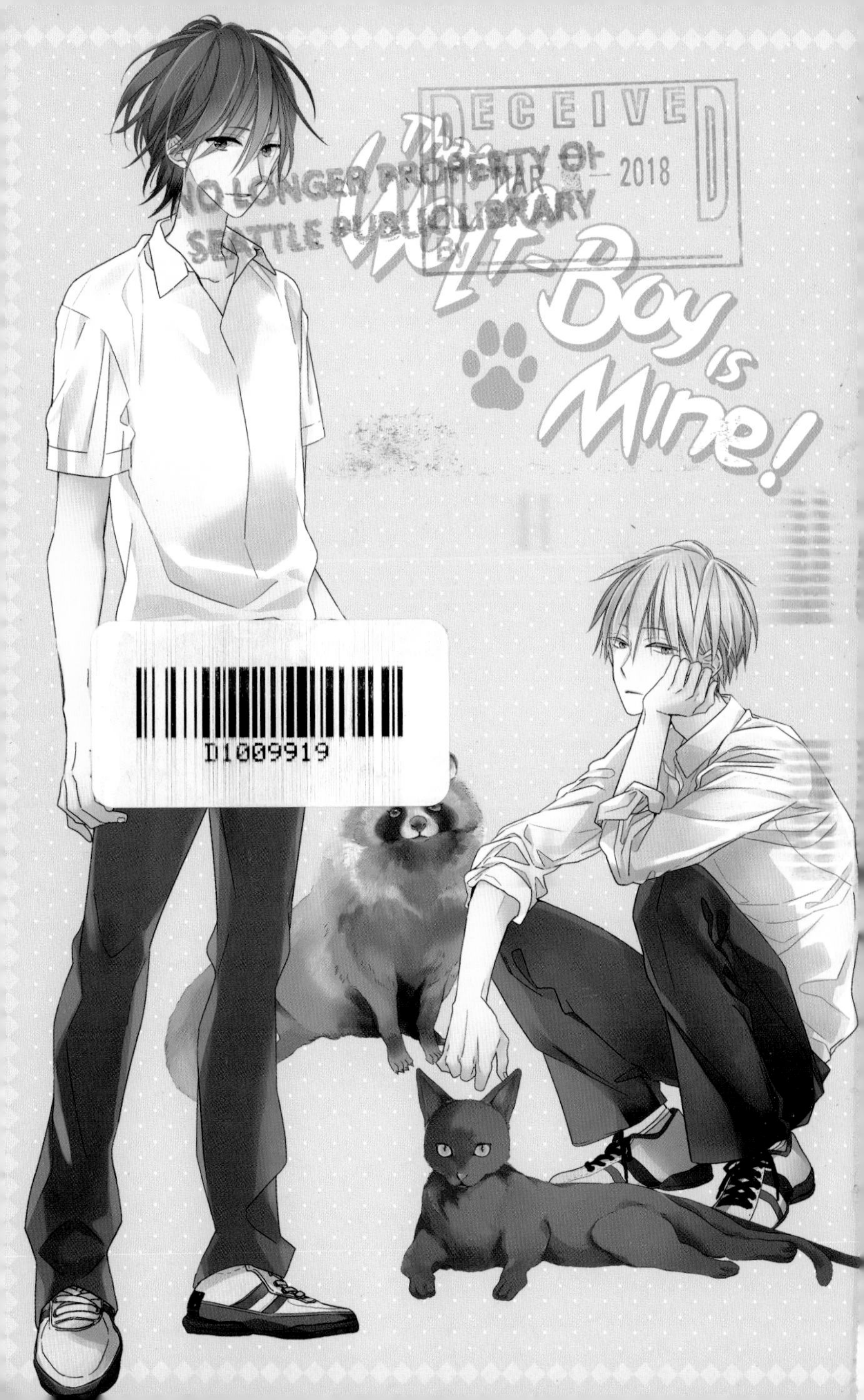
This Wolf-Boy is Mine!

# That Wolf-Boy is Mine!

## Contents

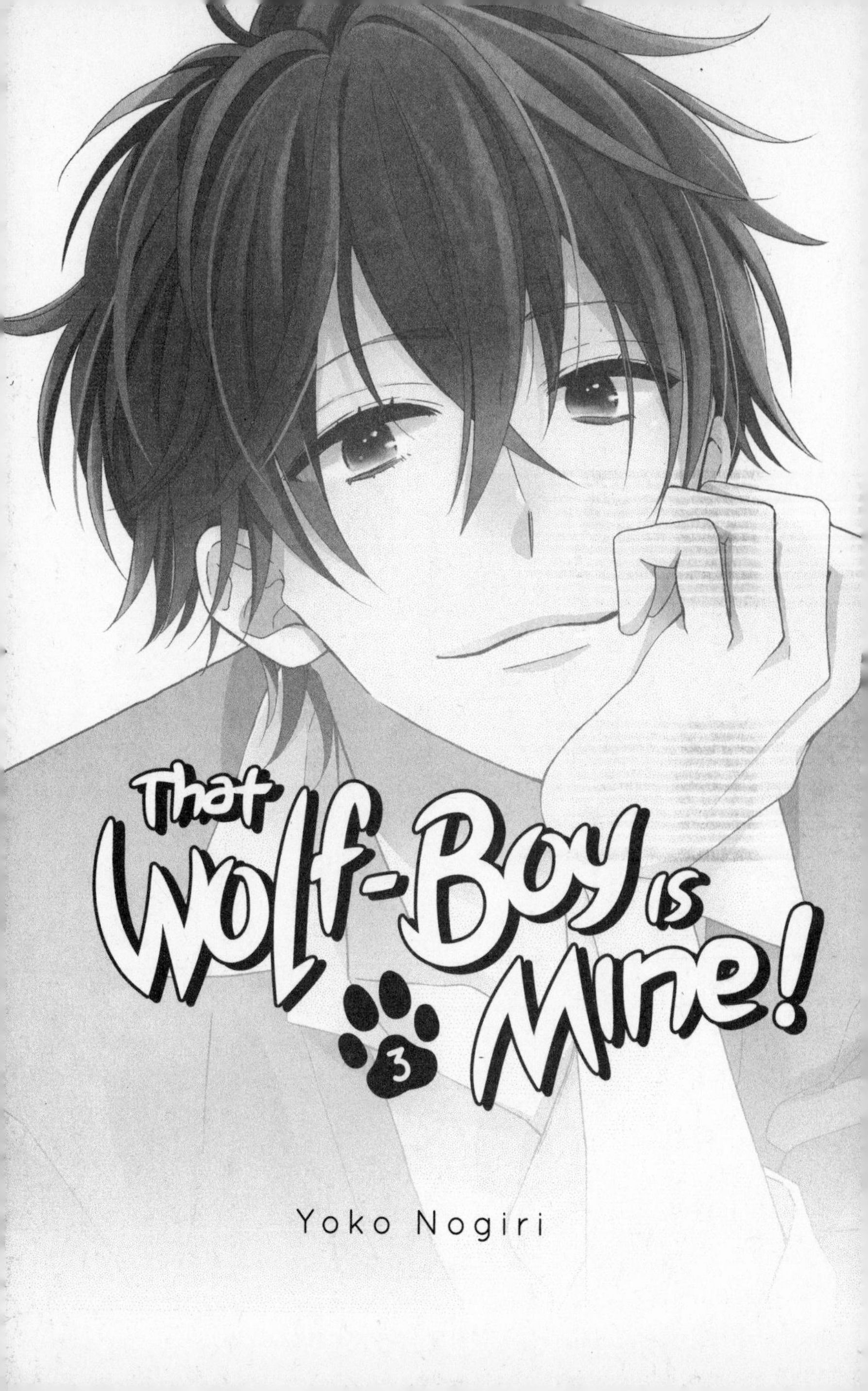
That Wolf-Boy is Mine!
3
Yoko Nogiri

# CHARACTER & STORY

**Sharing a secret with extraordinary boys?!**

# If you say no, I'll eat you up.

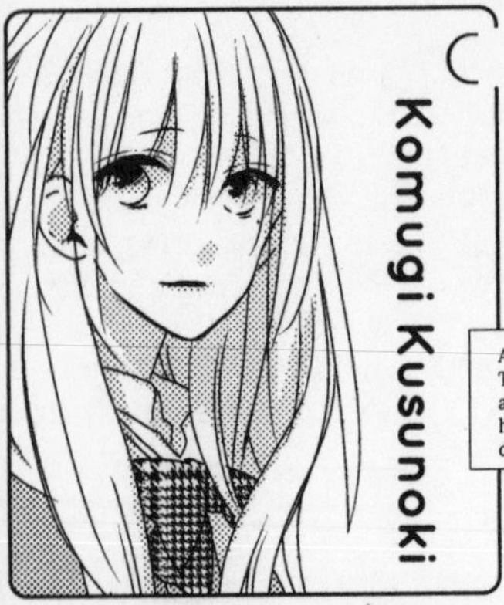

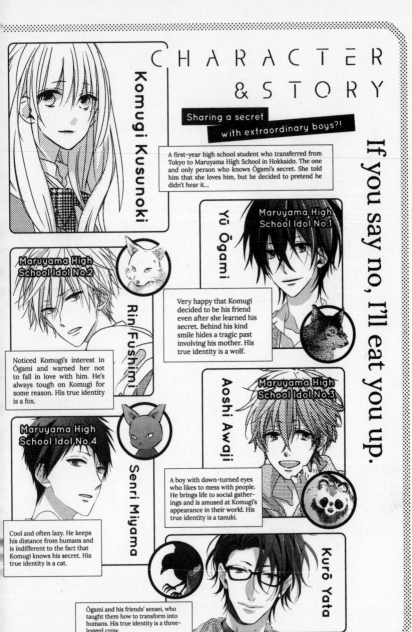

## Komugi Kusunoki

A first-year high school student who transferred from Tokyo to Maruyama High School in Hokkaido. The one and only person who knows Ōgami's secret. She told him that she loves him, but he decided to pretend he didn't hear it...

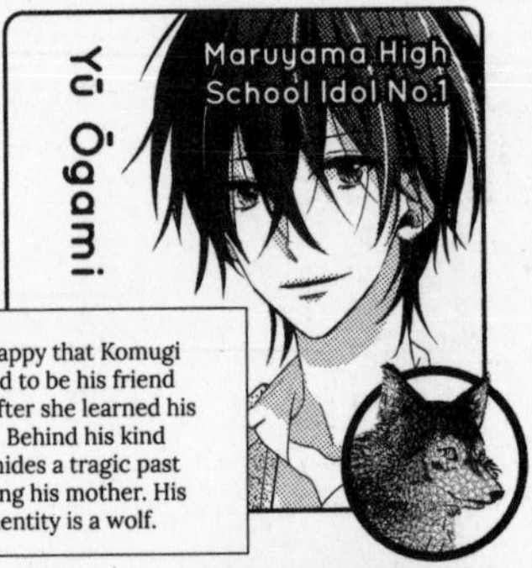

## Yū Ōgami

Maruyama High School Idol No.1

Very happy that Komugi decided to be his friend even after she learned his secret. Behind his kind smile hides a tragic past involving his mother. His true identity is a wolf.

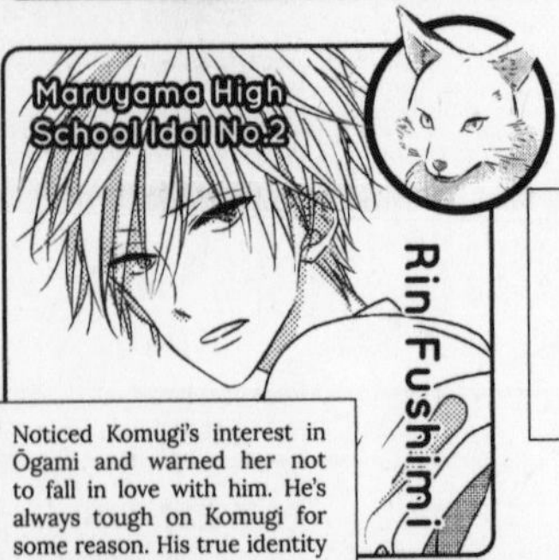

## Rin Fushimi

Maruyama High School Idol No.2

Noticed Komugi's interest in Ōgami and warned her not to fall in love with him. He's always tough on Komugi for some reason. His true identity is a fox.

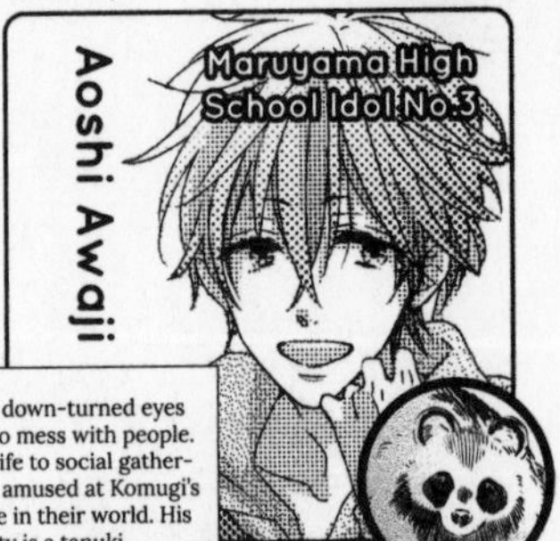

## Aoshi Awaji

Maruyama High School Idol No.3

A boy with down-turned eyes who likes to mess with people. He brings life to social gatherings and is amused at Komugi's appearance in their world. His true identity is a tanuki.

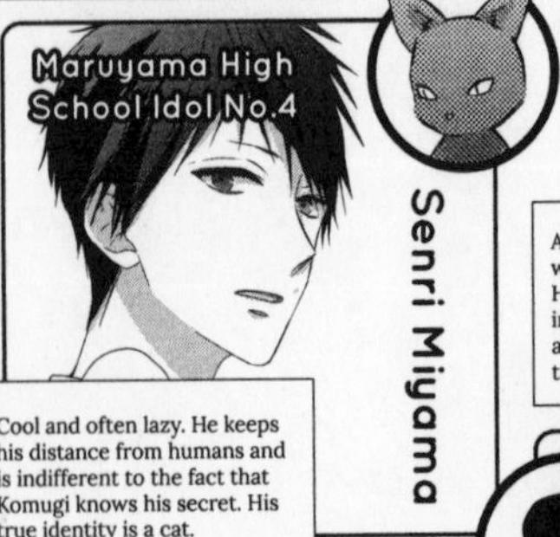

## Senri Miyama

Maruyama High School Idol No.4

Cool and often lazy. He keeps his distance from humans and is indifferent to the fact that Komugi knows his secret. His true identity is a cat.

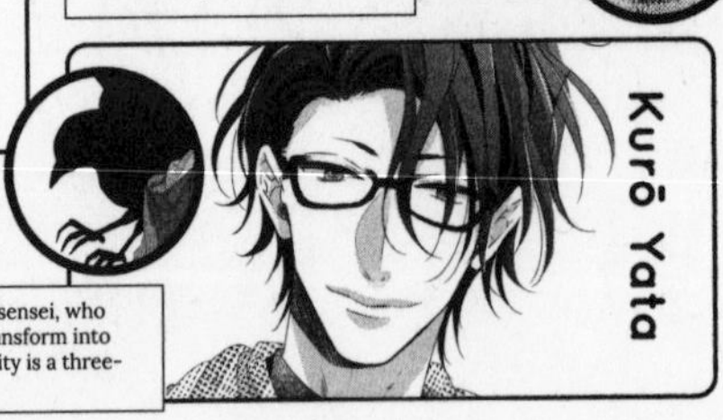

## Kurō Yata

Ōgami and his friends' sensei, who taught them how to transform into humans. His true identity is a three-legged crow.

The boy Komugi meets at her new school...is actually a wolf! Despite knowing his true identity, she can't help but feel close to him. When she confesses her love to him, he flat-out rejects her.

Then, out of the blue, Yata appears. He's the man who taught Yū Rin, Aoshi, and Senri how to transform into their human forms. Yata expresses an interest in Komugi, the girl who can't be hypnotized. But her heart is preoccupied with her longing to be by Yū's side.

When Yū starts to fear that Komugi is becoming distant, the way he reaches out to her ends up hurting her even more. She runs away in tears, straight into the arms of...?!

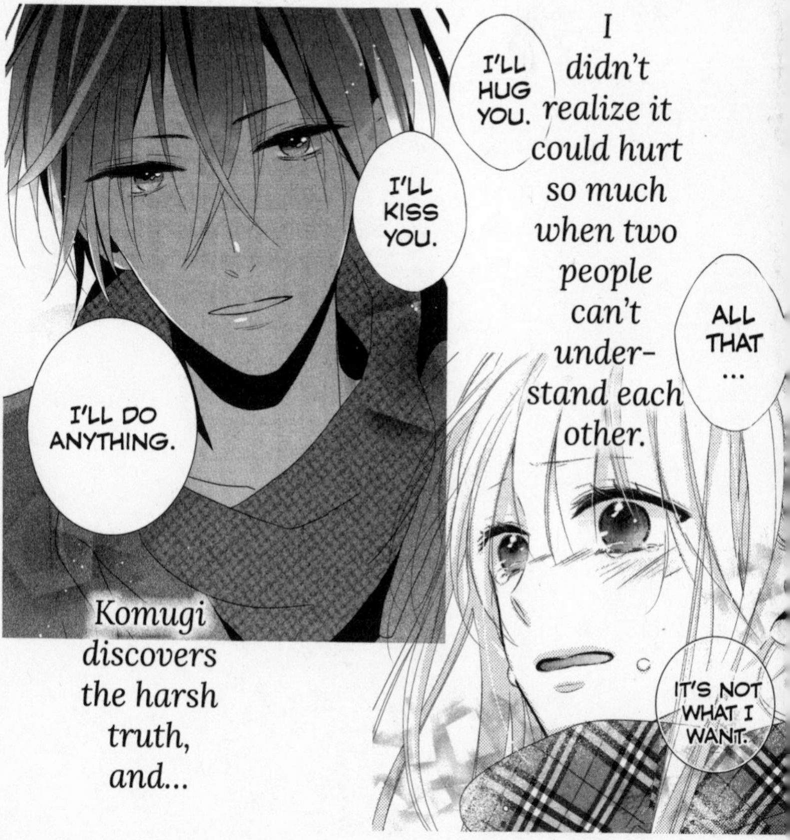
I didn't realize it could hurt so much when two people can't under-stand each other.
ALL THAT ...
IT'S NOT WHAT I WANT.
I'LL HUG YOU.
I'LL KISS YOU.
I'LL DO ANYTHING.
Komugi discovers the harsh truth, and...

# That Wolf-Boy is Mine!

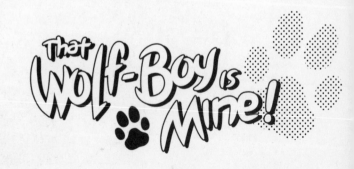

# Chapter 9

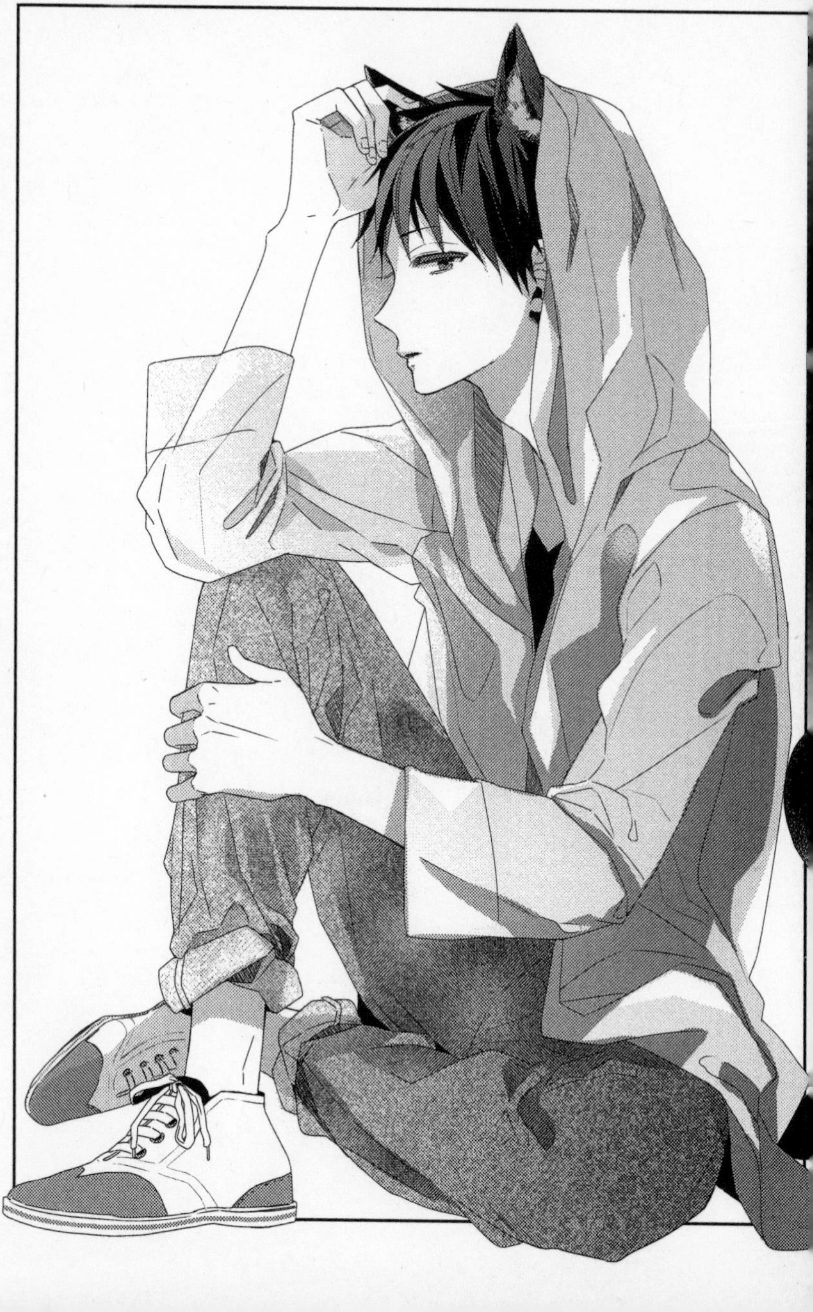

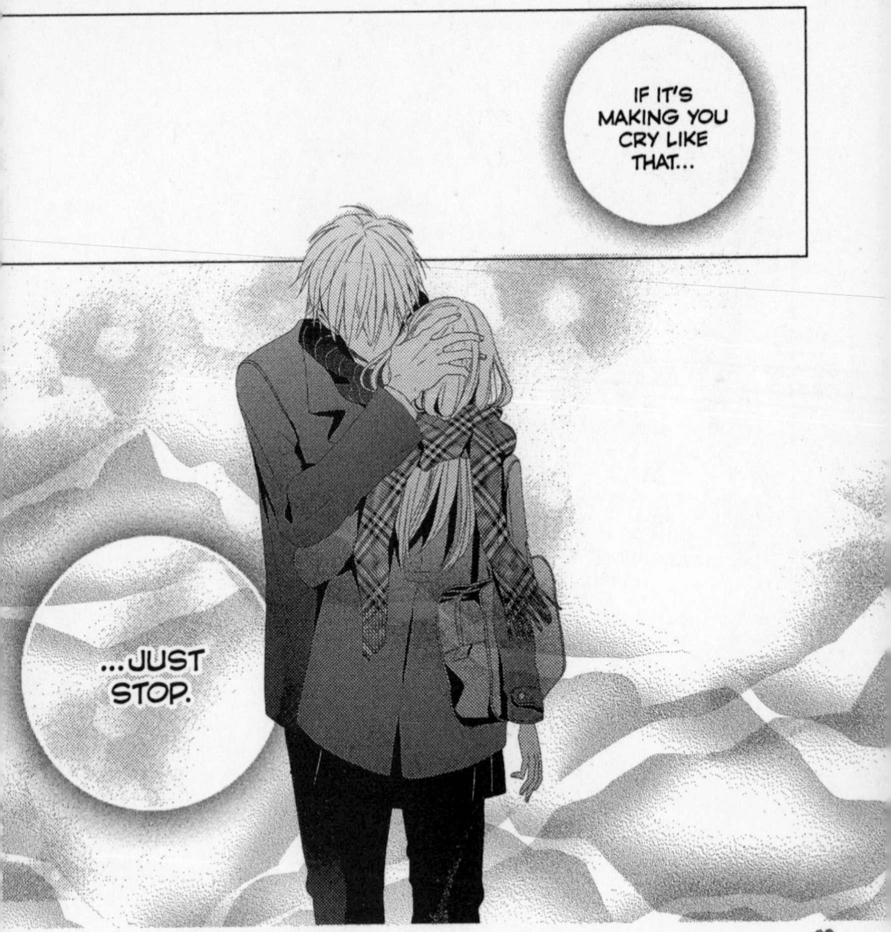
IF IT'S MAKING YOU CRY LIKE THAT...
...JUST STOP.

# That Wolf-Boy is Mine!

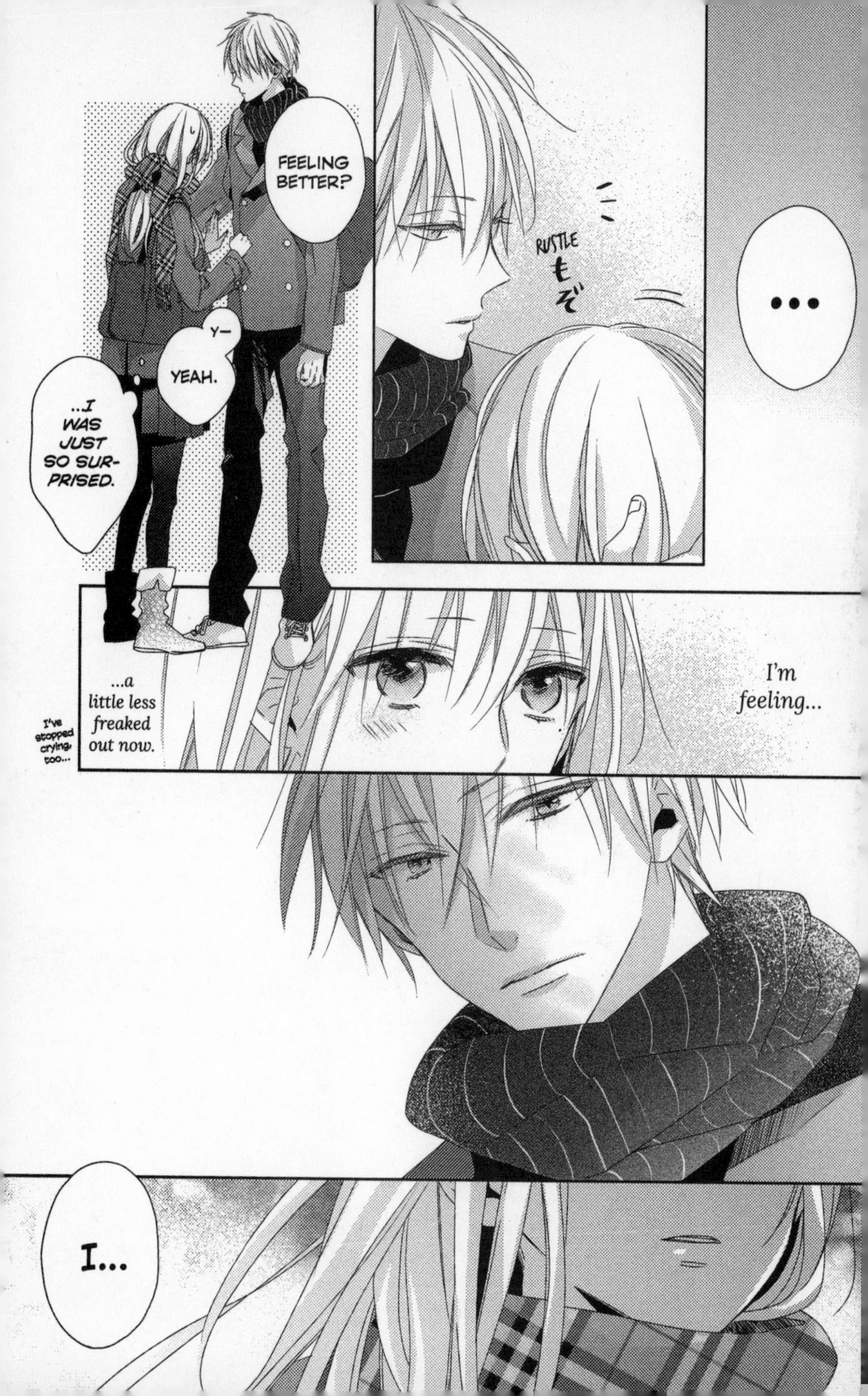
...
RUSTLE
もぞ
FEELING BETTER?
Y—
YEAH.
...I WAS JUST SO SURPRISED.
I'm feeling...
...a little less freaked out now.
I've stopped crying, too...
I...

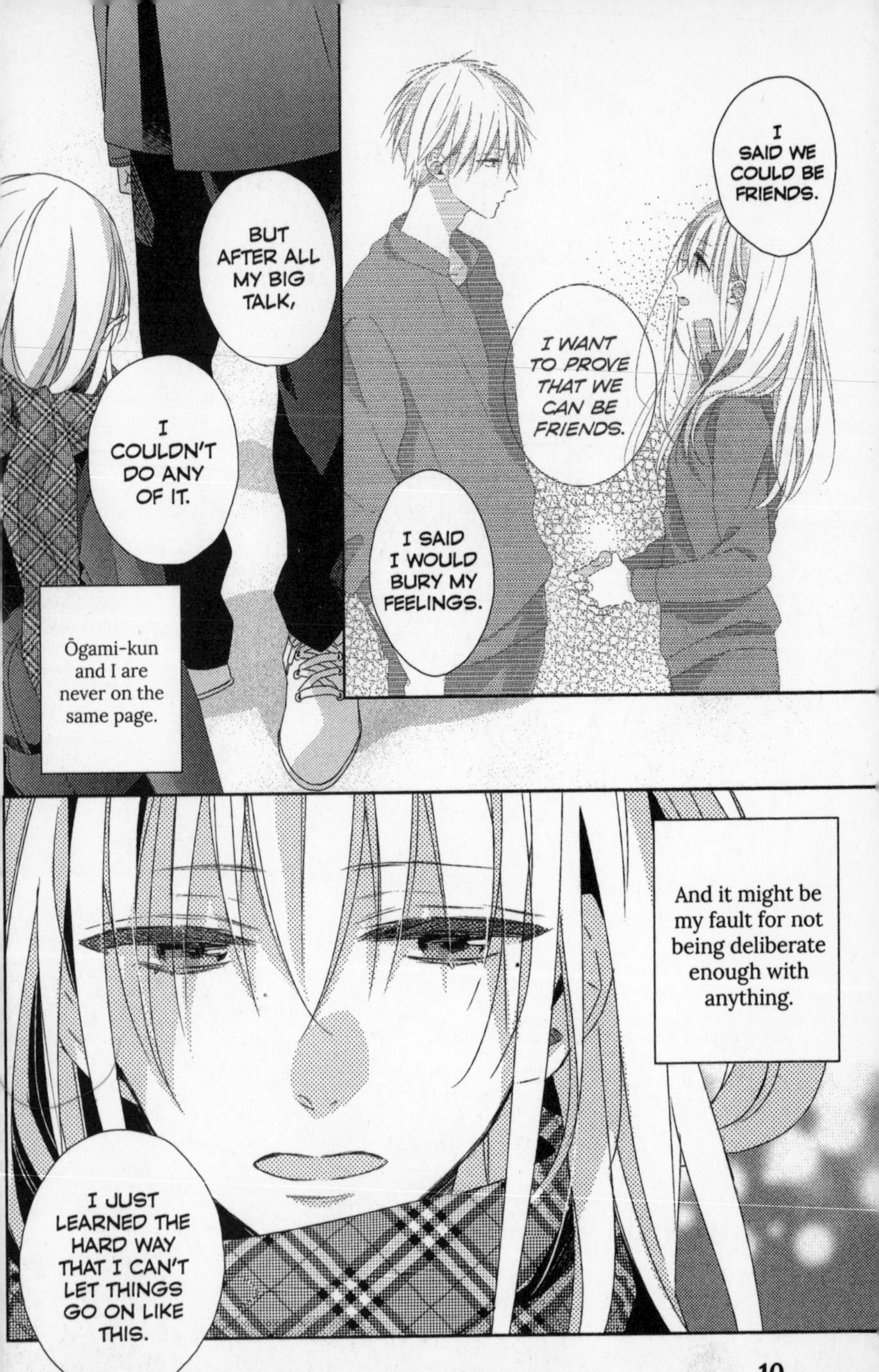
I SAID WE COULD BE FRIENDS.
I WANT TO PROVE THAT WE CAN BE FRIENDS.
I SAID I WOULD BURY MY FEELINGS.
BUT AFTER ALL MY BIG TALK,
I COULDN'T DO ANY OF IT.
Ōgami-kun and I are never on the same page.
And it might be my fault for not being deliberate enough with anything.
I JUST LEARNED THE HARD WAY THAT I CAN'T LET THINGS GO ON LIKE THIS.

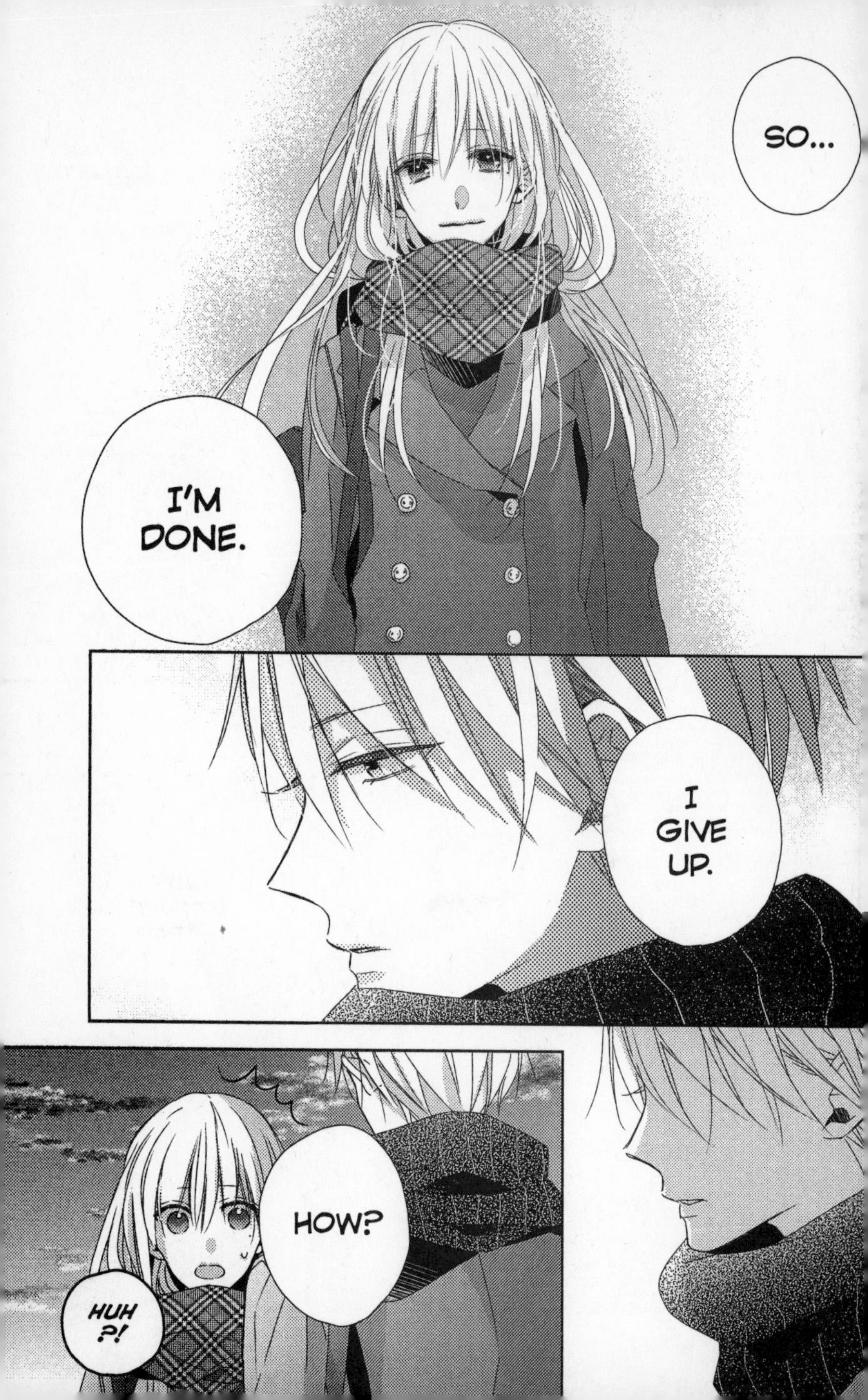
SO...
I'M DONE.
I GIVE UP.
HOW?
HUH?!

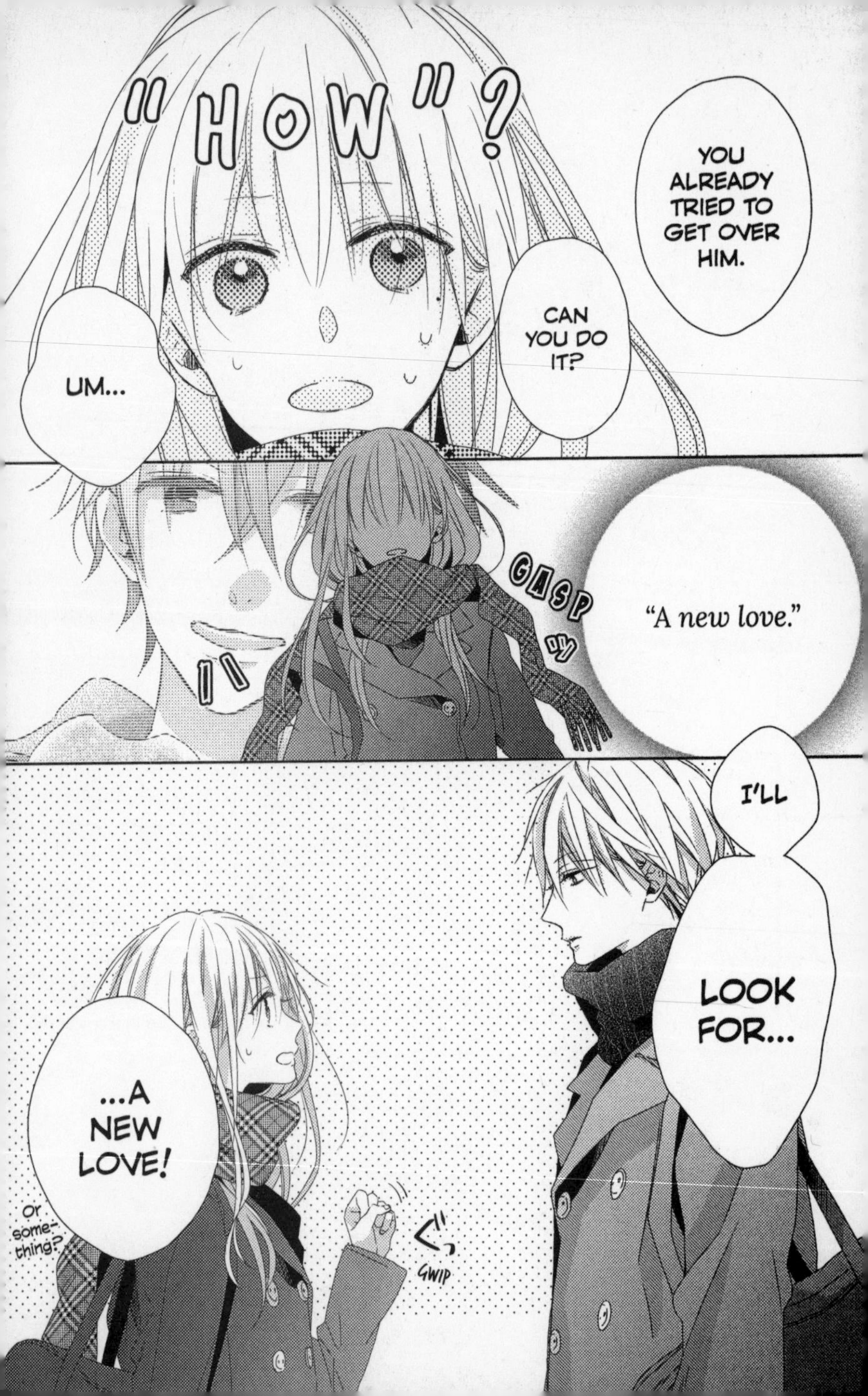
YOU ALREADY TRIED TO GET OVER HIM.
CAN YOU DO IT?
"HOW"?
UM...
"A new love."
GASP
I'LL
LOOK FOR...
...A NEW LOVE!
GWIP
Or some-thing?

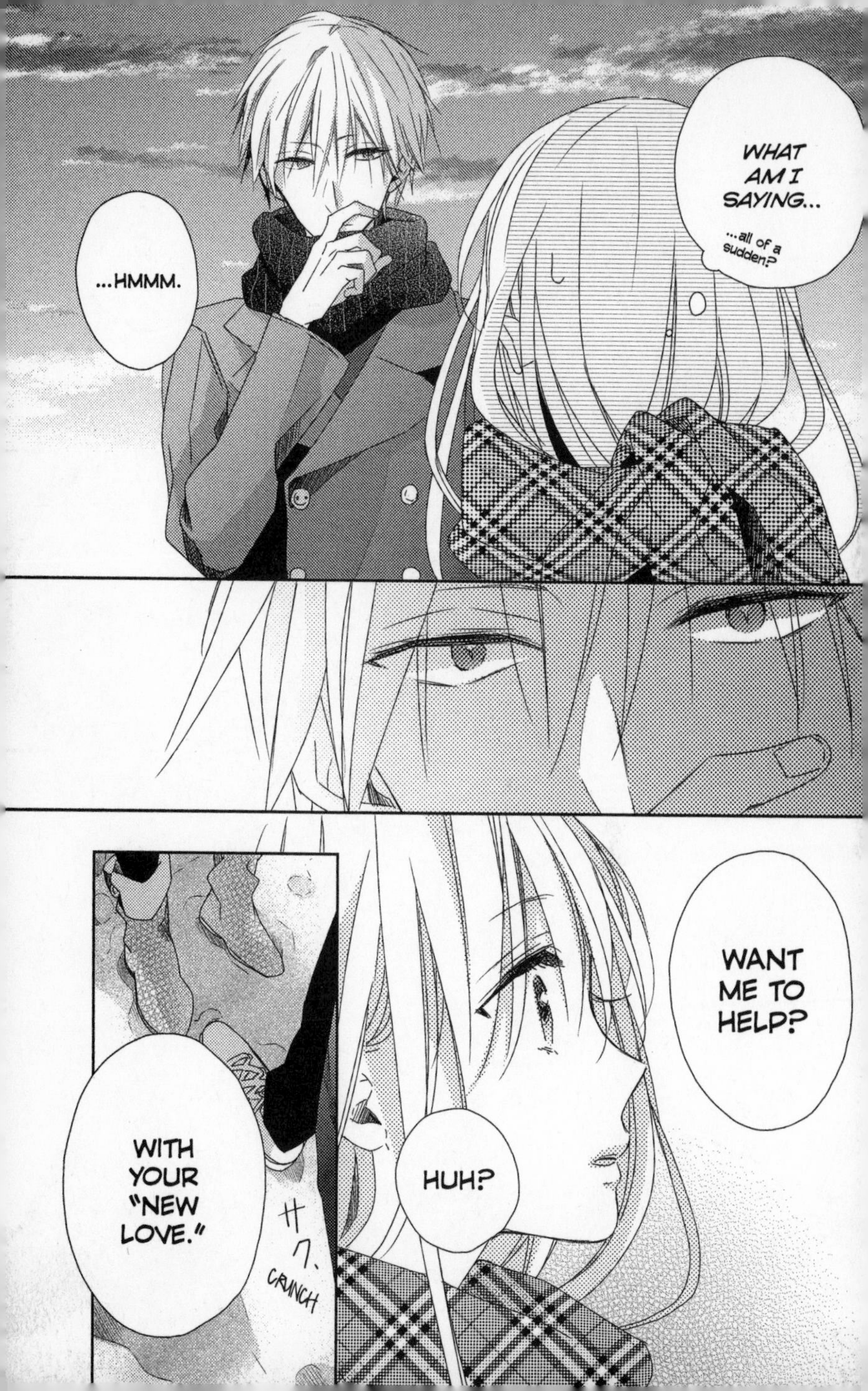
WHAT AM I SAYING...
...all of a sudden?
...HMMM.
WANT ME TO HELP?
HUH?
WITH YOUR "NEW LOVE."
CRUNCH

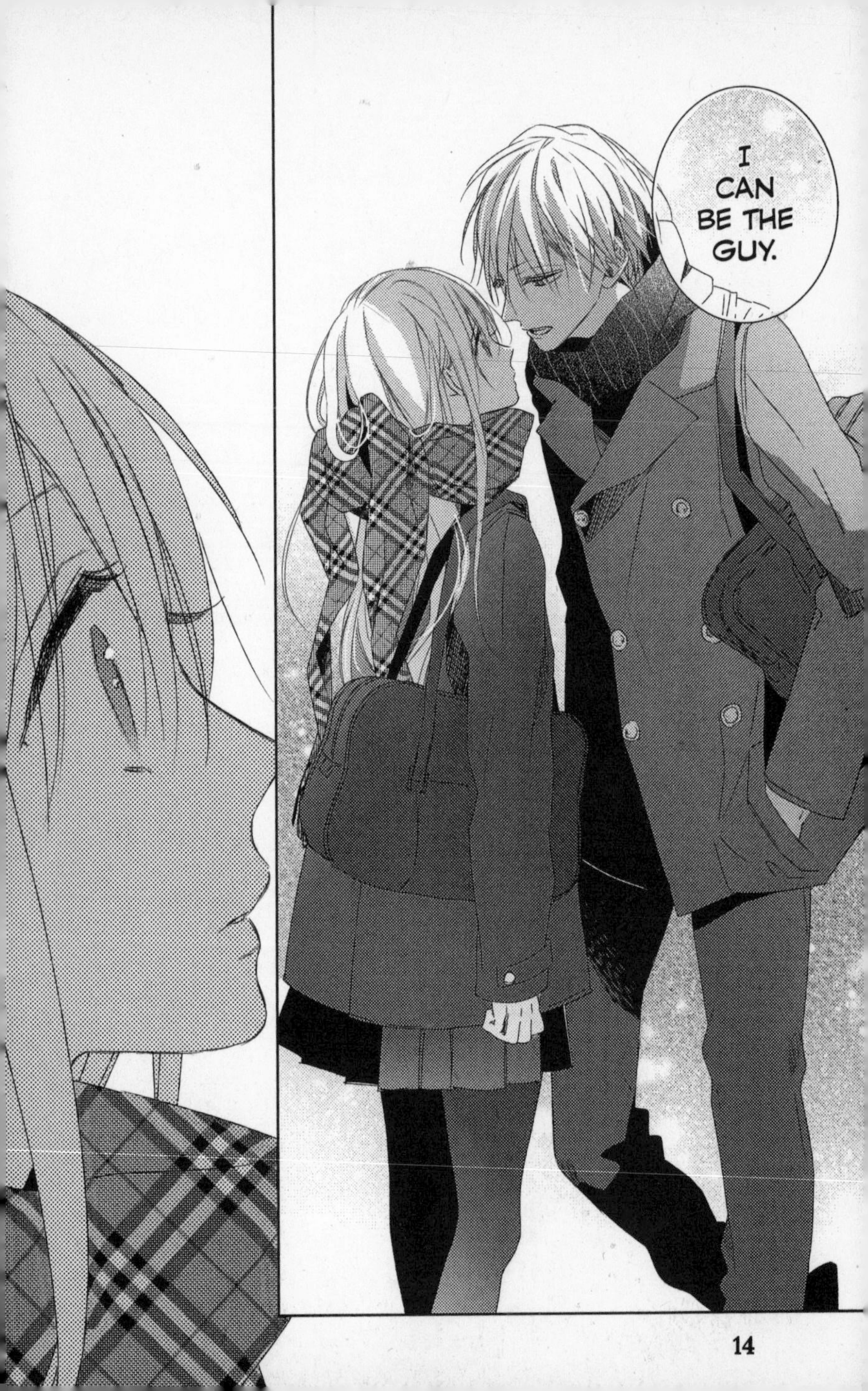
I CAN BE THE GUY.

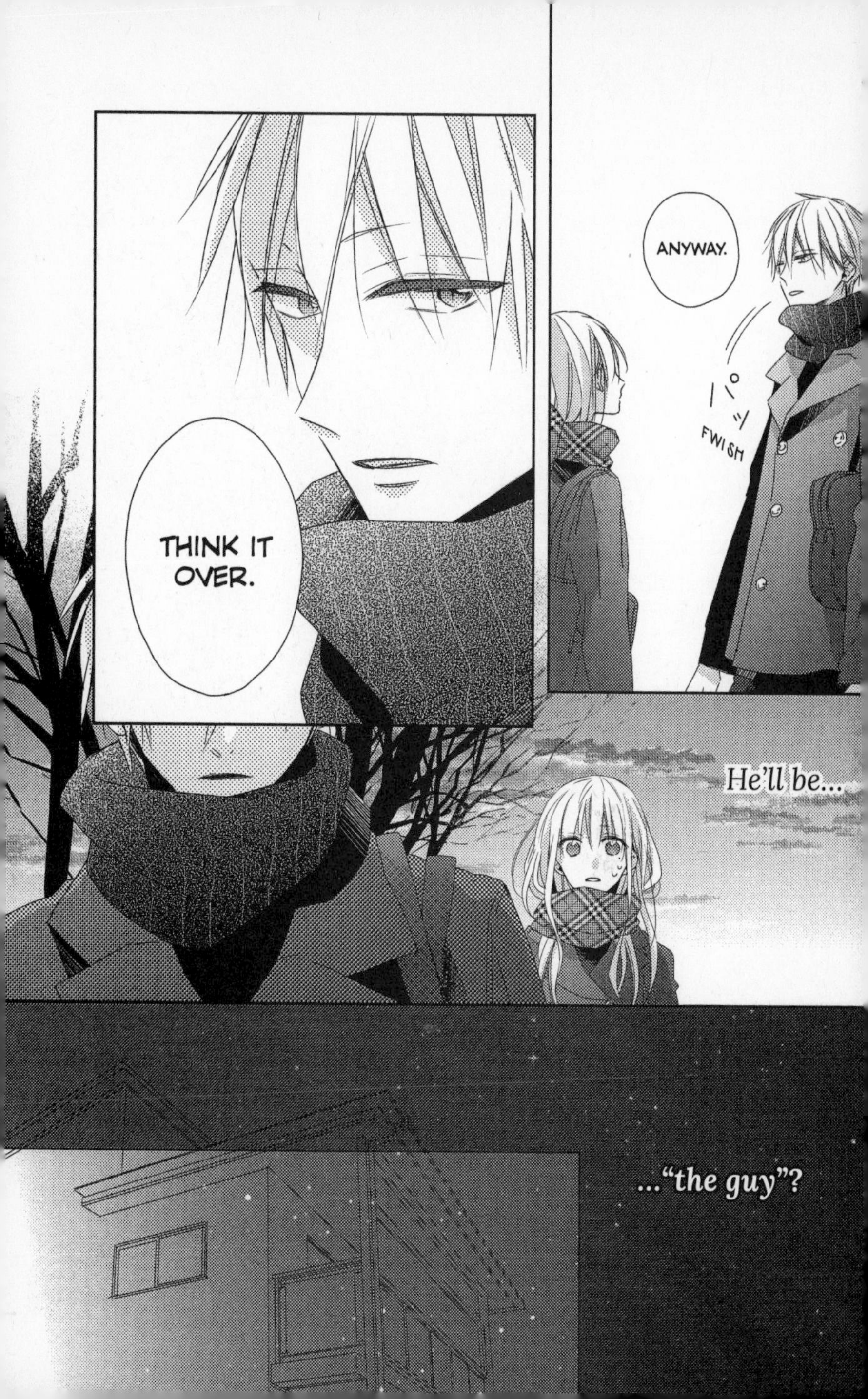
ANYWAY.
パッ
FWISH
THINK IT OVER.
He'll be...
..."the guy"?

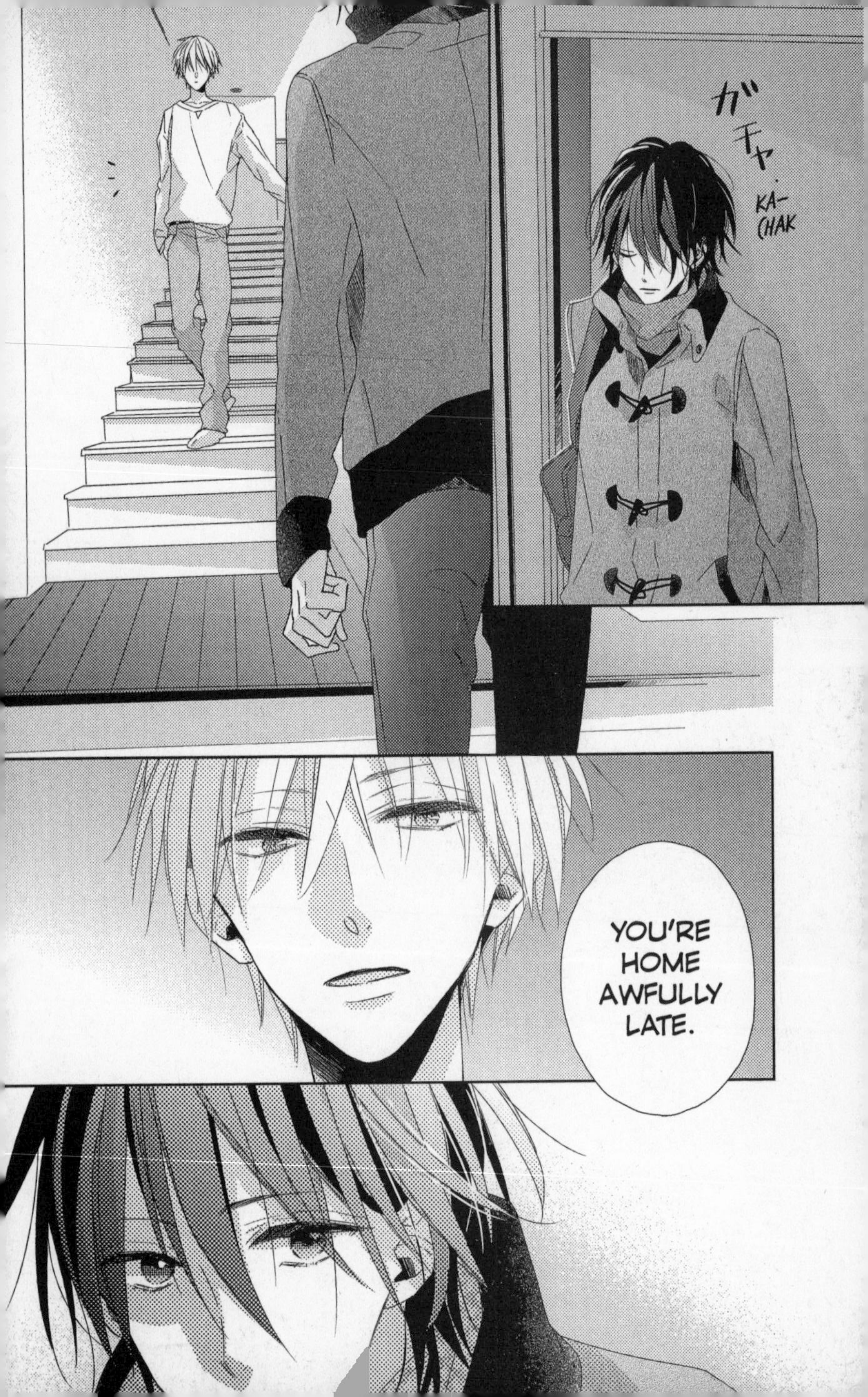
ガチャ
KA-CHAK
YOU'RE HOME AWFULLY LATE.

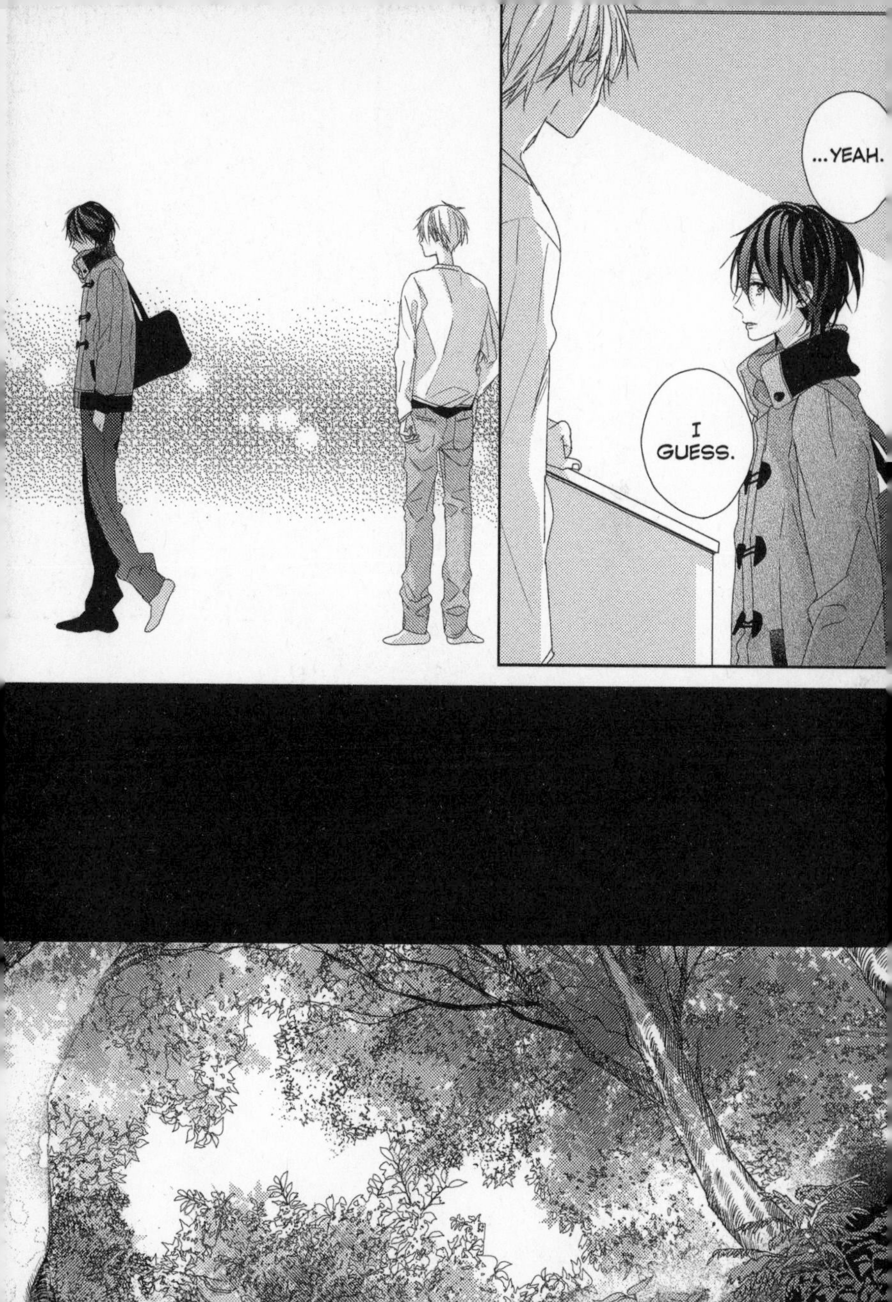
...YEAH.
I GUESS.

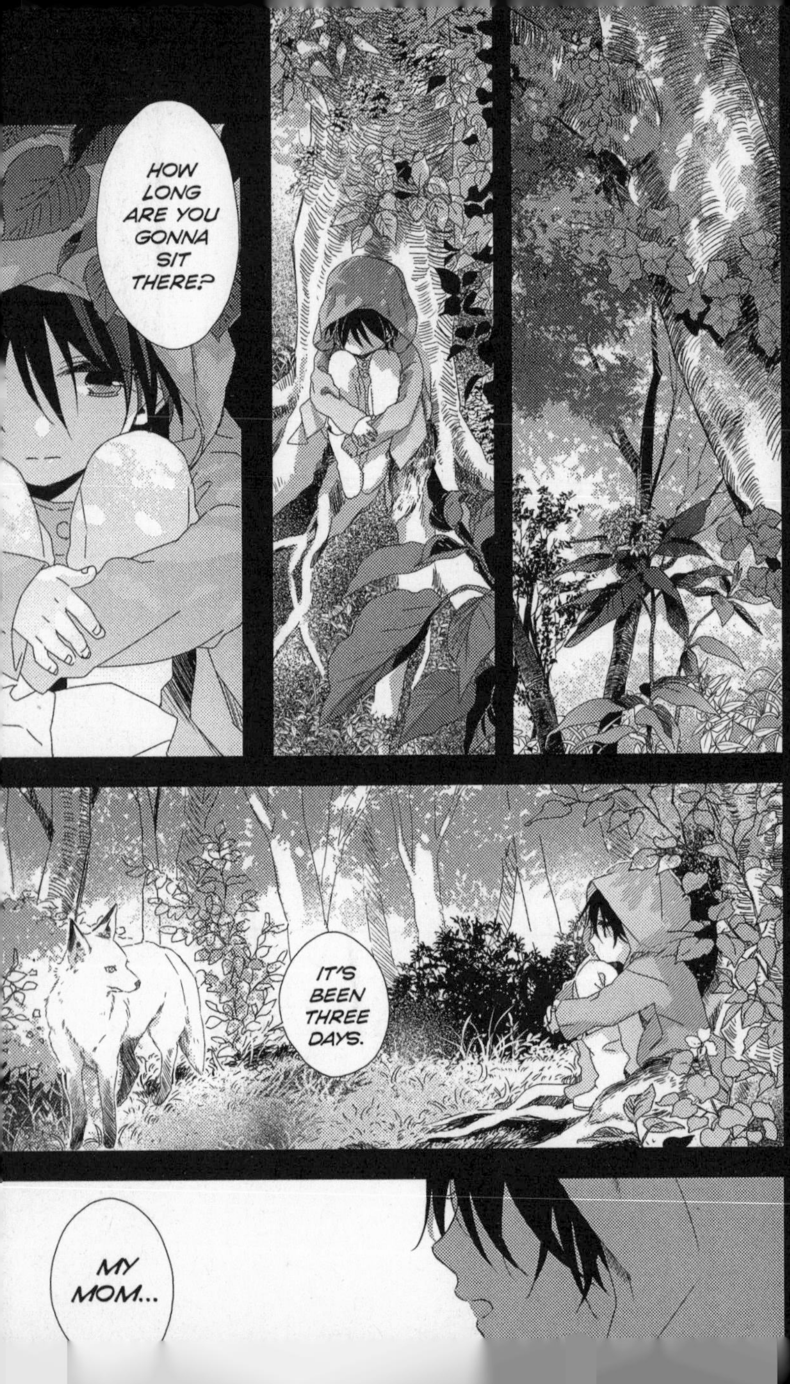
HOW LONG ARE YOU GONNA SIT THERE?
IT'S BEEN THREE DAYS.
MY MOM...

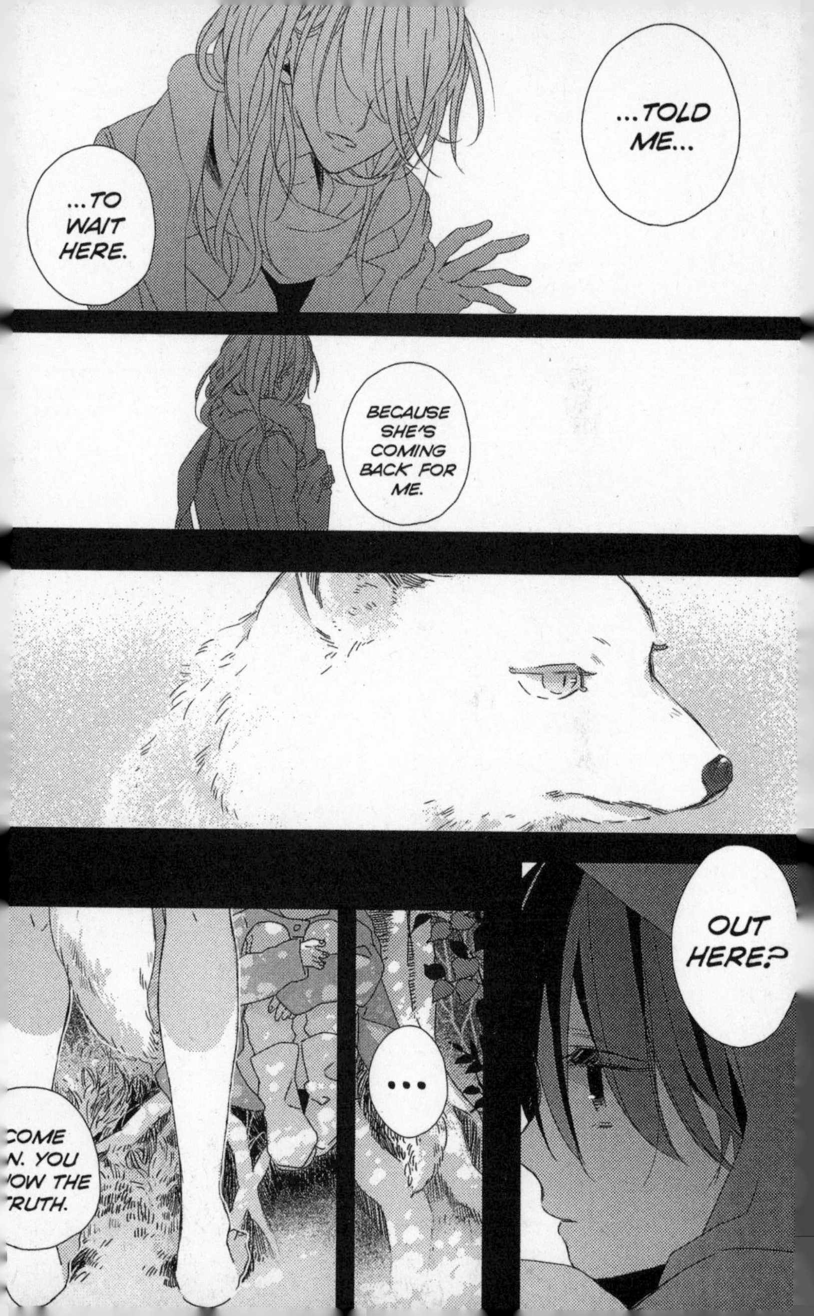
...TOLD ME...
...TO WAIT HERE.
BECAUSE SHE'S COMING BACK FOR ME.
OUT HERE?
...
COME N. YOU NOW THE TRUTH.

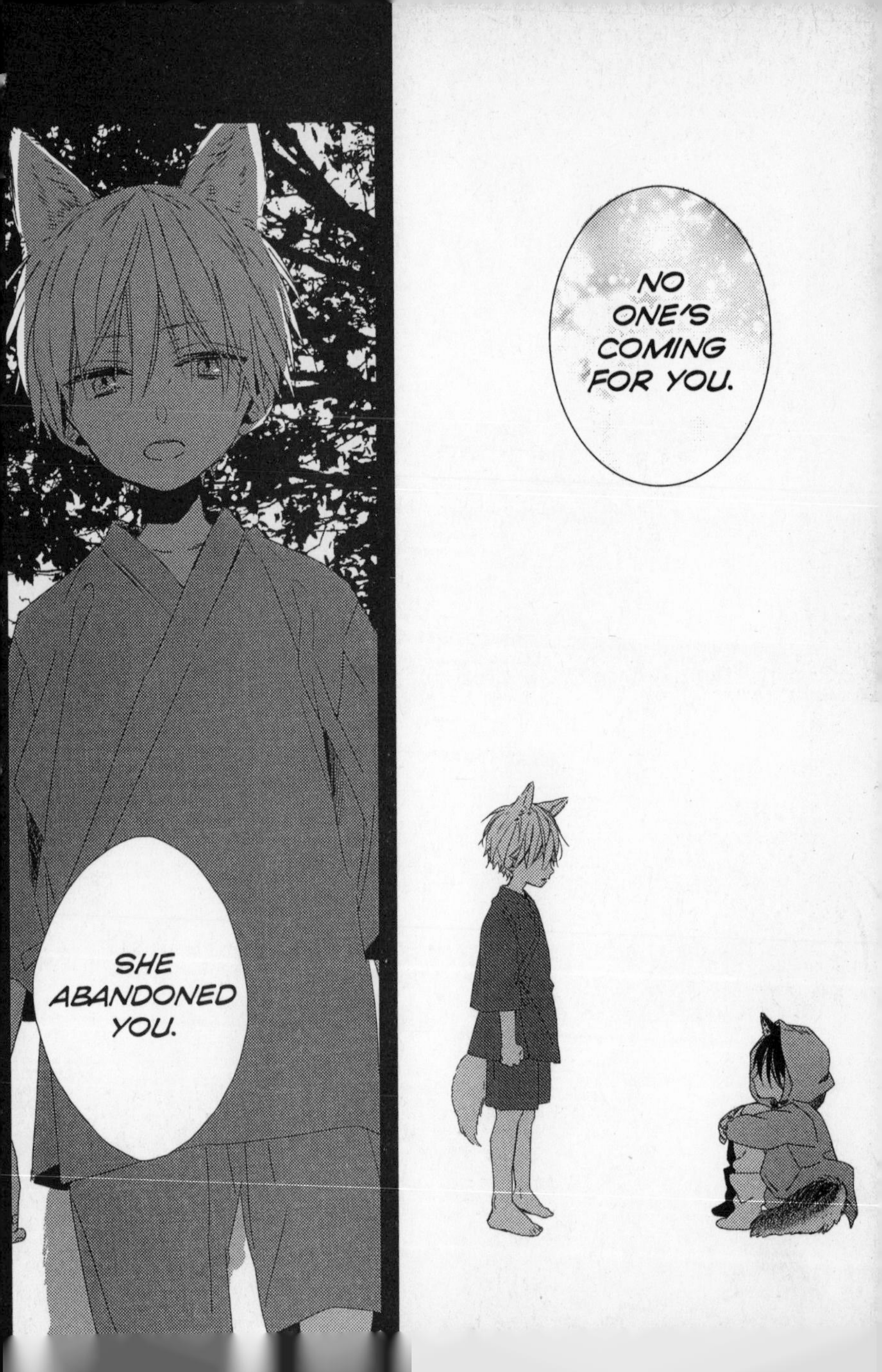
NO ONE'S COMING FOR YOU.
SHE ABANDONED YOU.

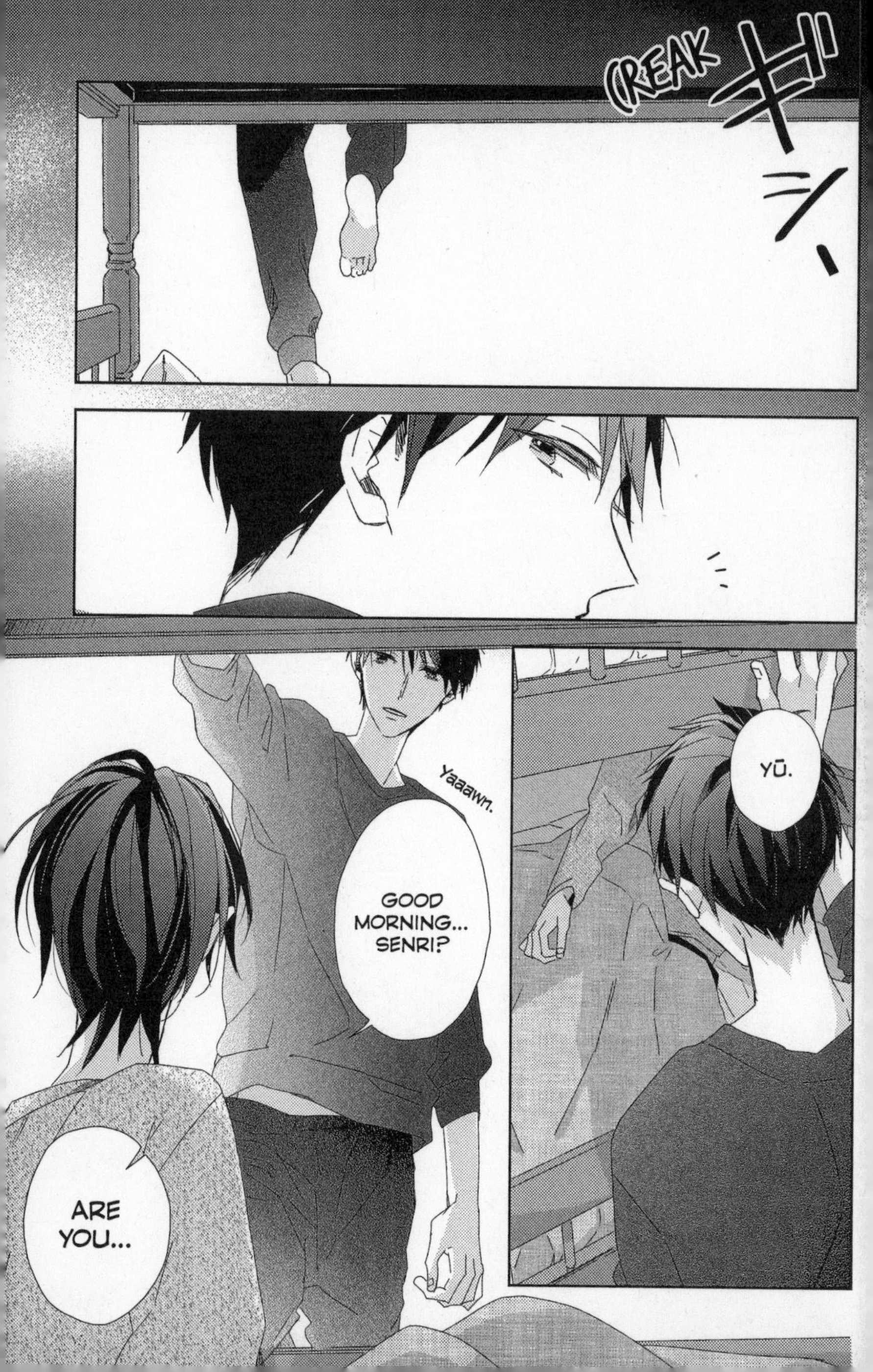
CREAK
YŪ.
Yaaawn.
GOOD MORNING... SENRI?
ARE YOU...

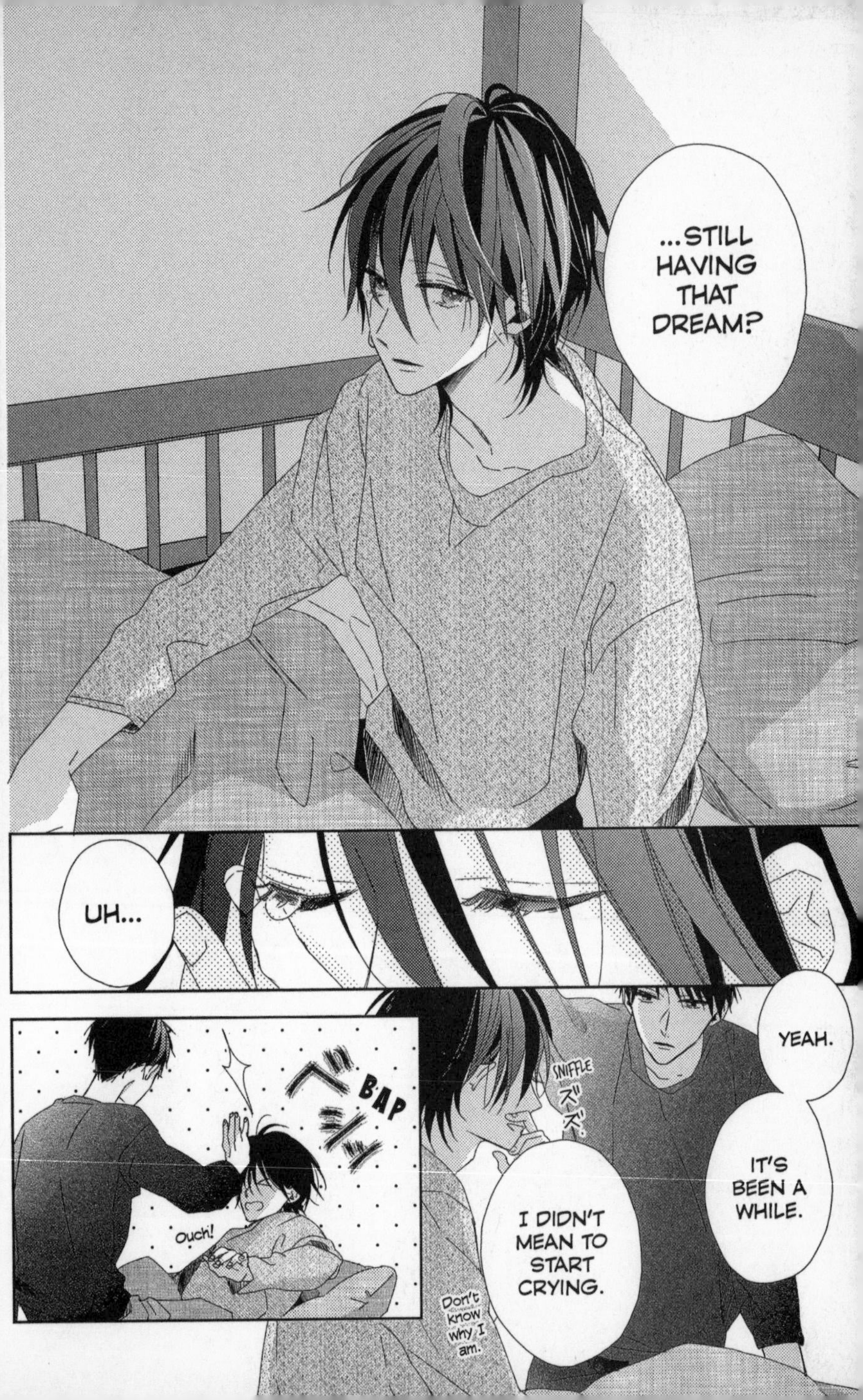
...STILL HAVING THAT DREAM?
UH...
YEAH.
IT'S BEEN A WHILE.
SNIFFLE
ズズ
I DIDN'T MEAN TO START CRYING.
Don't know why I am.
BAP
Ouch!

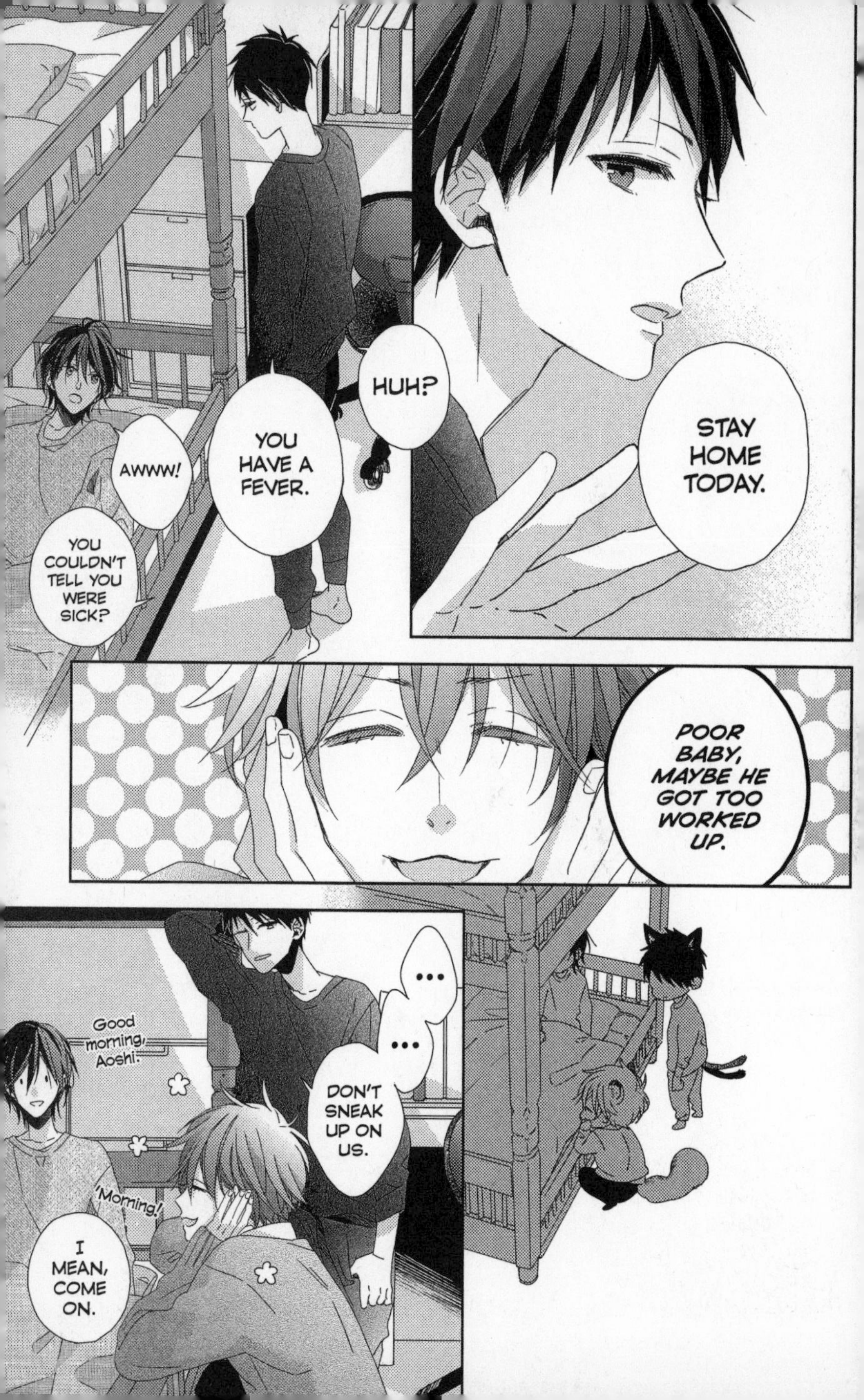
STAY HOME TODAY.
HUH?
YOU HAVE A FEVER.
AWWW!
YOU COULDN'T TELL YOU WERE SICK?
POOR BABY, MAYBE HE GOT TOO WORKED UP.
...
...
DON'T SNEAK UP ON US.
Good morning, Aoshi.
'Morning!
I MEAN, COME ON.

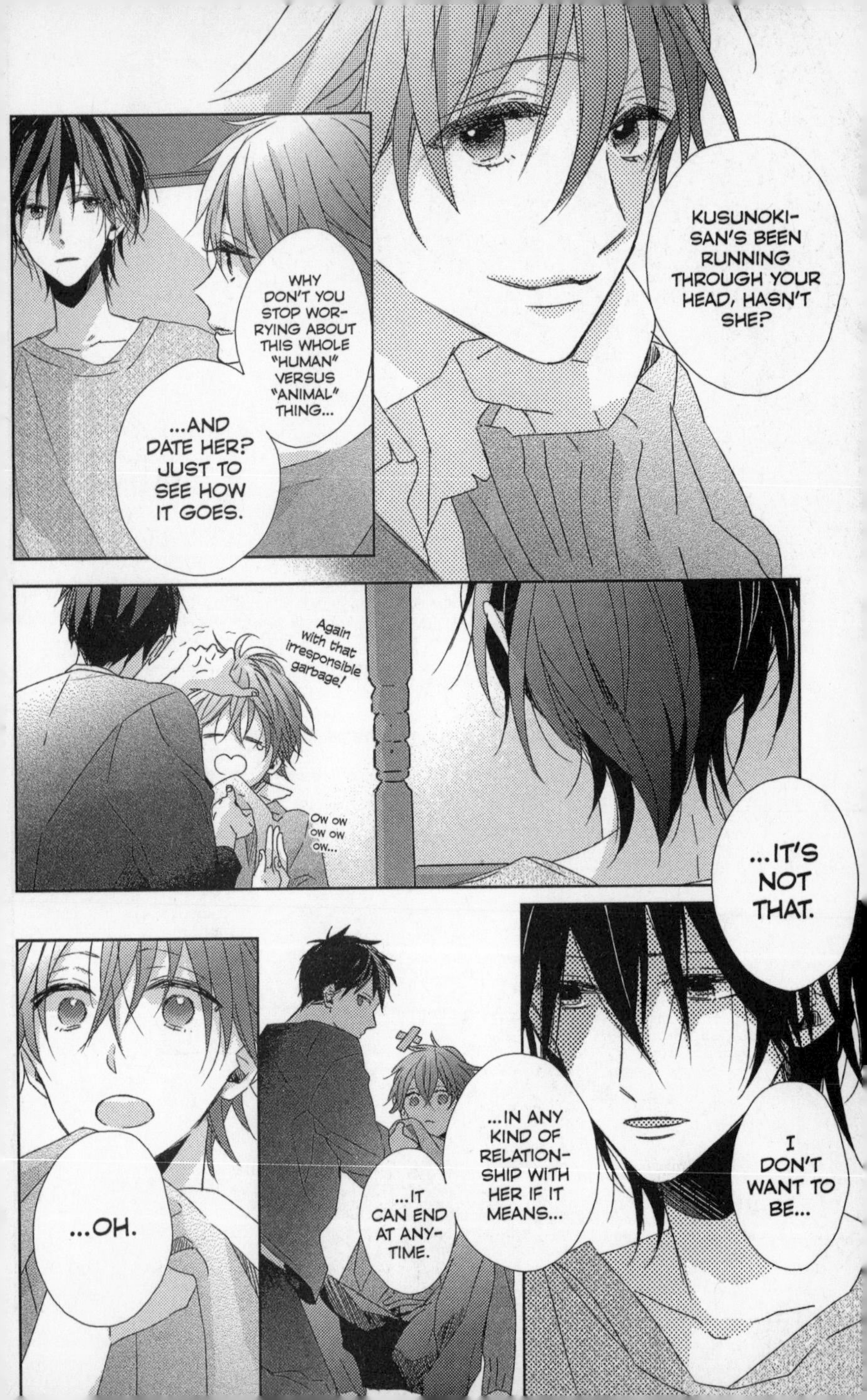
KUSUNOKI-SAN'S BEEN RUNNING THROUGH YOUR HEAD, HASN'T SHE?
WHY DON'T YOU STOP WORRYING ABOUT THIS WHOLE "HUMAN" VERSUS "ANIMAL" THING...
...AND DATE HER? JUST TO SEE HOW IT GOES.
...IT'S NOT THAT.
Again with that irresponsible garbage!
Ow ow ow ow ow...
I DON'T WANT TO BE...
...IN ANY KIND OF RELATIONSHIP WITH HER IF IT MEANS...
...IT CAN END AT ANYTIME.
...OH.

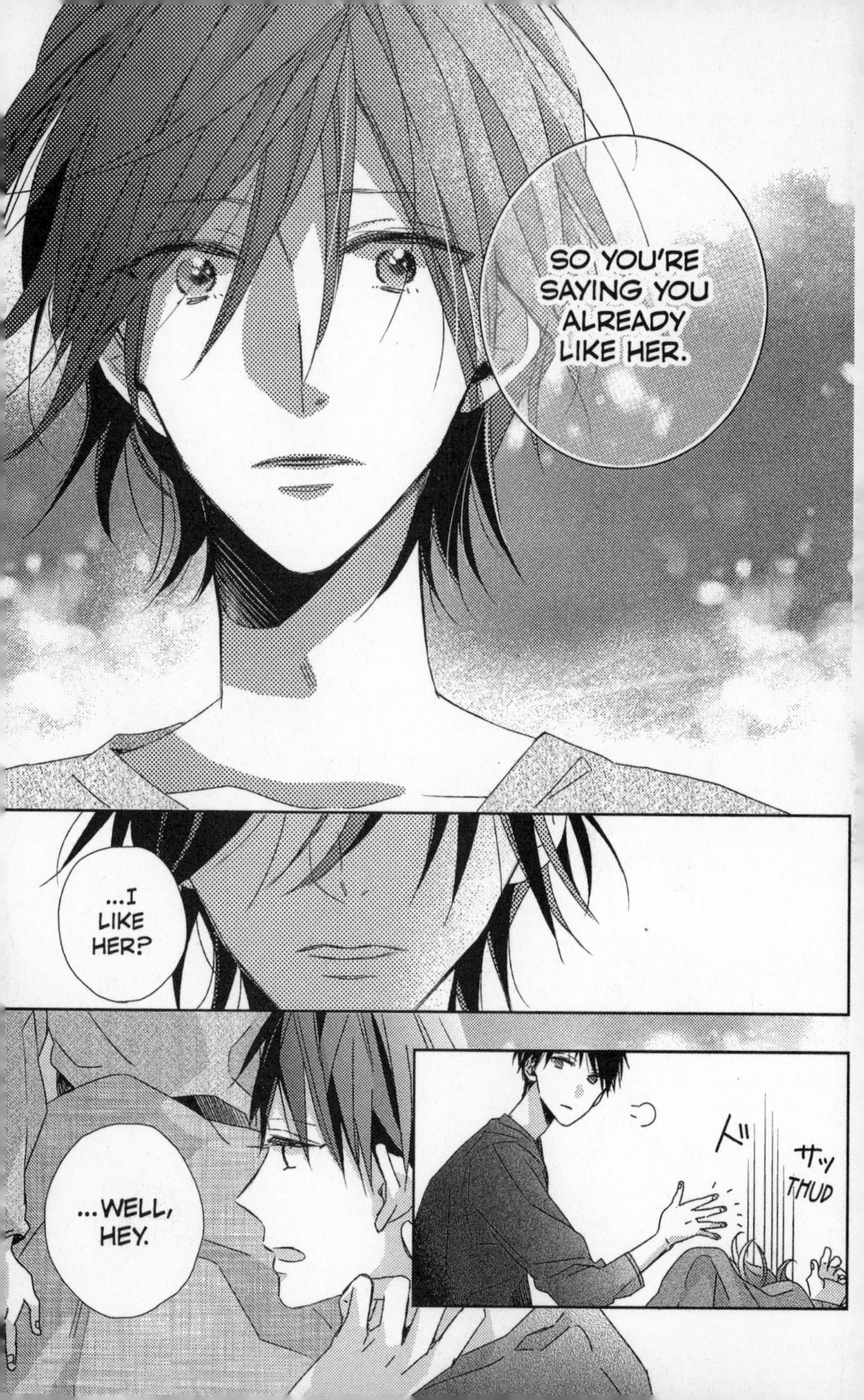
SO YOU'RE SAYING YOU ALREADY LIKE HER.
...I LIKE HER?
ド
サッ
THUD
...WELL, HEY.

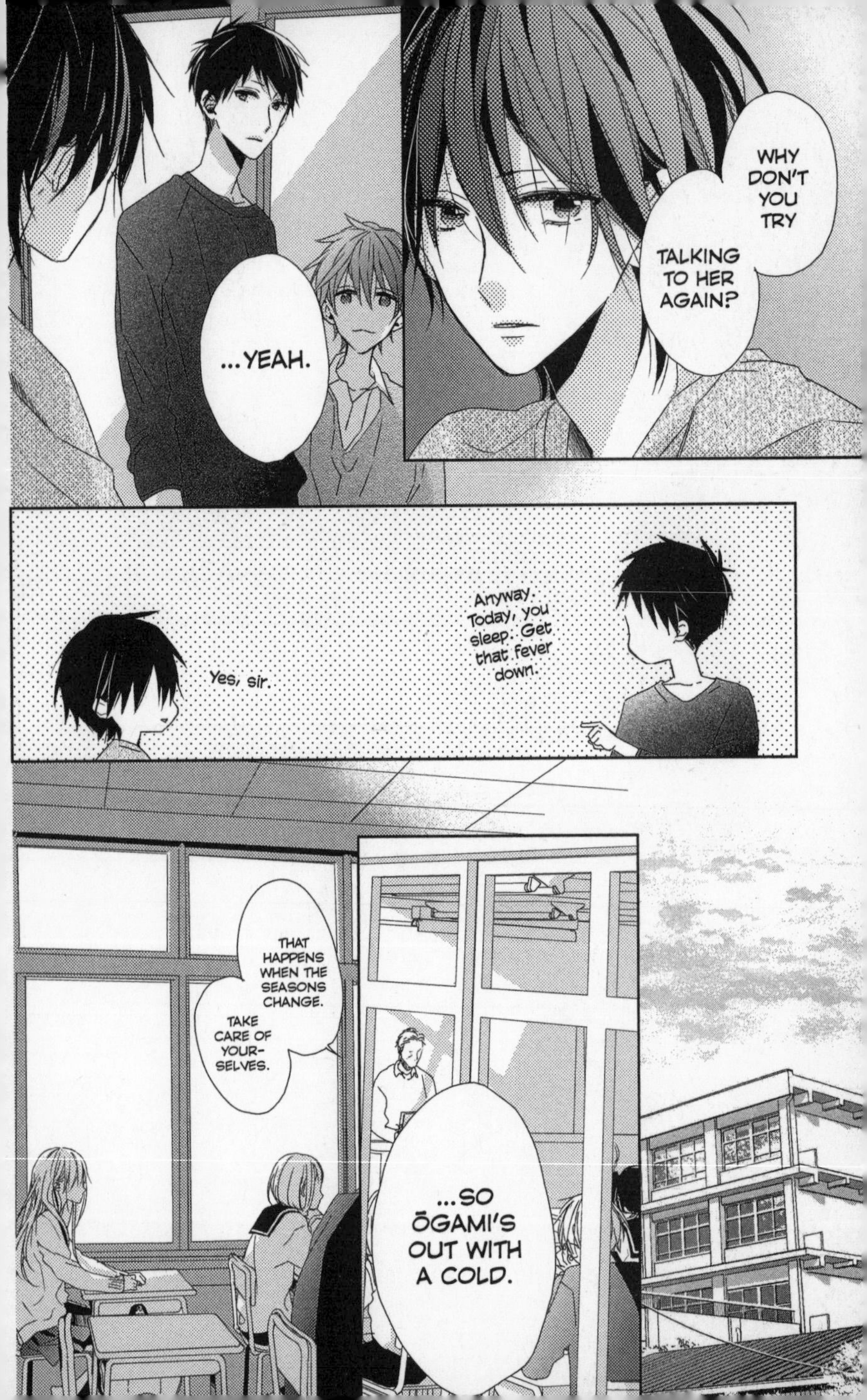
WHY DON'T YOU TRY
TALKING TO HER AGAIN?
...YEAH.
Anyway. Today, you sleep. Get that fever down.
Yes, sir.
...SO ŌGAMI'S OUT WITH A COLD.
THAT HAPPENS WHEN THE SEASONS CHANGE.
TAKE CARE OF YOUR-SELVES.

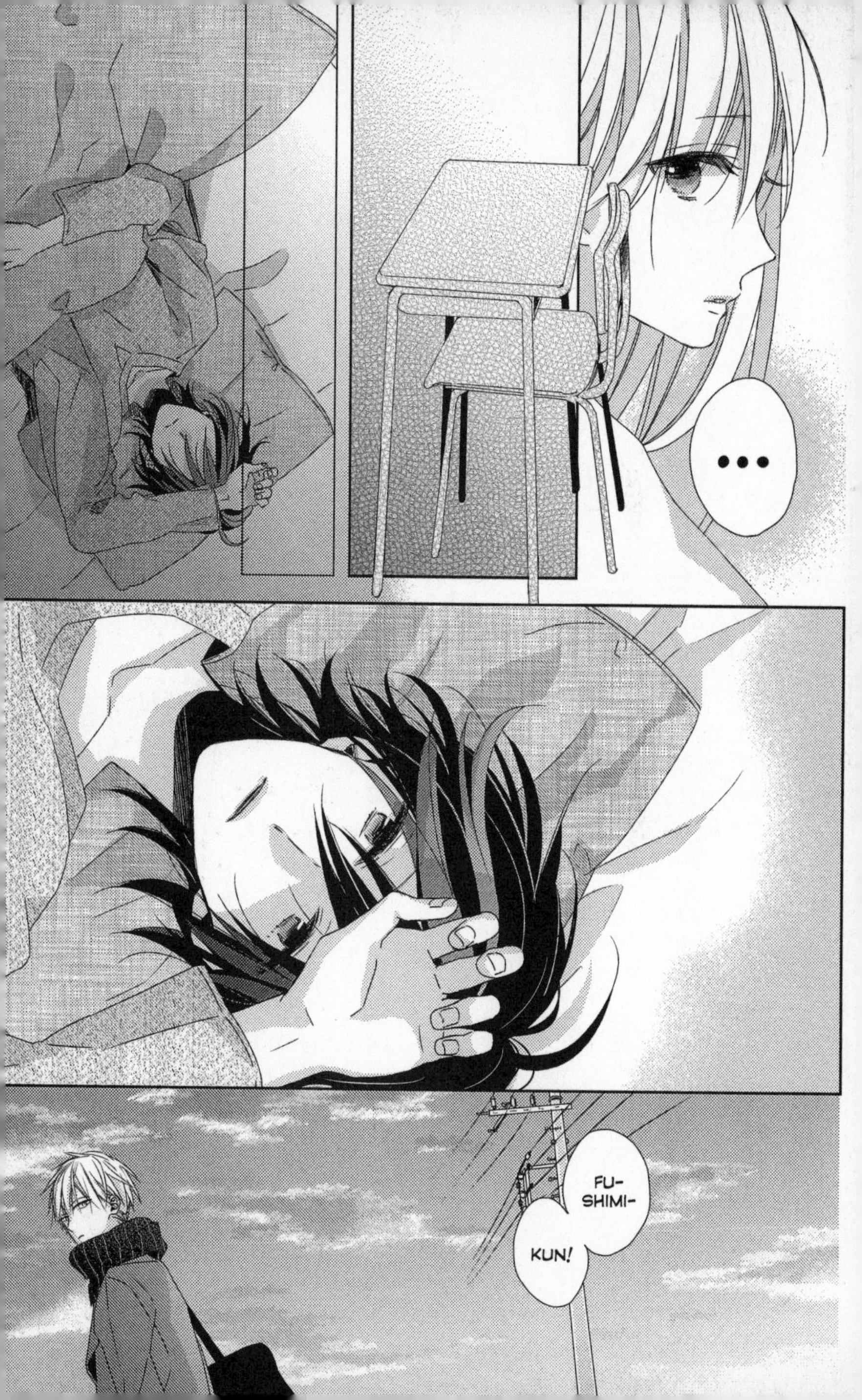
...
FU-SHIMI-
KUN!

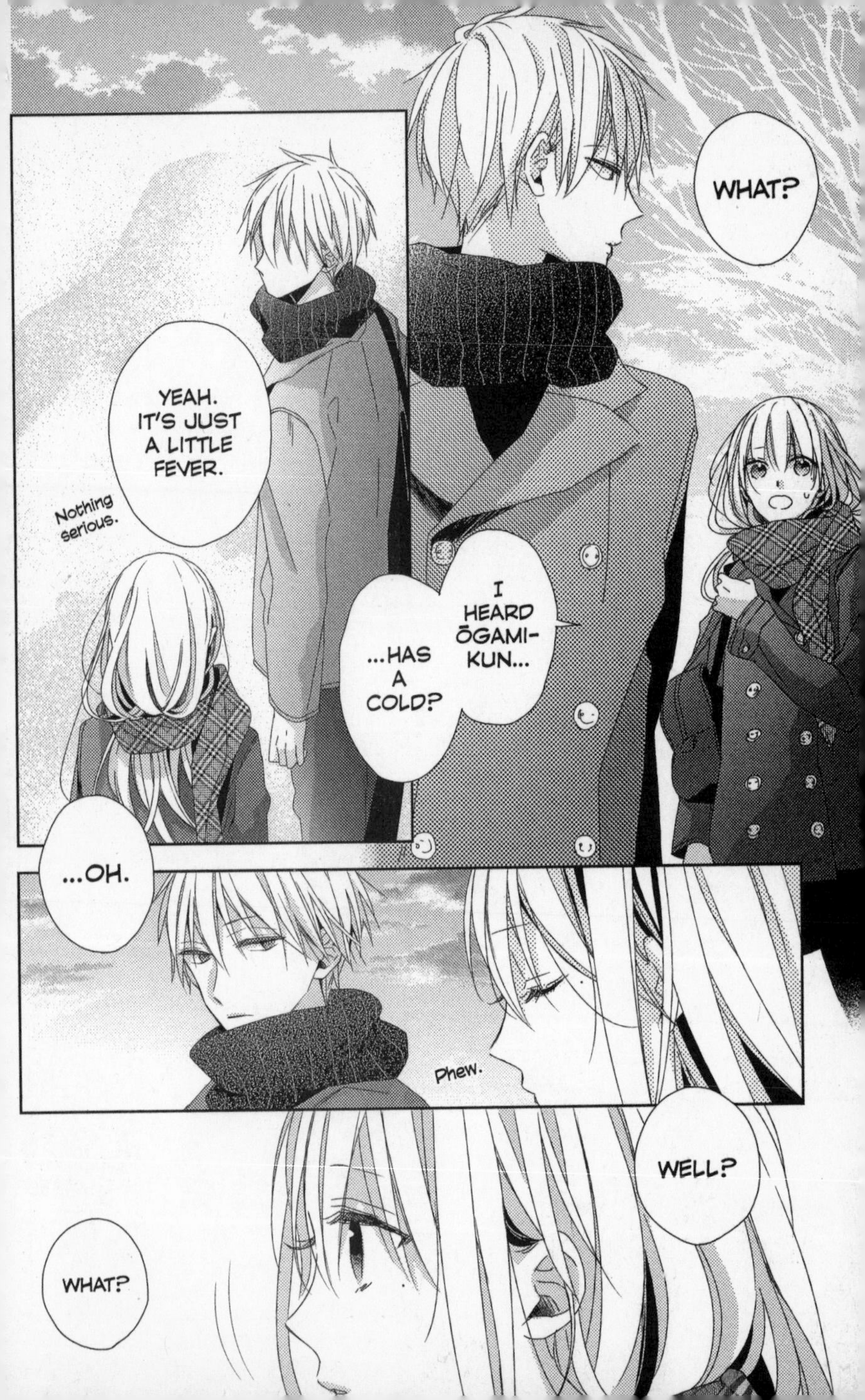
WHAT?
I HEARD ŌGAMI-KUN...
...HAS A COLD?
YEAH. IT'S JUST A LITTLE FEVER.
Nothing serious.
...OH.
Phew.
WELL?
WHAT?

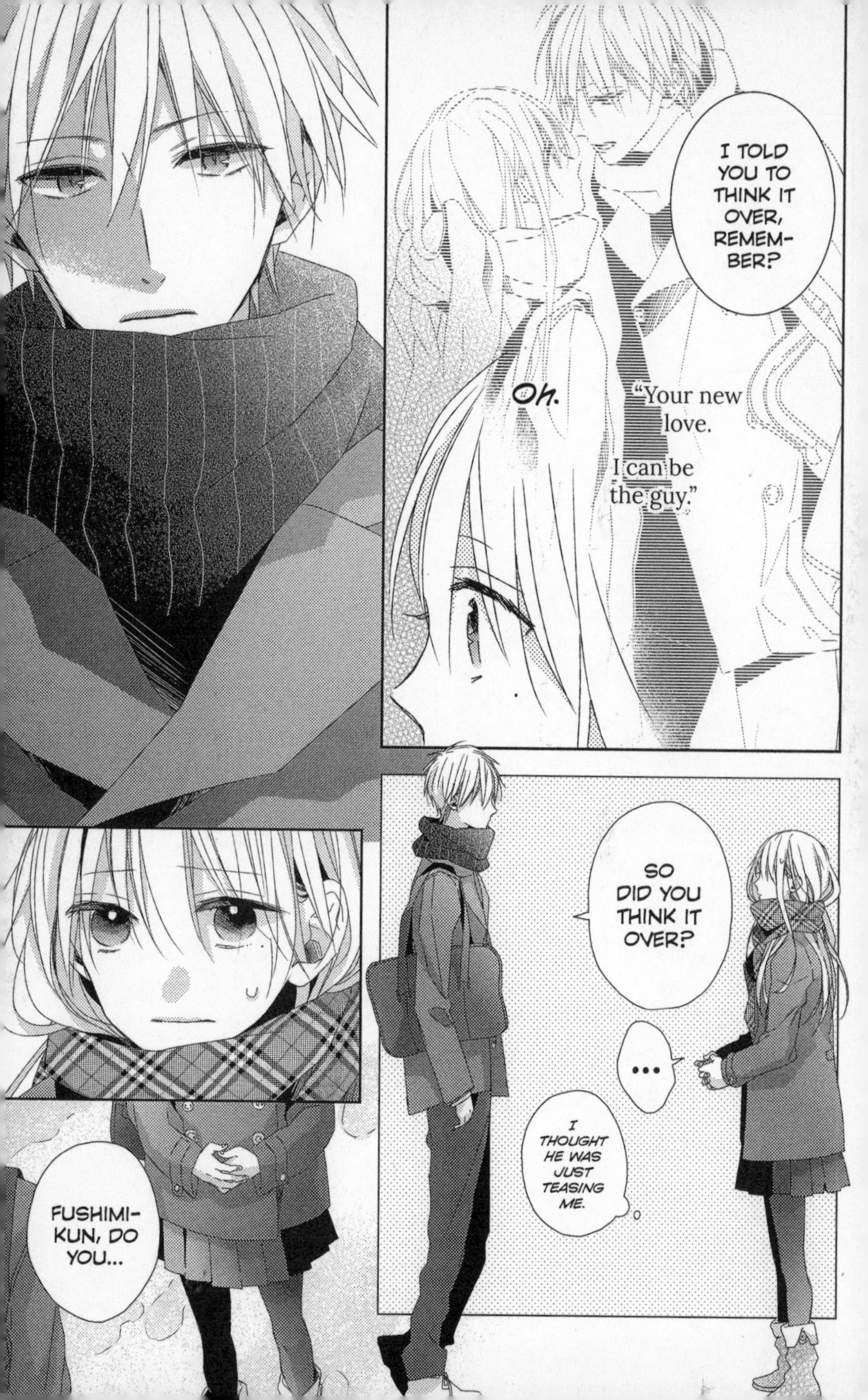
I TOLD YOU TO THINK IT OVER, REMEMBER?
Oh.
"Your new love.
I can be the guy."
SO DID YOU THINK IT OVER?
...
I THOUGHT HE WAS JUST TEASING ME.
FUSHIMI-KUN, DO YOU...

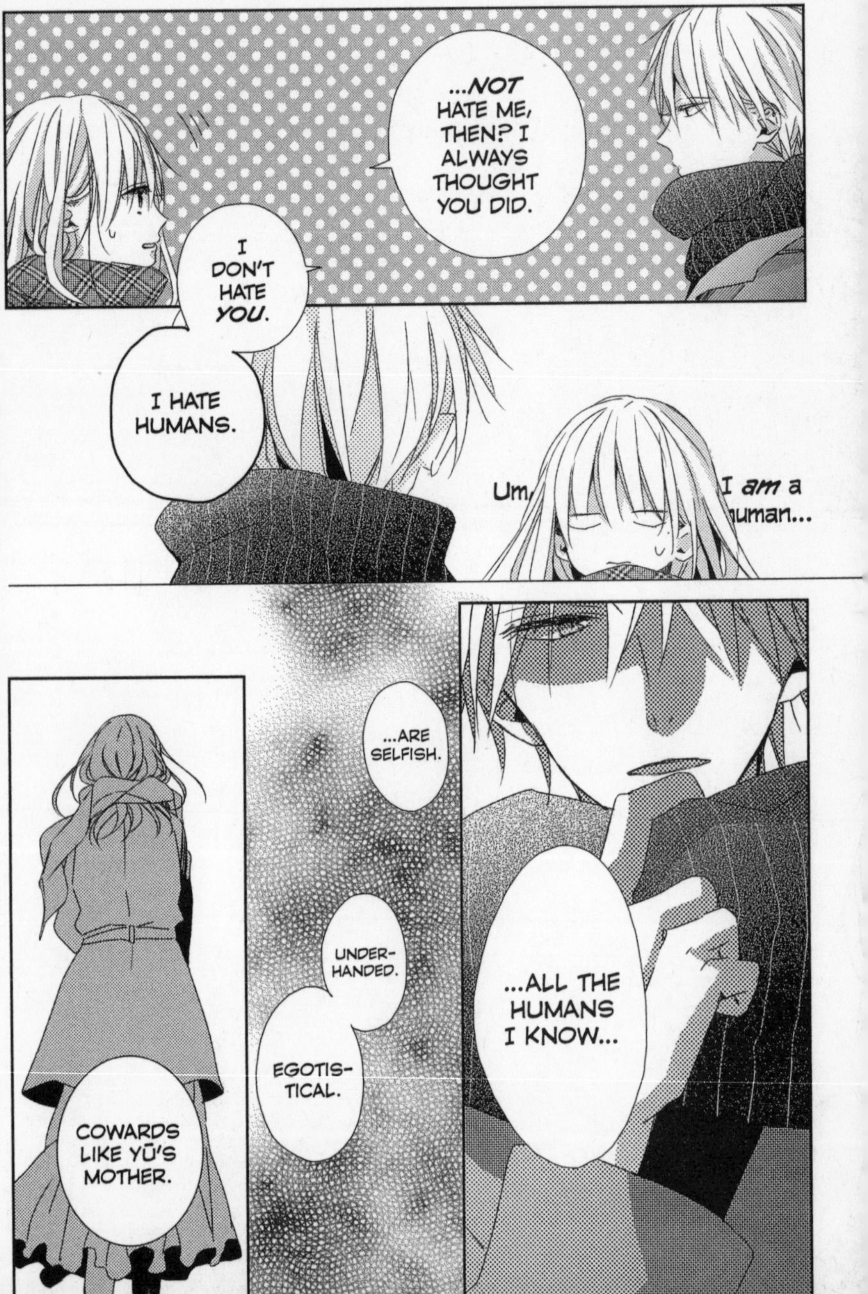
...*NOT* HATE ME, THEN? I ALWAYS THOUGHT YOU DID.
I DON'T HATE *YOU*.
I HATE HUMANS.
Um, I *am* a human...
...ALL THE HUMANS I KNOW...
...ARE SELFISH.
UNDER-HANDED.
EGOTIS-TICAL.
COWARDS LIKE YŪ'S MOTHER.

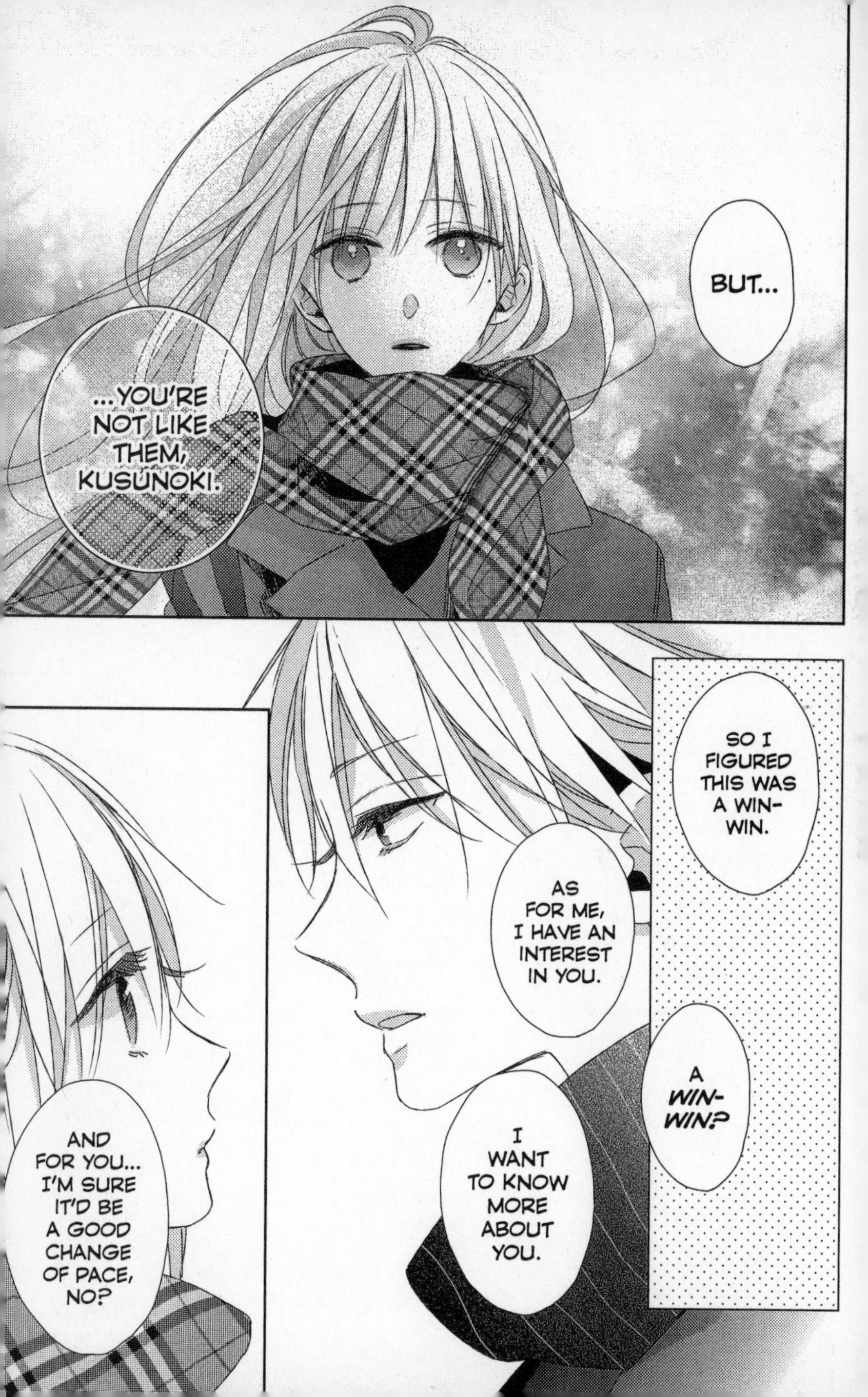
BUT...
...YOU'RE NOT LIKE THEM, KUSUNOKI.
SO I FIGURED THIS WAS A WIN-WIN.
A *WIN-WIN?*
AS FOR ME, I HAVE AN INTEREST IN YOU.
I WANT TO KNOW MORE ABOUT YOU.
AND FOR YOU... I'M SURE IT'D BE A GOOD CHANGE OF PACE, NO?

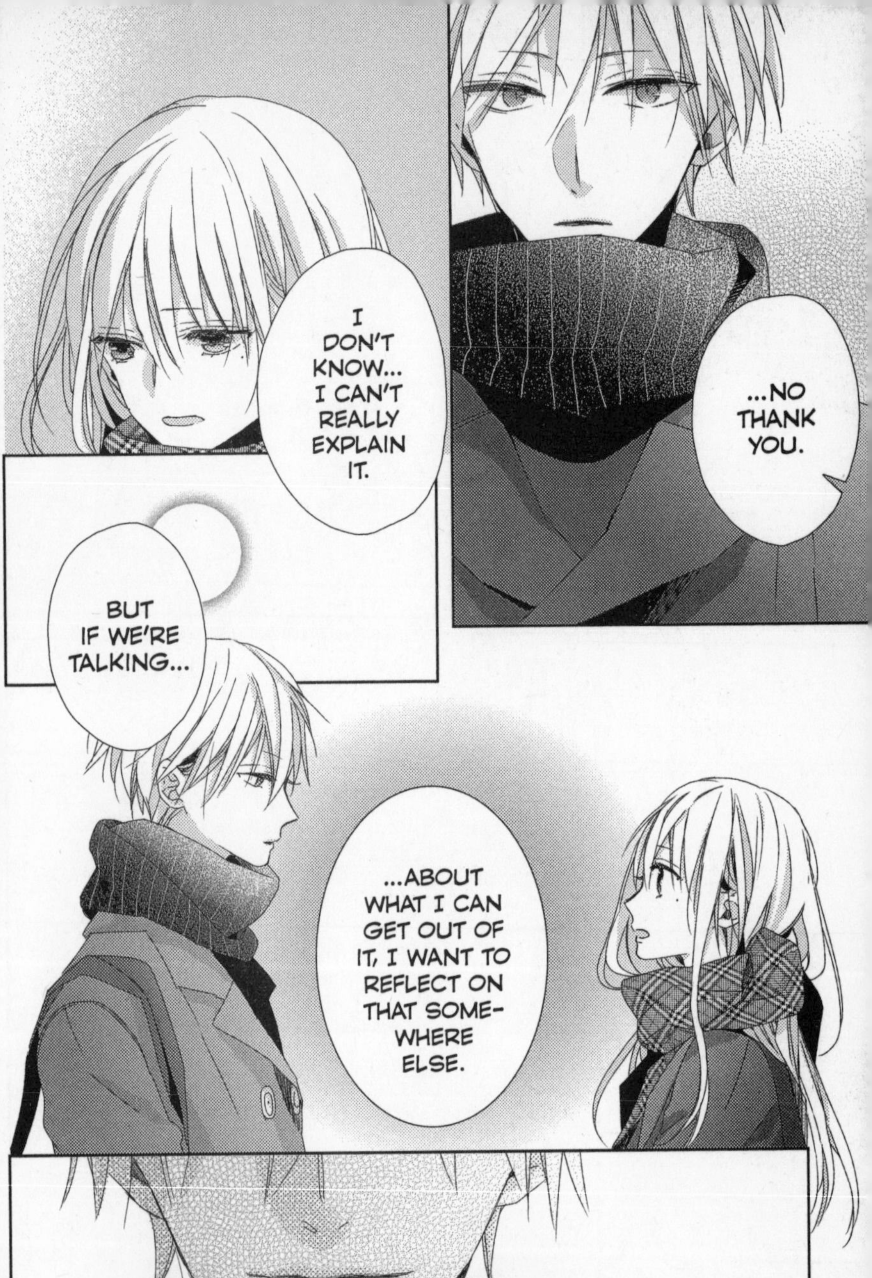
...NO THANK YOU.
I DON'T KNOW... I CAN'T REALLY EXPLAIN IT.
BUT IF WE'RE TALKING...
...ABOUT WHAT I CAN GET OUT OF IT, I WANT TO REFLECT ON THAT SOME-WHERE ELSE.

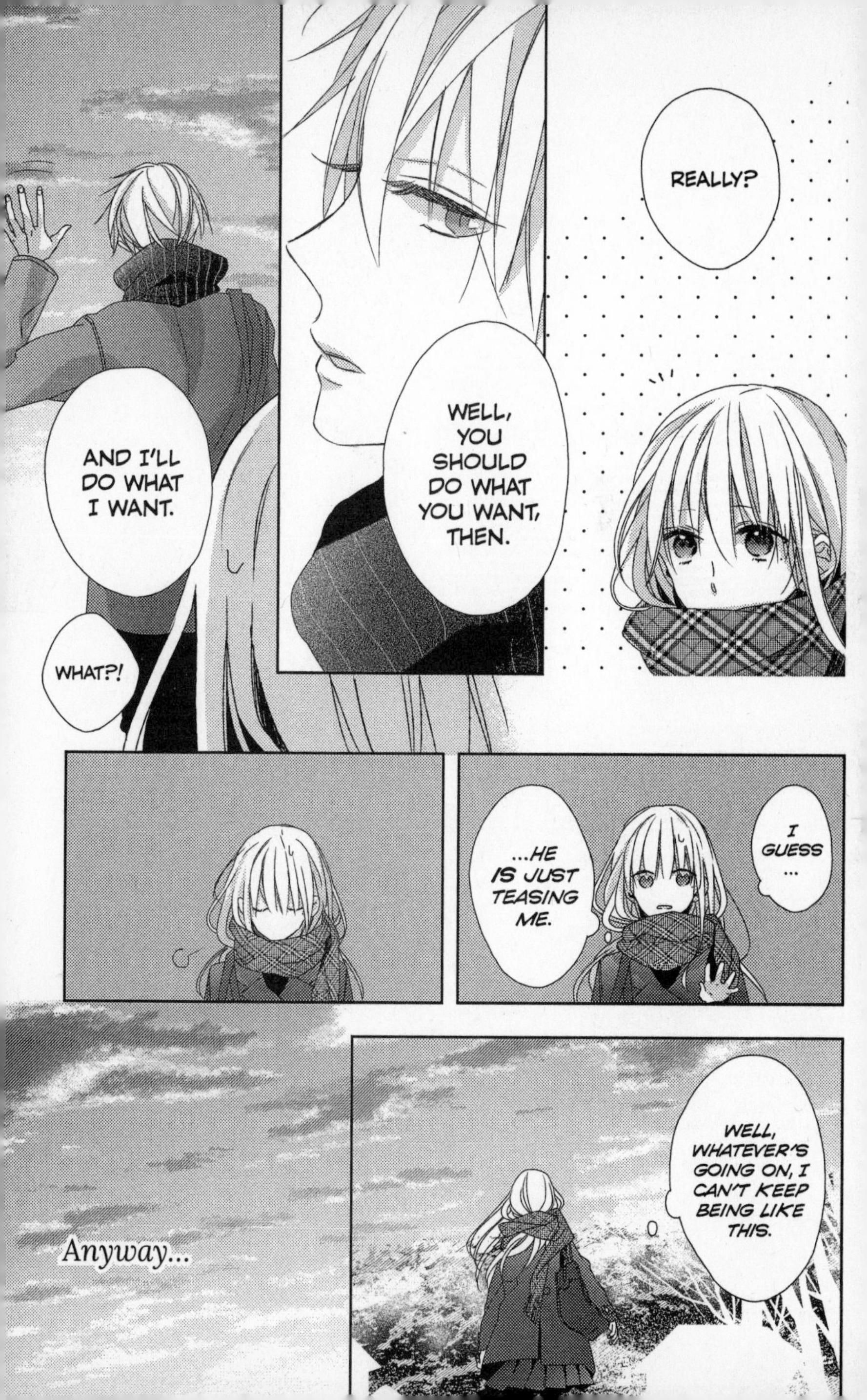
REALLY?
WELL, YOU SHOULD DO WHAT YOU WANT, THEN.
AND I'LL DO WHAT I WANT.
WHAT?!
I GUESS...
...HE IS JUST TEASING ME.
WELL, WHATEVER'S GOING ON, I CAN'T KEEP BEING LIKE THIS.
Anyway...

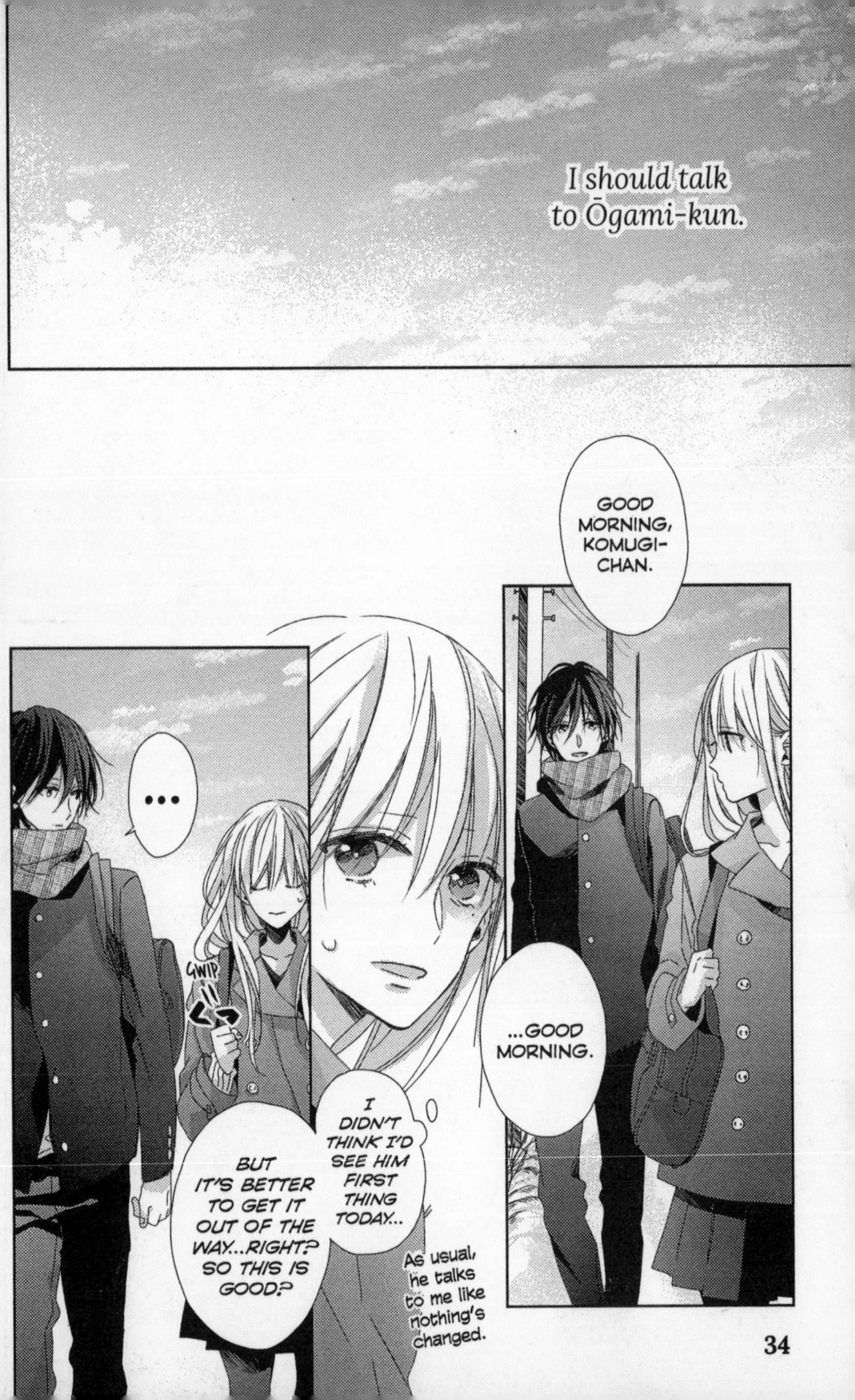
I should talk to Ōgami-kun.
GOOD MORNING, KOMUGI-CHAN.
...GOOD MORNING.
I DIDN'T THINK I'D SEE HIM FIRST THING TODAY...
BUT IT'S BETTER TO GET IT OUT OF THE WAY...RIGHT? SO THIS IS GOOD?
As usual, he talks to me like nothing's changed.
...
GWIP

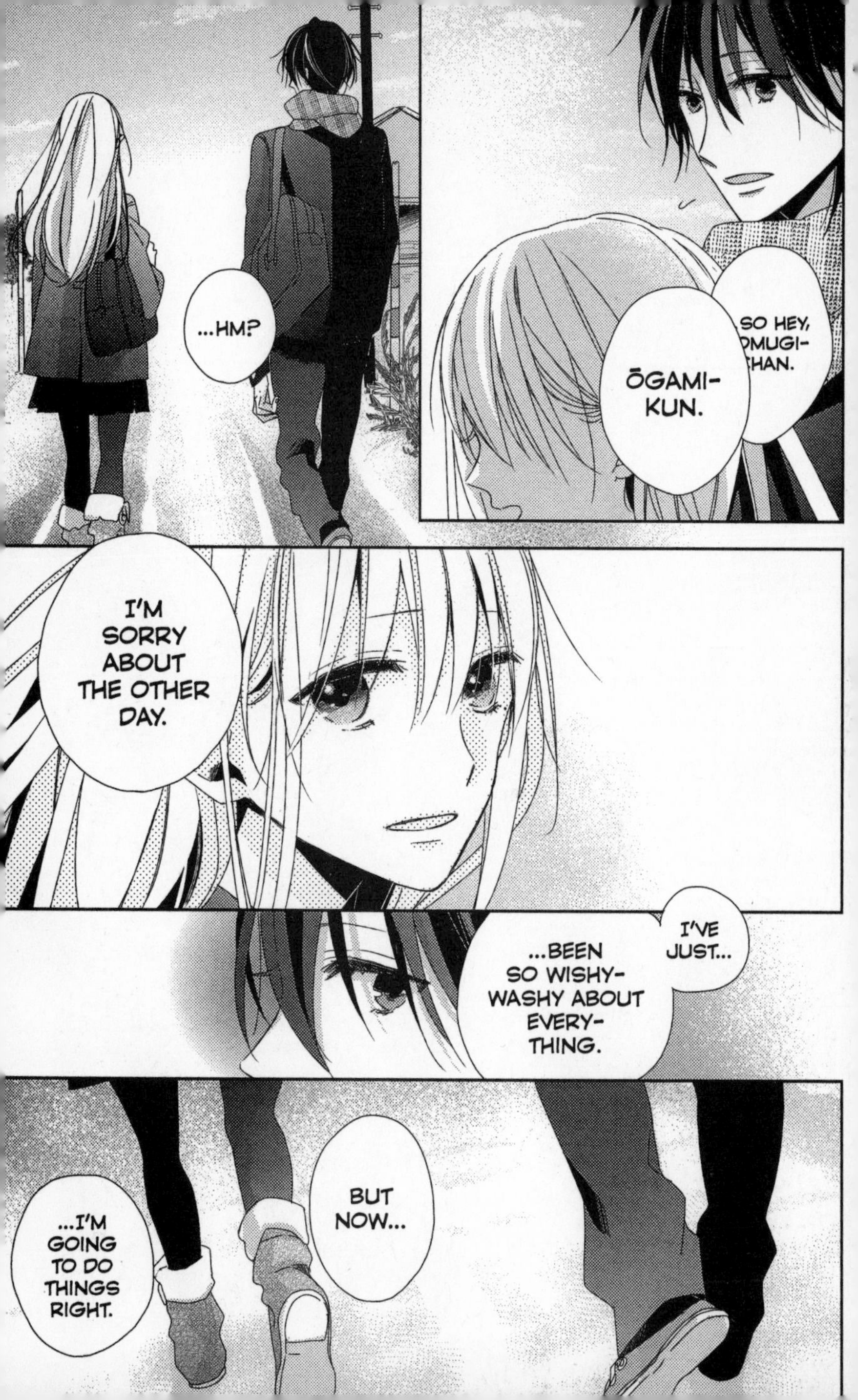
SO HEY, OMUGI- HAN.
ŌGAMI-KUN.
...HM?
I'M SORRY ABOUT THE OTHER DAY.
I'VE JUST...
...BEEN SO WISHY-WASHY ABOUT EVERYTHING.
BUT NOW...
...I'M GOING TO DO THINGS RIGHT.

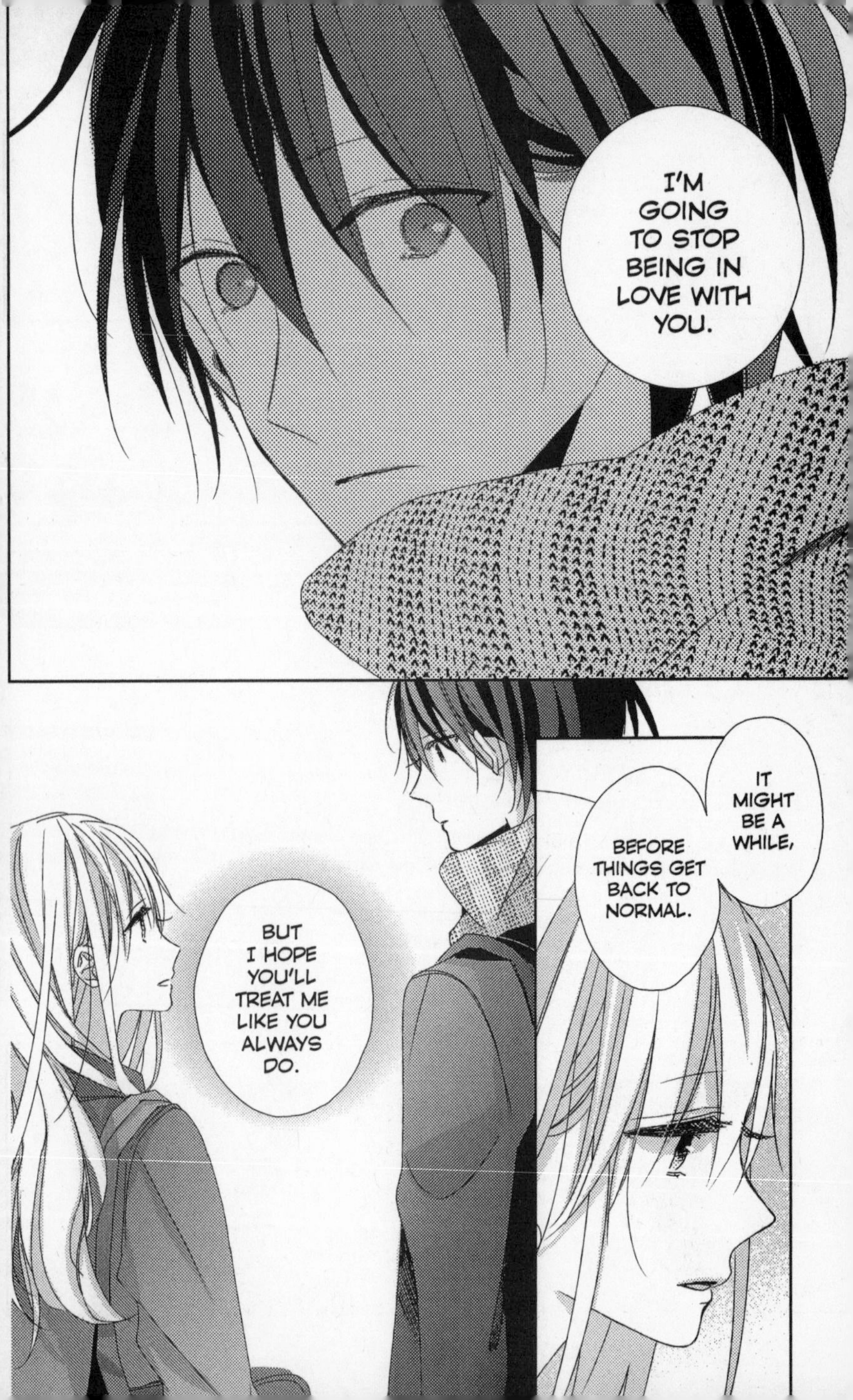
I'M GOING TO STOP BEING IN LOVE WITH YOU.
IT MIGHT BE A WHILE,
BEFORE THINGS GET BACK TO NORMAL.
BUT I HOPE YOU'LL TREAT ME LIKE YOU ALWAYS DO.

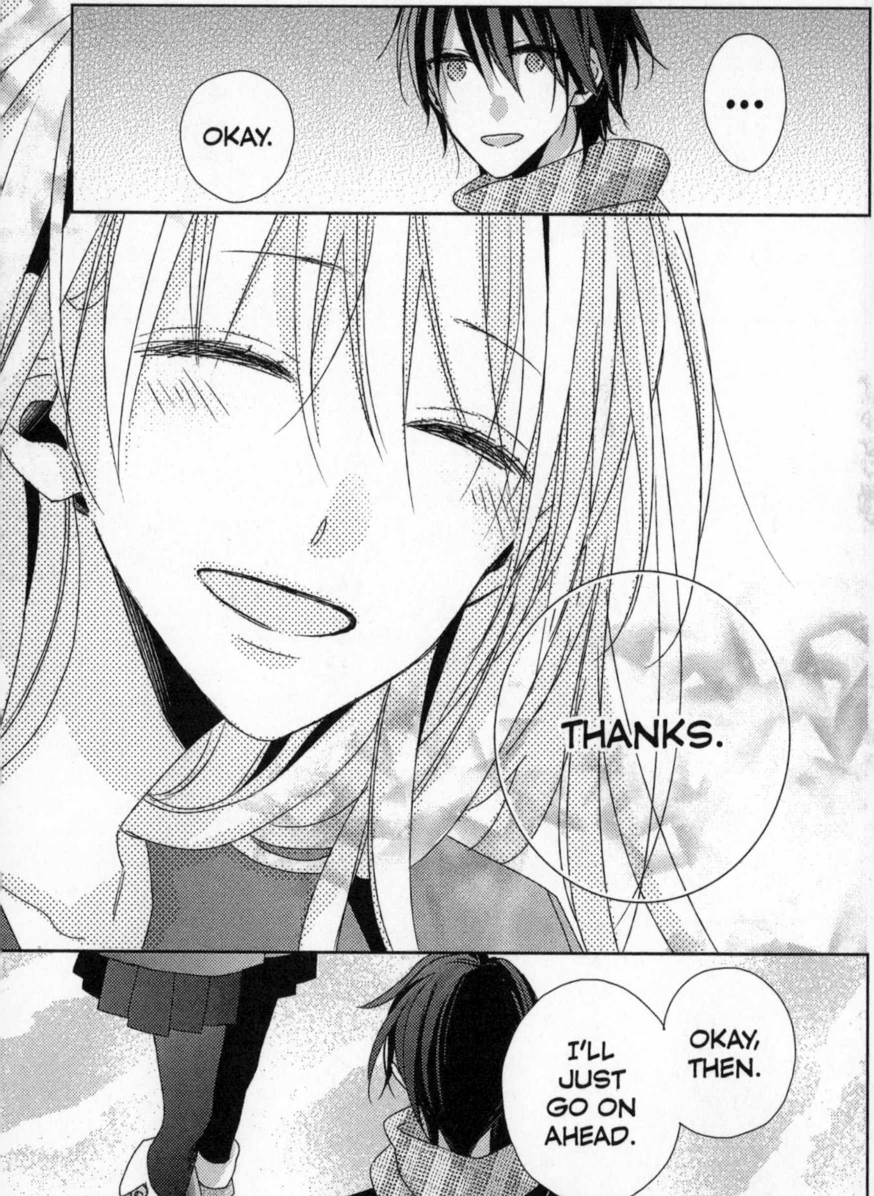
...
OKAY.
THANKS.
OKAY, THEN.
I'LL JUST GO ON AHEAD.

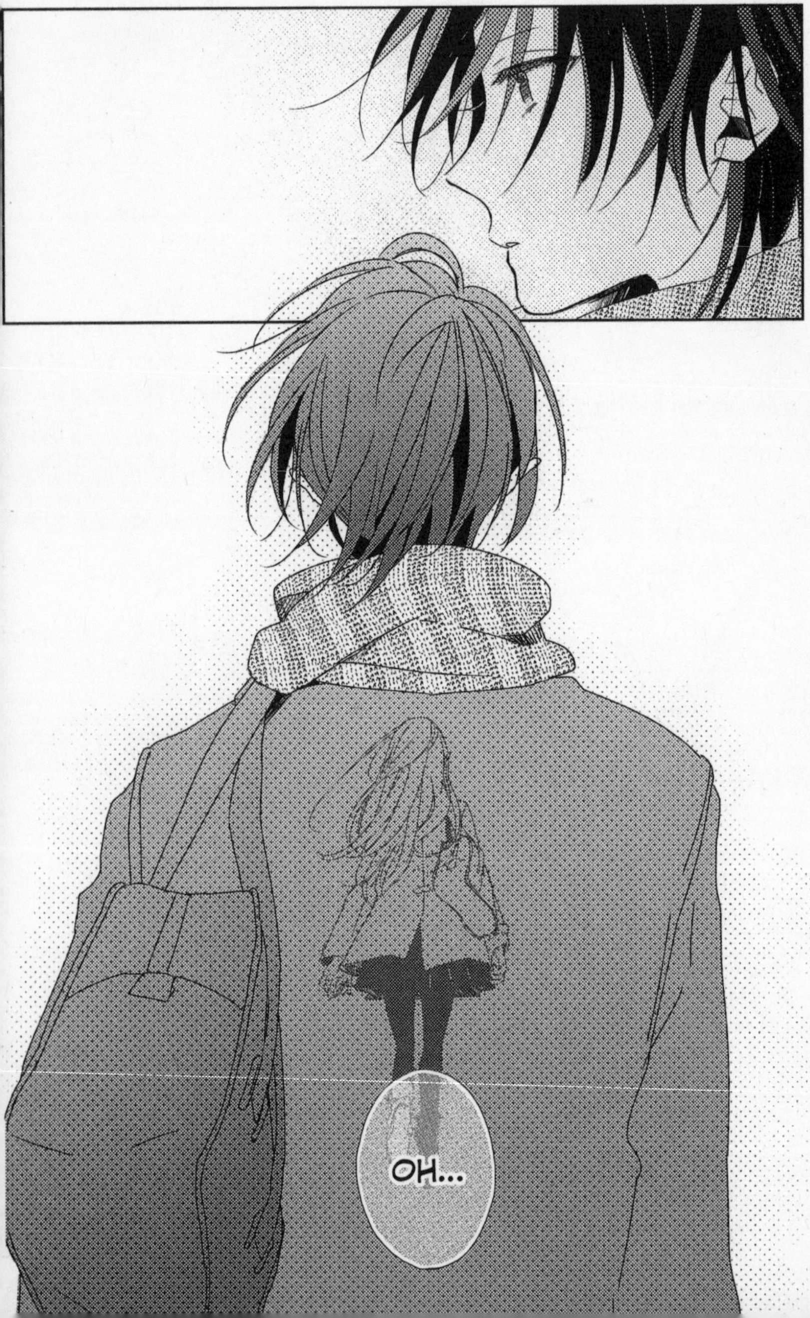
OH...

# Chapter 10

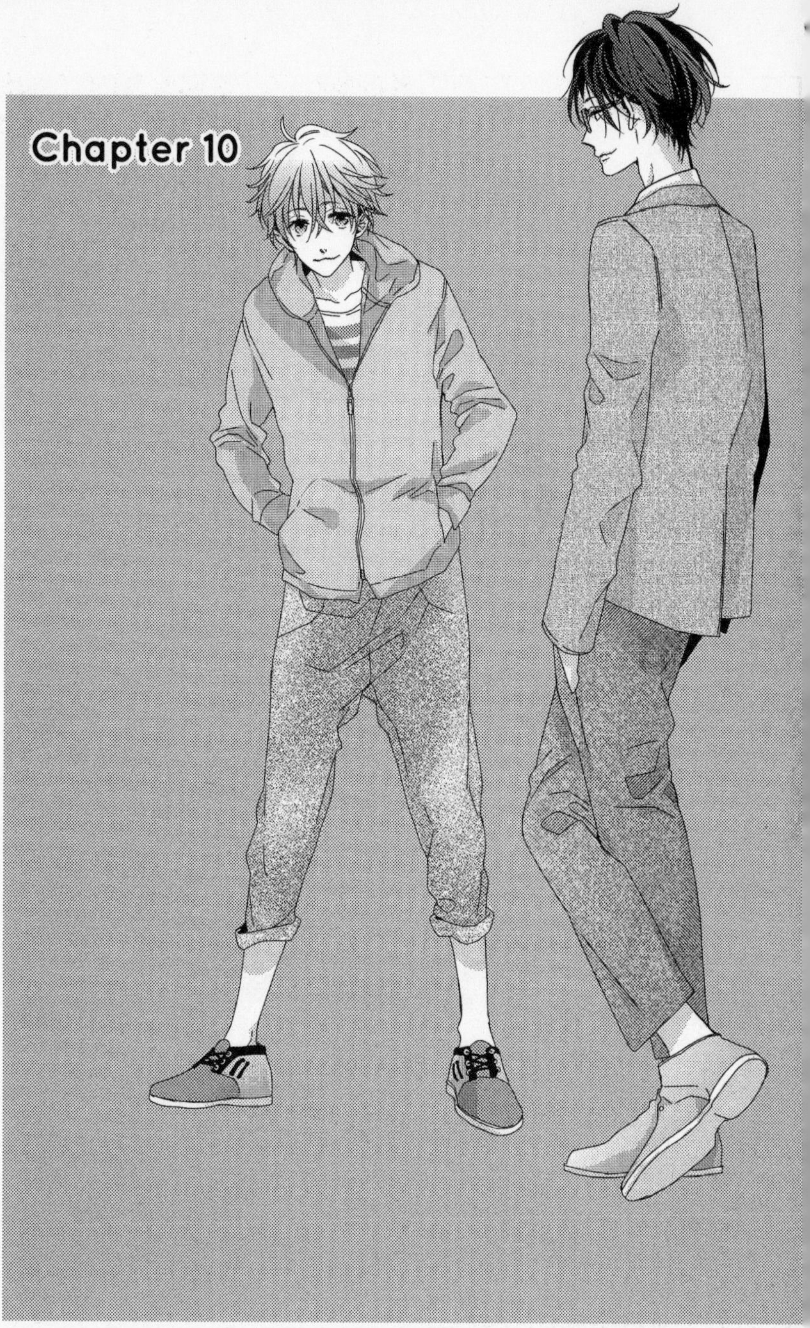

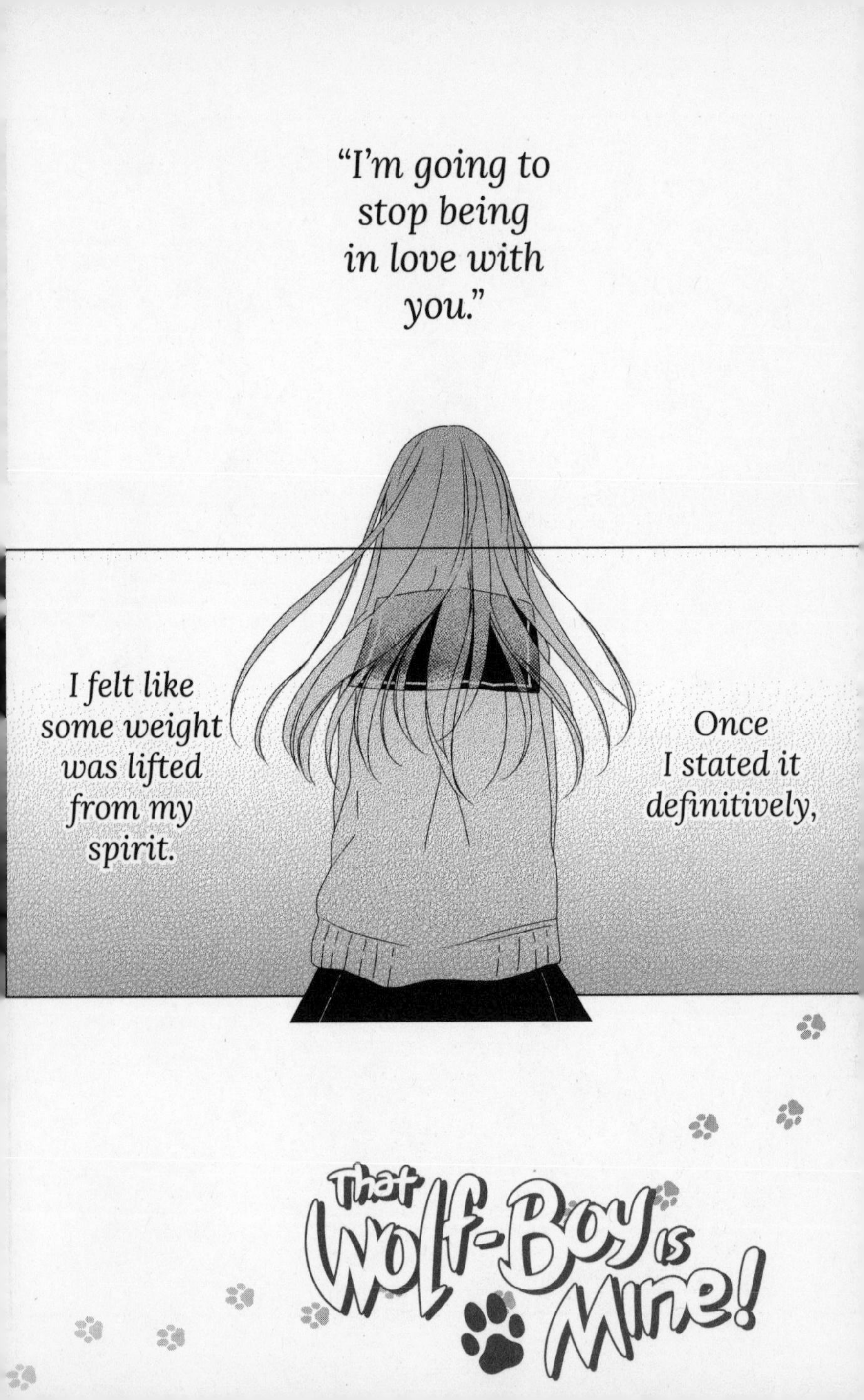
"I'm going to stop being in love with you."
Once I stated it definitively,
I felt like some weight was lifted from my spirit.
That Wolf-Boy is Mine!

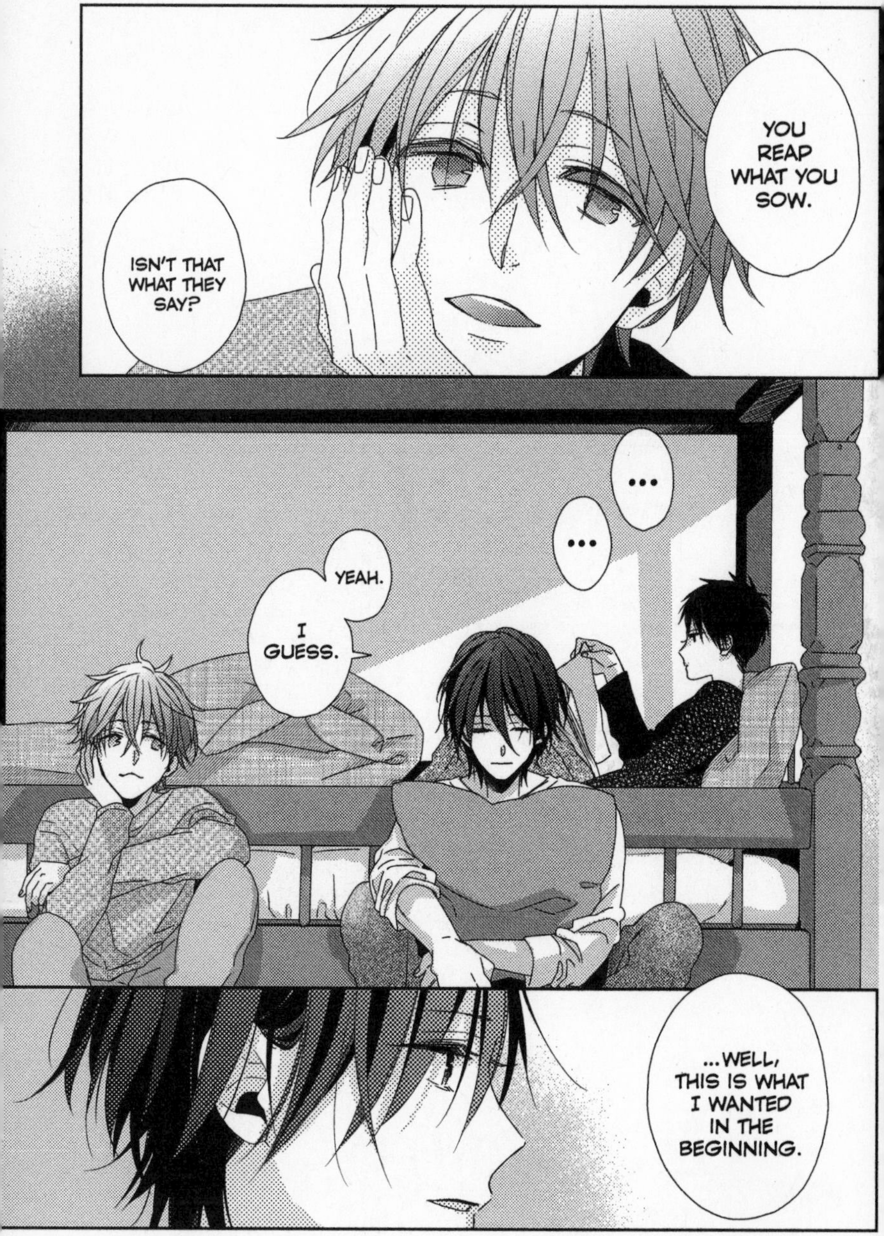
YOU REAP WHAT YOU SOW.
ISN'T THAT WHAT THEY SAY?
...
...
YEAH.
I GUESS.
...WELL, THIS IS WHAT I WANTED IN THE BEGINNING.

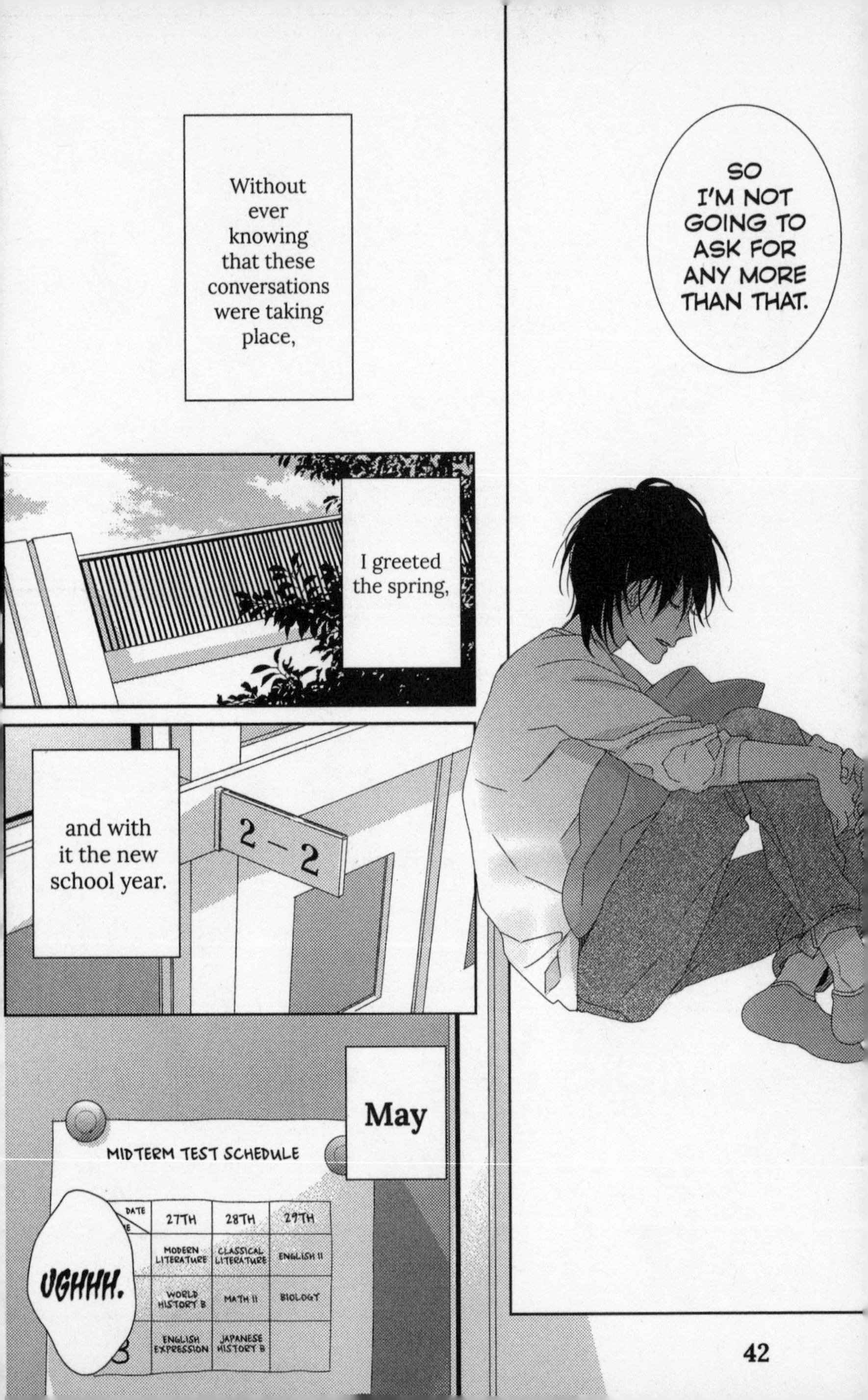
SO I'M NOT GOING TO ASK FOR ANY MORE THAN THAT.
Without ever knowing that these conversations were taking place,
I greeted the spring,
and with it the new school year.
2-2
May
MIDTERM TEST SCHEDULE
DATE
27TH
28TH
29TH
MODERN LITERATURE
CLASSICAL LITERATURE
ENGLISH II
WORLD HISTORY B
MATH II
BIOLOGY
ENGLISH EXPRESSION
JAPANESE HISTORY B
UGHHH.

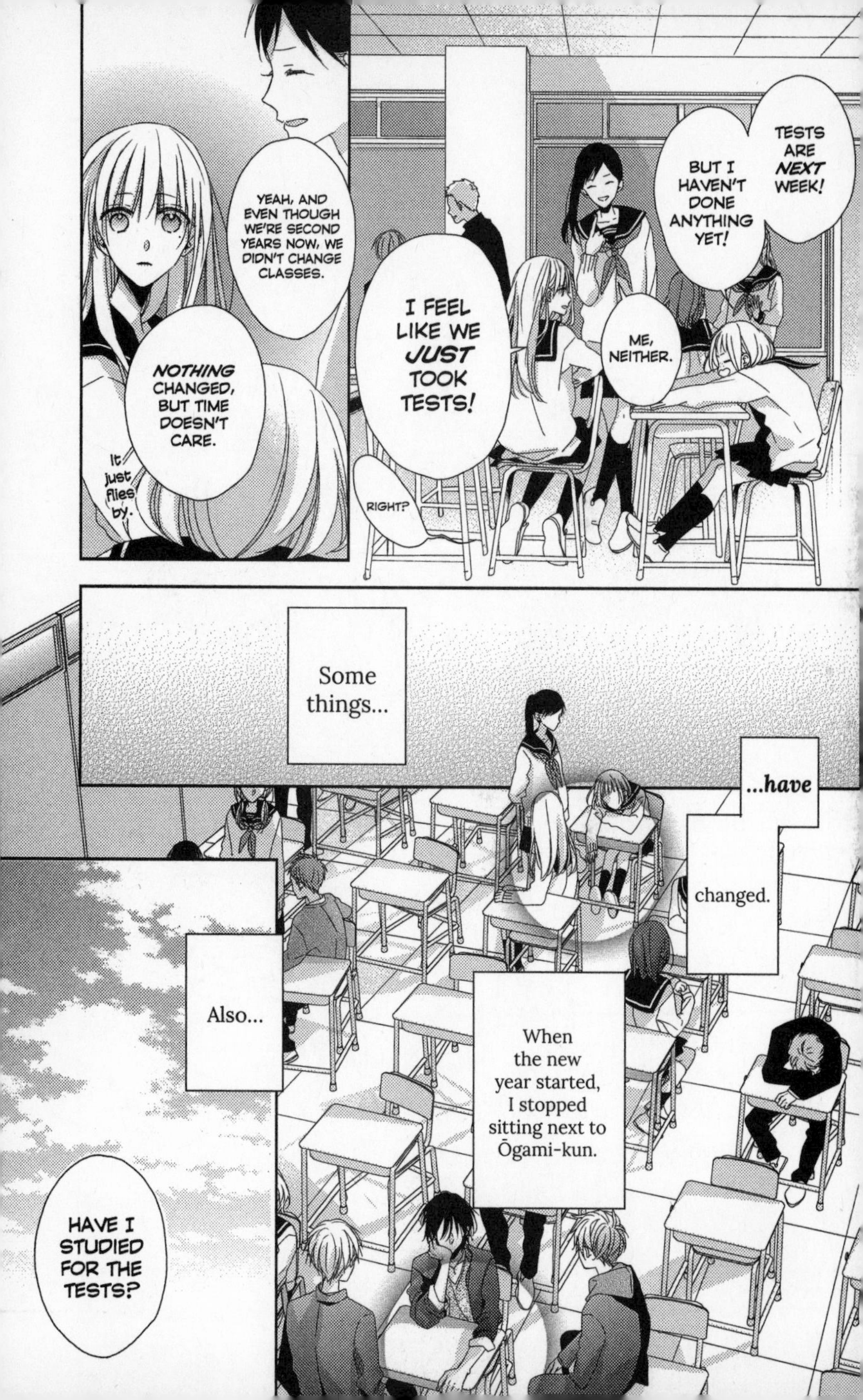
TESTS ARE NEXT WEEK!
BUT I HAVEN'T DONE ANYTHING YET!
ME, NEITHER.
I FEEL LIKE WE JUST TOOK TESTS!
RIGHT?
YEAH, AND EVEN THOUGH WE'RE SECOND YEARS NOW, WE DIDN'T CHANGE CLASSES.
NOTHING CHANGED, BUT TIME DOESN'T CARE.
It just flies by.
Some things...
...have
changed.
Also...
When the new year started, I stopped sitting next to Ōgami-kun.
HAVE I STUDIED FOR THE TESTS?

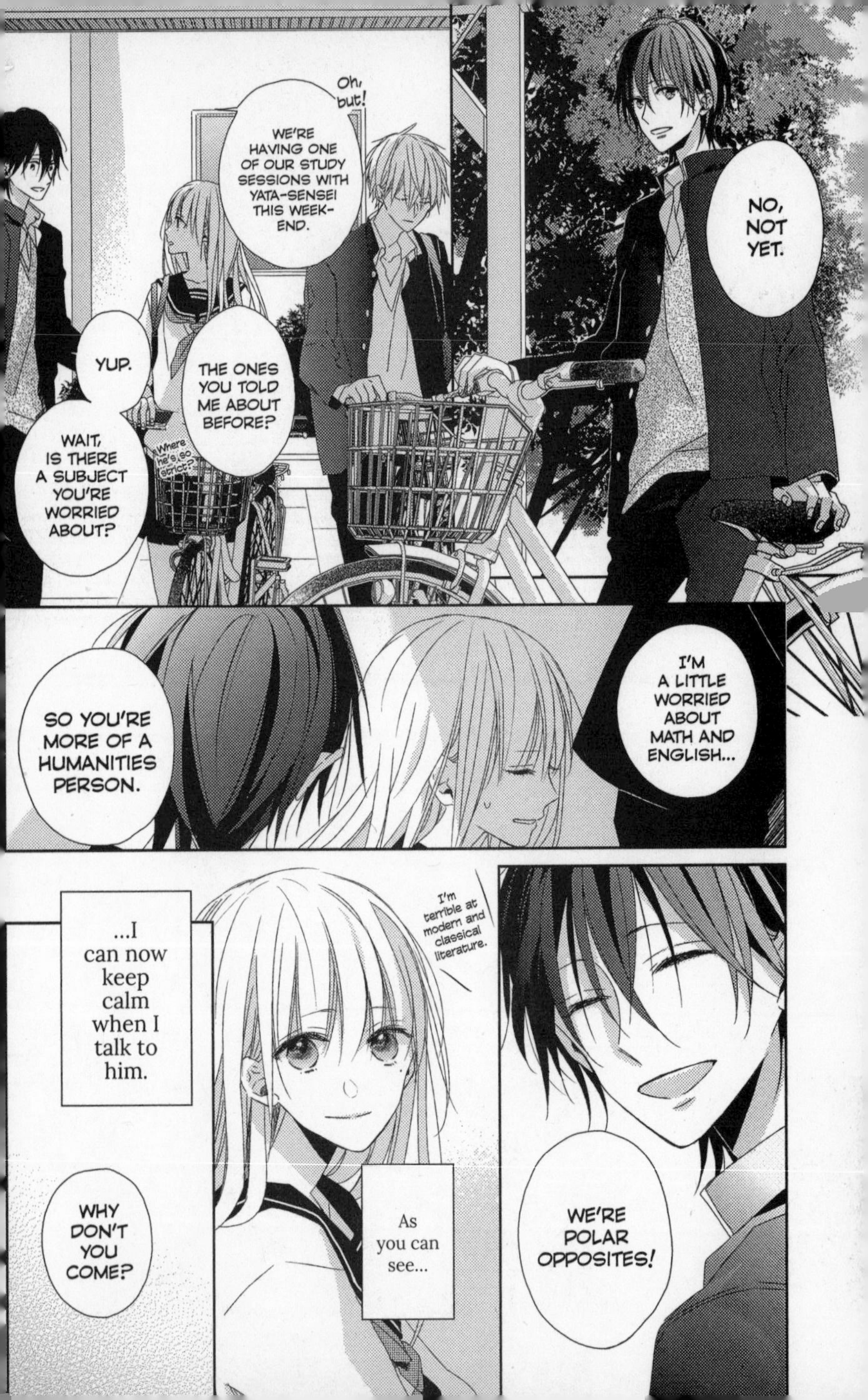
NO, NOT YET.
Oh, but!
WE'RE HAVING ONE OF OUR STUDY SESSIONS WITH YATA-SENSEI THIS WEEK-END.
THE ONES YOU TOLD ME ABOUT BEFORE?
YUP.
Where he's so strict?
WAIT, IS THERE A SUBJECT YOU'RE WORRIED ABOUT?
I'M A LITTLE WORRIED ABOUT MATH AND ENGLISH...
SO YOU'RE MORE OF A HUMANITIES PERSON.
I'm terrible at modern and classical literature.
WE'RE POLAR OPPOSITES!
As you can see...
...I can now keep calm when I talk to him.
WHY DON'T YOU COME?

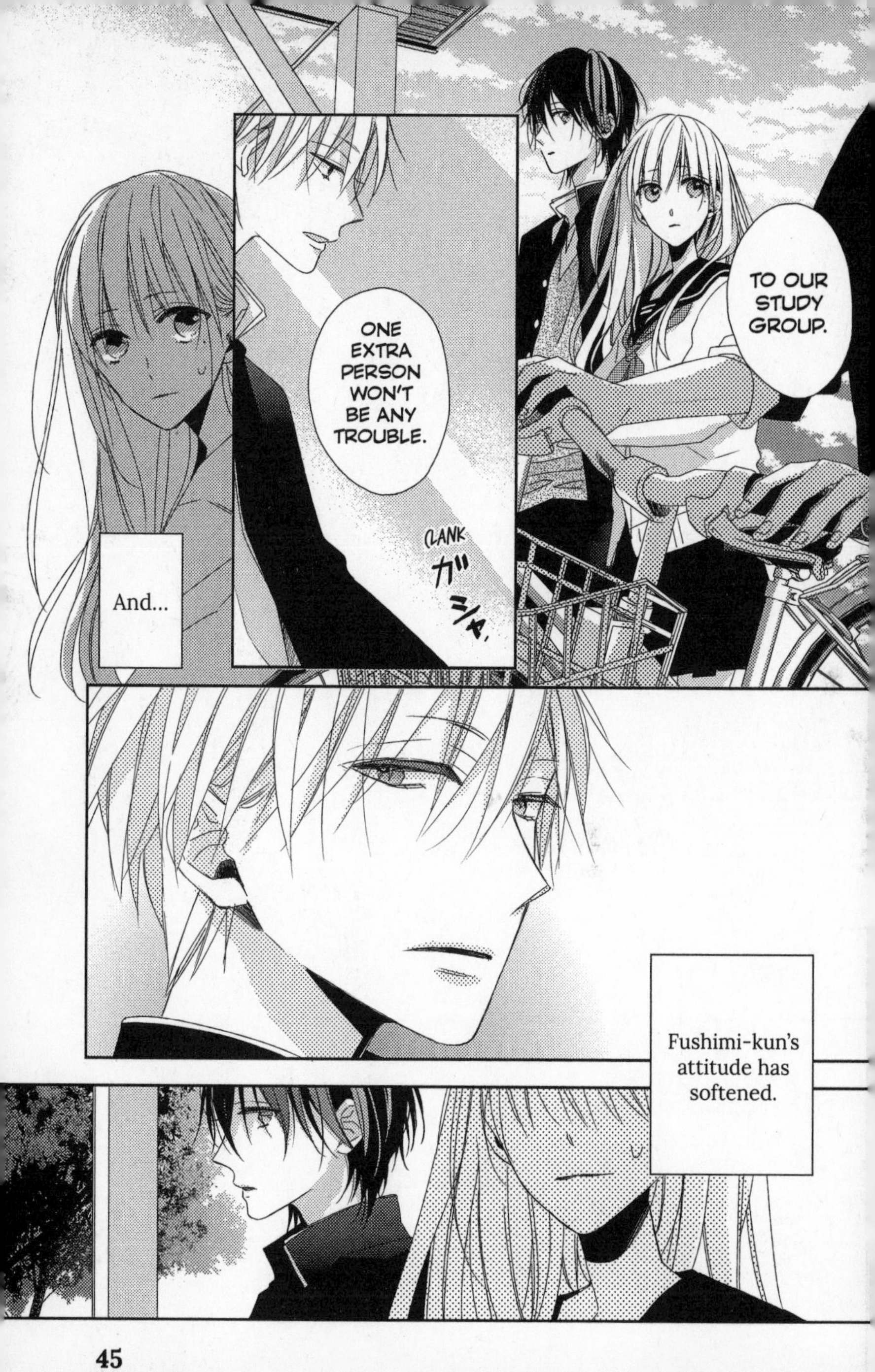
TO OUR STUDY GROUP.
ONE EXTRA PERSON WON'T BE ANY TROUBLE.
CLANK
ガシャ
And...
Fushimi-kun's attitude has softened.

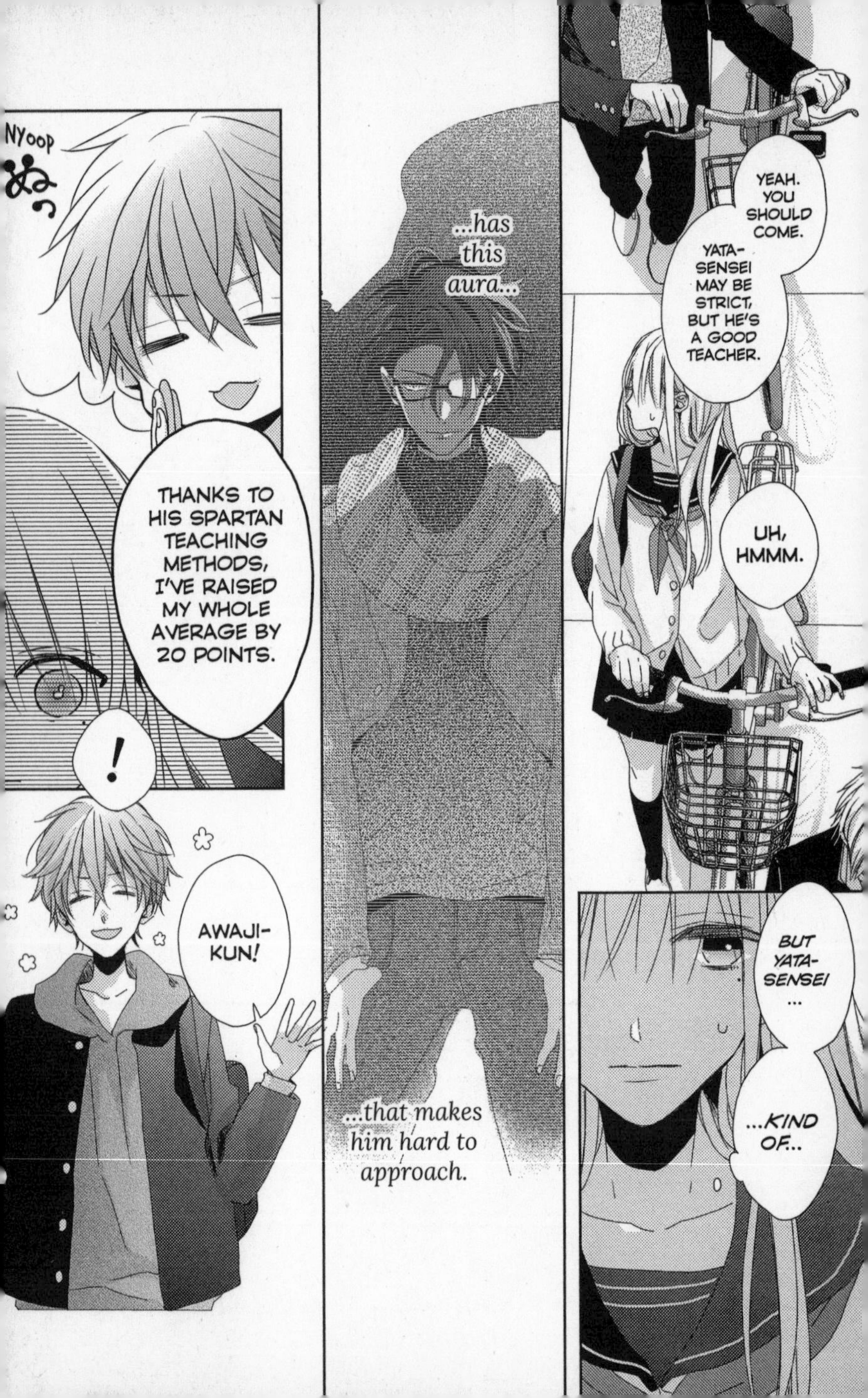
YEAH. YOU SHOULD COME.
YATA-SENSEI MAY BE STRICT, BUT HE'S A GOOD TEACHER.
UH, HMMM.
BUT YATA-SENSEI...
...KIND OF...
...has this aura...
...that makes him hard to approach.
NYOOP
ぬっ
THANKS TO HIS SPARTAN TEACHING METHODS, I'VE RAISED MY WHOLE AVERAGE BY 20 POINTS.
!
AWAJI-KUN!

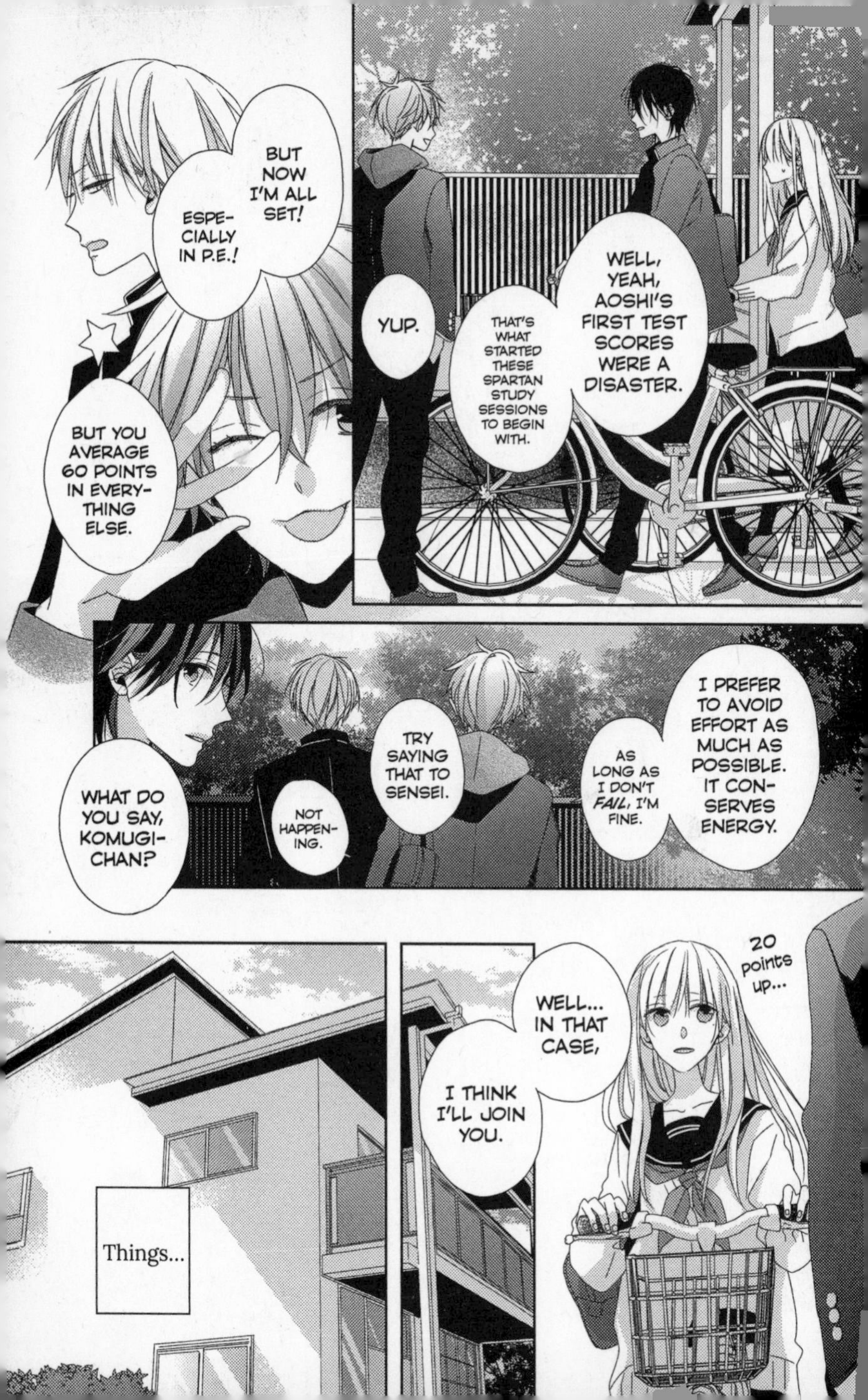
WELL, YEAH, AOSHI'S FIRST TEST SCORES WERE A DISASTER.
THAT'S WHAT STARTED THESE SPARTAN STUDY SESSIONS TO BEGIN WITH.
YUP.
BUT NOW I'M ALL SET!
ESPECIALLY IN P.E.!
BUT YOU AVERAGE 60 POINTS IN EVERYTHING ELSE.
I PREFER TO AVOID EFFORT AS MUCH AS POSSIBLE. IT CONSERVES ENERGY.
AS LONG AS I DON'T *FAIL*, I'M FINE.
TRY SAYING THAT TO SENSEI.
NOT HAPPENING.
WHAT DO YOU SAY, KOMUGI-CHAN?
20 points up...
WELL... IN THAT CASE,
I THINK I'LL JOIN YOU.
Things...

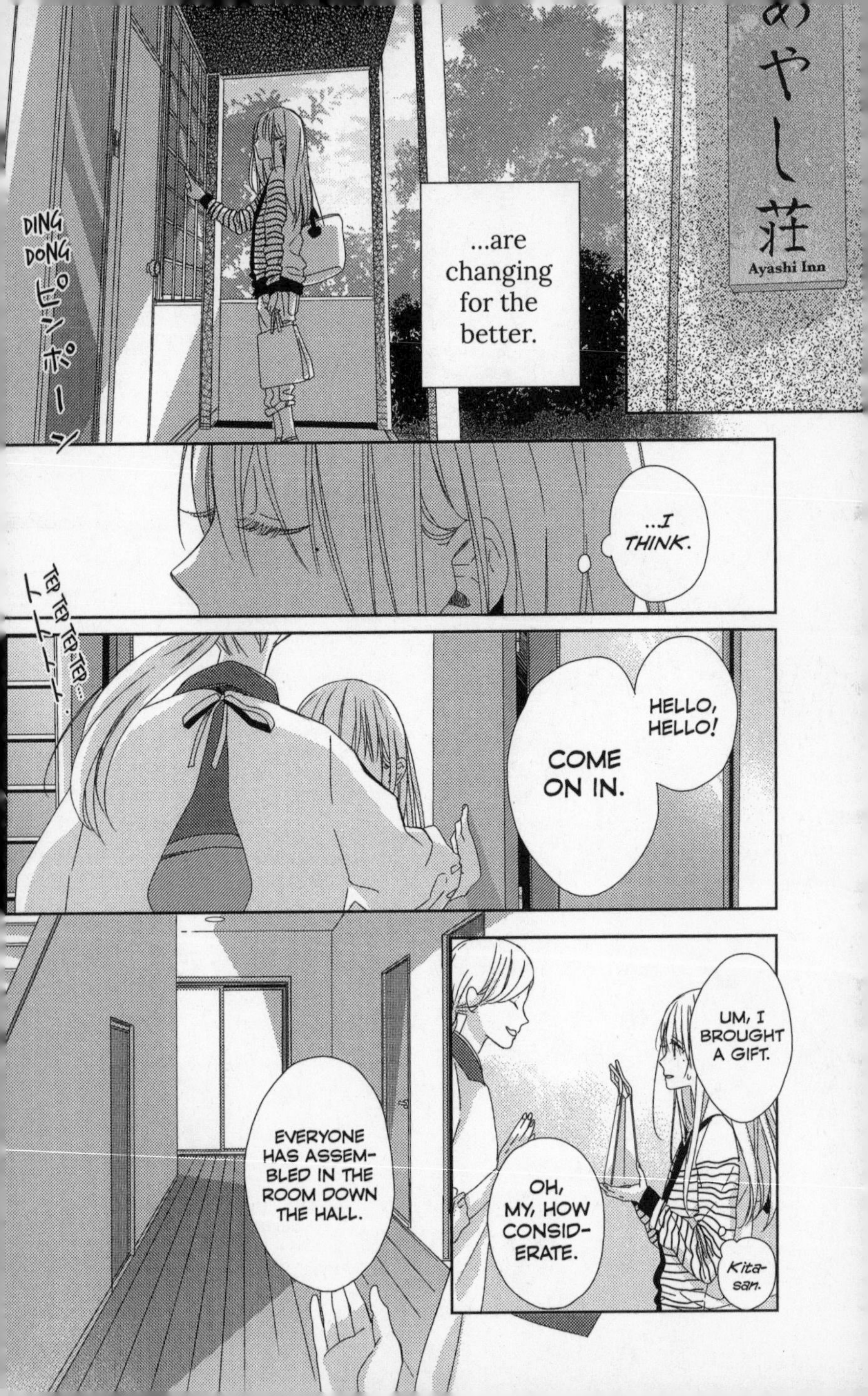

やし荘
Ayashi Inn
...are changing for the better.
DING DONG
ピンポーン
...I THINK.
TEP TEP TEP TEP...
トトトト
HELLO, HELLO!
COME ON IN.
UM, I BROUGHT A GIFT.
Kita-san.
OH, MY, HOW CONSIDERATE.
EVERYONE HAS ASSEMBLED IN THE ROOM DOWN THE HALL.

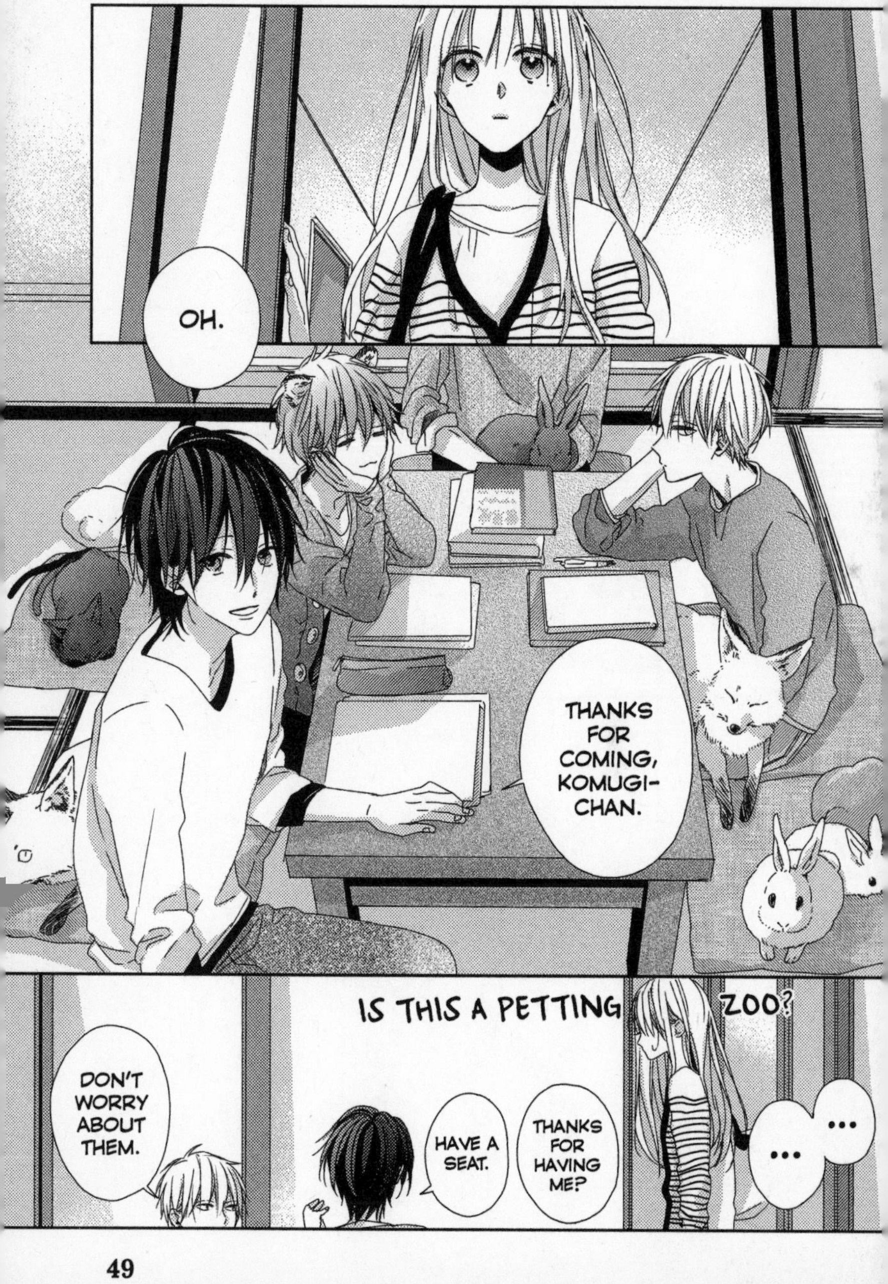
OH.
THANKS FOR COMING, KOMUGI-CHAN.
... ...
IS THIS A PETTING ZOO?
THANKS FOR HAVING ME?
HAVE A SEAT.
DON'T WORRY ABOUT THEM.

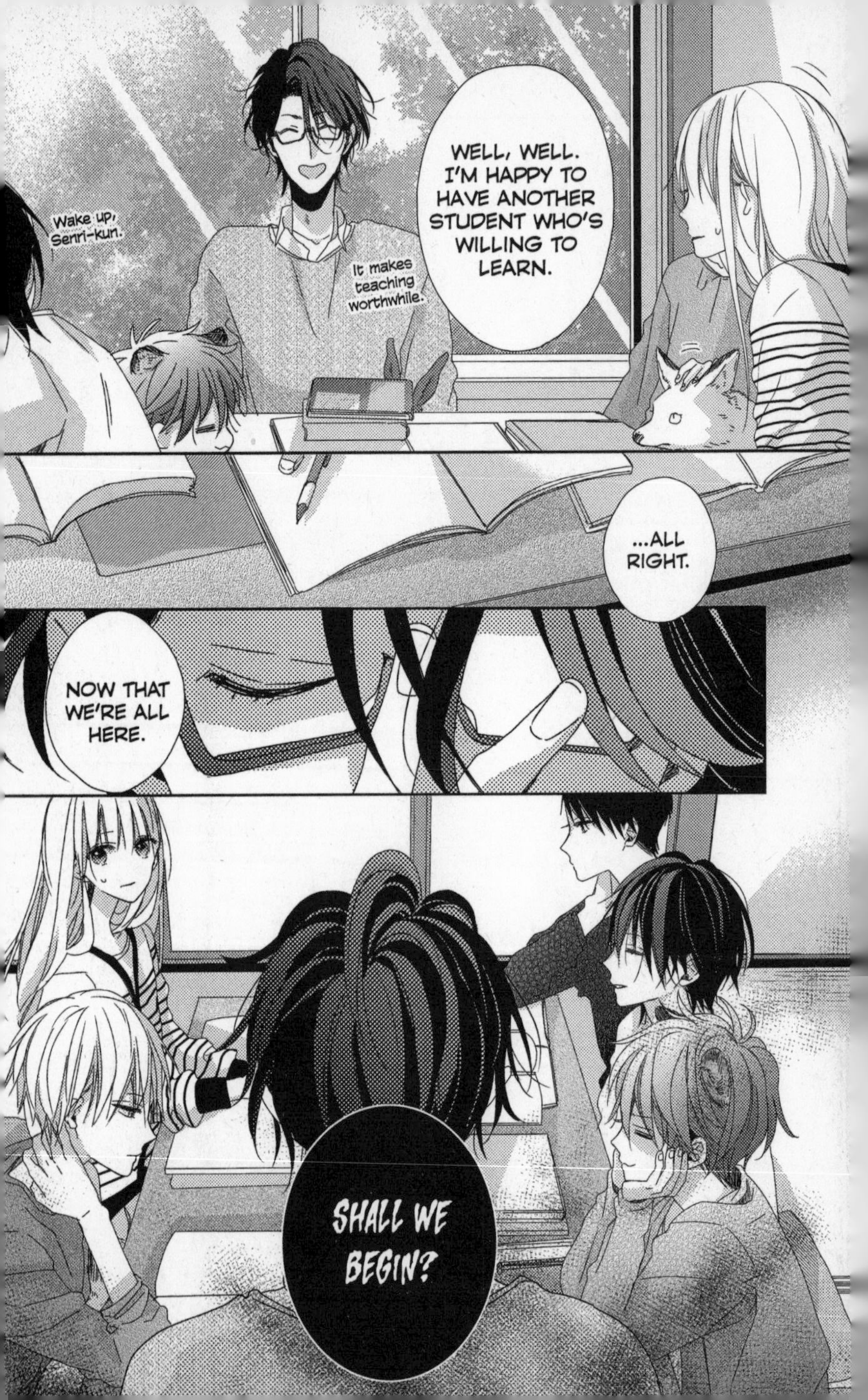
WELL, WELL. I'M HAPPY TO HAVE ANOTHER STUDENT WHO'S WILLING TO LEARN.
It makes teaching worthwhile.
Wake up, Senri-kun.
...ALL RIGHT.
NOW THAT WE'RE ALL HERE.
SHALL WE BEGIN?

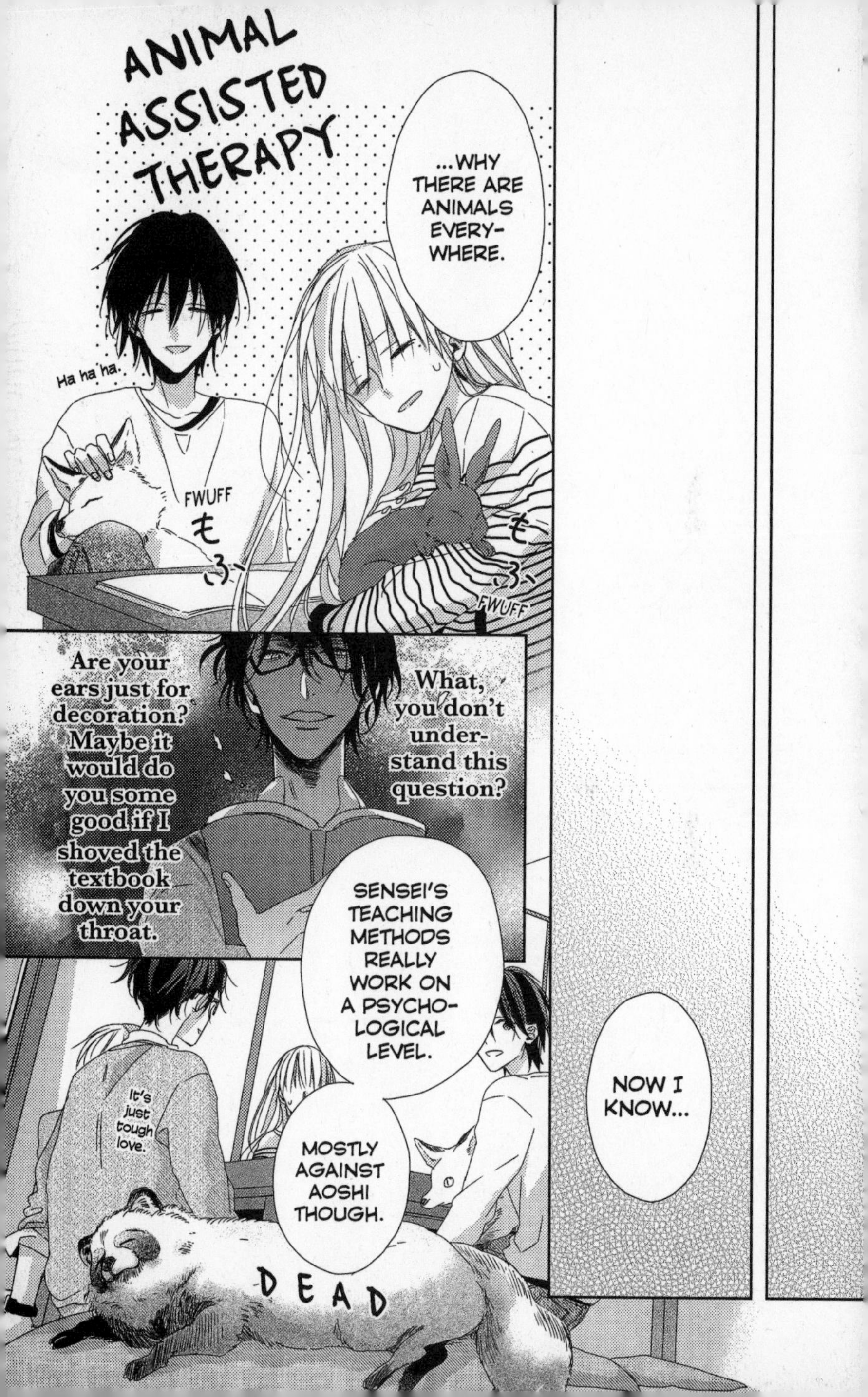
NOW I KNOW...
...WHY THERE ARE ANIMALS EVERYWHERE.
ANIMAL ASSISTED THERAPY
もふ FWUFF
Ha ha ha.
もふ FWUFF
What, you don't understand this question?
Are your ears just for decoration? Maybe it would do you some good if I shoved the textbook down your throat.
SENSEI'S TEACHING METHODS REALLY WORK ON A PSYCHOLOGICAL LEVEL.
MOSTLY AGAINST AOSHI THOUGH.
It's just tough love.
DEAD

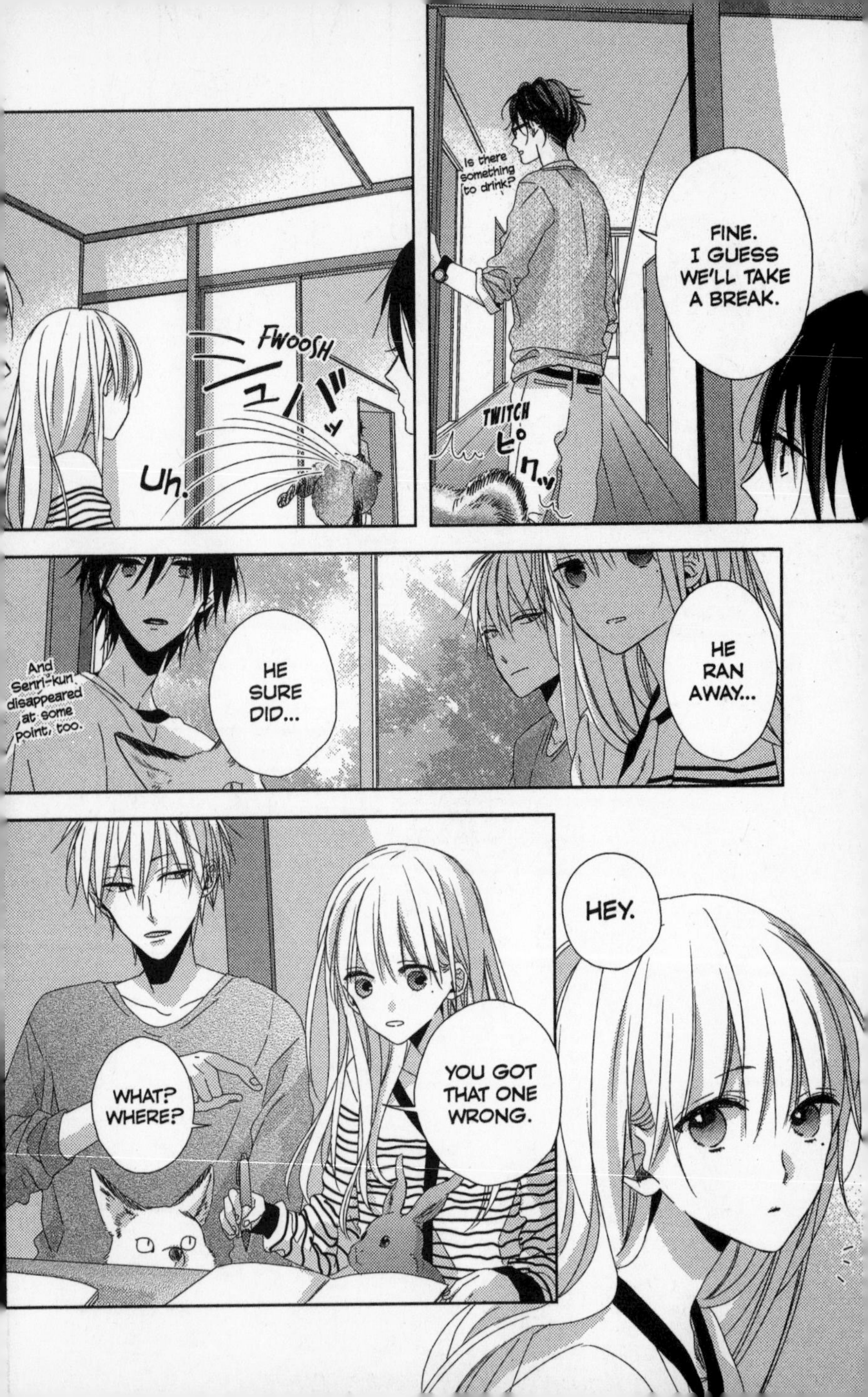
FINE. I GUESS WE'LL TAKE A BREAK.
Is there something to drink?
TWITCH
FWOOSH
Uh.
HE RAN AWAY...
HE SURE DID...
And Senri-kun disappeared at some point, too.
HEY.
YOU GOT THAT ONE WRONG.
WHAT? WHERE?

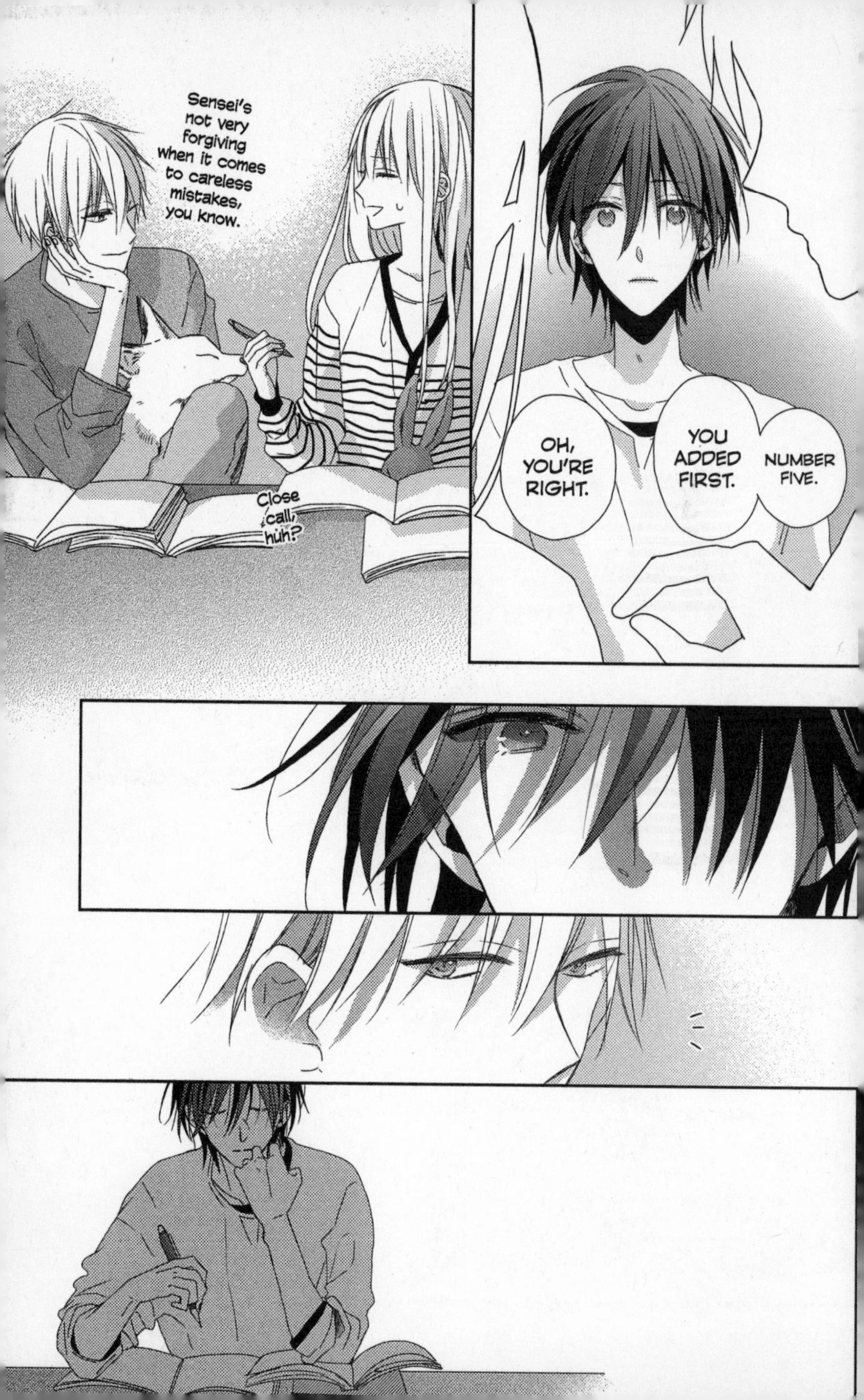
NUMBER FIVE.
YOU ADDED FIRST.
OH, YOU'RE RIGHT.
Sensei's not very forgiving when it comes to careless mistakes, you know.
Close call, huh?

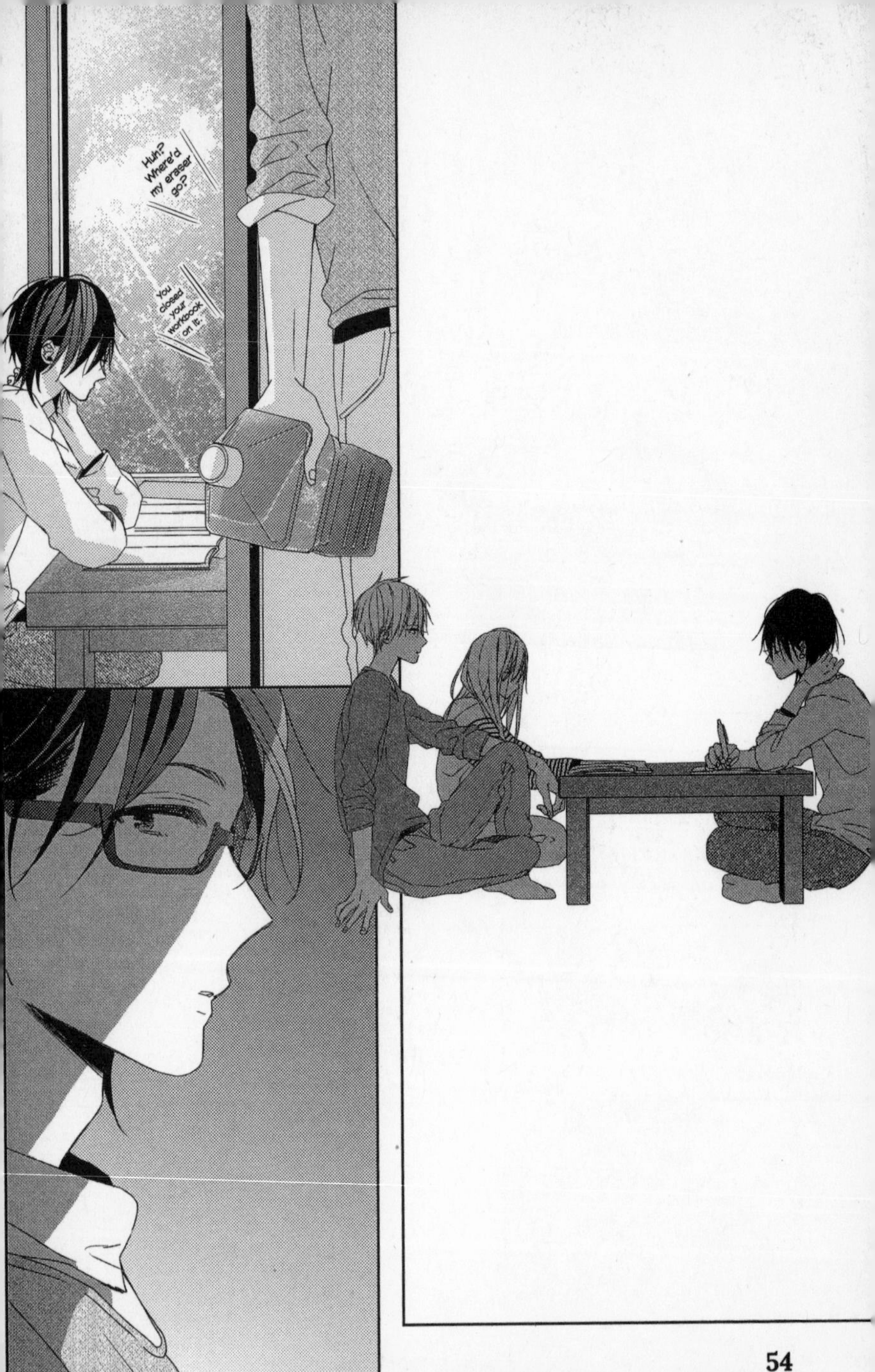

Huh? Where'd my eraser go?
You closed your workbook on it.

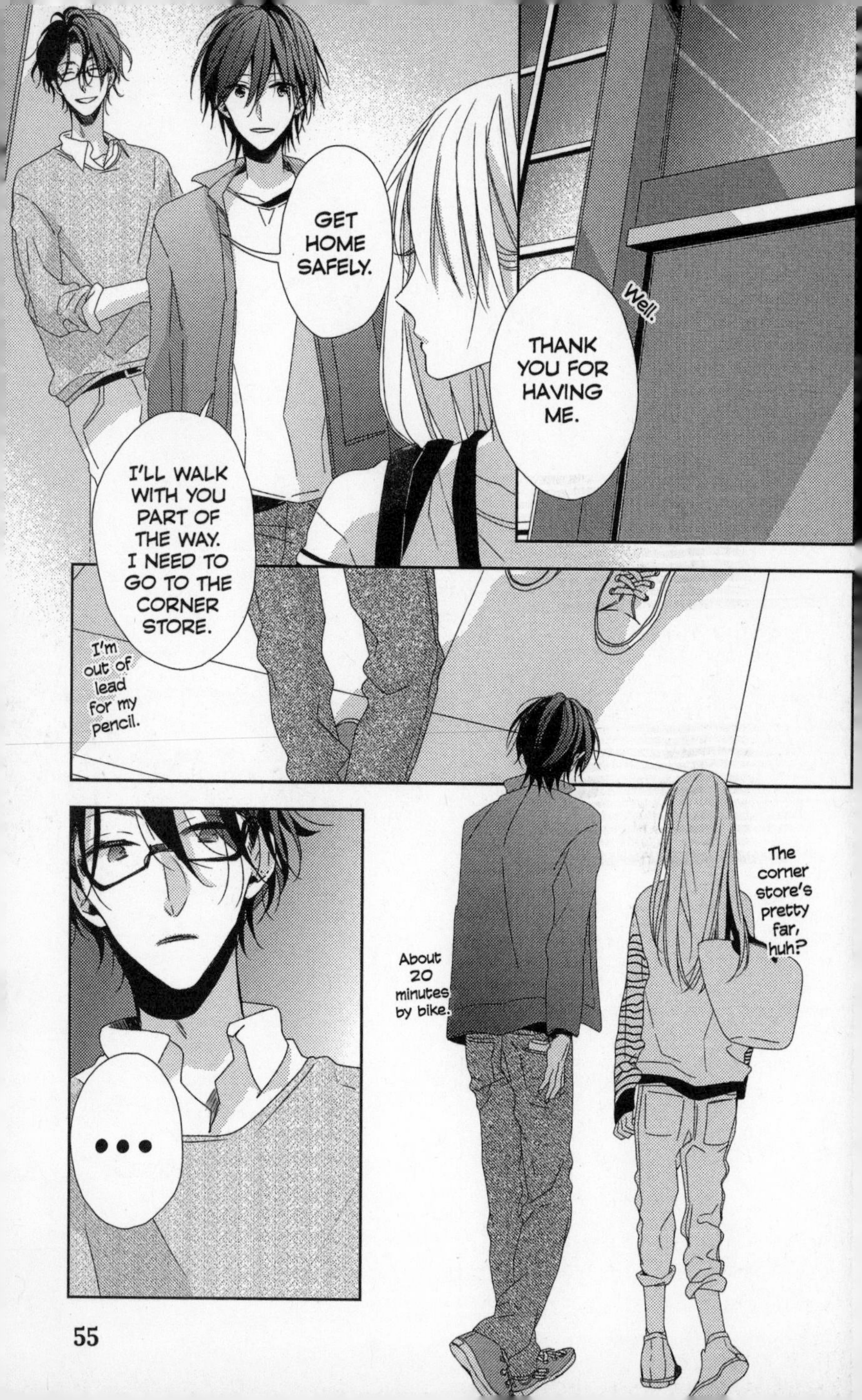
Well.
THANK YOU FOR HAVING ME.
GET HOME SAFELY.
I'LL WALK WITH YOU PART OF THE WAY. I NEED TO GO TO THE CORNER STORE.
I'm out of lead for my pencil.
The corner store's pretty far, huh?
About 20 minutes by bike.
...

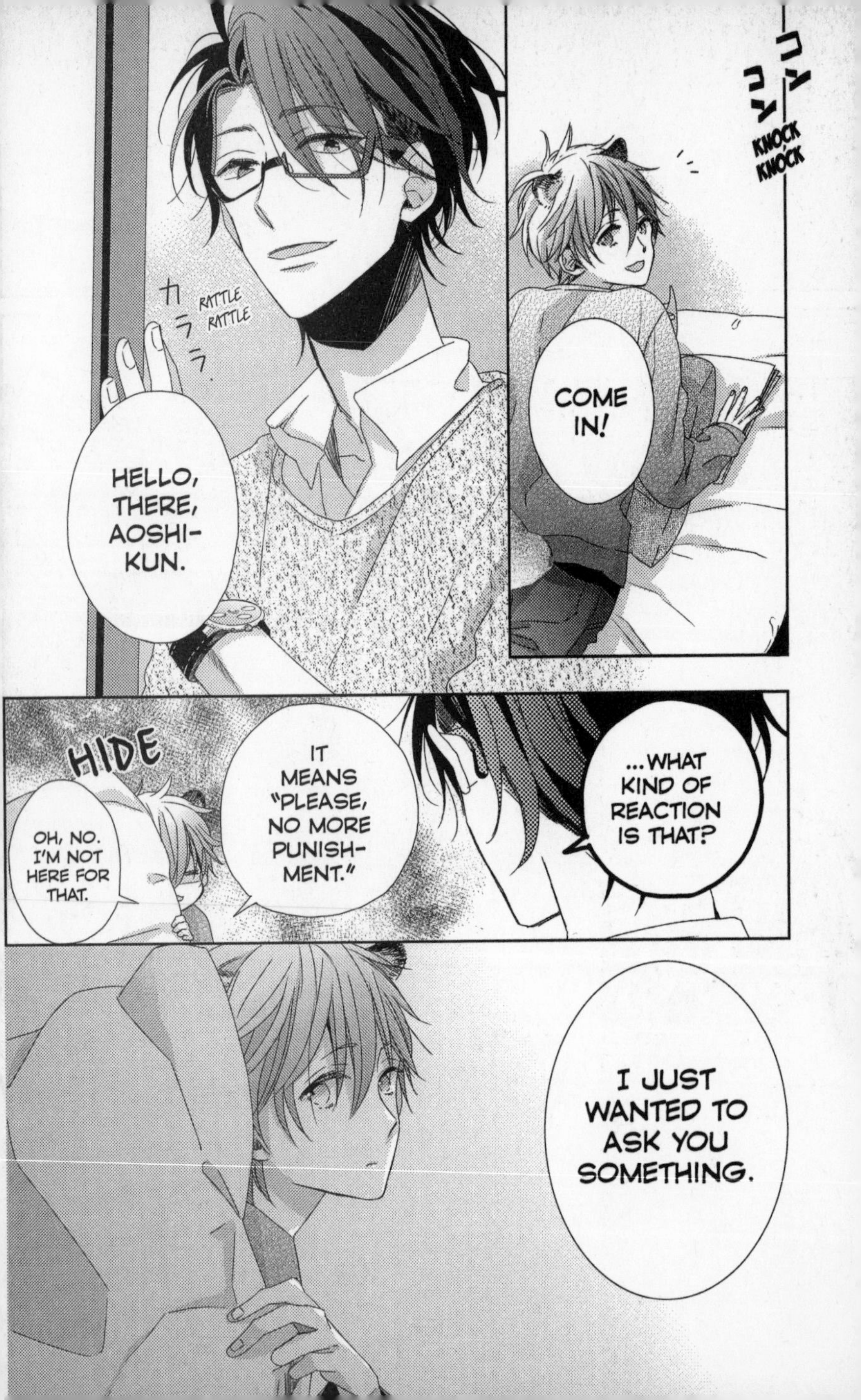
コンコン
KNOCK KNOCK
COME IN!
カラララ
RATTLE RATTLE
HELLO, THERE, AOSHI-KUN.
...WHAT KIND OF REACTION IS THAT?
IT MEANS "PLEASE, NO MORE PUNISHMENT."
HIDE
OH, NO. I'M NOT HERE FOR THAT.
I JUST WANTED TO ASK YOU SOMETHING.

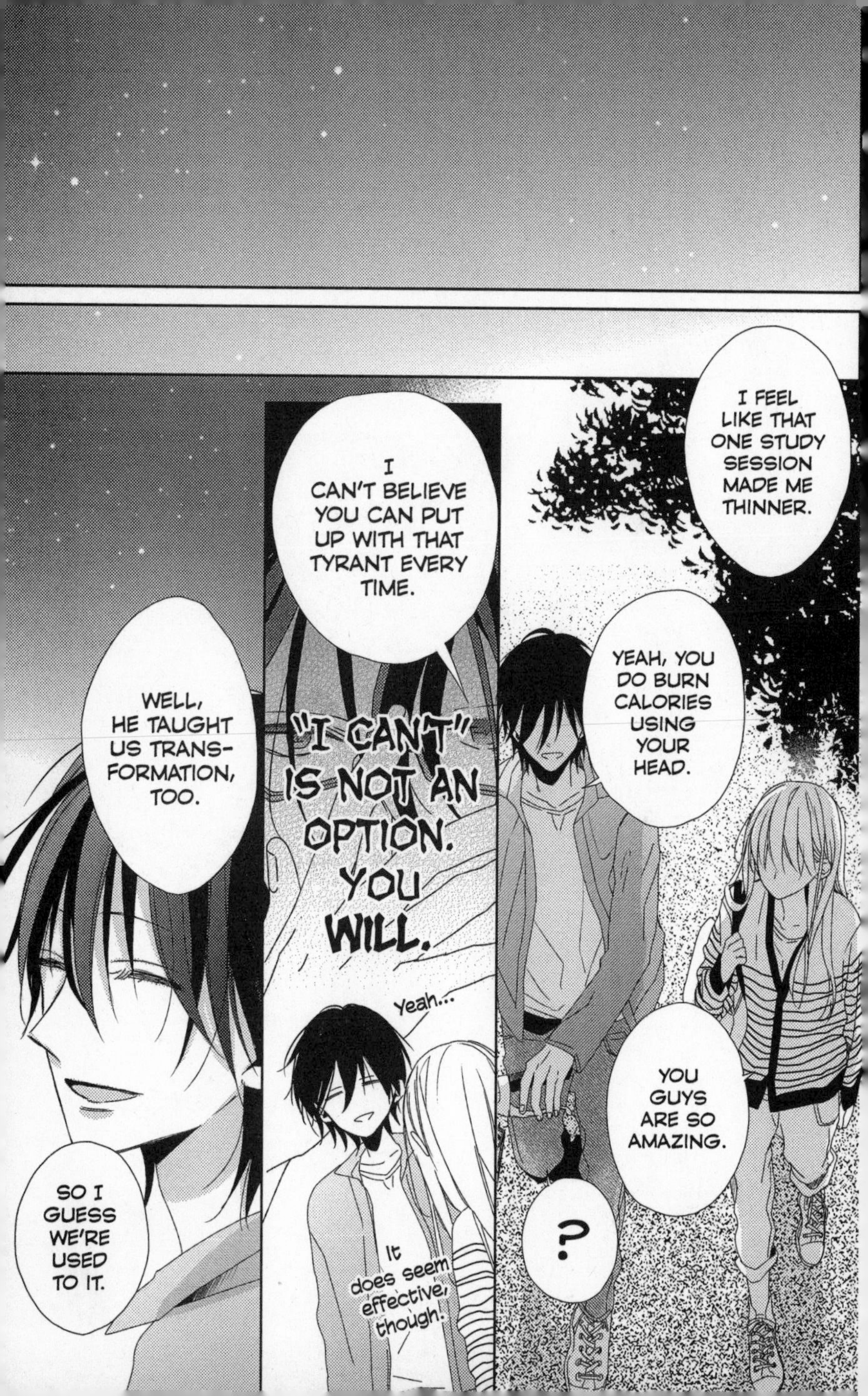
I FEEL LIKE THAT ONE STUDY SESSION MADE ME THINNER.
YEAH, YOU DO BURN CALORIES USING YOUR HEAD.
YOU GUYS ARE SO AMAZING.
?
I CAN'T BELIEVE YOU CAN PUT UP WITH THAT TYRANT EVERY TIME.
"I CAN'T" IS NOT AN OPTION. YOU WILL.
Yeah...
It does seem effective, though.
WELL, HE TAUGHT US TRANS-FORMATION, TOO.
SO I GUESS WE'RE USED TO IT.

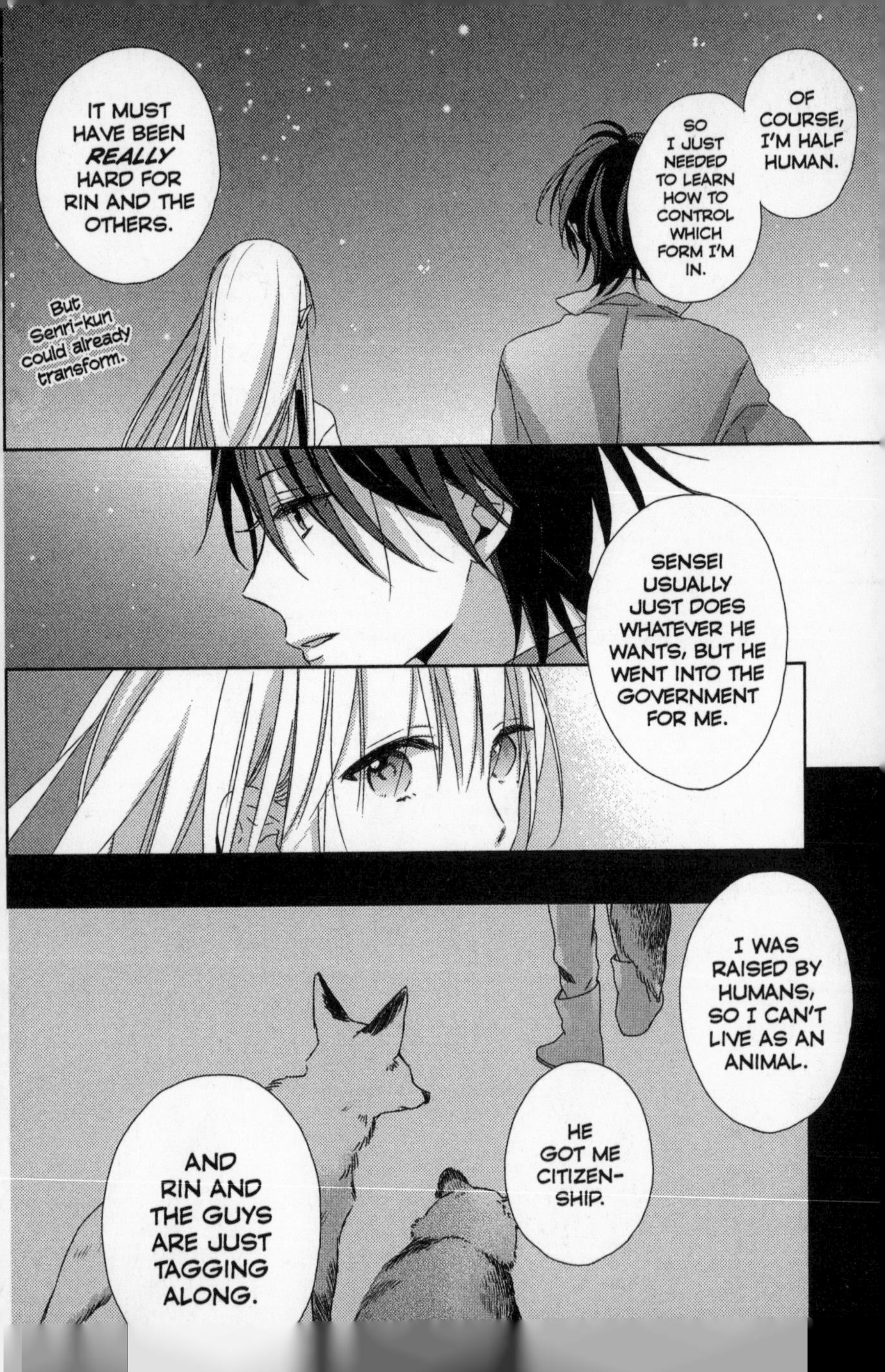
OF COURSE, I'M HALF HUMAN.
SO I JUST NEEDED TO LEARN HOW TO CONTROL WHICH FORM I'M IN.
IT MUST HAVE BEEN REALLY HARD FOR RIN AND THE OTHERS.
But Senri-kun could already transform.
SENSEI USUALLY JUST DOES WHATEVER HE WANTS, BUT HE WENT INTO THE GOVERNMENT FOR ME.
I WAS RAISED BY HUMANS, SO I CAN'T LIVE AS AN ANIMAL.
HE GOT ME CITIZEN-SHIP.
AND RIN AND THE GUYS ARE JUST TAGGING ALONG.

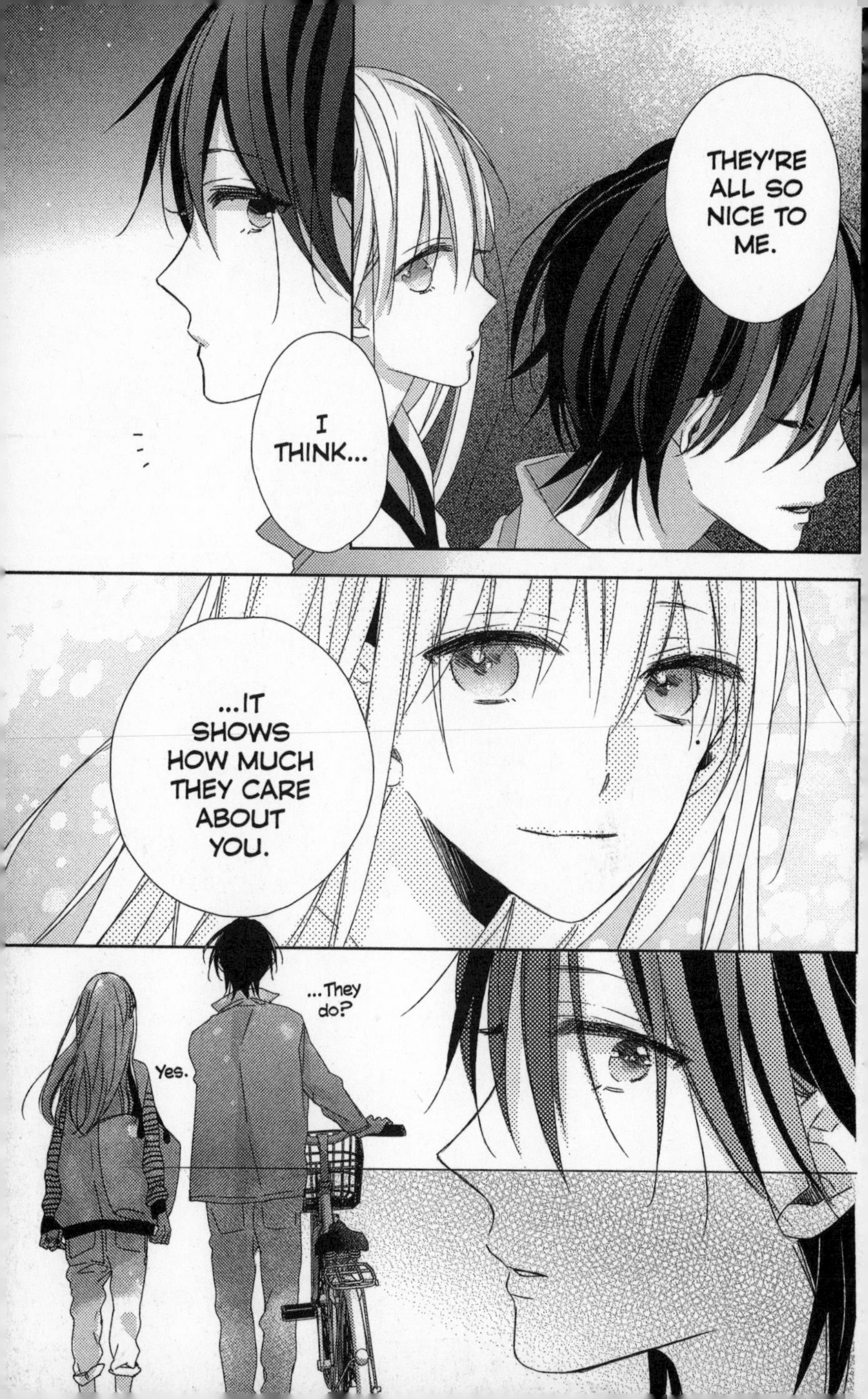
THEY'RE ALL SO NICE TO ME.
I THINK...
...IT SHOWS HOW MUCH THEY CARE ABOUT YOU.
...They do?
Yes.

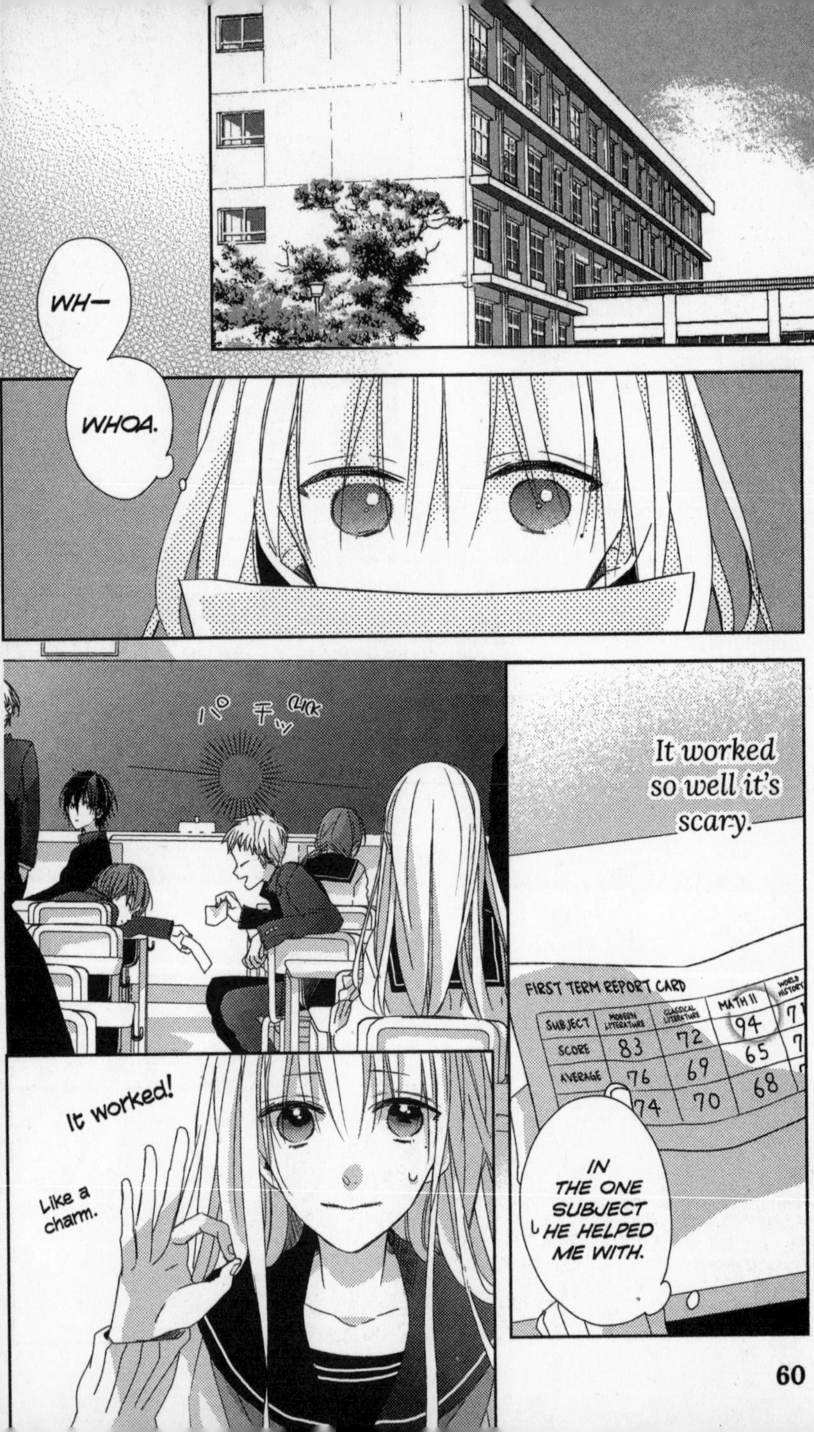
WH–
WHOA.
It worked so well it's scary.
FIRST TERM REPORT CARD
SUBJECT
MODERN LITERATURE
CLASSICAL LITERATURE
MATH II
WORLD HISTORY
SCORE 83 72 94
AVERAGE 76 69 65
74 70 68
IN THE ONE SUBJECT HE HELPED ME WITH.
パ チッ CLICK
It worked!
Like a charm.

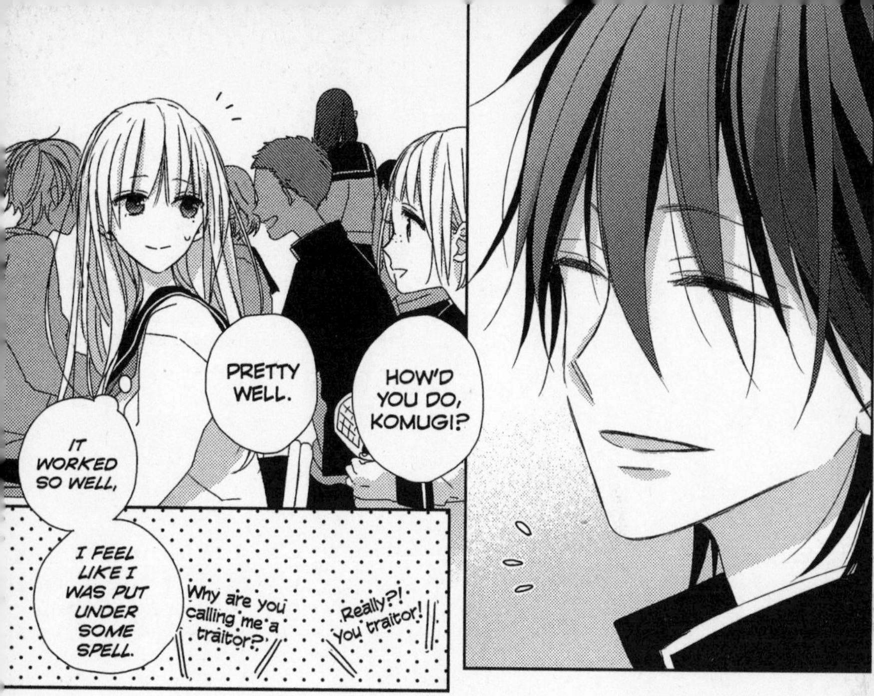
HOW'D YOU DO, KOMUGI?
PRETTY WELL.
IT WORKED SO WELL,
I FEEL LIKE I WAS PUT UNDER SOME SPELL.
Really?! You traitor!
Why are you calling me a traitor?

It's all moving in a good direction.

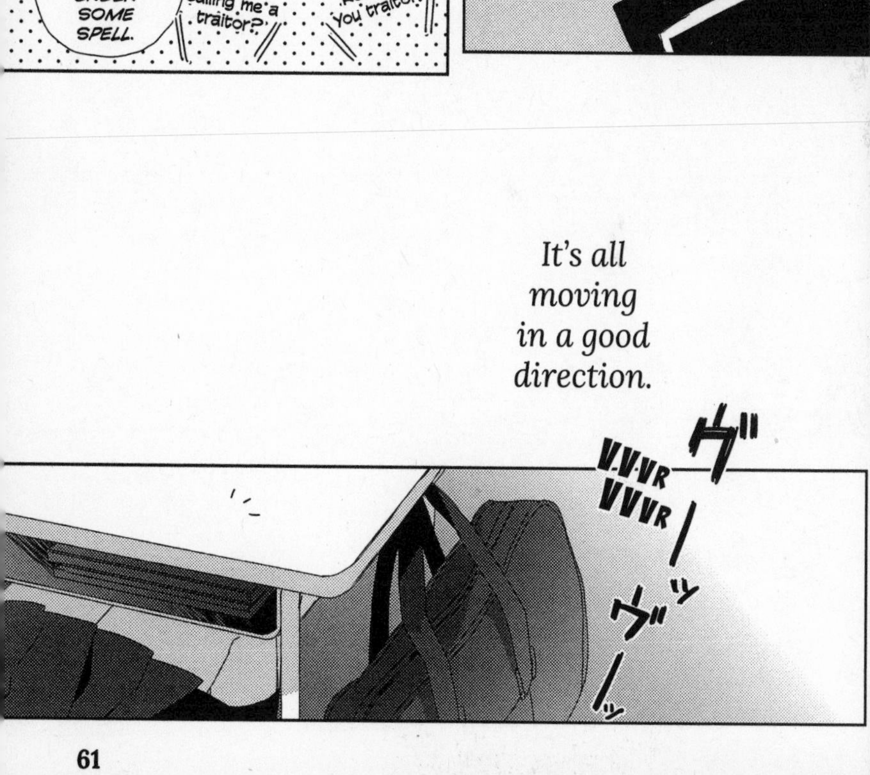
V-V-VR VVVR

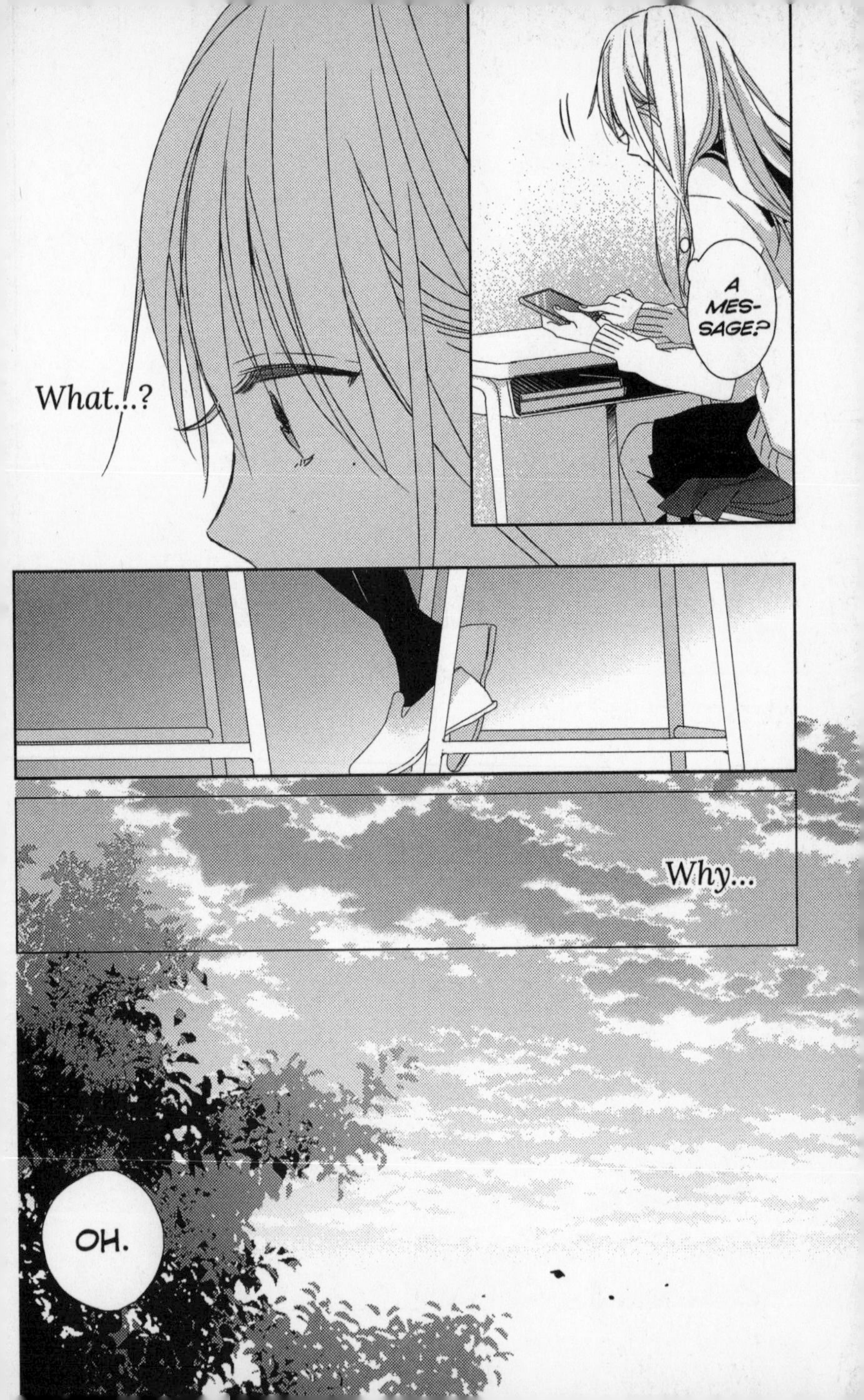
A MES-SAGE?
What...?
Why...
OH.

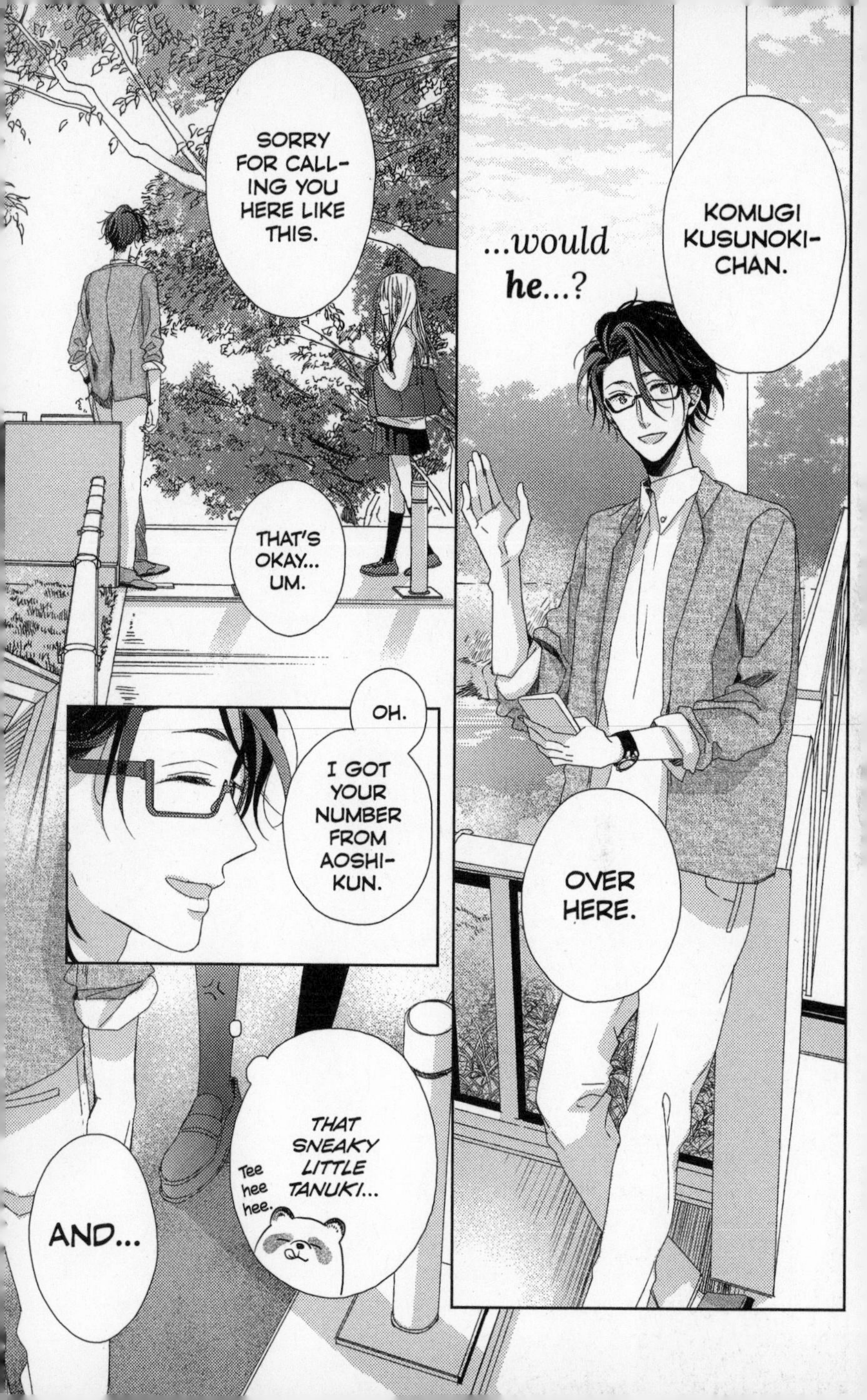
KOMUGI KUSUNOKI-CHAN.
...would he...?
OVER HERE.
SORRY FOR CALLING YOU HERE LIKE THIS.
THAT'S OKAY... UM.
OH.
I GOT YOUR NUMBER FROM AOSHI-KUN.
THAT SNEAKY LITTLE TANUKI...
Tee hee hee.
AND...

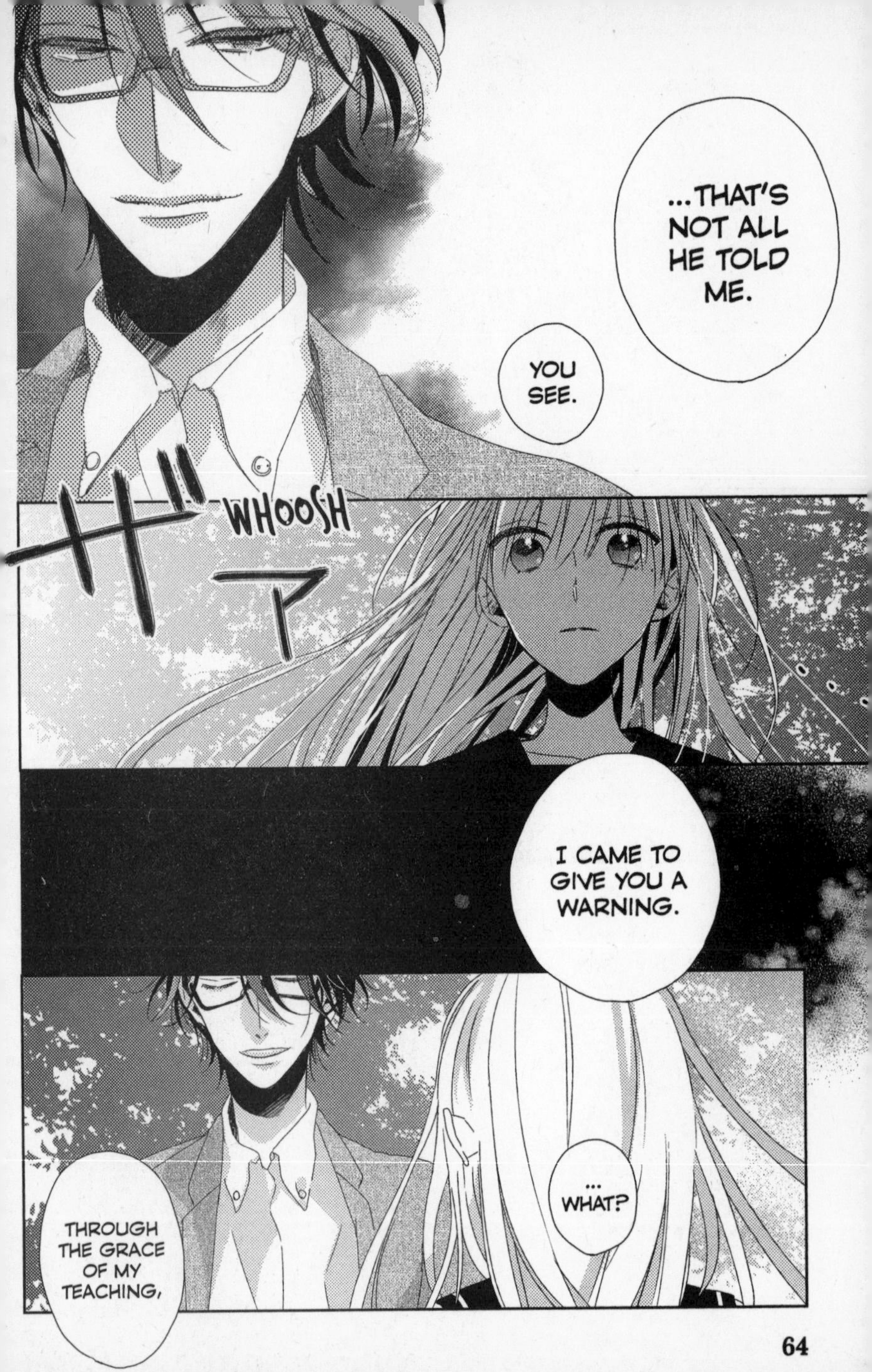
...THAT'S NOT ALL HE TOLD ME.
YOU SEE.
ザア
WHOOSH
I CAME TO GIVE YOU A WARNING.
...WHAT?
THROUGH THE GRACE OF MY TEACHING,

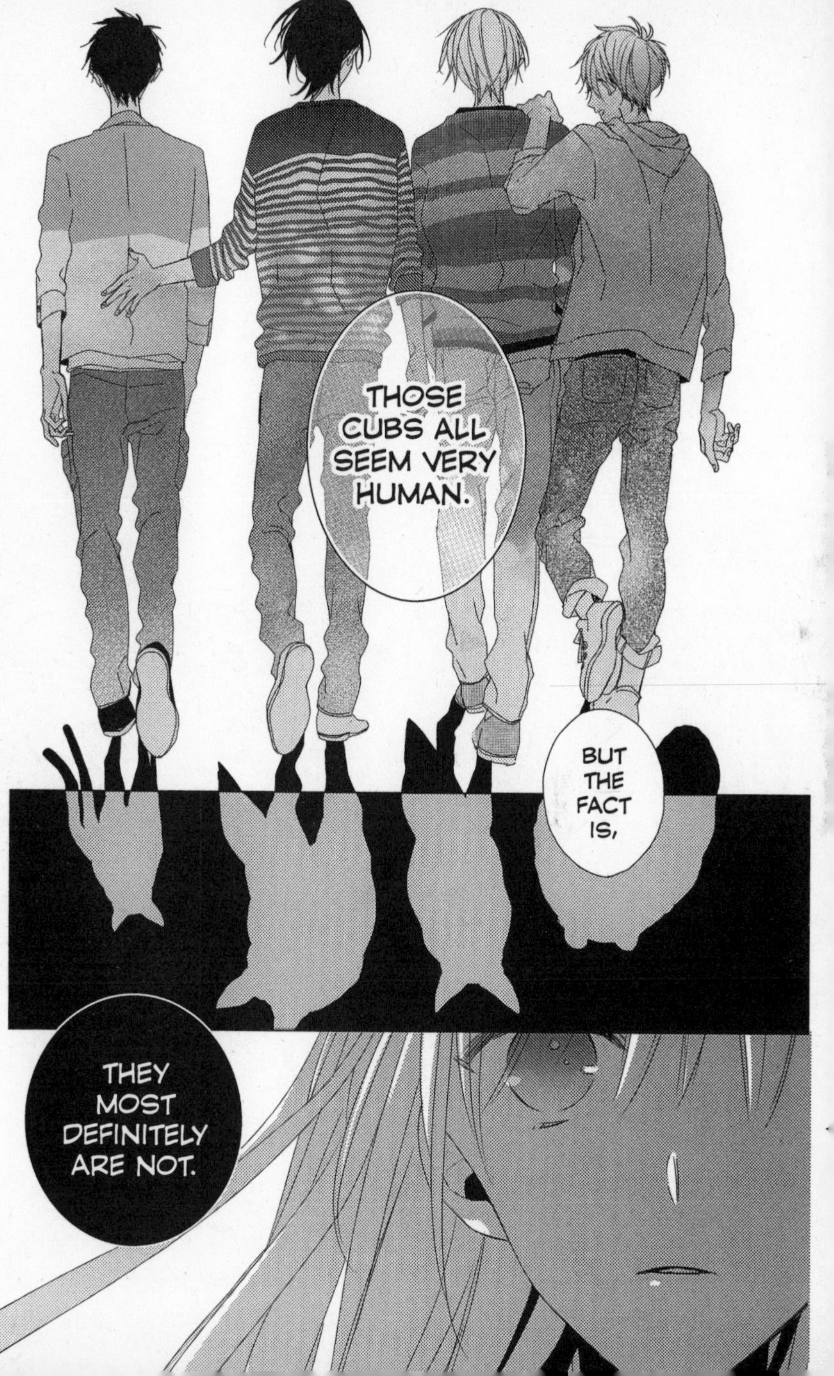
THOSE CUBS ALL SEEM VERY HUMAN.
BUT THE FACT IS,
THEY MOST DEFINITELY ARE NOT.

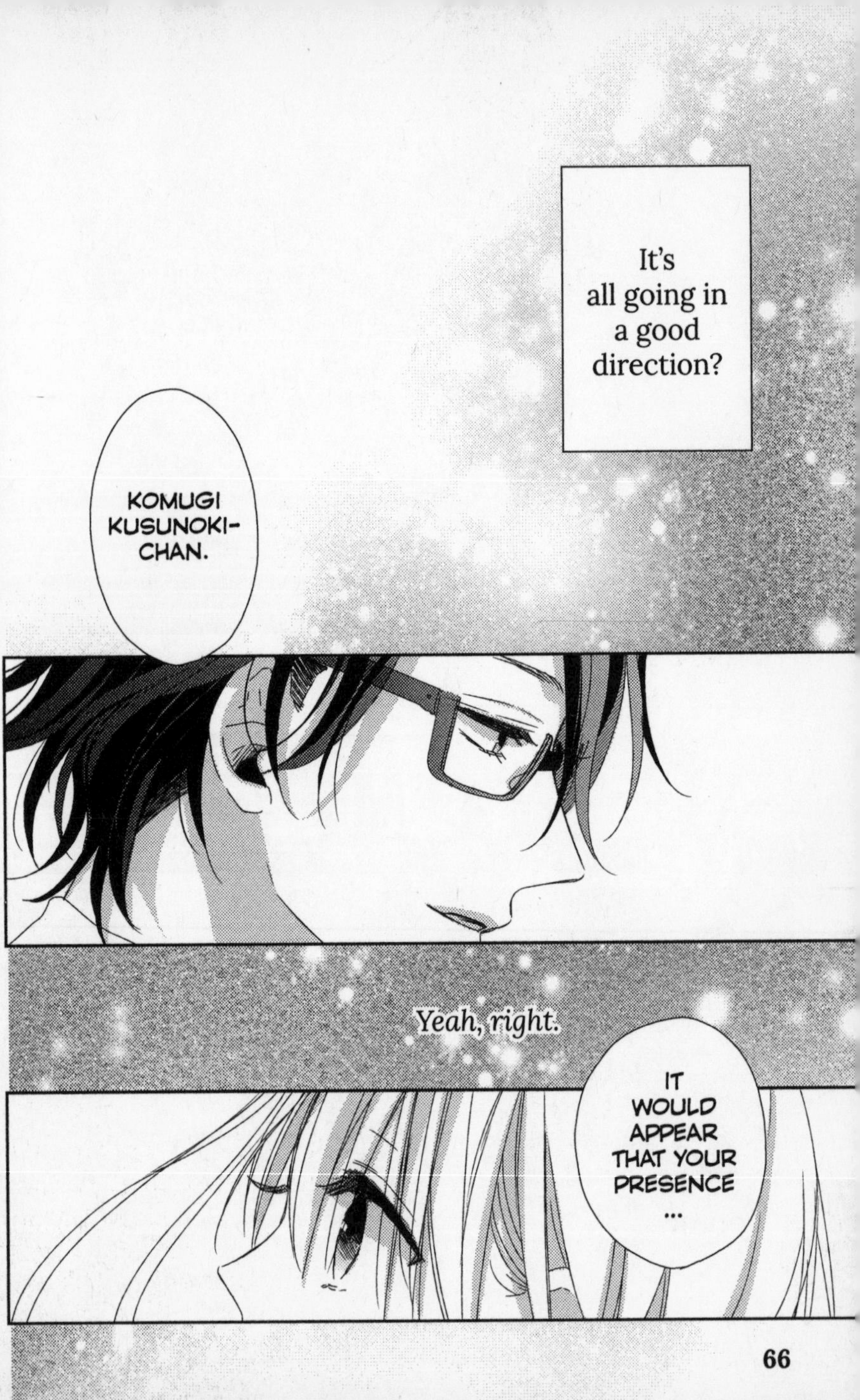
It's all going in a good direction?
KOMUGI KUSUNOKI-CHAN.
Yeah, right.
IT WOULD APPEAR THAT YOUR PRESENCE ...

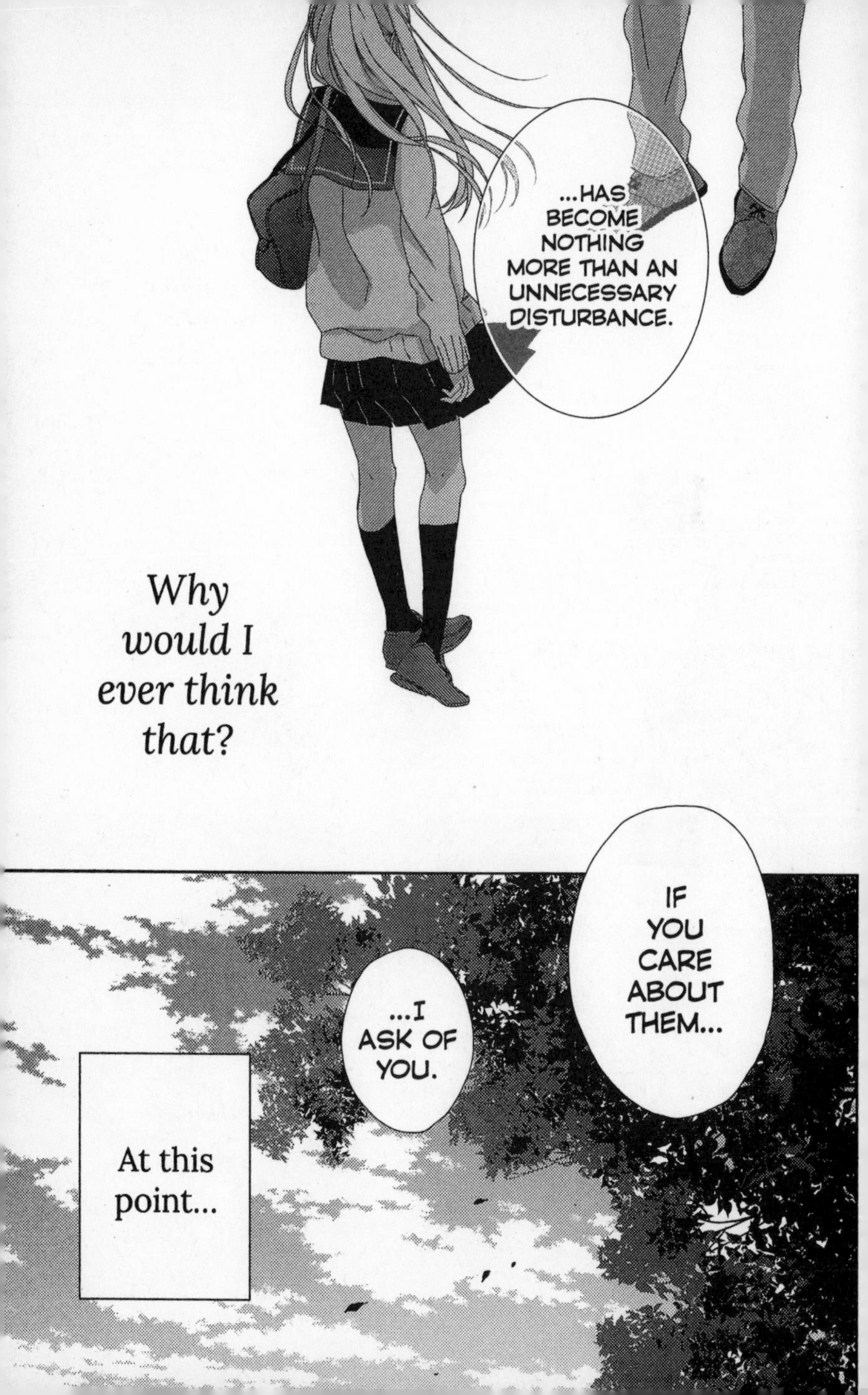
...HAS BECOME NOTHING MORE THAN AN UNNECESSARY DISTURBANCE.
Why would I ever think that?
IF YOU CARE ABOUT THEM...
...I ASK OF YOU.
At this point...

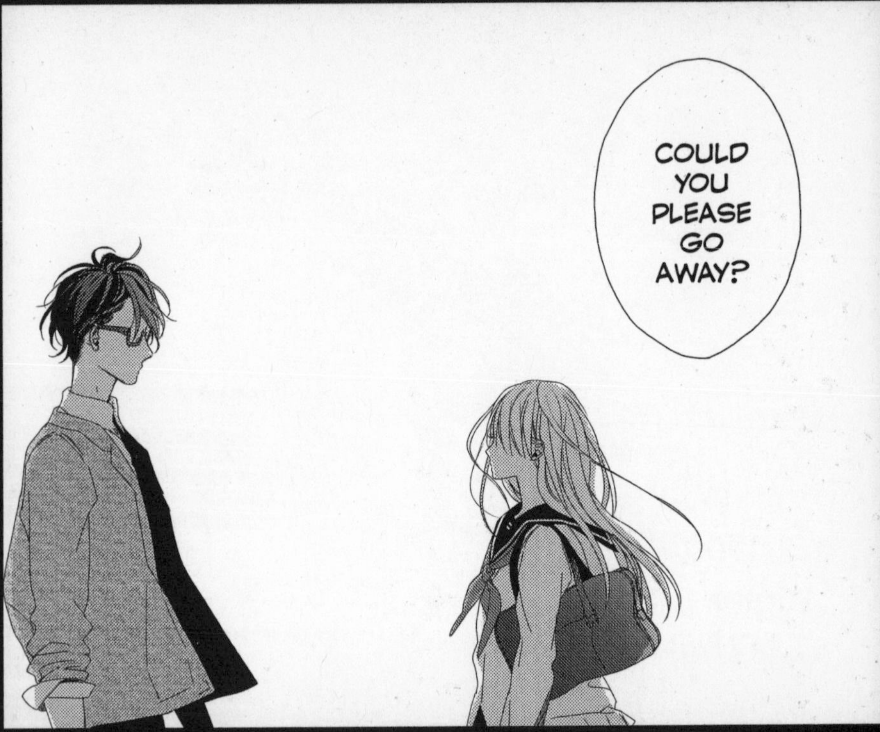
COULD YOU PLEASE GO AWAY?

*...I knew nothing.*

# Chapter 11

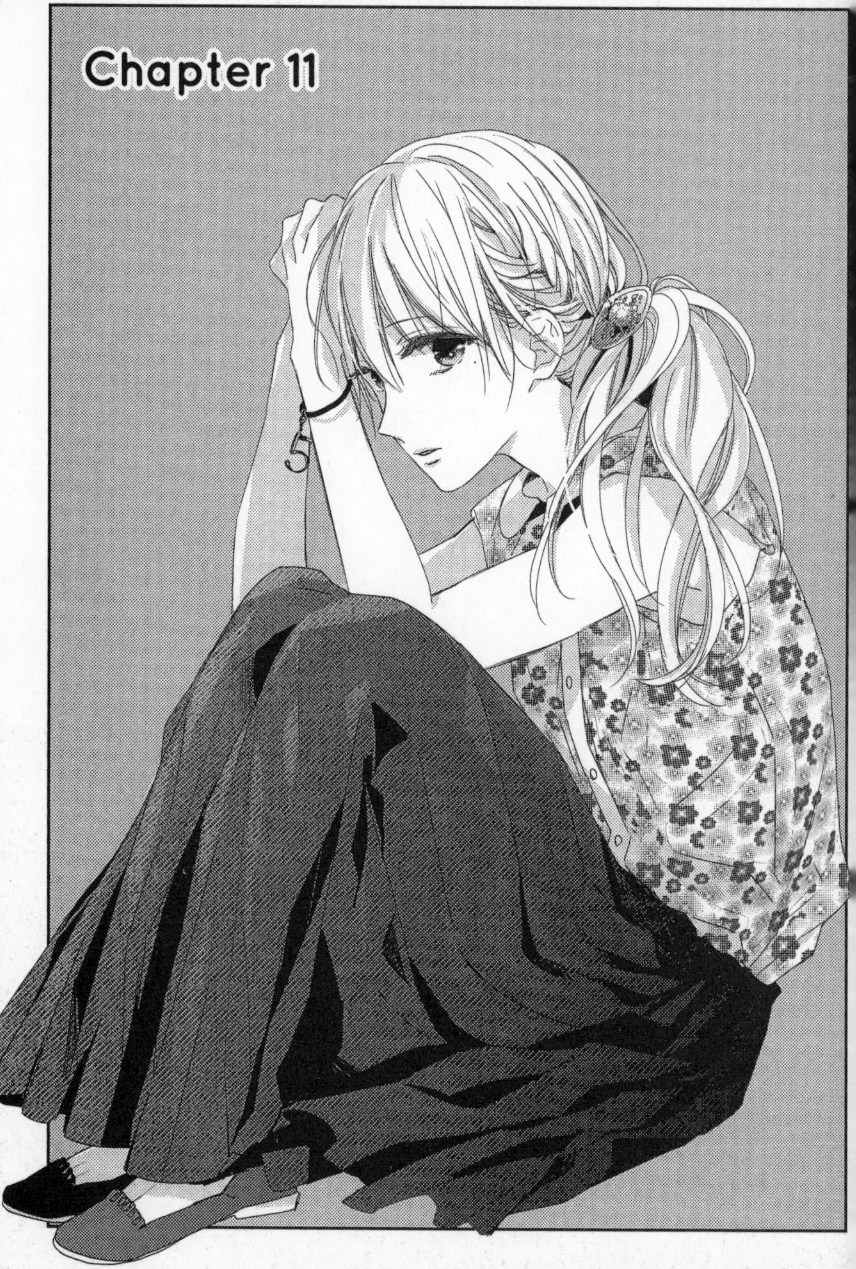

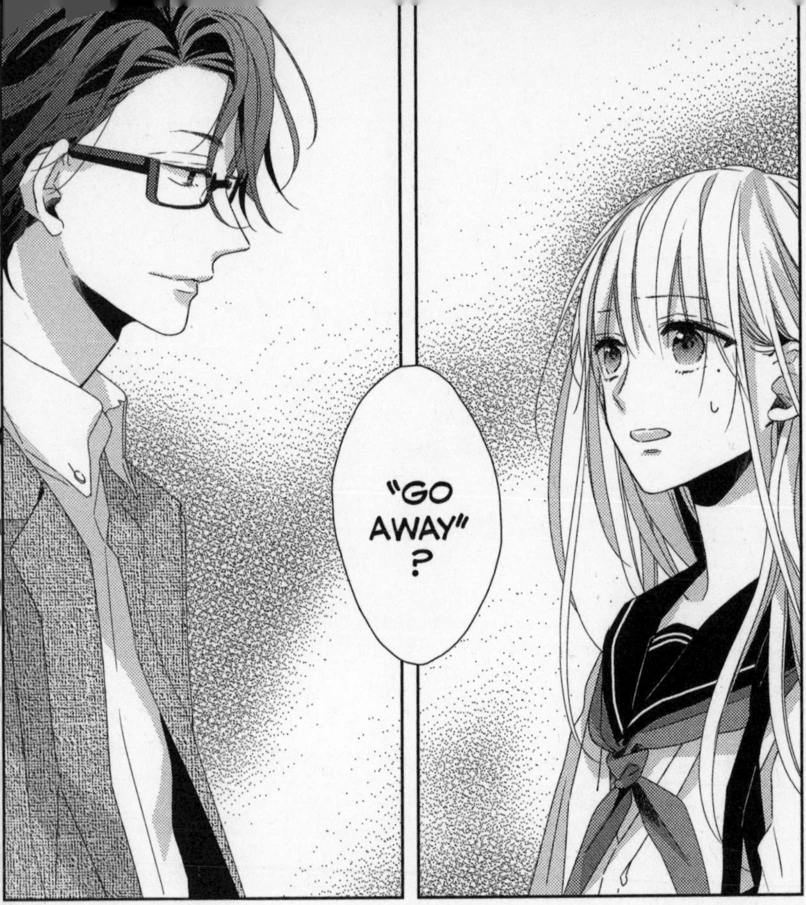
"GO AWAY"?

That Wolf-Boy is Mine!

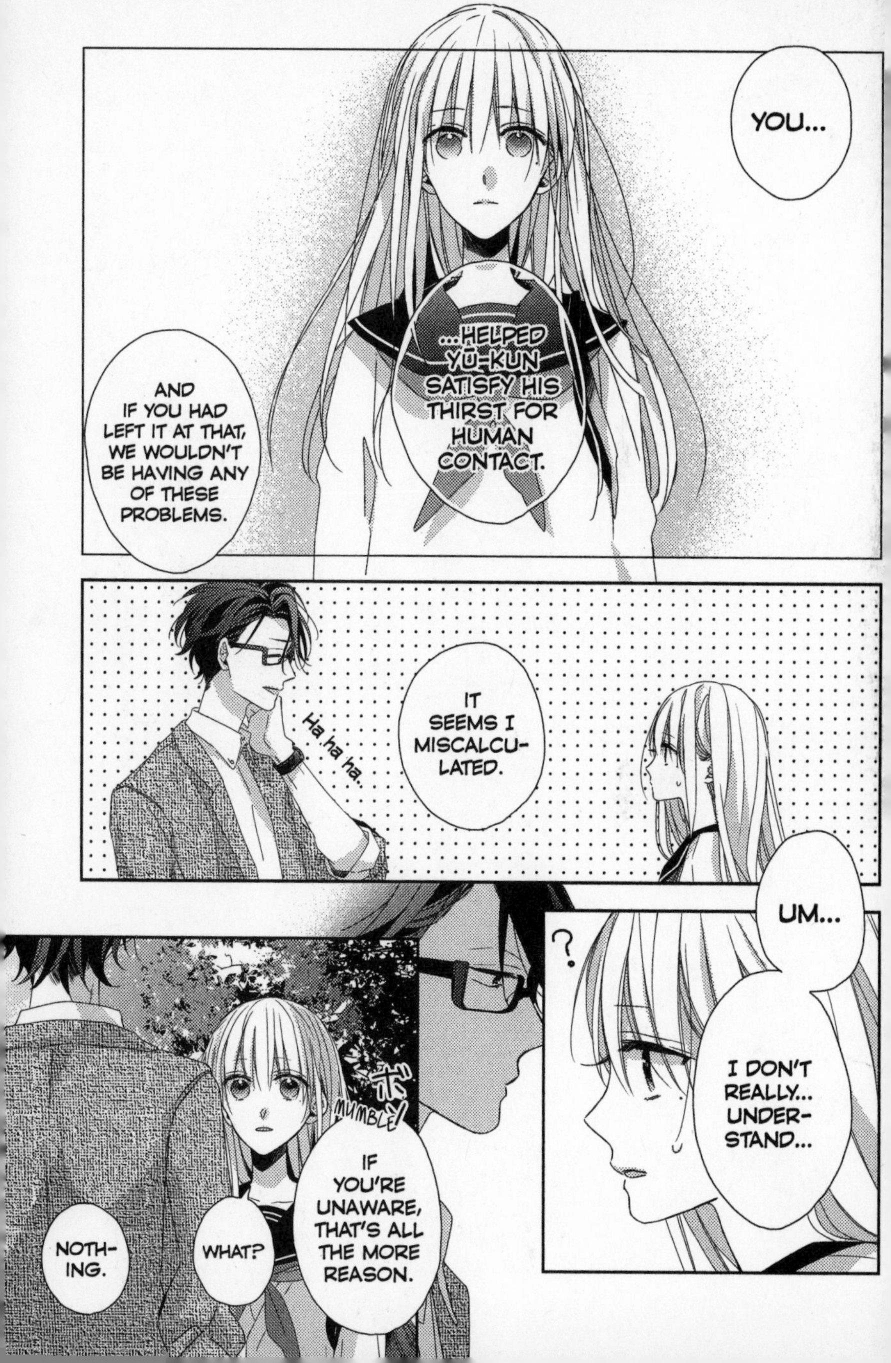
YOU...
...HELPED YŪ-KUN SATISFY HIS THIRST FOR HUMAN CONTACT.
AND IF YOU HAD LEFT IT AT THAT, WE WOULDN'T BE HAVING ANY OF THESE PROBLEMS.
IT SEEMS I MISCALCULATED.
Ha ha ha...
UM...
I DON'T REALLY... UNDERSTAND...
MUMBLE
IF YOU'RE UNAWARE, THAT'S ALL THE MORE REASON.
WHAT?
NOTH-ING.

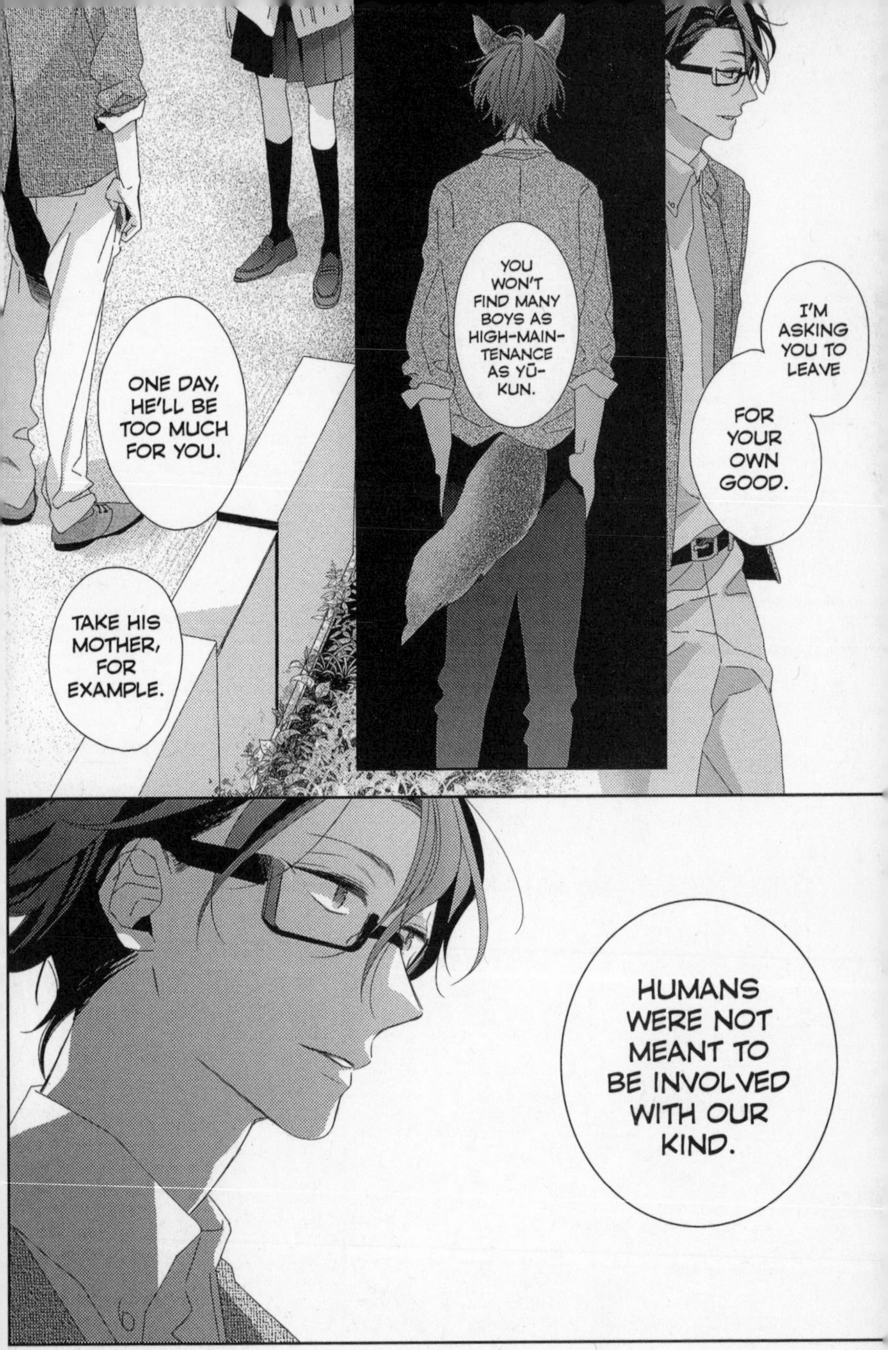
I'M ASKING YOU TO LEAVE
FOR YOUR OWN GOOD.
YOU WON'T FIND MANY BOYS AS HIGH-MAINTENANCE AS YŪ-KUN.
ONE DAY, HE'LL BE TOO MUCH FOR YOU.
TAKE HIS MOTHER, FOR EXAMPLE.
HUMANS WERE NOT MEANT TO BE INVOLVED WITH OUR KIND.

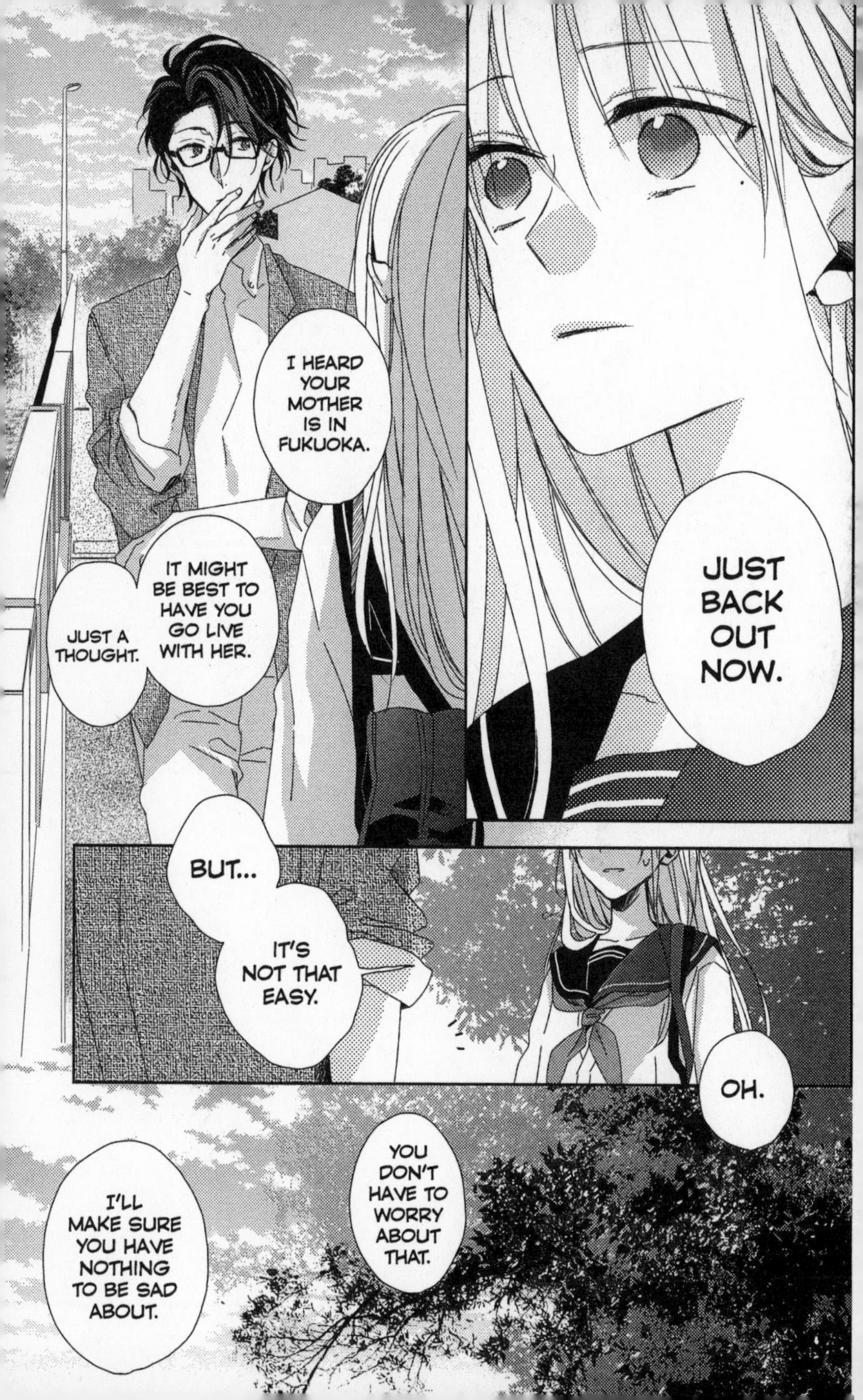
JUST BACK OUT NOW.
I HEARD YOUR MOTHER IS IN FUKUOKA.
IT MIGHT BE BEST TO HAVE YOU GO LIVE WITH HER.
JUST A THOUGHT.
BUT...
IT'S NOT THAT EASY.
OH.
YOU DON'T HAVE TO WORRY ABOUT THAT.
I'LL MAKE SURE YOU HAVE NOTHING TO BE SAD ABOUT.

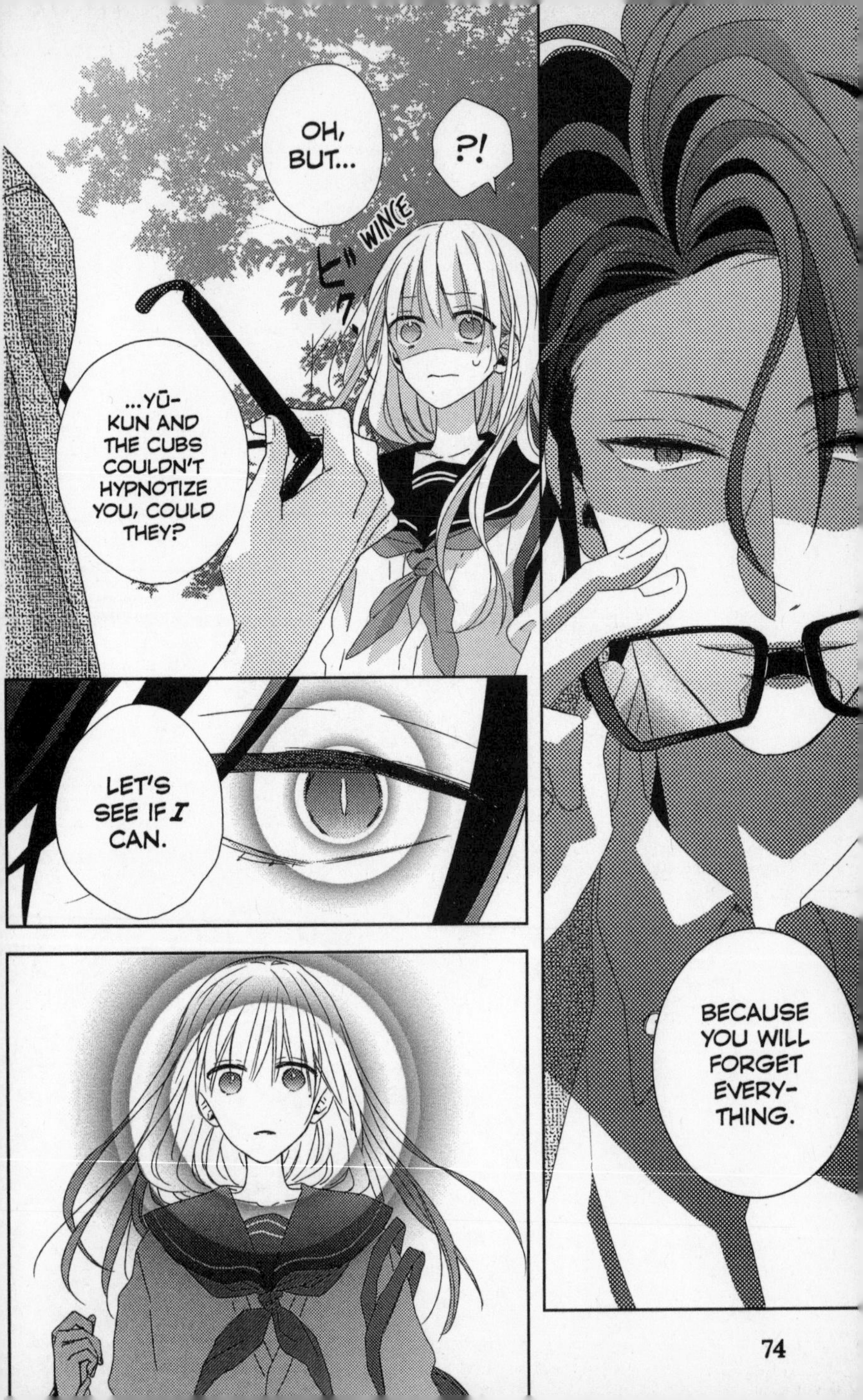
OH, BUT...
?!
WINCE
...YŪ-KUN AND THE CUBS COULDN'T HYPNOTIZE YOU, COULD THEY?
LET'S SEE IF I CAN.
BECAUSE YOU WILL FORGET EVERY-THING.

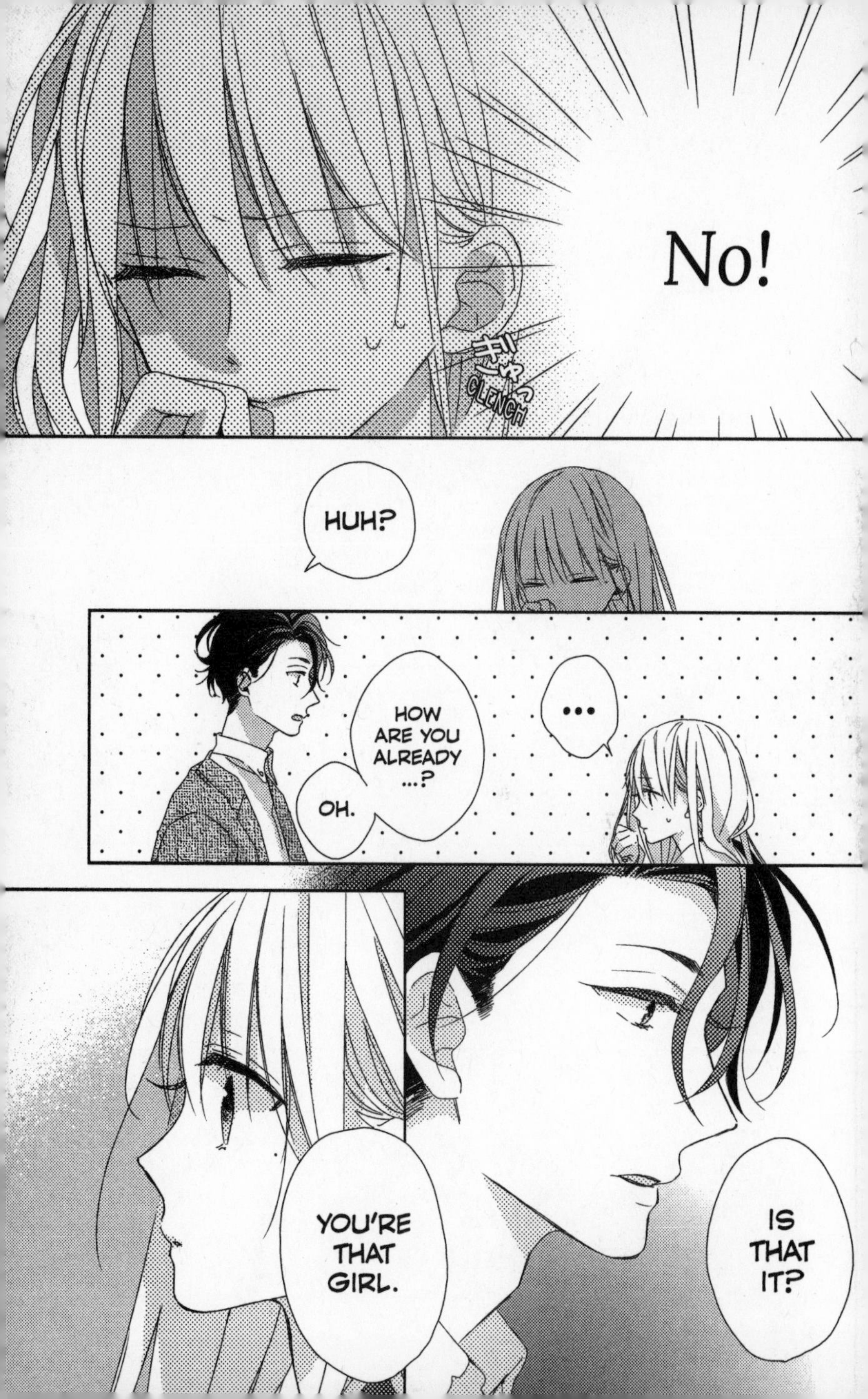
No!
CLENCH
HUH?
...
HOW ARE YOU ALREADY ...?
OH.
YOU'RE THAT GIRL.
IS THAT IT?

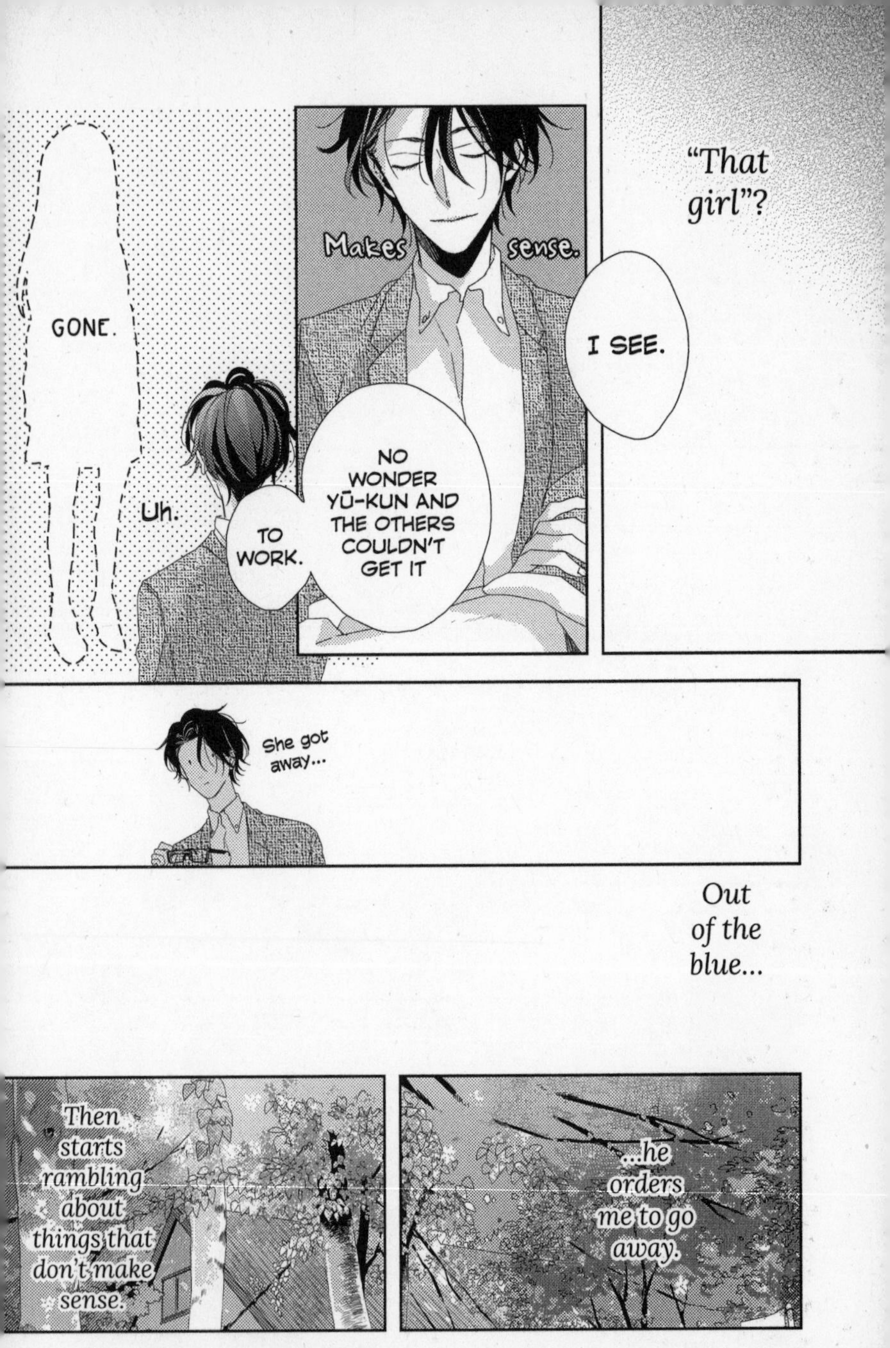
"That girl"?
Makes sense.
I SEE.
NO WONDER YŪ-KUN AND THE OTHERS COULDN'T GET IT
TO WORK.
Uh.
GONE.
She got away...
Out of the blue...
...he orders me to go away.
Then starts rambling about things that don't make sense.

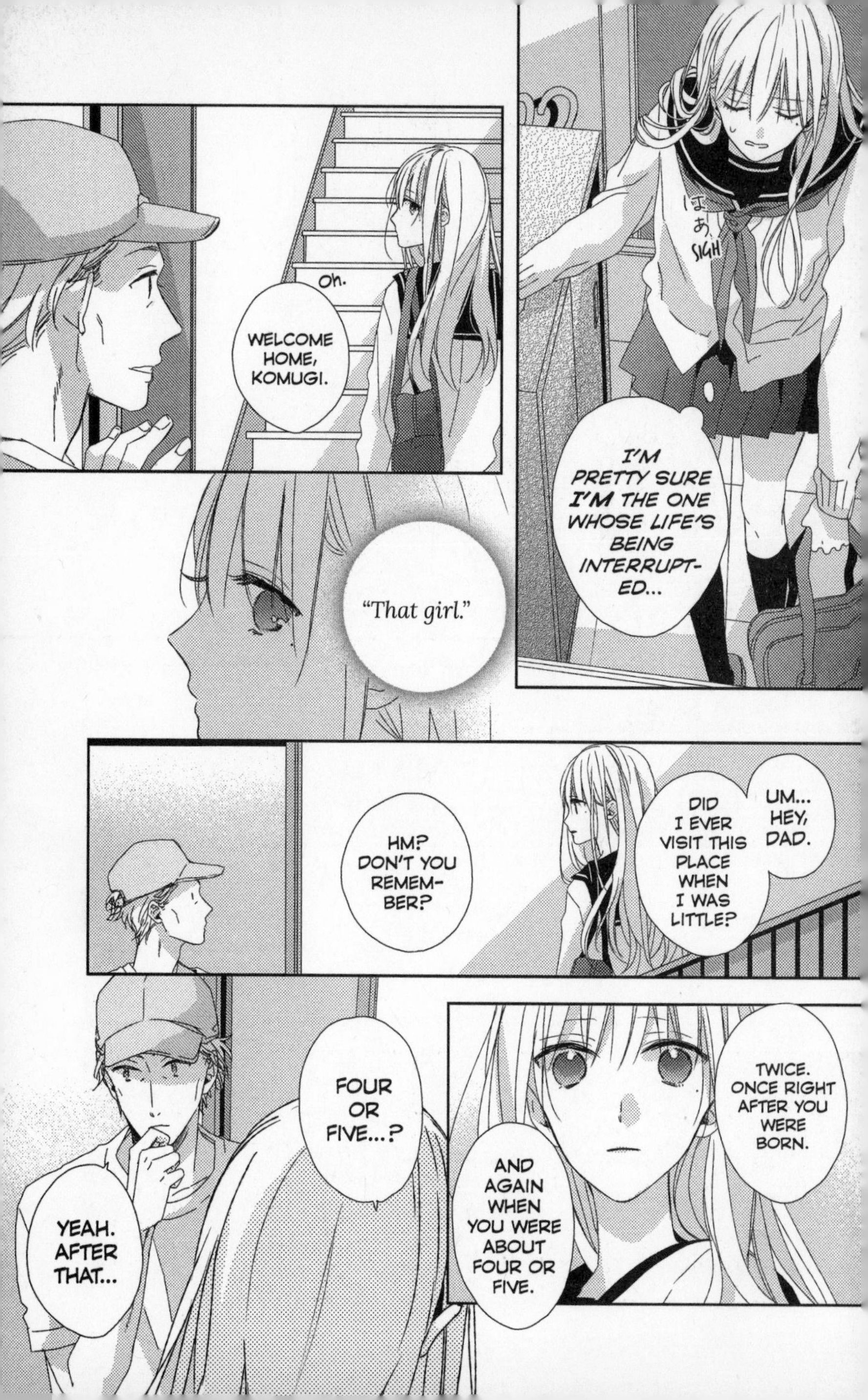
はあ
SIGH
I'M PRETTY SURE *I'M* THE ONE WHOSE LIFE'S BEING INTERRUPTED...
Oh.
WELCOME HOME, KOMUGI.
"That girl."
UM... HEY, DAD.
DID I EVER VISIT THIS PLACE WHEN I WAS LITTLE?
HM? DON'T YOU REMEMBER?
TWICE. ONCE RIGHT AFTER YOU WERE BORN.
AND AGAIN WHEN YOU WERE ABOUT FOUR OR FIVE.
FOUR OR FIVE...?
YEAH. AFTER THAT...

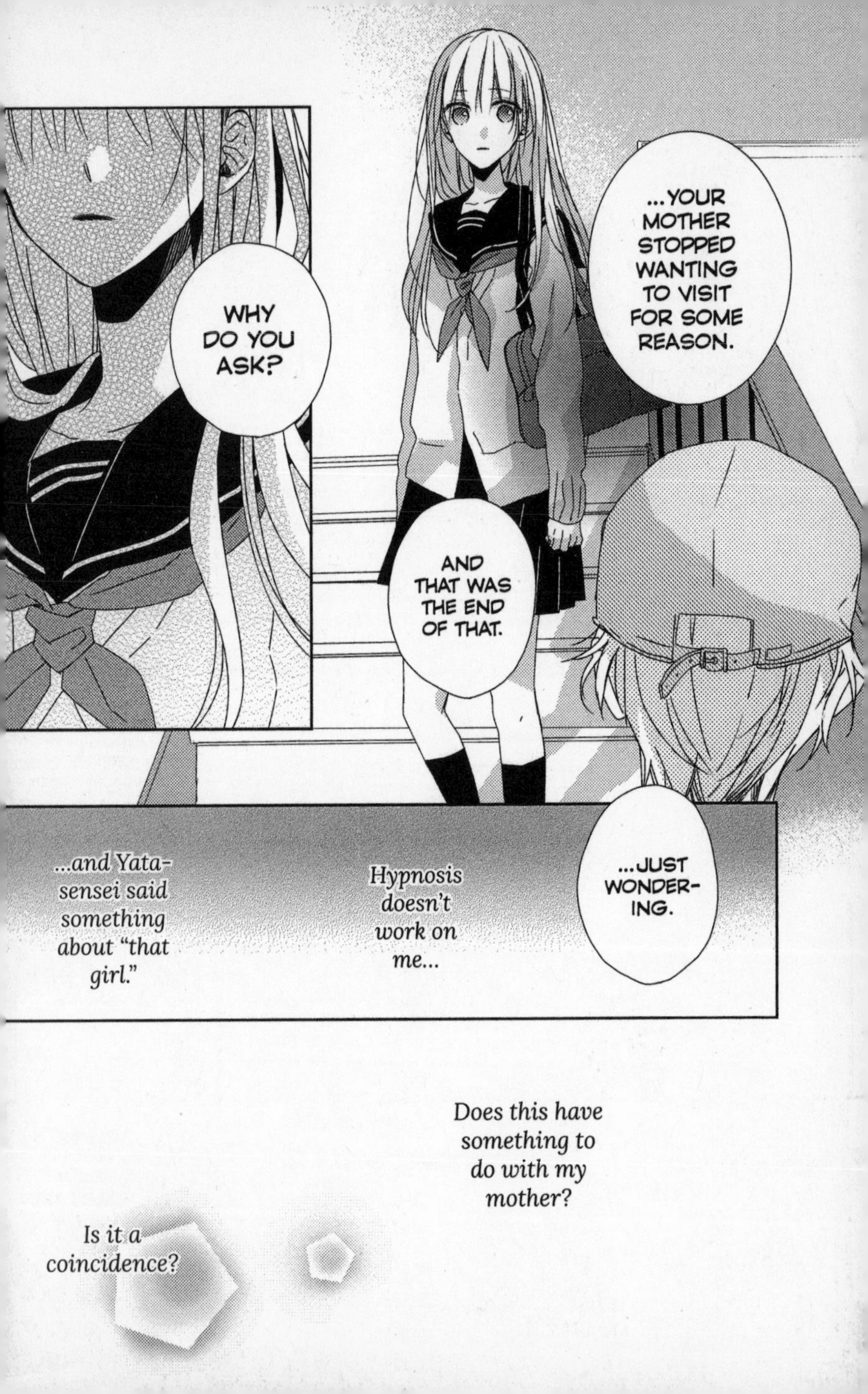
...YOUR MOTHER STOPPED WANTING TO VISIT FOR SOME REASON.
AND THAT WAS THE END OF THAT.
WHY DO YOU ASK?
...JUST WONDER-ING.
Hypnosis doesn't work on me...
...and Yata-sensei said something about "that girl."
Does this have something to do with my mother?
Is it a coincidence?

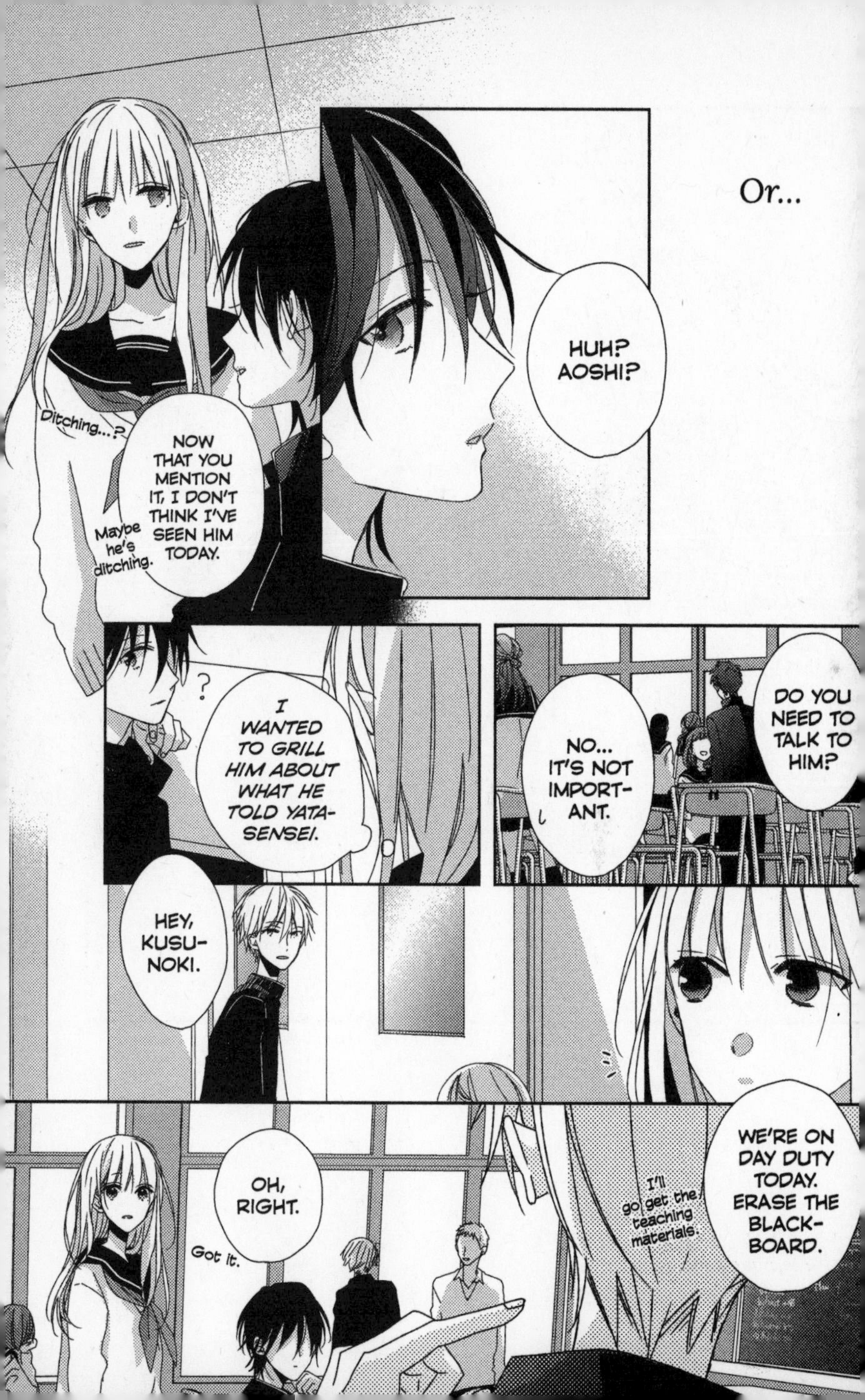
Or...
HUH? AOSHI?
NOW THAT YOU MENTION IT, I DON'T THINK I'VE SEEN HIM TODAY.
Maybe he's ditching.
Ditching...?
DO YOU NEED TO TALK TO HIM?
NO... IT'S NOT IMPORT-ANT.
I WANTED TO GRILL HIM ABOUT WHAT HE TOLD YATA-SENSEI.
HEY, KUSU-NOKI.
WE'RE ON DAY DUTY TODAY. ERASE THE BLACK-BOARD.
I'll go get the teaching materials.
OH, RIGHT.
Got it.

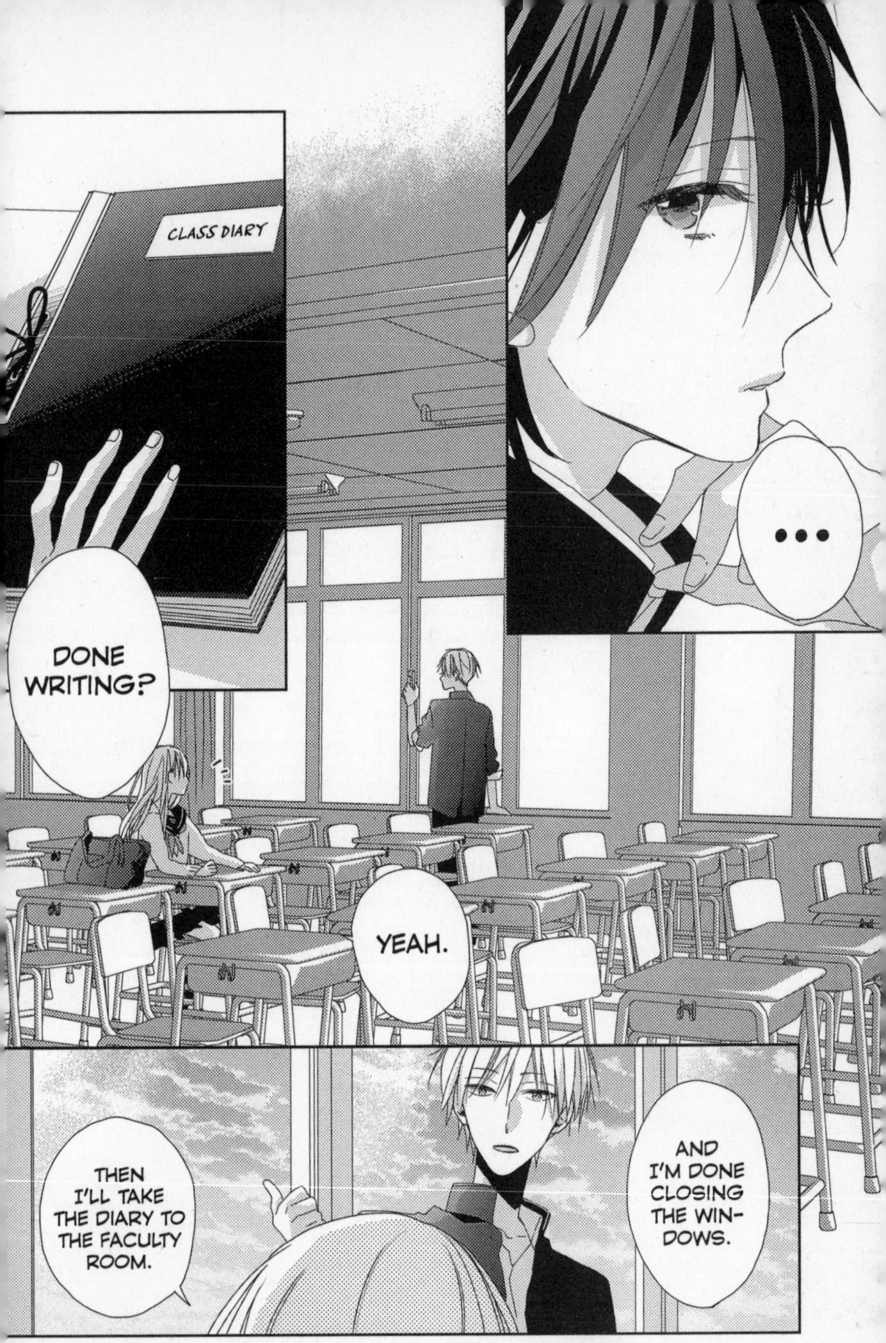
...
CLASS DIARY
DONE WRITING?
YEAH.
AND I'M DONE CLOSING THE WIN-DOWS.
THEN I'LL TAKE THE DIARY TO THE FACULTY ROOM.

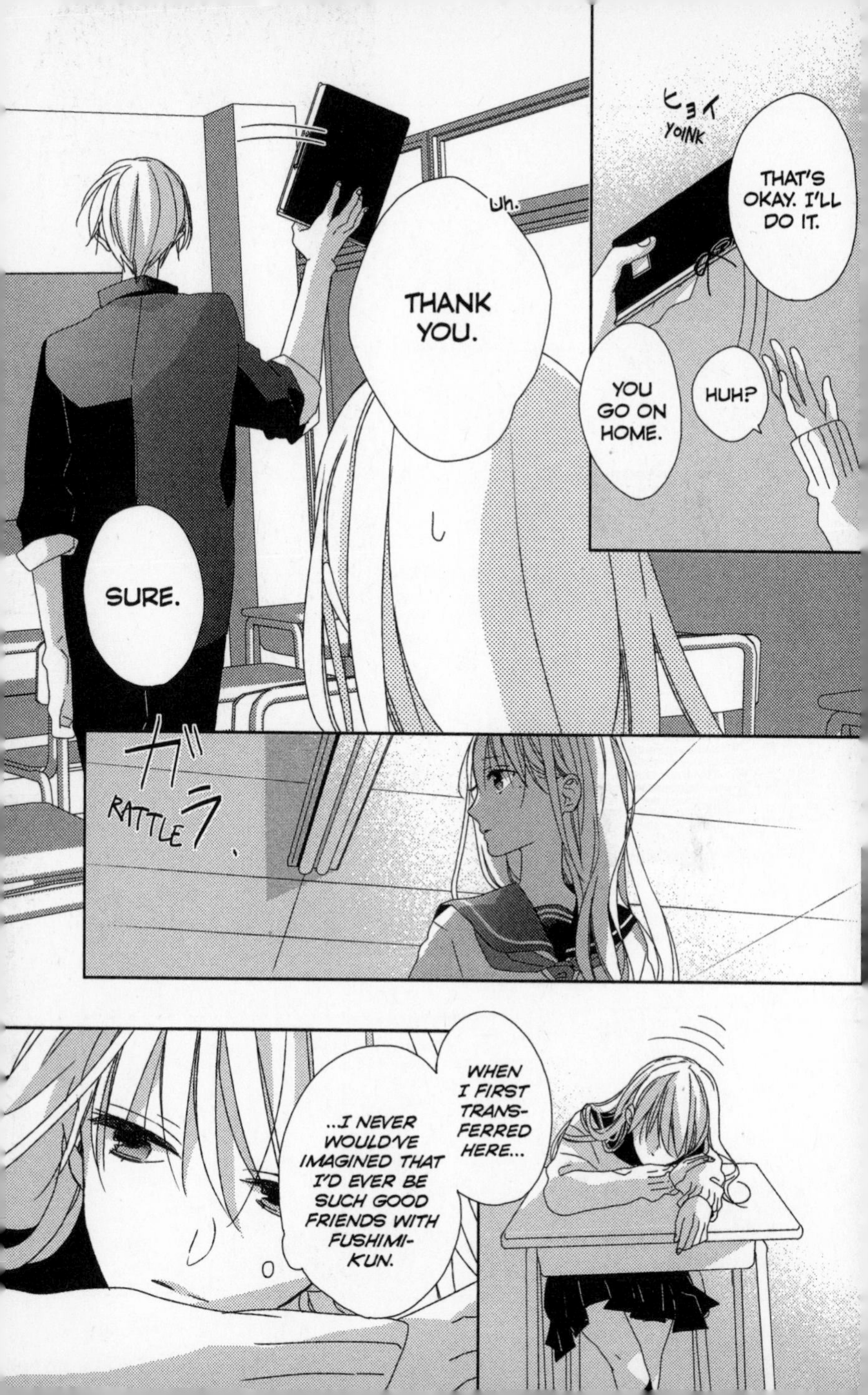

ヒョイ
YOINK
THAT'S OKAY. I'LL DO IT.
HUH?
YOU GO ON HOME.
Uh.
THANK YOU.
SURE.
ガラ
RATTLE
WHEN I FIRST TRANSFERRED HERE...
...I NEVER WOULD'VE IMAGINED THAT I'D EVER BE SUCH GOOD FRIENDS WITH FUSHIMI-KUN.

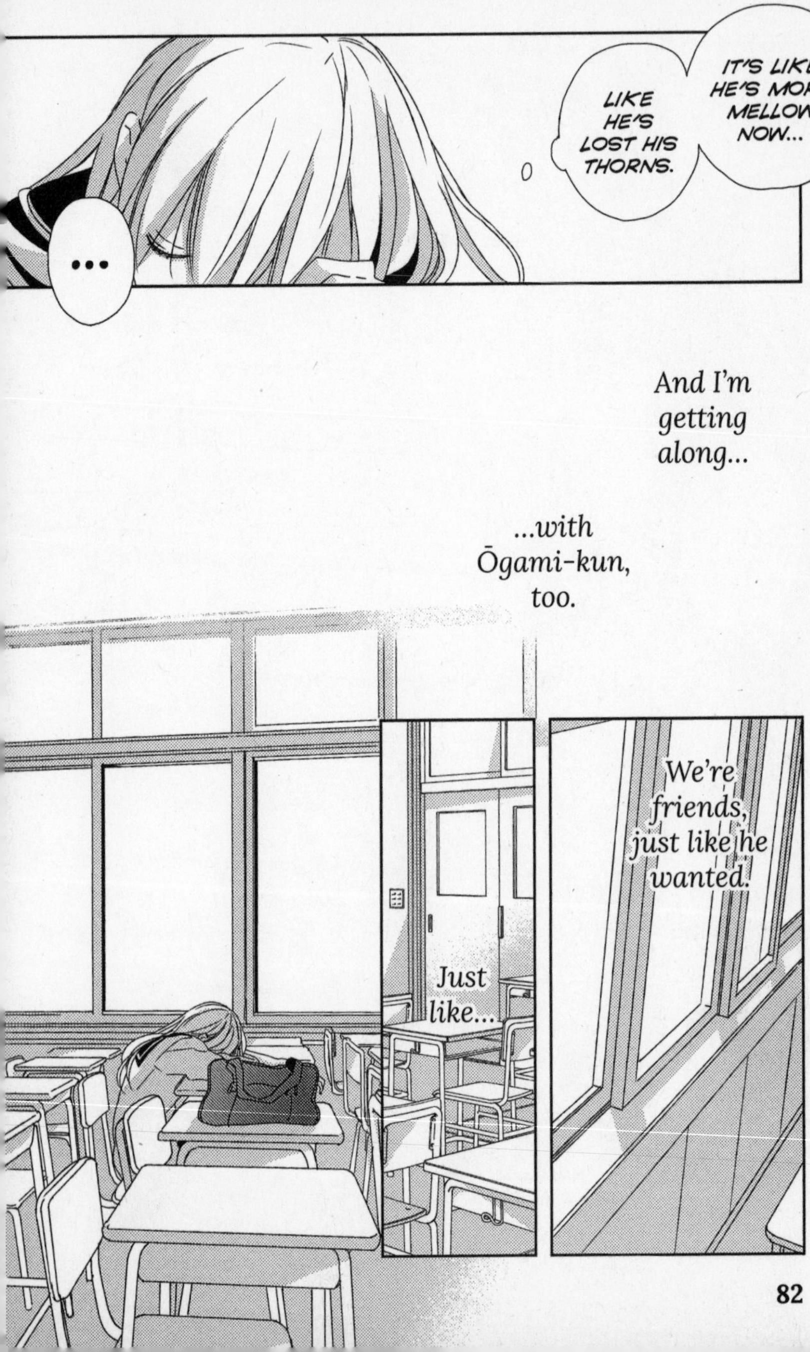
IT'S LIKE HE'S MORE MELLOW NOW...
LIKE HE'S LOST HIS THORNS.
...
And I'm getting along...
...with Ōgami-kun, too.
We're friends, just like he wanted.
Just like...

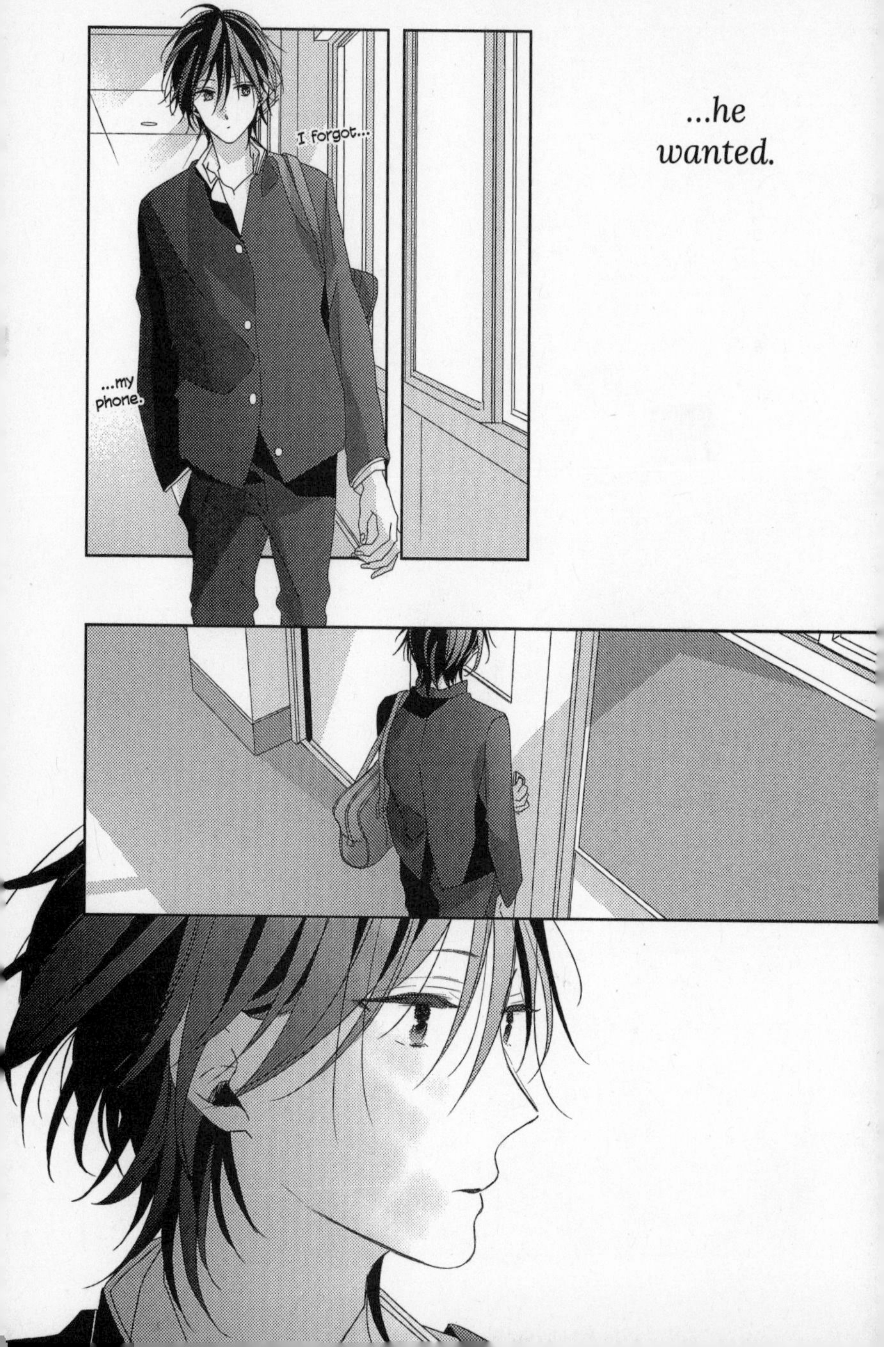
...he wanted.
I forgot...
...my phone.

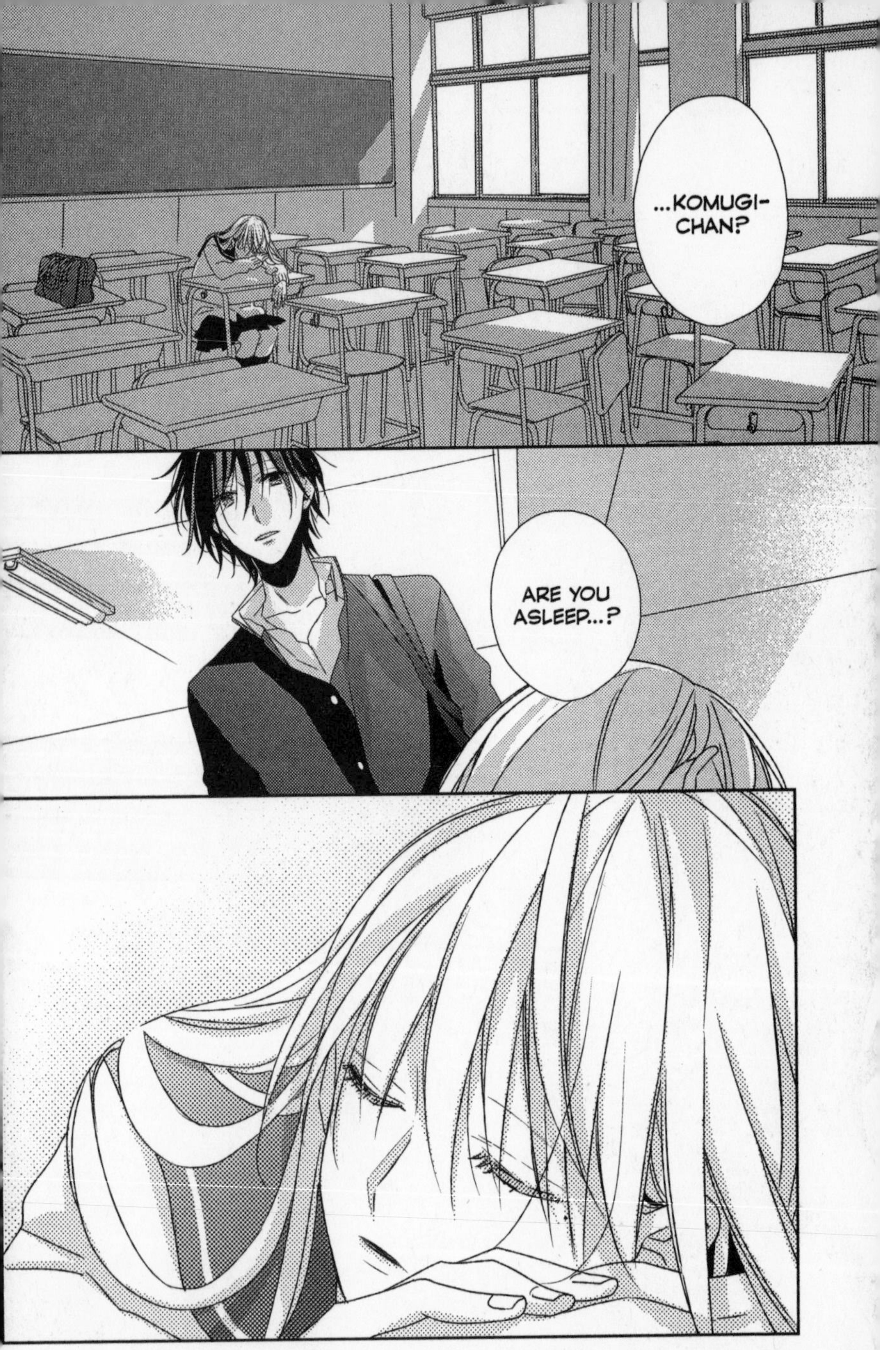
...KOMUGI-
CHAN?
ARE YOU
ASLEEP...?

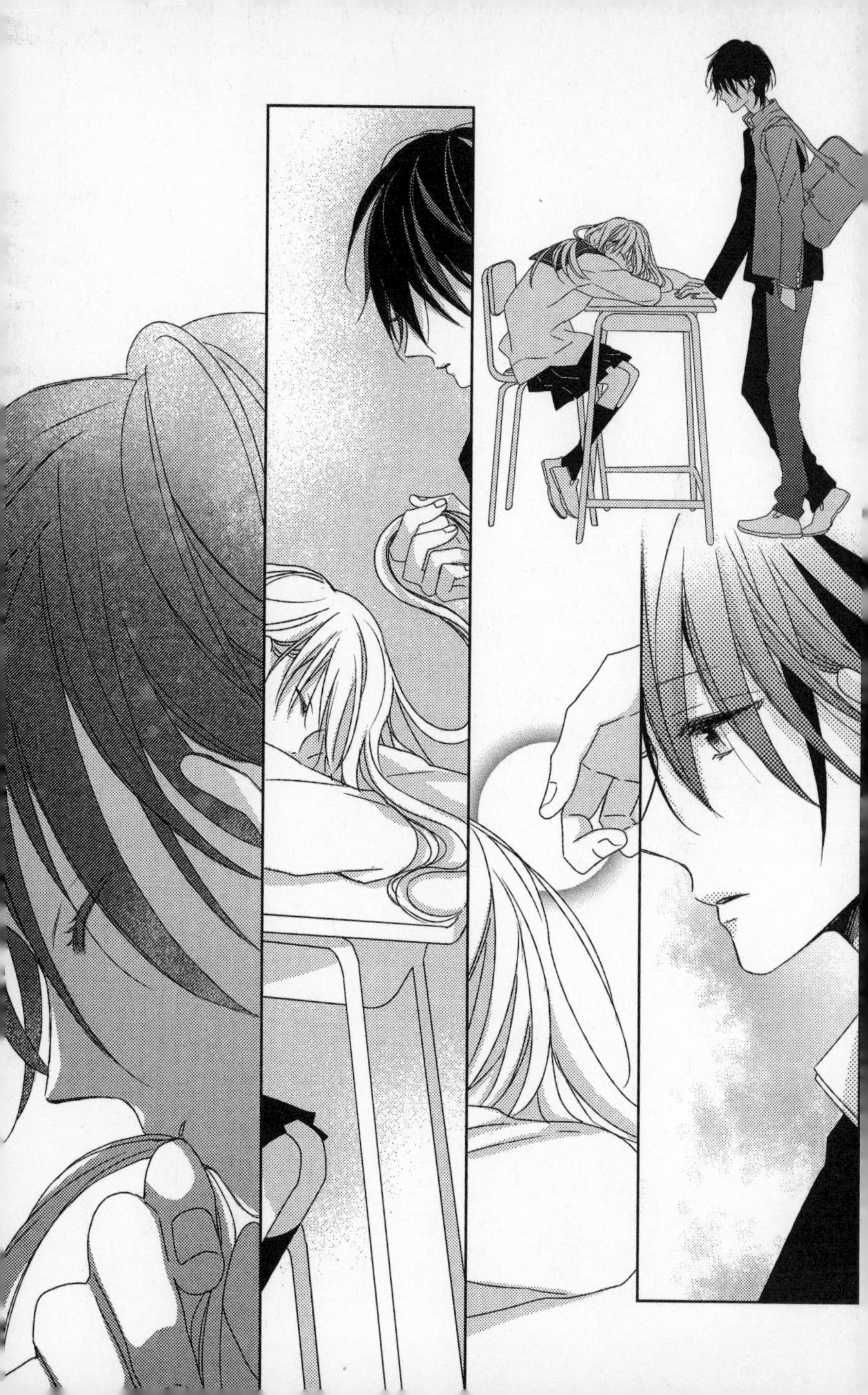

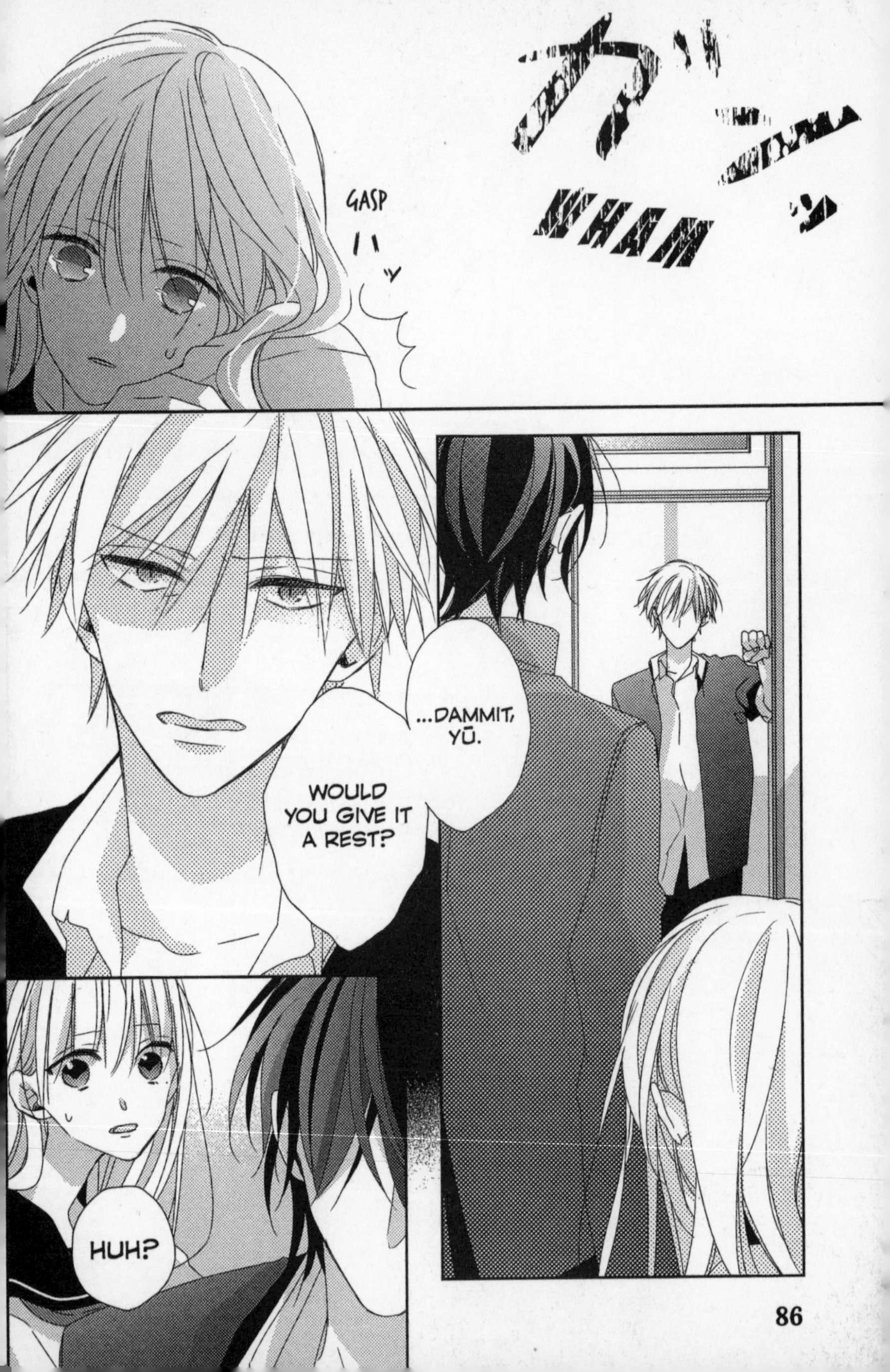
WHAM
GASP
...DAMMIT, YŪ.
WOULD YOU GIVE IT A REST?
HUH?

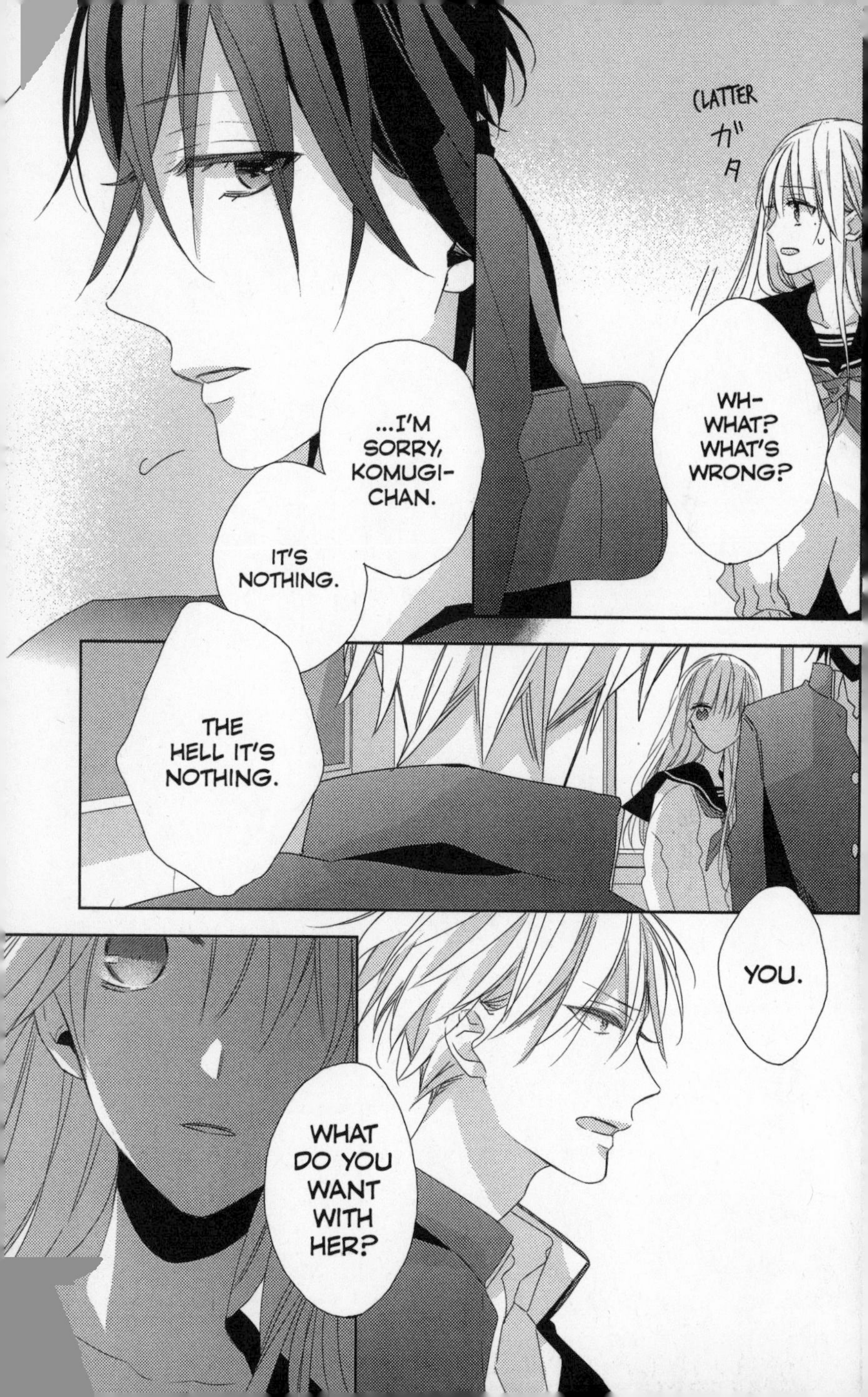
CLATTER
ガタ
WH- WHAT? WHAT'S WRONG?
...I'M SORRY, KOMUGI-CHAN.
IT'S NOTHING.
THE HELL IT'S NOTHING.
YOU.
WHAT DO YOU WANT WITH HER?

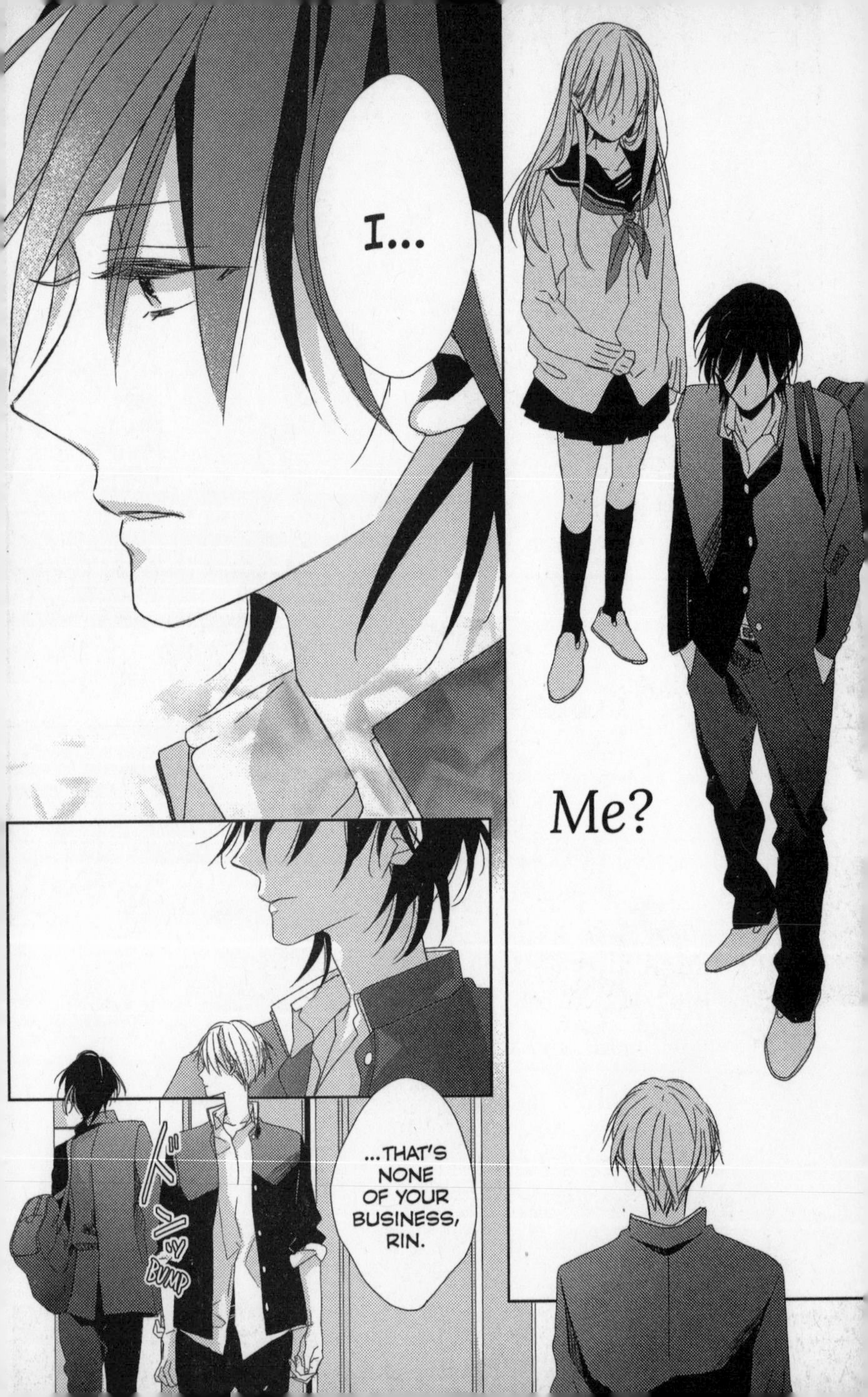
Me?
I...
...THAT'S NONE OF YOUR BUSINESS, RIN.
BUMP

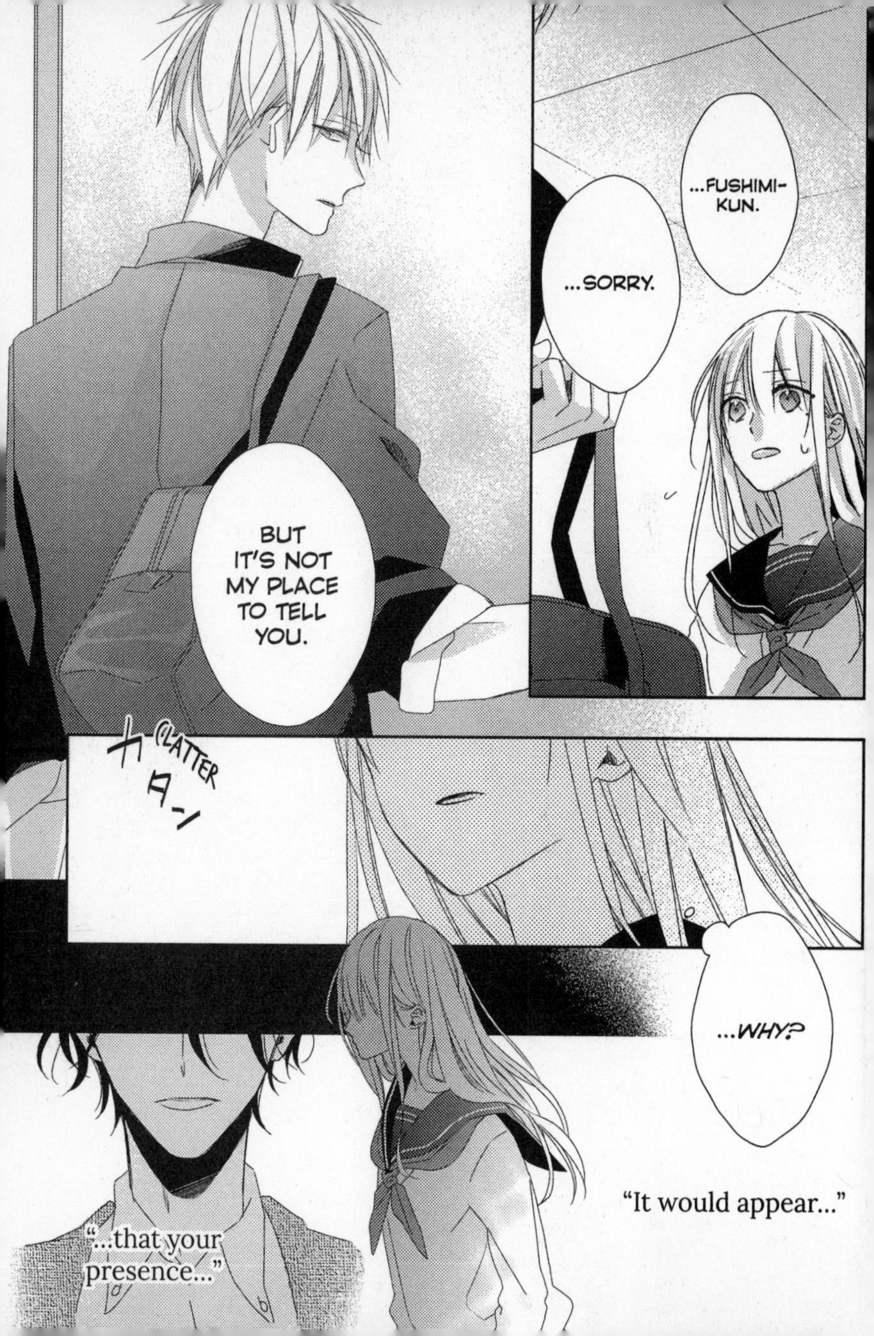
...FUSHIMI-KUN.
...SORRY.
BUT IT'S NOT MY PLACE TO TELL YOU.
CLATTER
...WHY?
"It would appear..."
"...that your presence..."

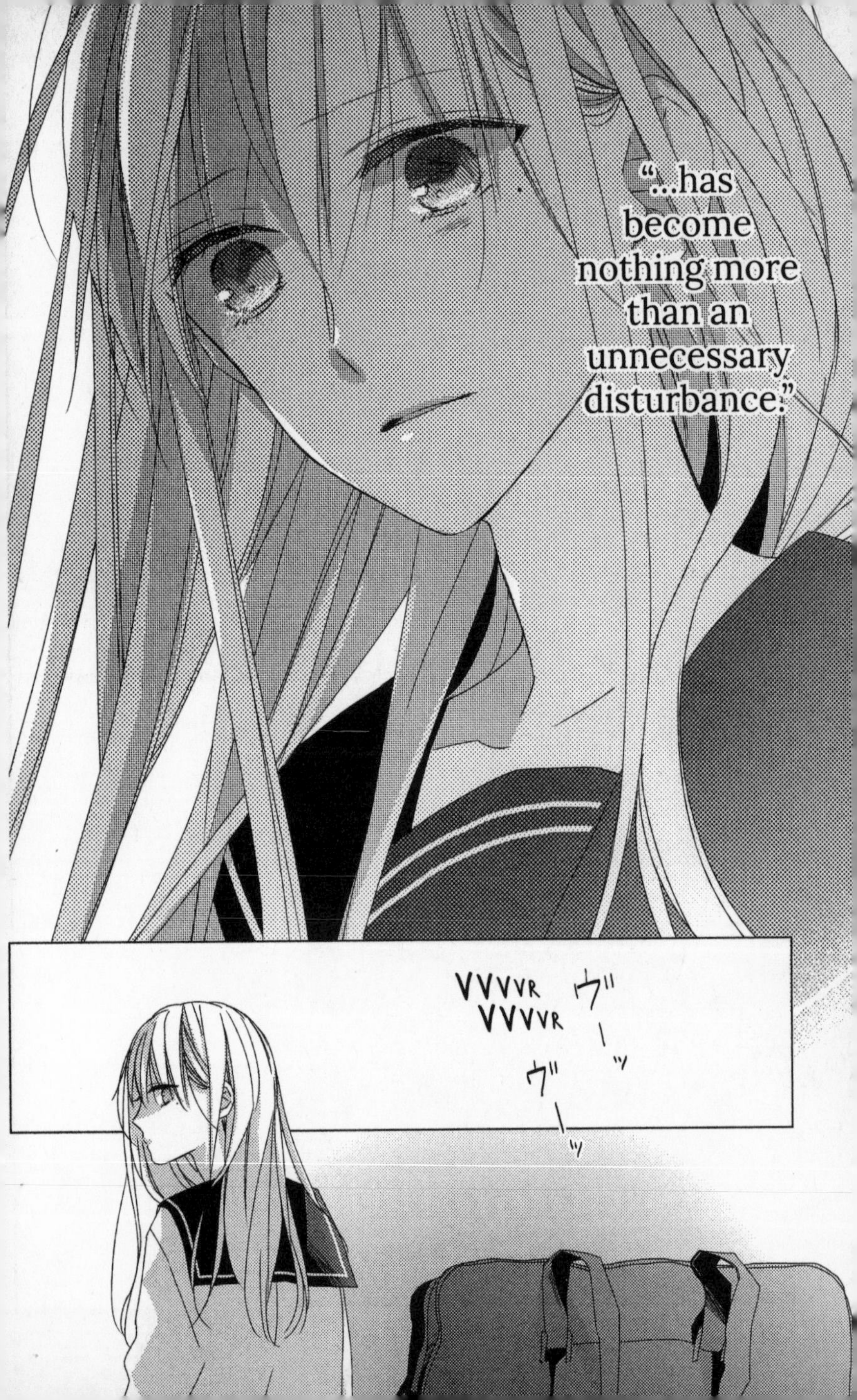
"...has become nothing more than an unnecessary disturbance."
VVVVR VVVVR
ヴーッ
ヴーッ

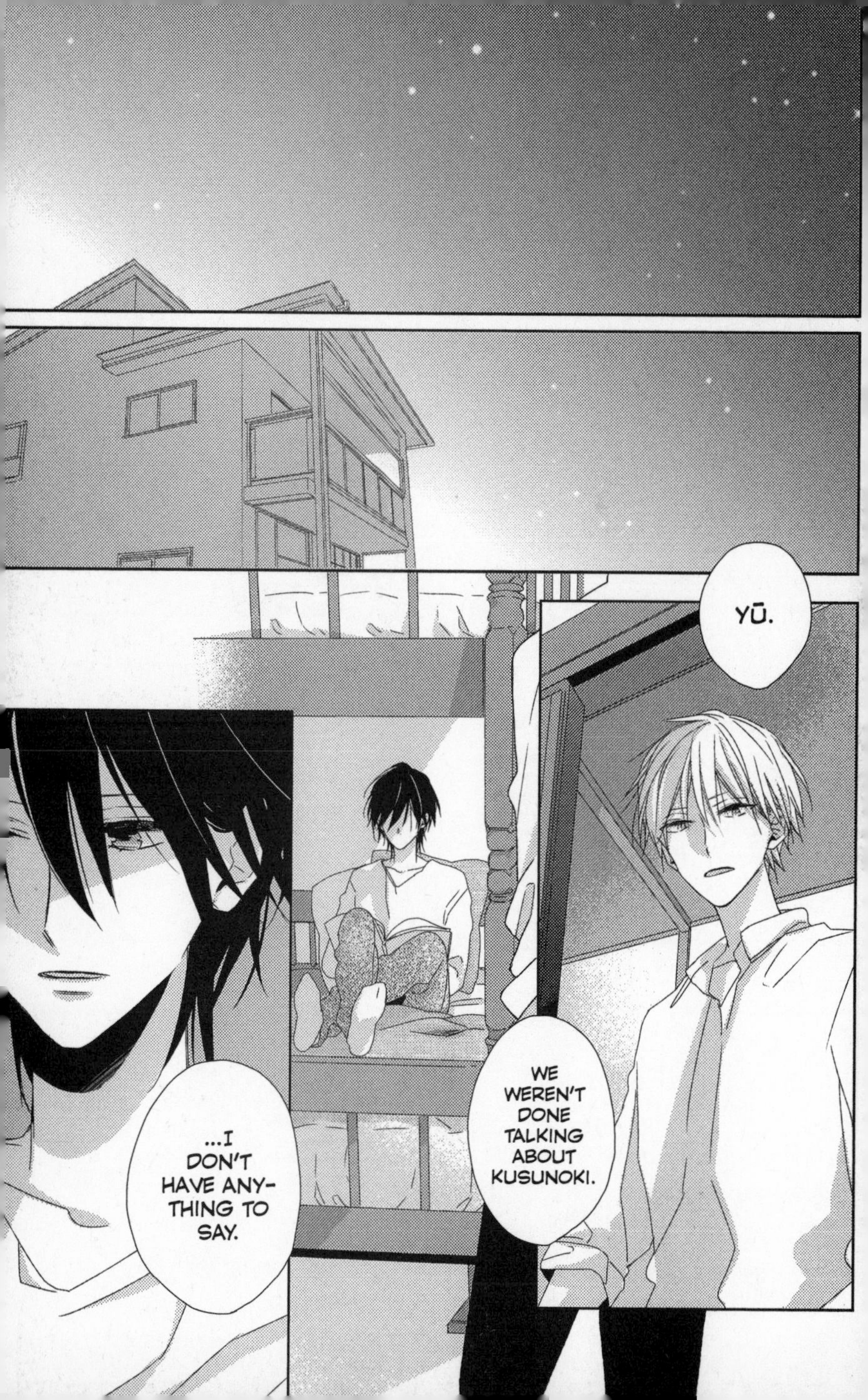
YŪ.
WE WEREN'T DONE TALKING ABOUT KUSUNOKI.
...I DON'T HAVE ANY-THING TO SAY.

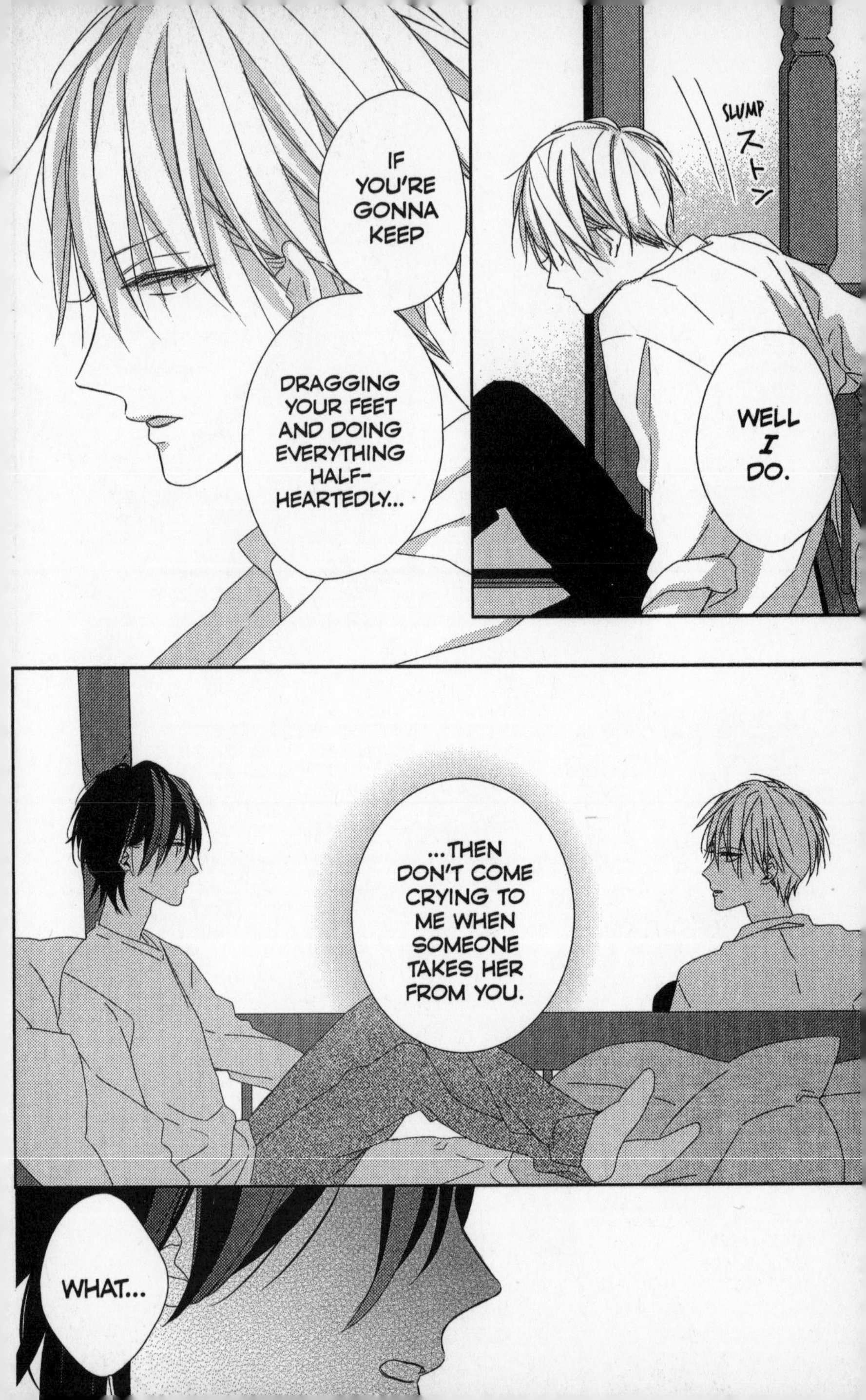

SLUMP
ストン
WELL I DO.
IF YOU'RE GONNA KEEP
DRAGGING YOUR FEET AND DOING EVERYTHING HALF-HEARTEDLY...
...THEN DON'T COME CRYING TO ME WHEN SOMEONE TAKES HER FROM YOU.
WHAT...

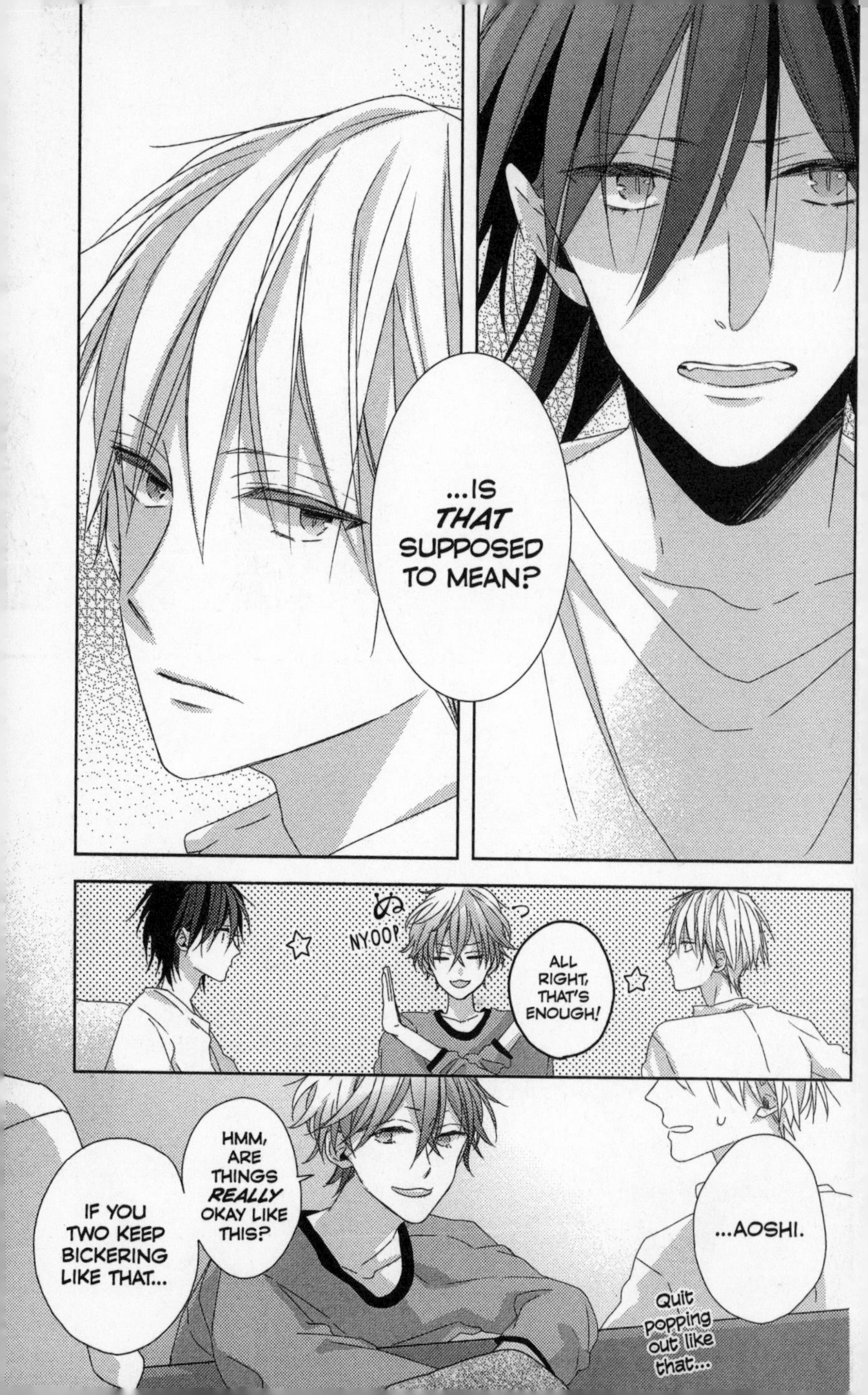
...IS *THAT* SUPPOSED TO MEAN?
ALL RIGHT, THAT'S ENOUGH!
NYOOP
ぬっ
...AOSHI.
Quit popping out like that...
HMM, ARE THINGS *REALLY* OKAY LIKE THIS?
IF YOU TWO KEEP BICKERING LIKE THAT...

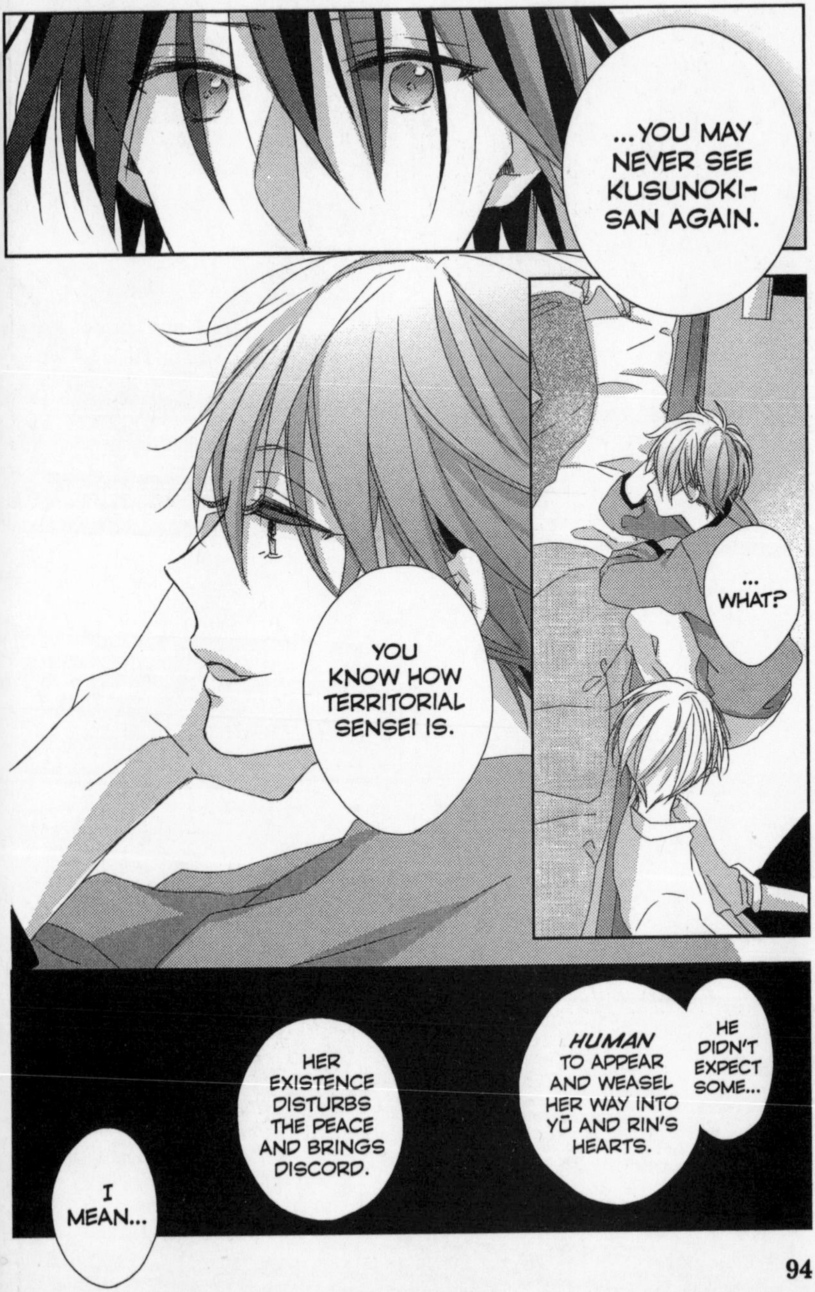
...YOU MAY NEVER SEE KUSUNOKI-SAN AGAIN.
... WHAT?
YOU KNOW HOW TERRITORIAL SENSEI IS.
HE DIDN'T EXPECT SOME...
*HUMAN* TO APPEAR AND WEASEL HER WAY INTO YŪ AND RIN'S HEARTS.
HER EXISTENCE DISTURBS THE PEACE AND BRINGS DISCORD.
I MEAN...

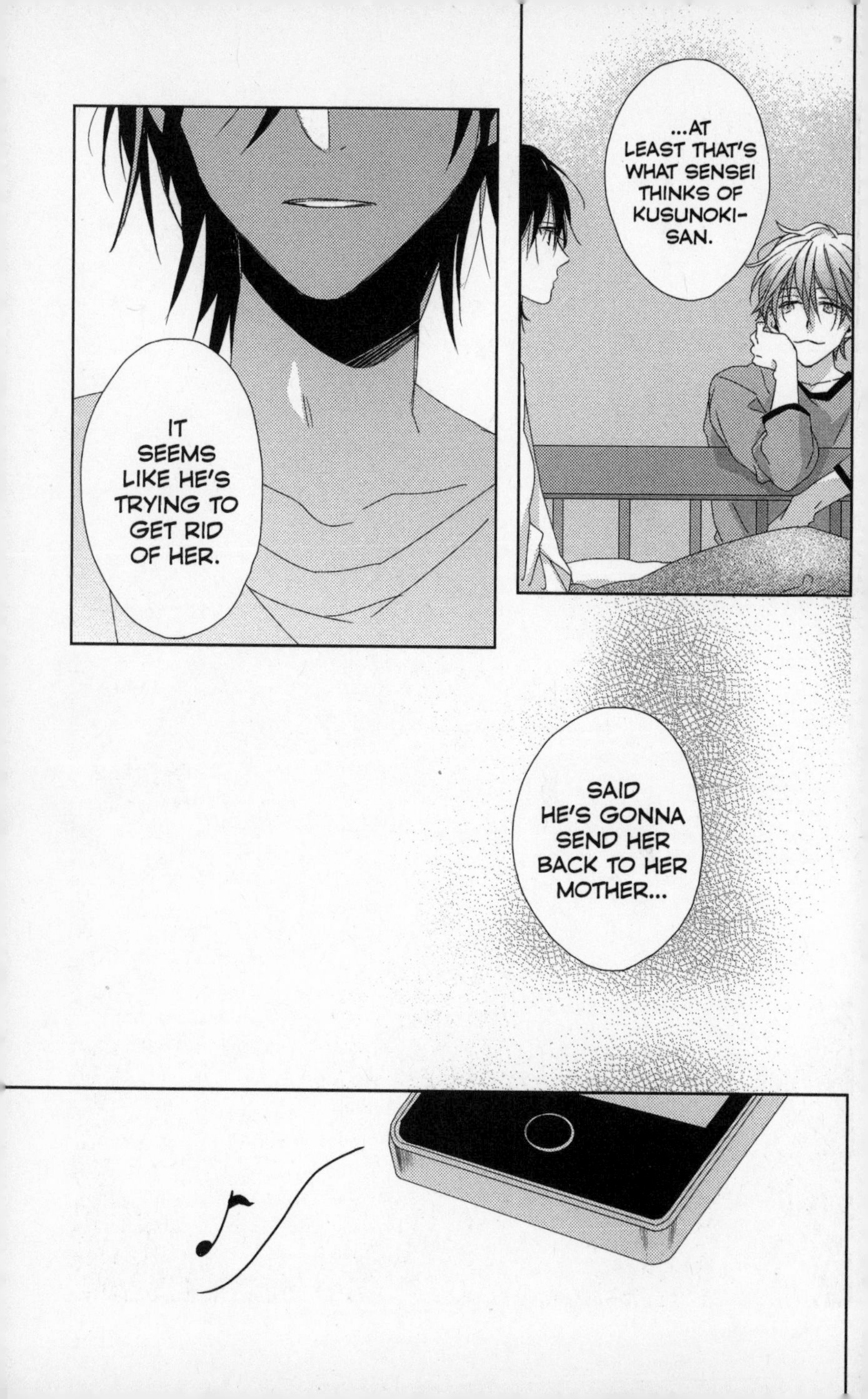
...AT LEAST THAT'S WHAT SENSEI THINKS OF KUSUNOKI-SAN.
IT SEEMS LIKE HE'S TRYING TO GET RID OF HER.
SAID HE'S GONNA SEND HER BACK TO HER MOTHER...

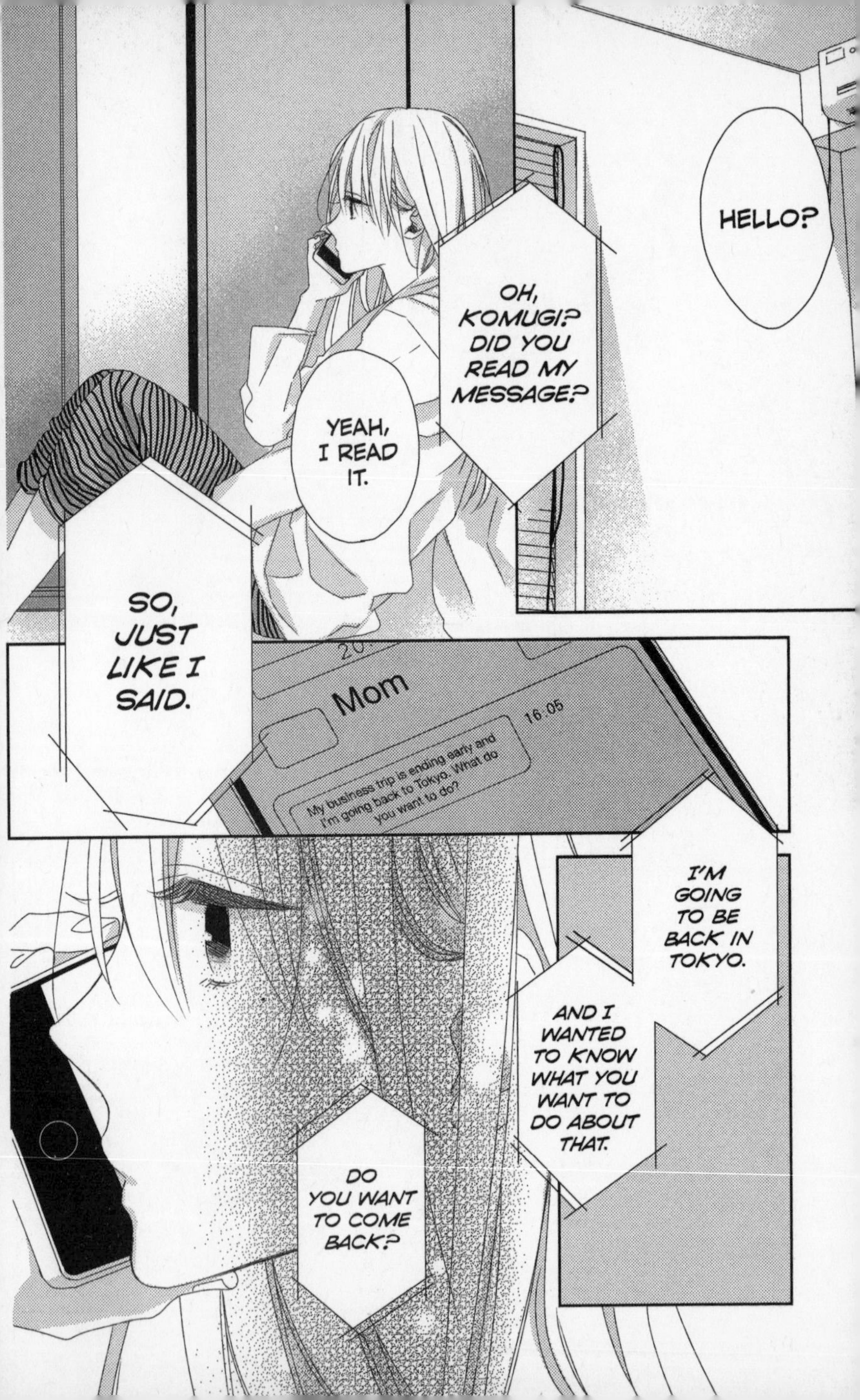
HELLO?
OH, KOMUGI? DID YOU READ MY MESSAGE?
YEAH, I READ IT.
SO, JUST LIKE I SAID.
Mom
16:05
My business trip is ending early and I'm going back to Tokyo. What do you want to do?
I'M GOING TO BE BACK IN TOKYO.
AND I WANTED TO KNOW WHAT YOU WANT TO DO ABOUT THAT.
DO YOU WANT TO COME BACK?

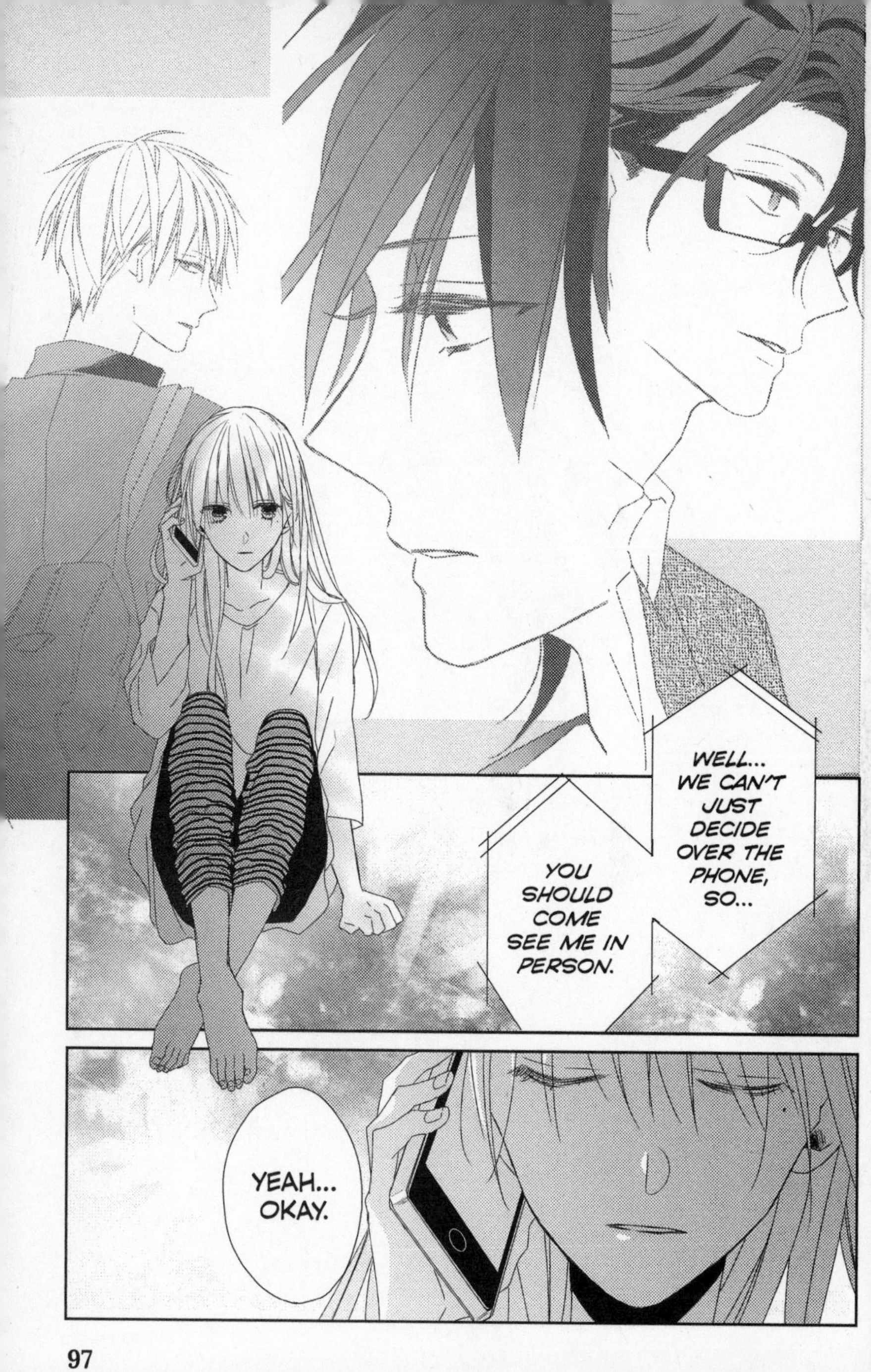
WELL... WE CAN'T JUST DECIDE OVER THE PHONE, SO...
YOU SHOULD COME SEE ME IN PERSON.
YEAH... OKAY.

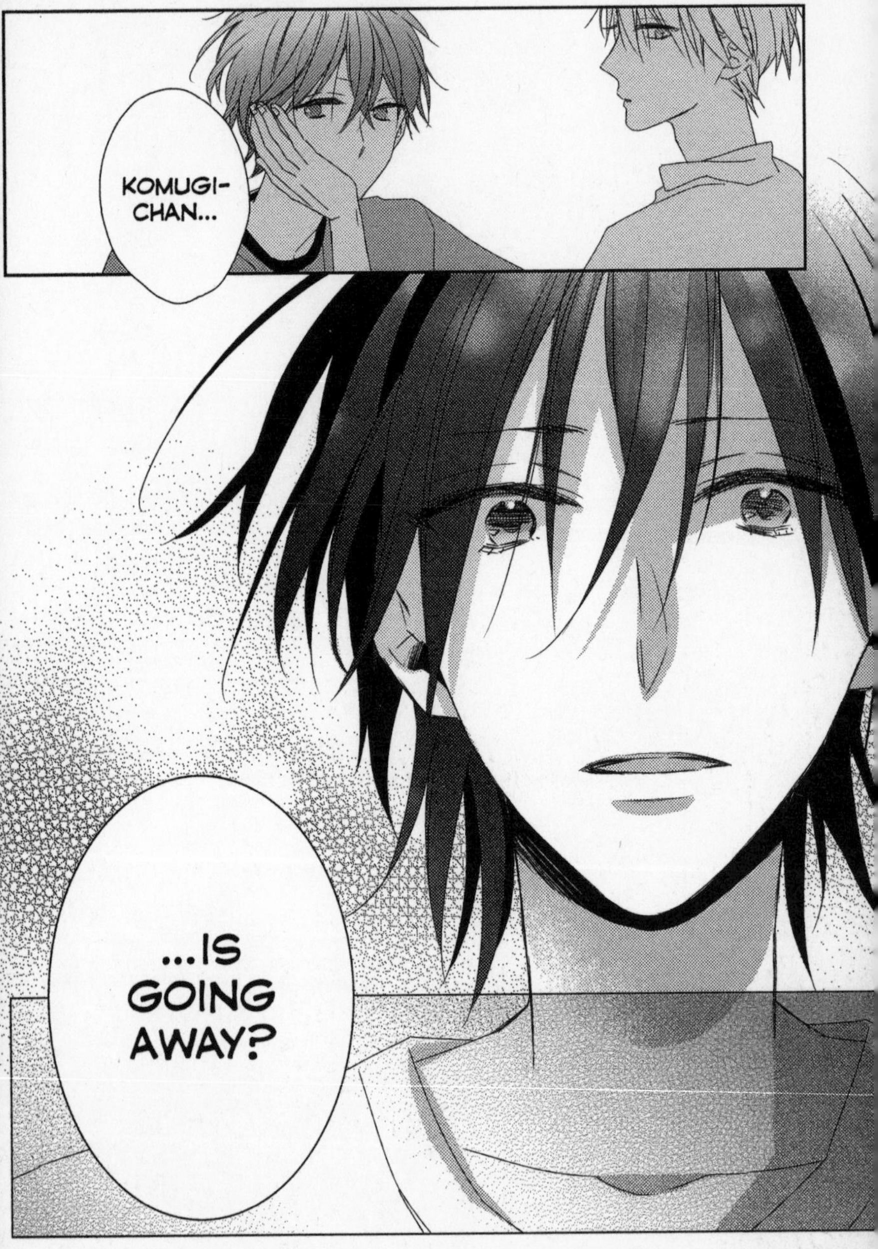
KOMUGI-CHAN...
...IS GOING AWAY?

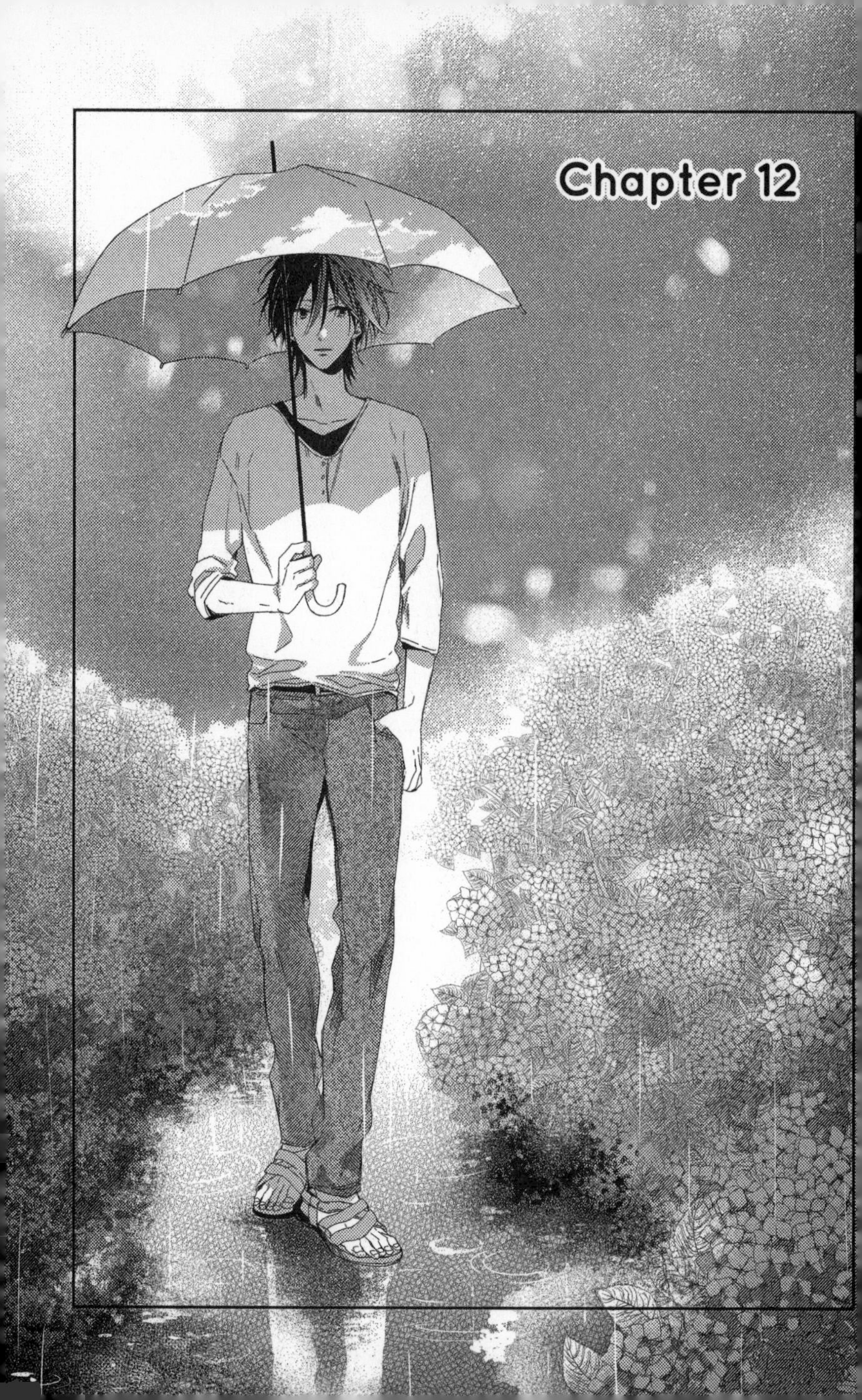
Chapter 12

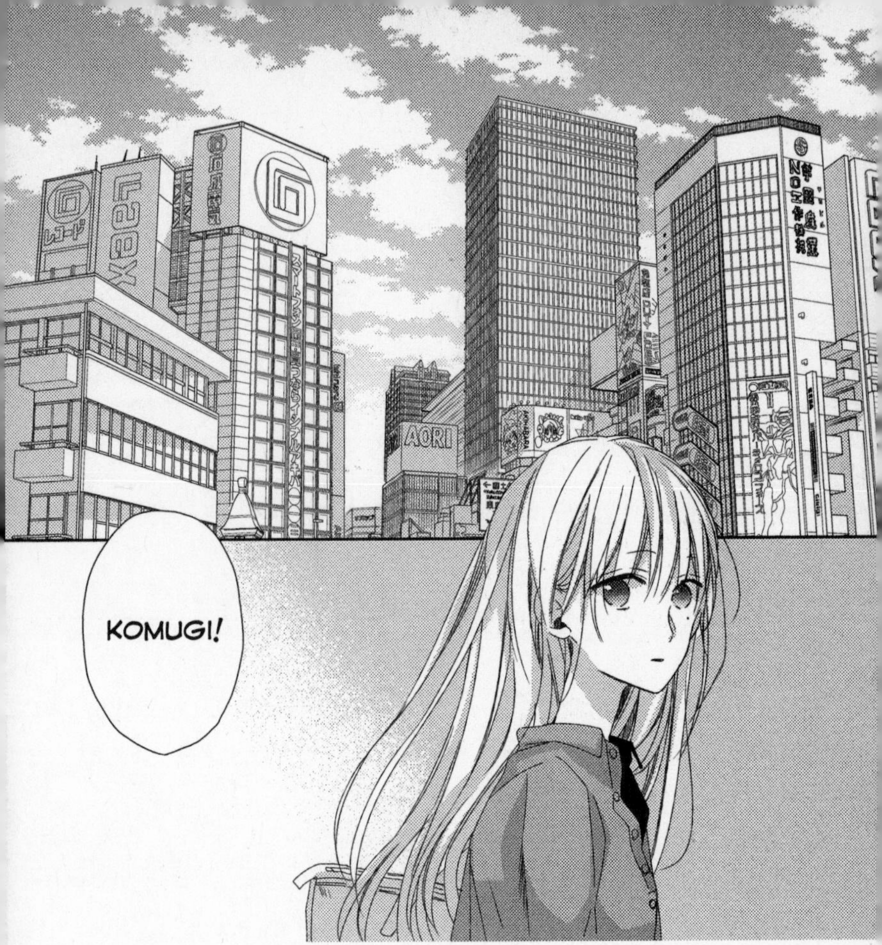
KOMUGI!

# That Wolf-Boy is Mine!

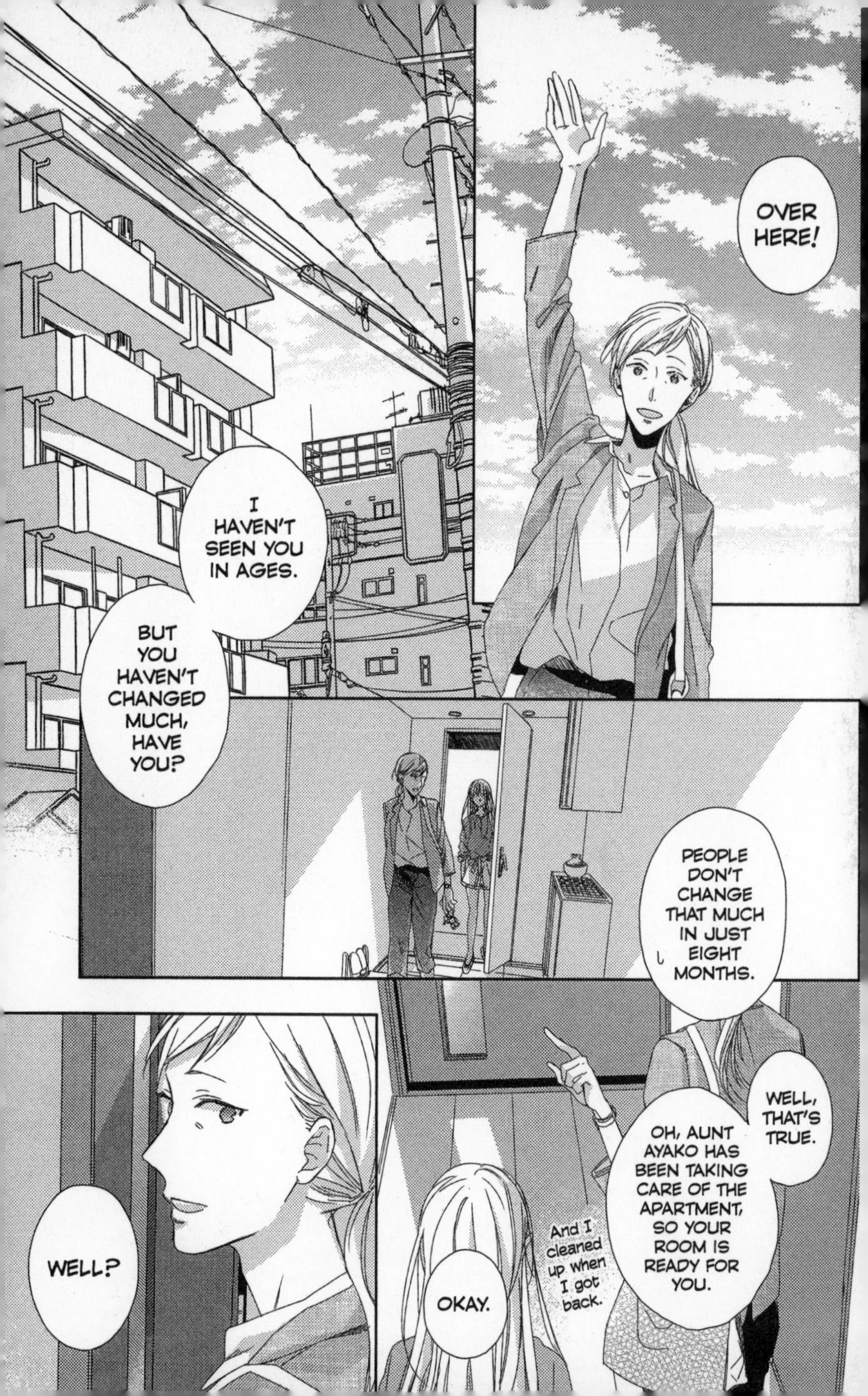
OVER HERE!
I HAVEN'T SEEN YOU IN AGES.
BUT YOU HAVEN'T CHANGED MUCH, HAVE YOU?
PEOPLE DON'T CHANGE THAT MUCH IN JUST EIGHT MONTHS.
WELL, THAT'S TRUE.
OH, AUNT AYAKO HAS BEEN TAKING CARE OF THE APARTMENT, SO YOUR ROOM IS READY FOR YOU.
And I cleaned up when I got back.
OKAY.
WELL?

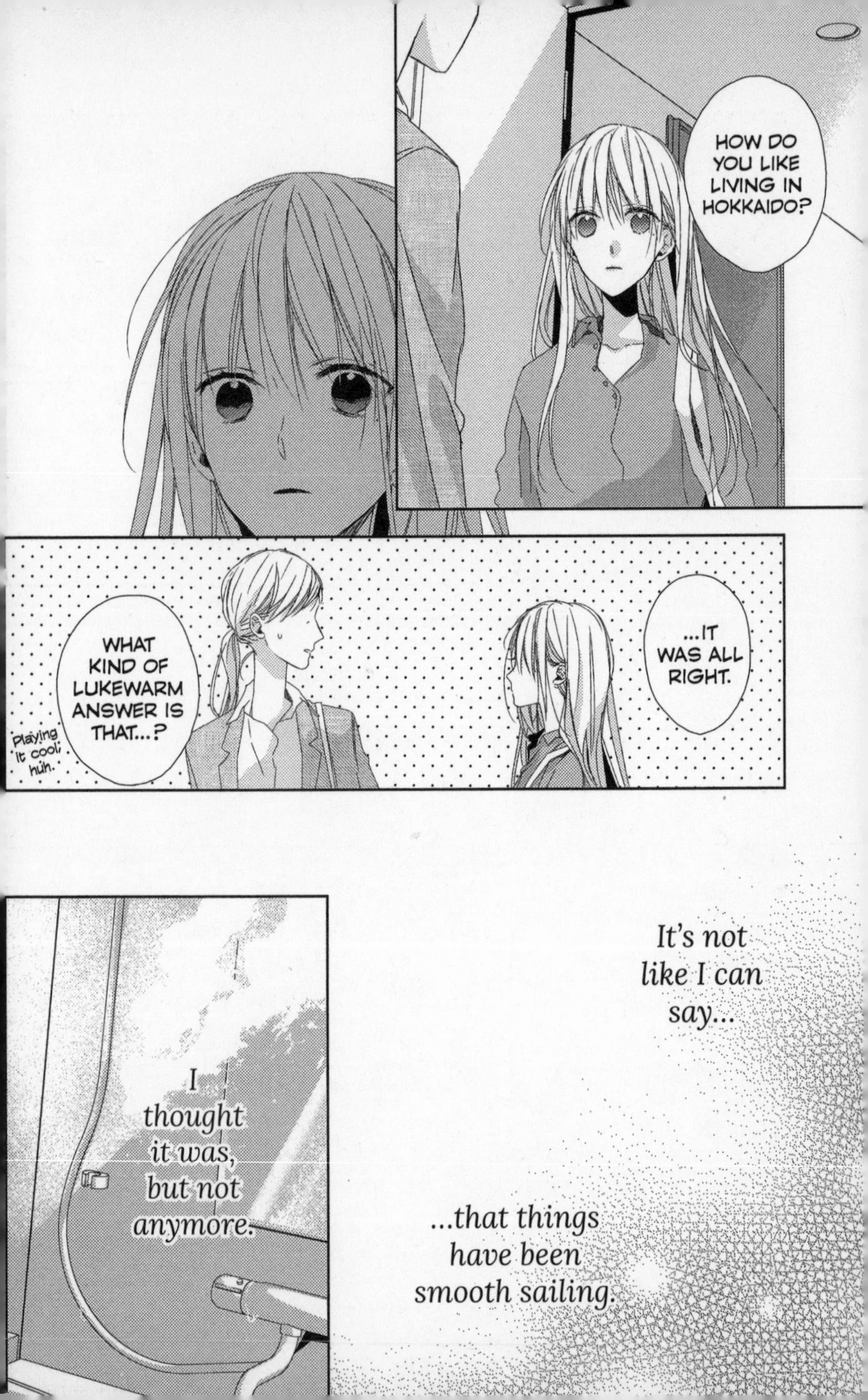
HOW DO YOU LIKE LIVING IN HOKKAIDO?
...IT WAS ALL RIGHT.
WHAT KIND OF LUKEWARM ANSWER IS THAT...?
Playing it cool, huh.
It's not like I can say...
...that things have been smooth sailing.
I thought it was, but not anymore.

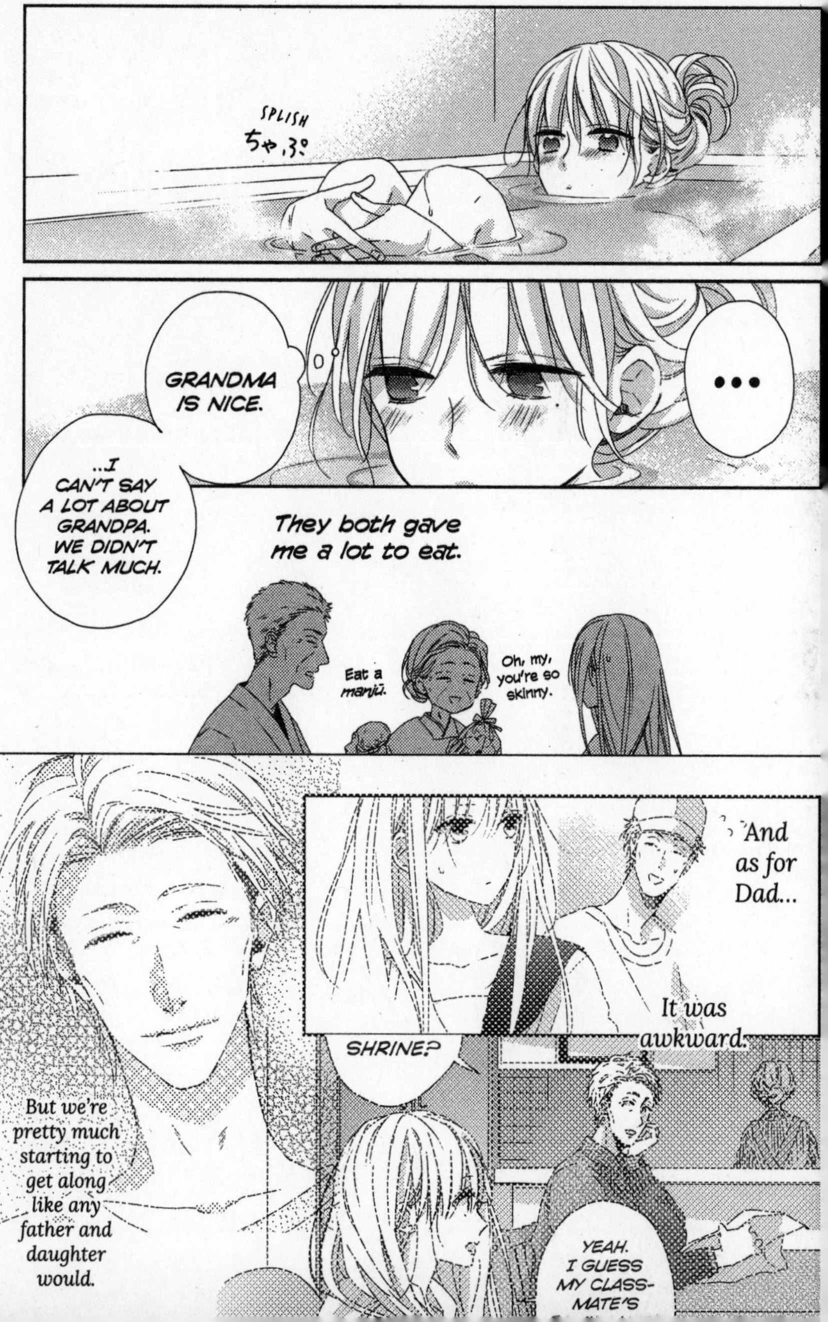
SPLISH
ちゃぷ
...
GRANDMA IS NICE.
...I CAN'T SAY A LOT ABOUT GRANDPA. WE DIDN'T TALK MUCH.
They both gave me a lot to eat.
Oh, my, you're so skinny.
Eat a *manjū*.
And as for Dad...
It was awkward.
SHRINE?
YEAH. I GUESS MY CLASS-MATE'S
But we're pretty much starting to get along like any father and daughter would.

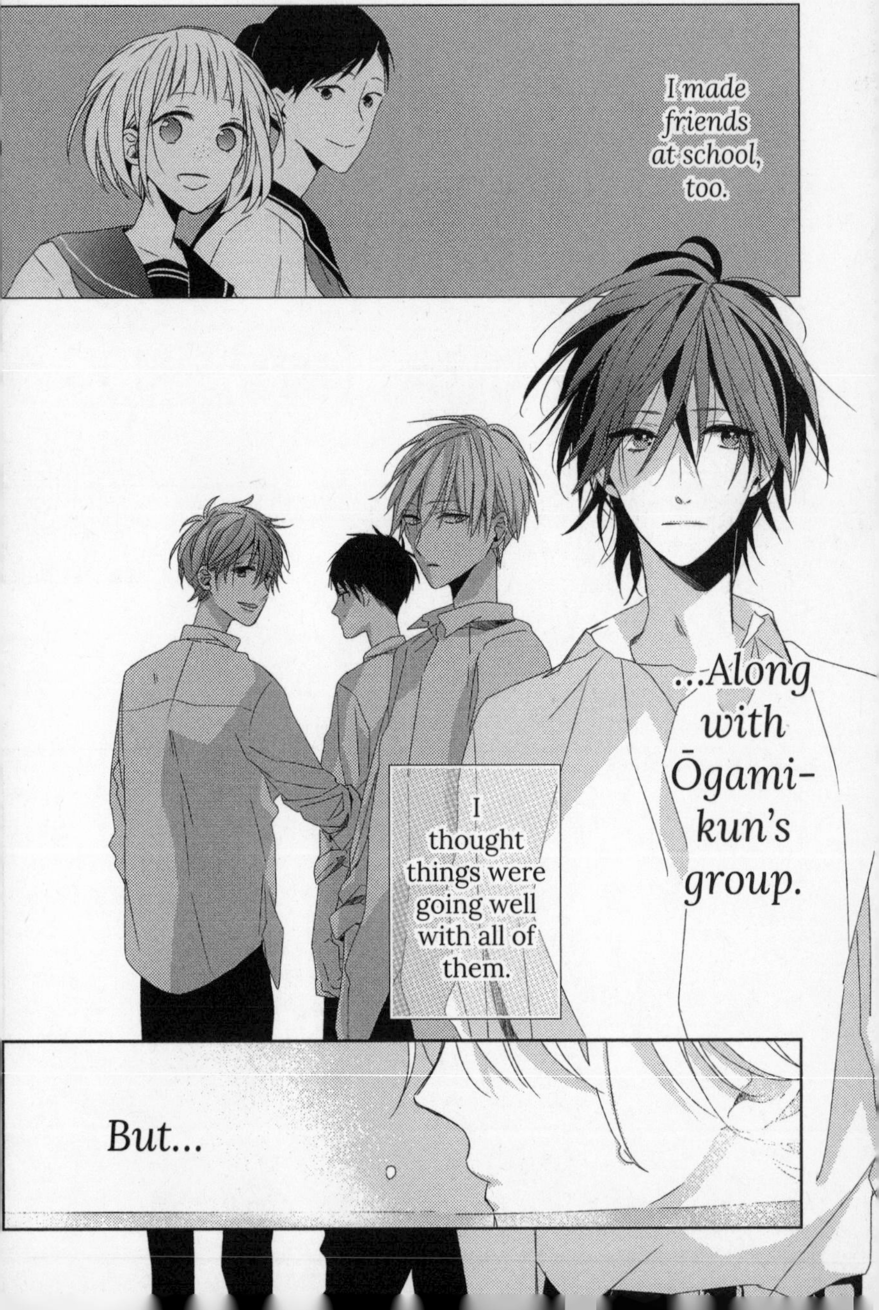
I made friends at school, too.
...Along with Ōgami-kun's group.
I thought things were going well with all of them.
But...

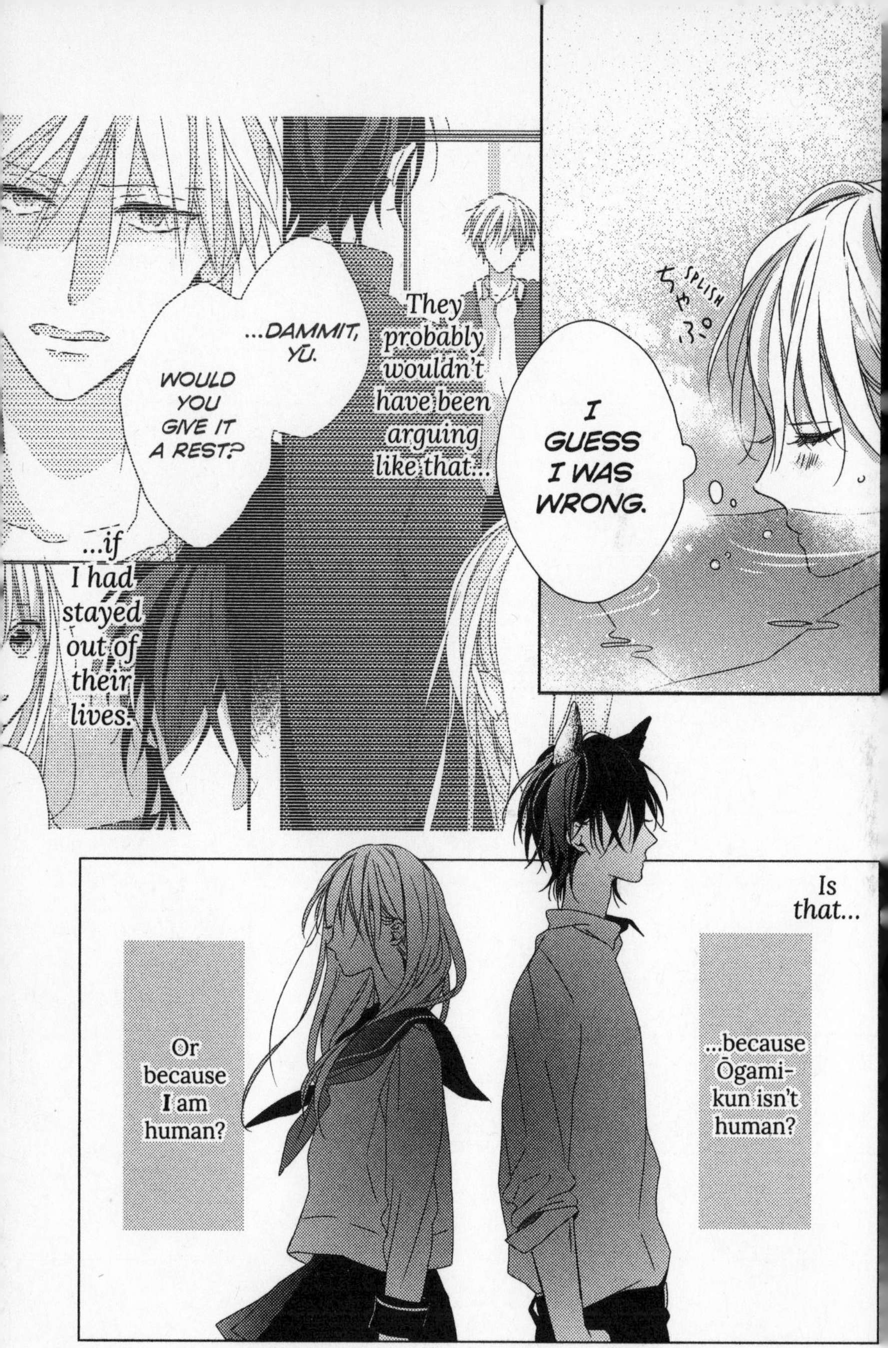
SPLISH
I GUESS I WAS WRONG.
They probably wouldn't have been arguing like that...
...DAMMIT, YŪ.
WOULD YOU GIVE IT A REST?
...if I had stayed out of their lives.
Is that...
...because Ōgami-kun isn't human?
Or because I am human?

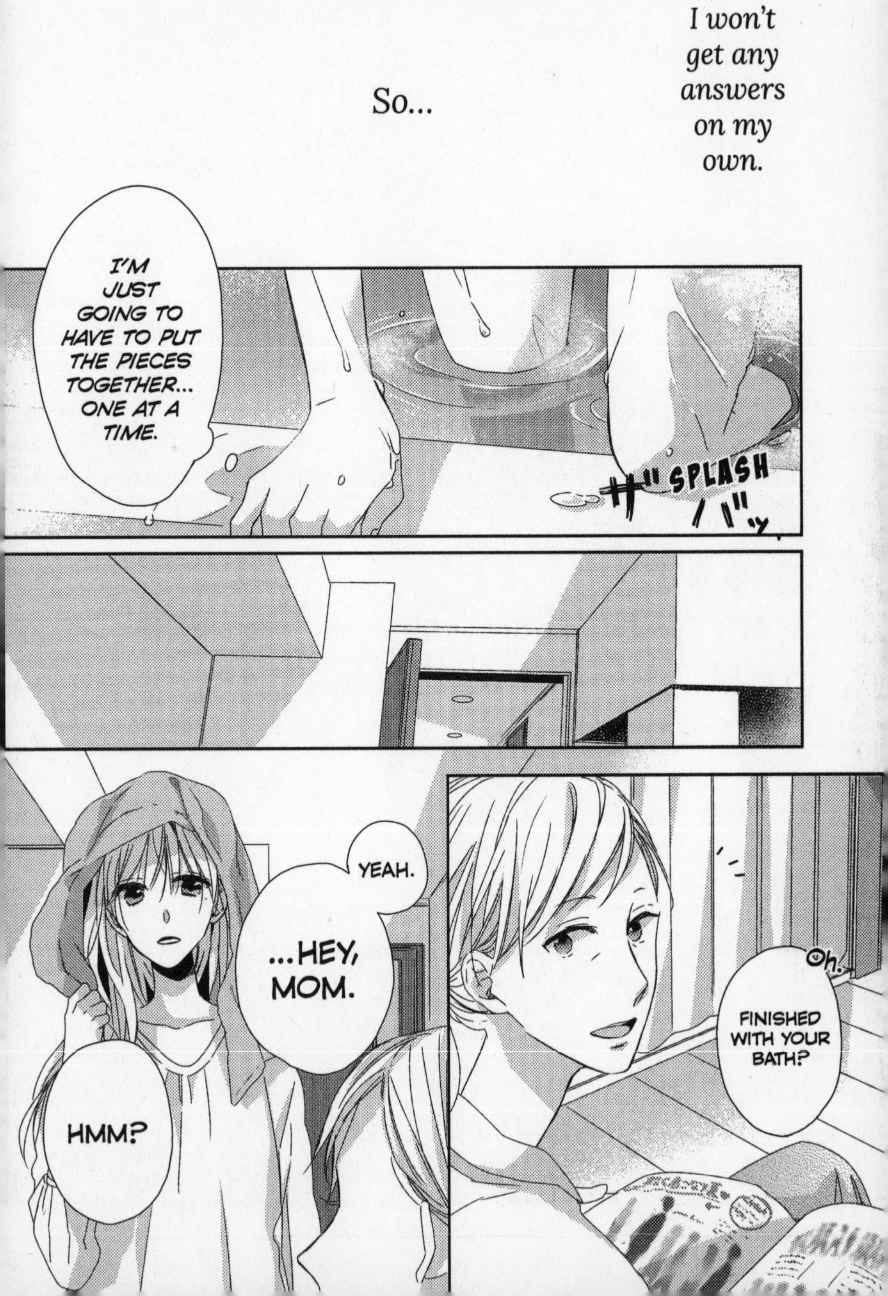
I won't get any answers on my own.
So...
I'M JUST GOING TO HAVE TO PUT THE PIECES TOGETHER... ONE AT A TIME.
SPLASH
Oh.
FINISHED WITH YOUR BATH?
YEAH.
...HEY, MOM.
HMM?

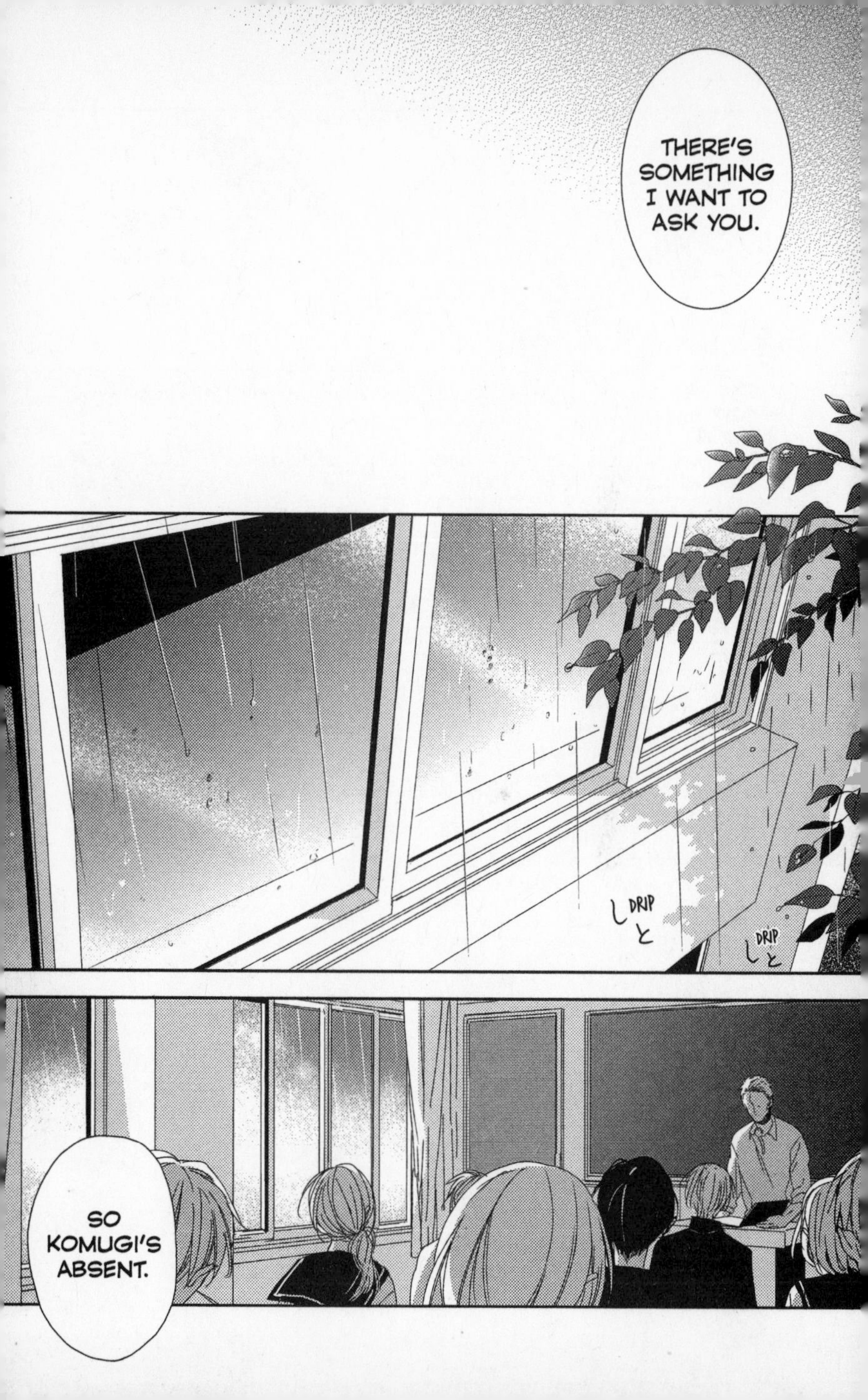
THERE'S SOMETHING I WANT TO ASK YOU.
DRIP
しと
DRIP
しと
SO KOMUGI'S ABSENT.

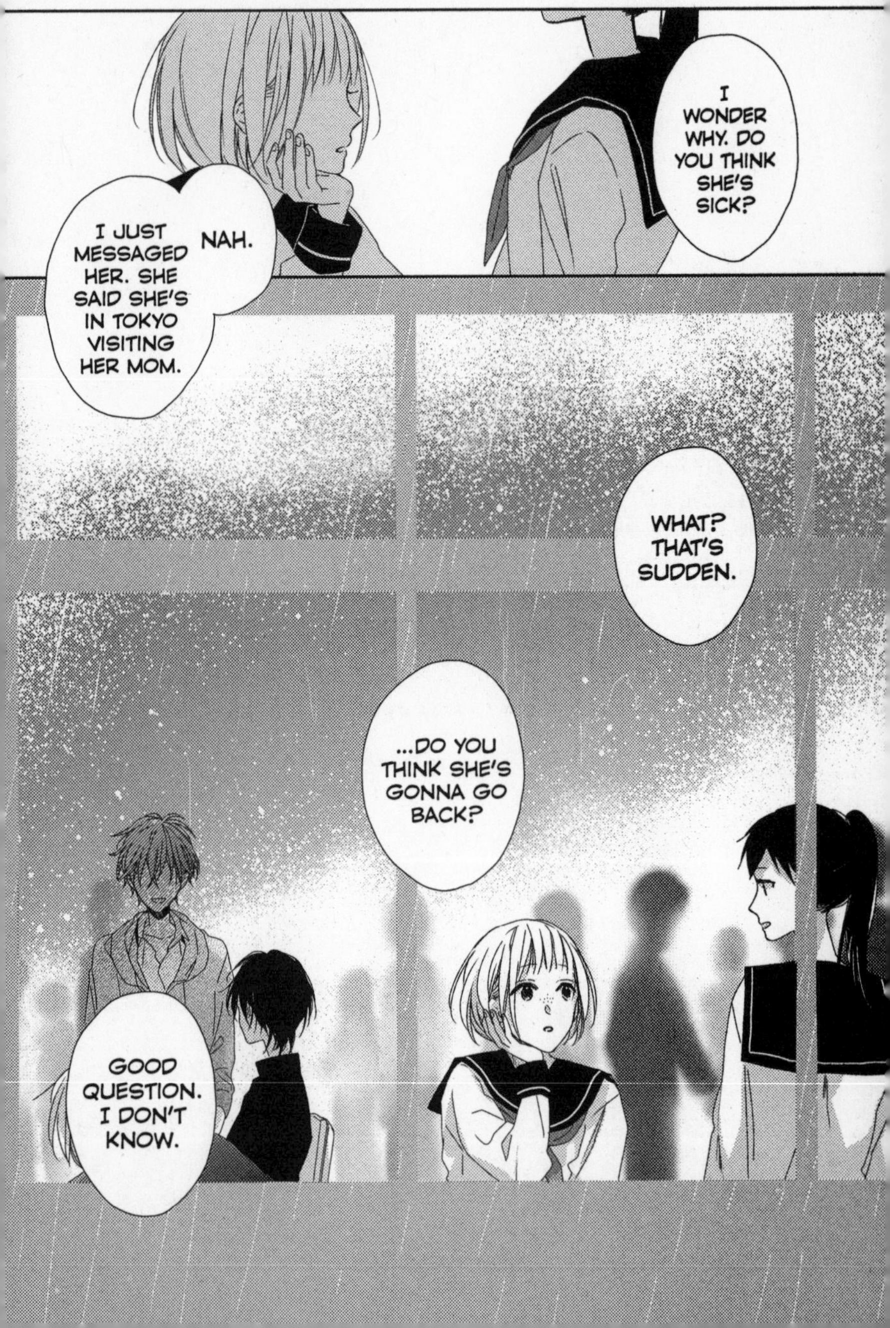
I WONDER WHY. DO YOU THINK SHE'S SICK?
NAH.
I JUST MESSAGED HER. SHE SAID SHE'S IN TOKYO VISITING HER MOM.
WHAT? THAT'S SUDDEN.
...DO YOU THINK SHE'S GONNA GO BACK?
GOOD QUESTION. I DON'T KNOW.

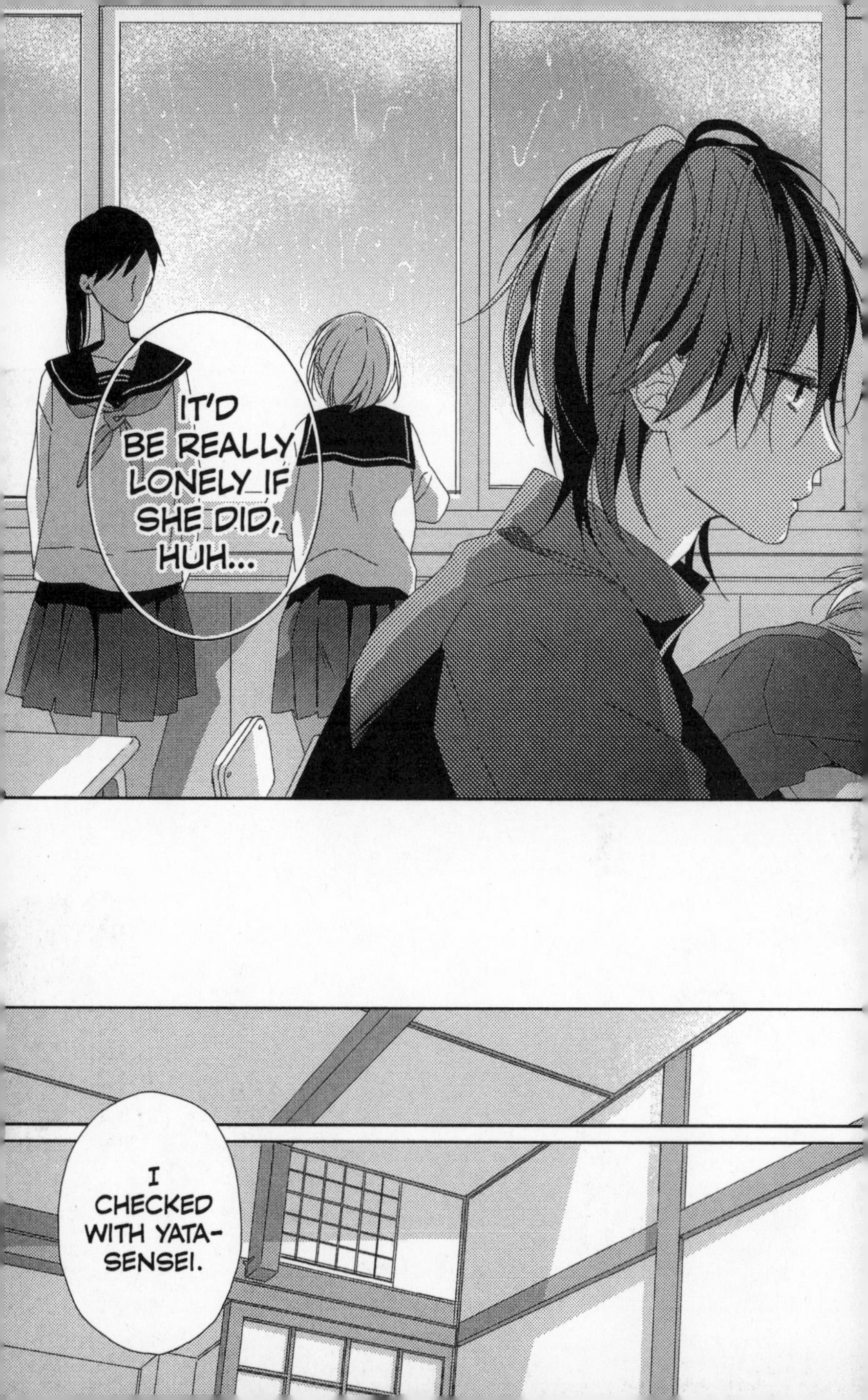
IT'D BE REALLY LONELY IF SHE DID, HUH...
I CHECKED WITH YATA-SENSEI.

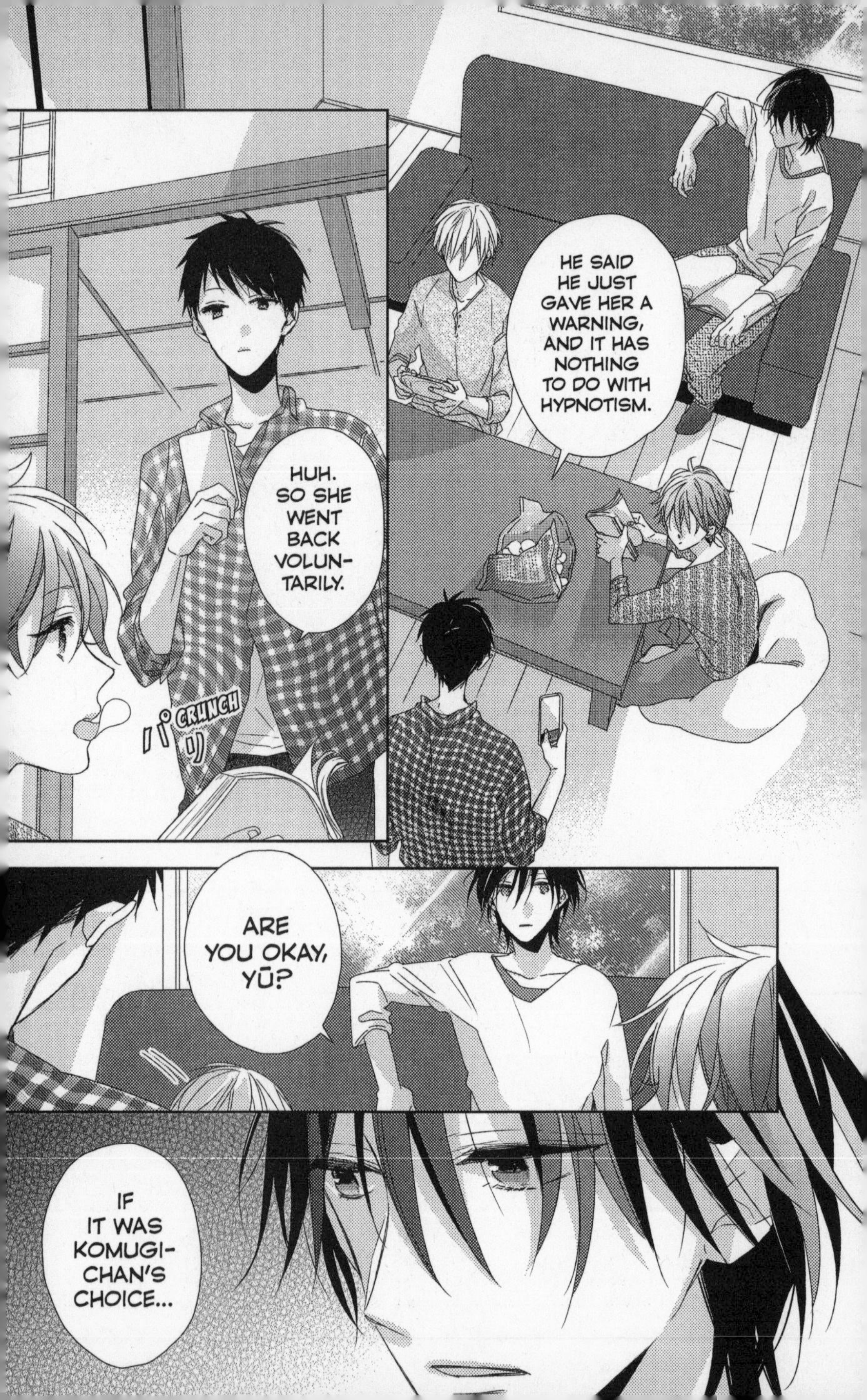
HE SAID HE JUST GAVE HER A WARNING, AND IT HAS NOTHING TO DO WITH HYPNOTISM.
HUH. SO SHE WENT BACK VOLUN-TARILY.
CRUNCH
ARE YOU OKAY, YŪ?
IF IT WAS KOMUGI-CHAN'S CHOICE...

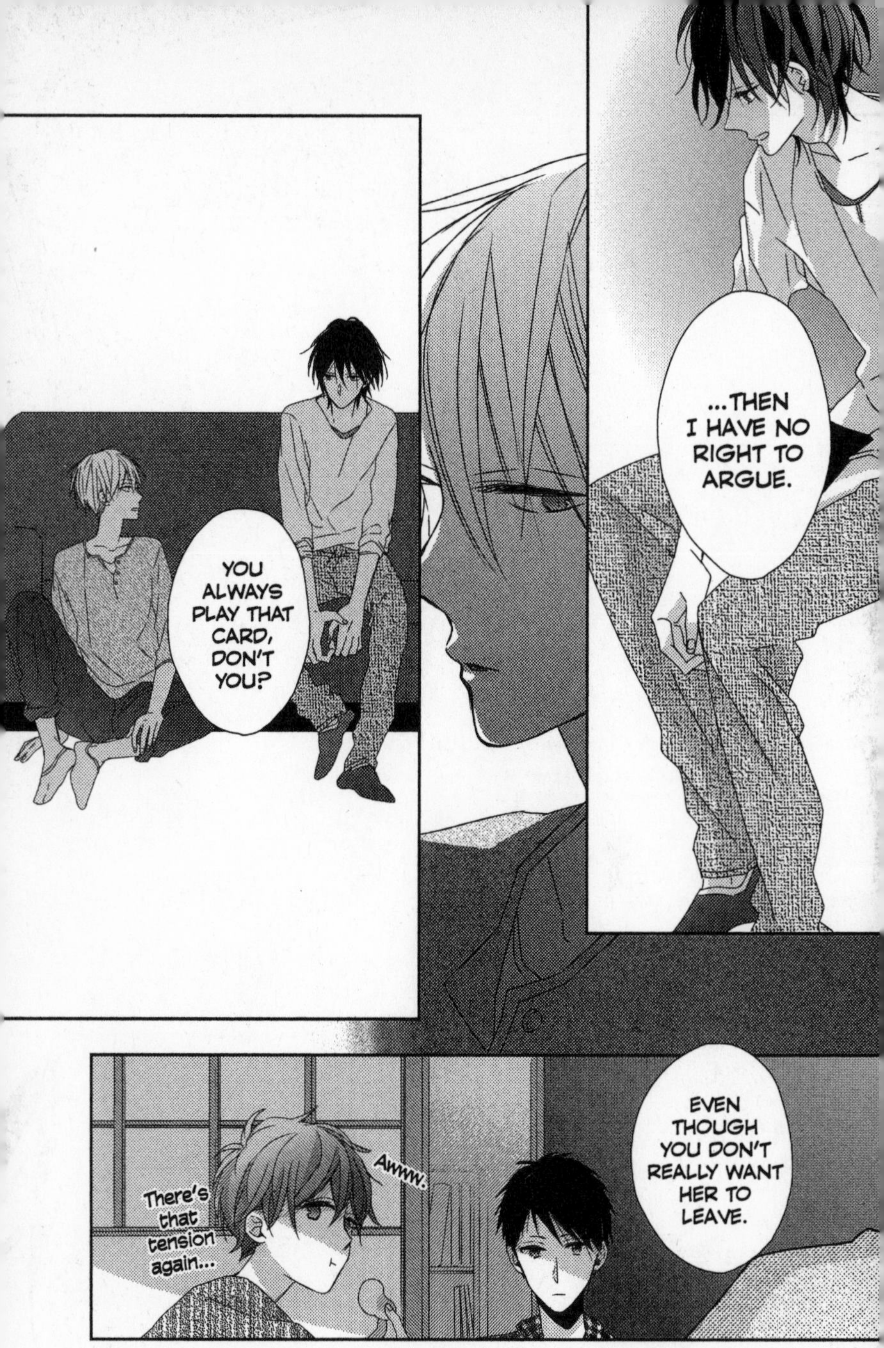
...THEN I HAVE NO RIGHT TO ARGUE.
YOU ALWAYS PLAY THAT CARD, DON'T YOU?
EVEN THOUGH YOU DON'T REALLY WANT HER TO LEAVE.
Awww.
There's that tension again...

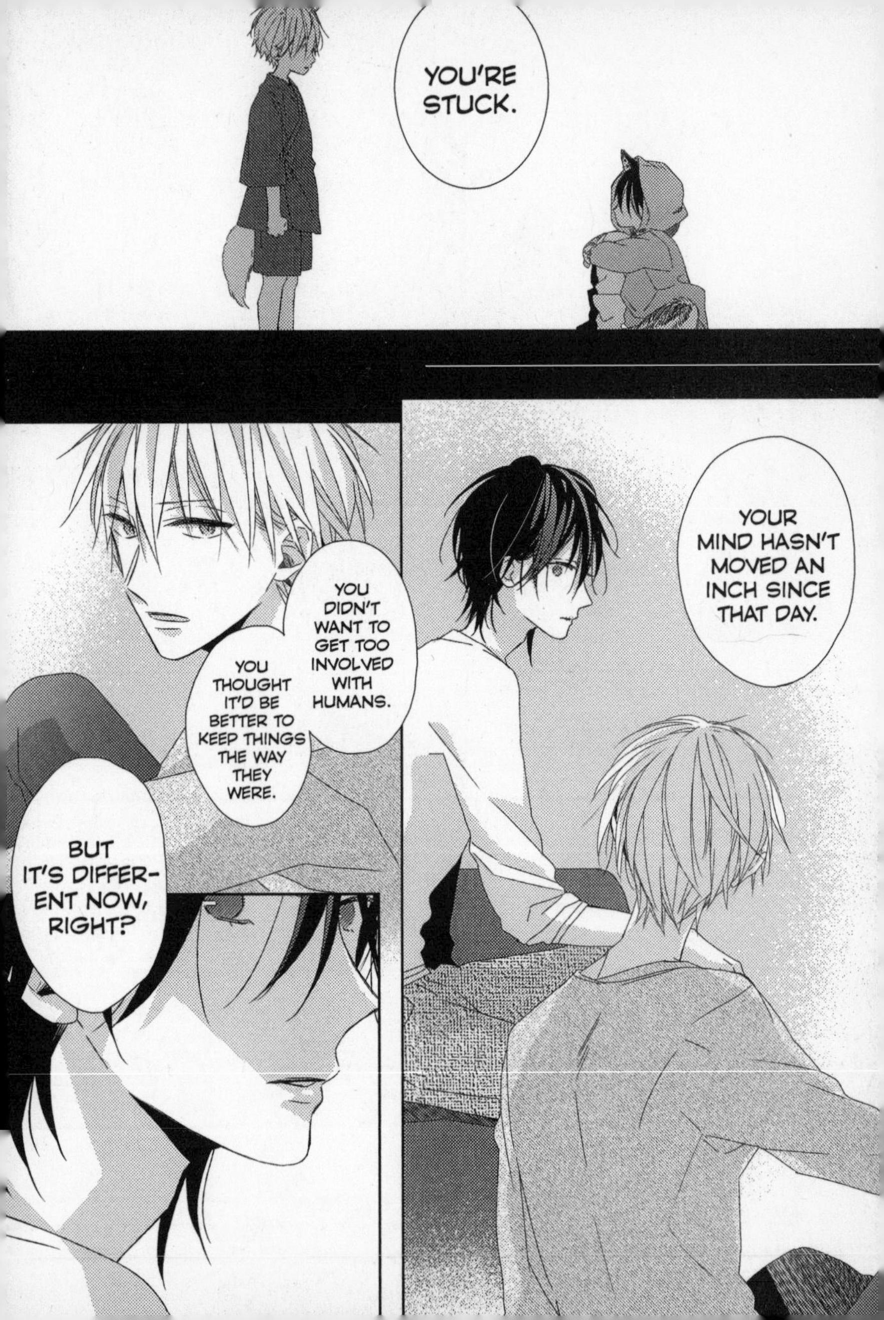
YOU'RE STUCK.
YOUR MIND HASN'T MOVED AN INCH SINCE THAT DAY.
YOU DIDN'T WANT TO GET TOO INVOLVED WITH HUMANS.
YOU THOUGHT IT'D BE BETTER TO KEEP THINGS THE WAY THEY WERE.
BUT IT'S DIFFER-ENT NOW, RIGHT?

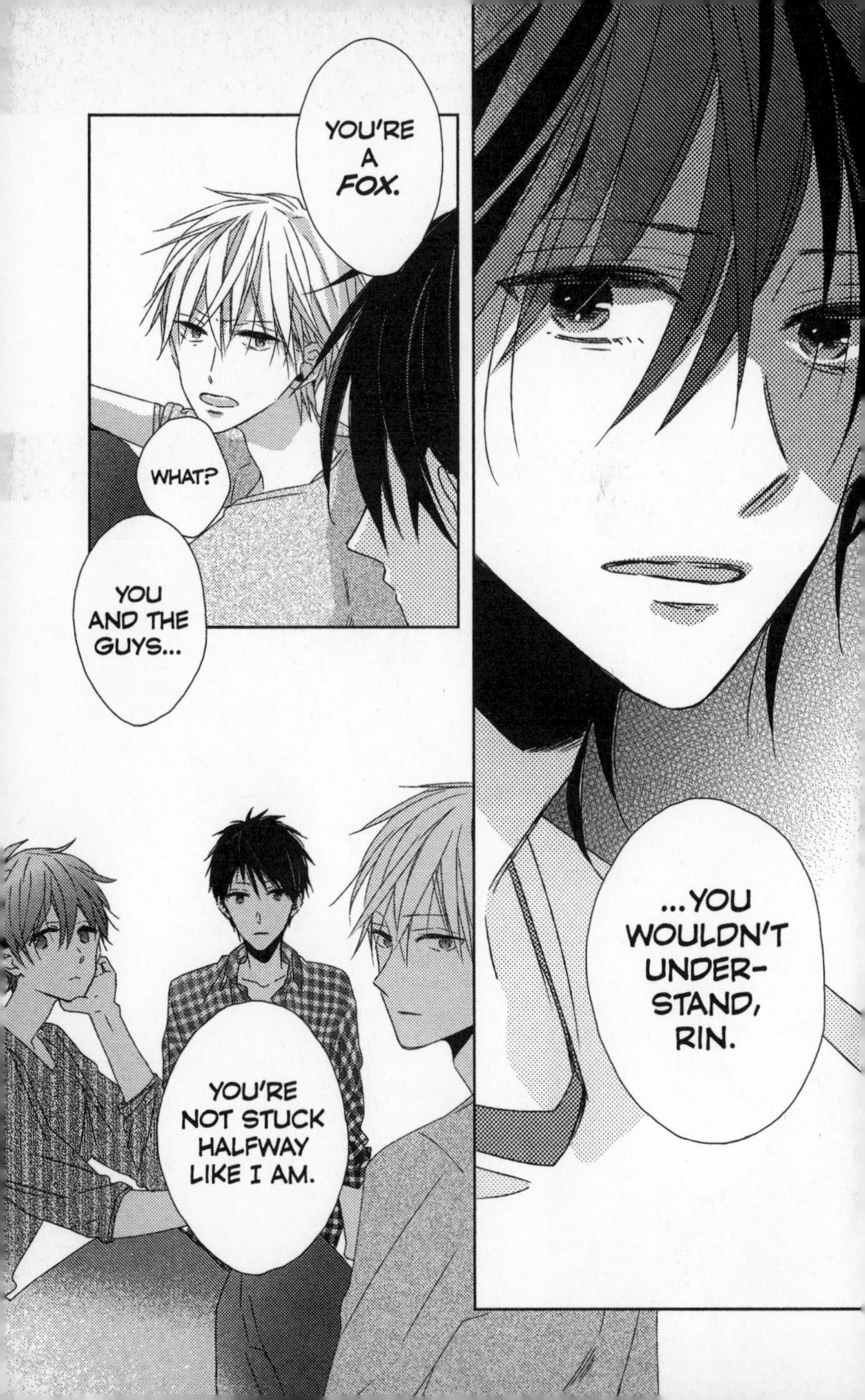
...YOU WOULDN'T UNDER-STAND, RIN.
YOU'RE A *FOX.*
WHAT?
YOU AND THE GUYS...
YOU'RE NOT STUCK HALFWAY LIKE I AM.

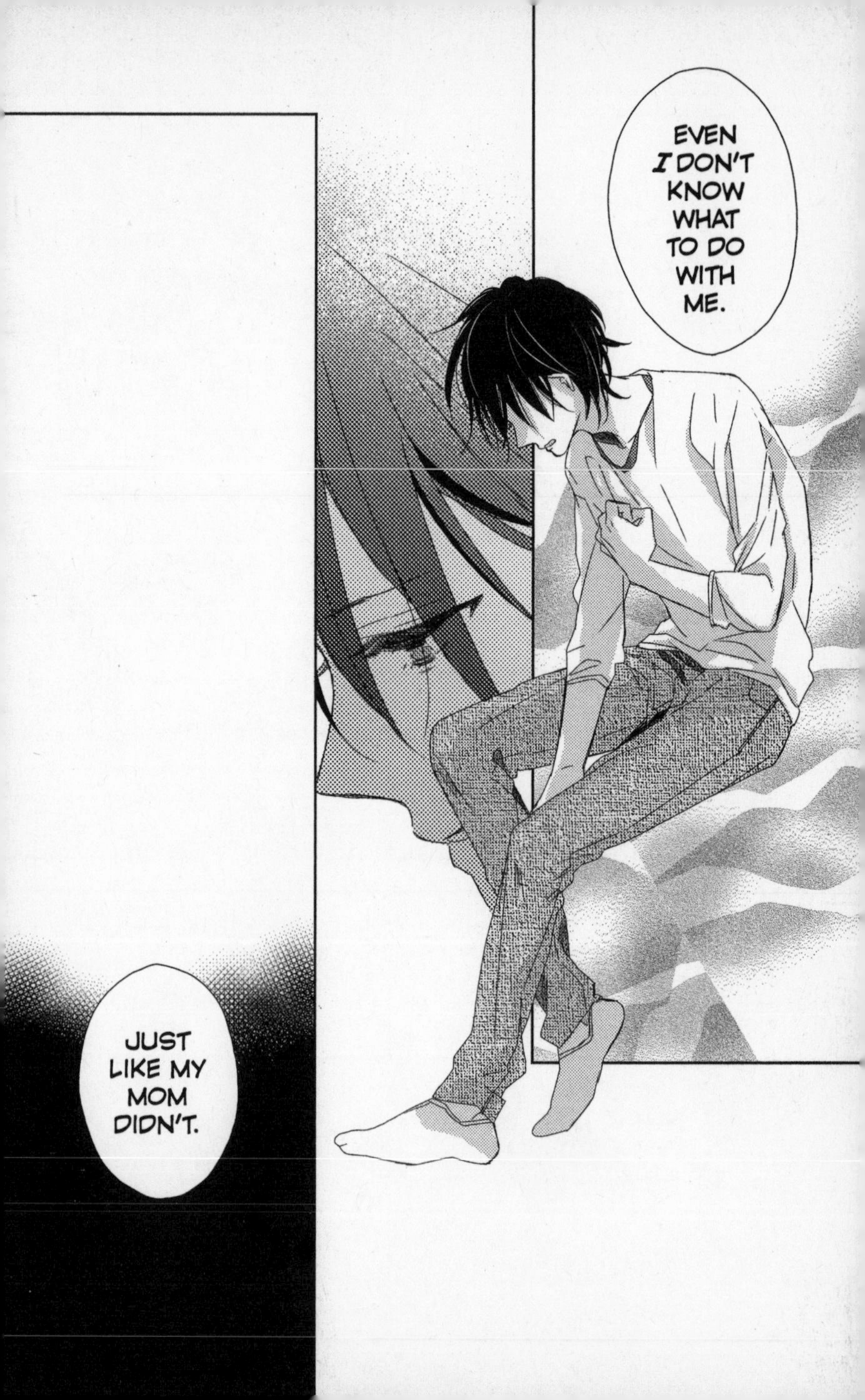
EVEN *I* DON'T KNOW WHAT TO DO WITH ME.
JUST LIKE MY MOM DIDN'T.

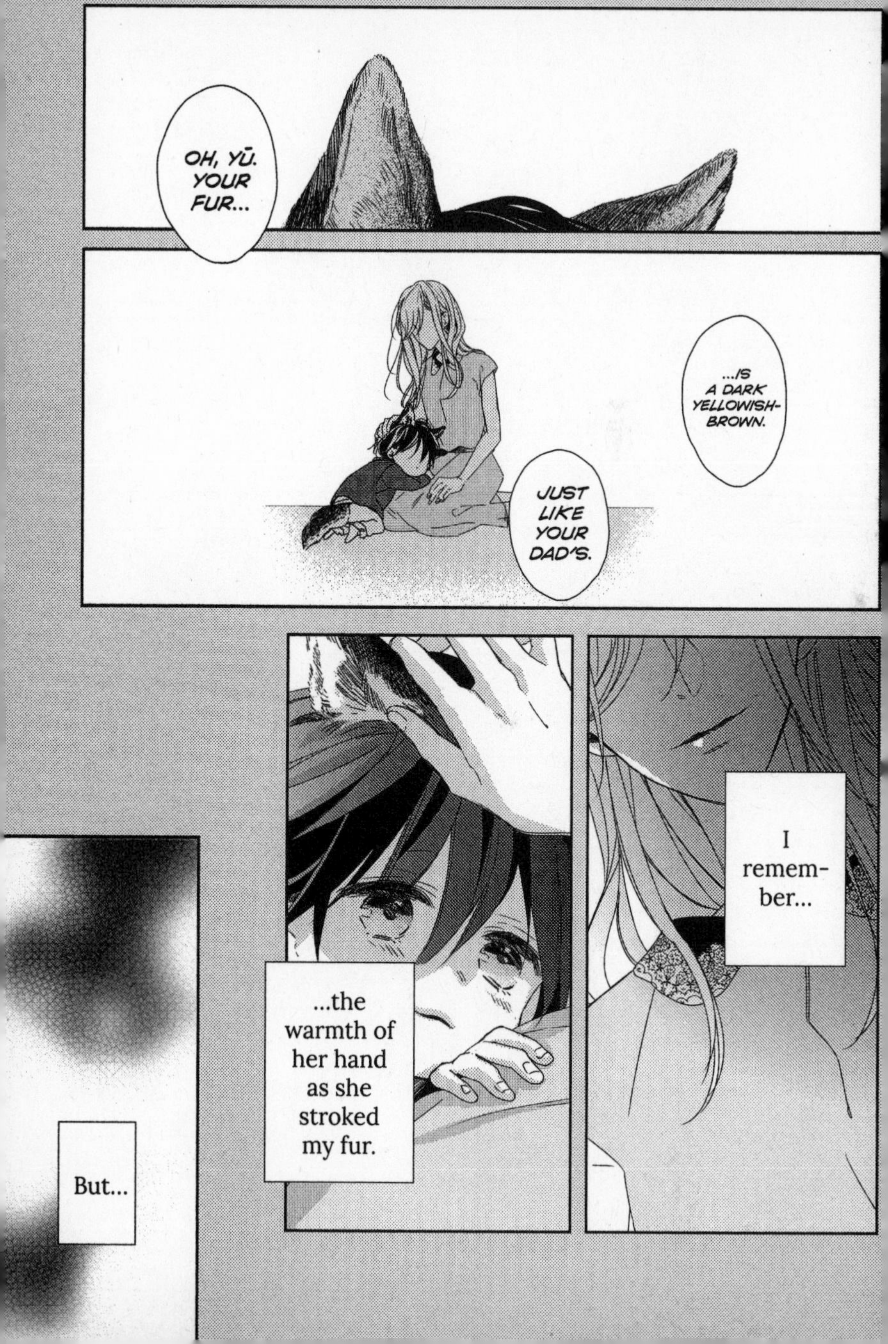
OH, YŪ. YOUR FUR...
...IS A DARK YELLOWISH-BROWN.
JUST LIKE YOUR DAD'S.
I remember...
...the warmth of her hand as she stroked my fur.
But...

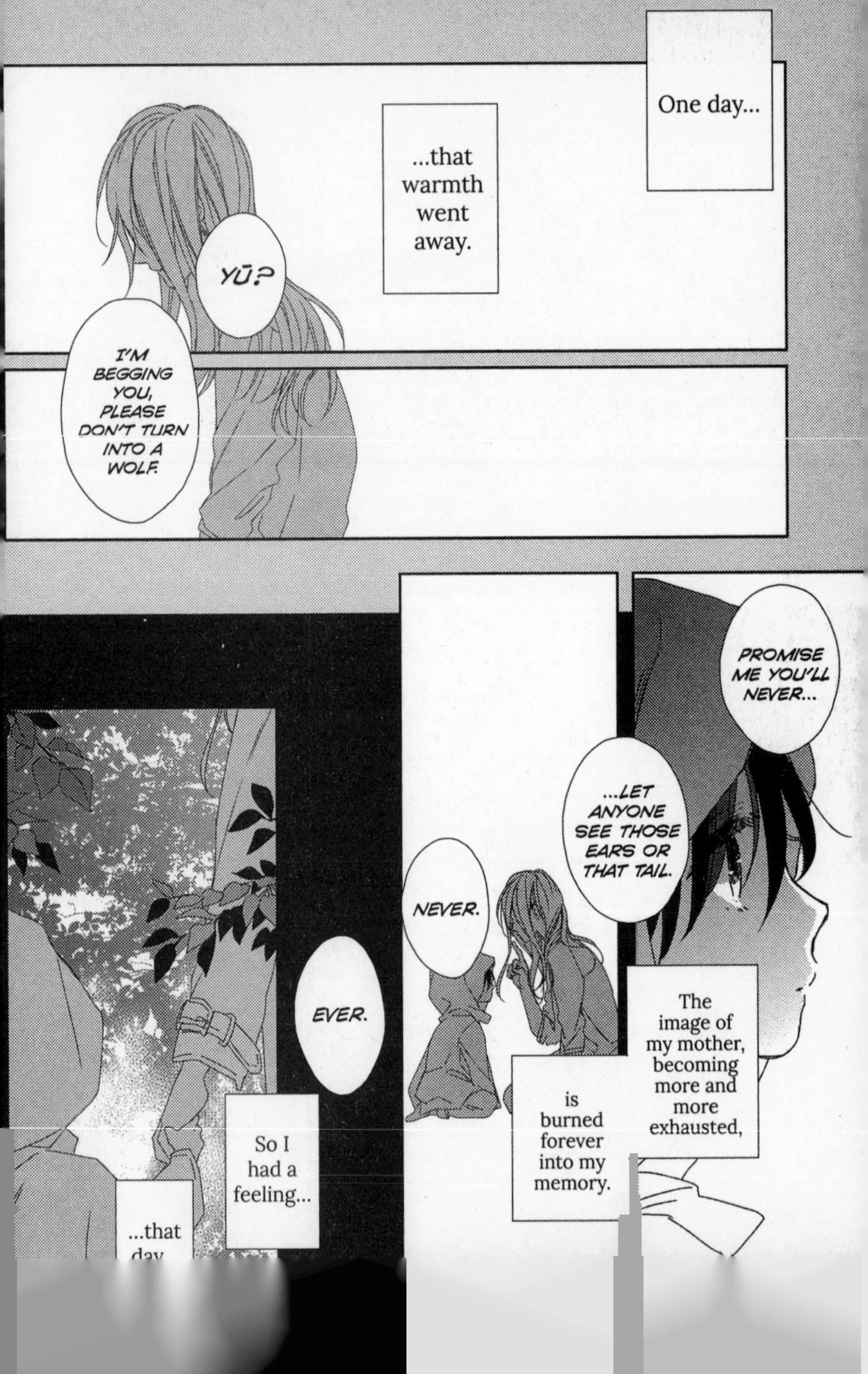
One day...
...that warmth went away.
YŪ?
I'M BEGGING YOU, PLEASE DON'T TURN INTO A WOLF.
PROMISE ME YOU'LL NEVER...
...LET ANYONE SEE THOSE EARS OR THAT TAIL.
NEVER.
The image of my mother, becoming more and more exhausted,
is burned forever into my memory.
EVER.
So I had a feeling...
...that

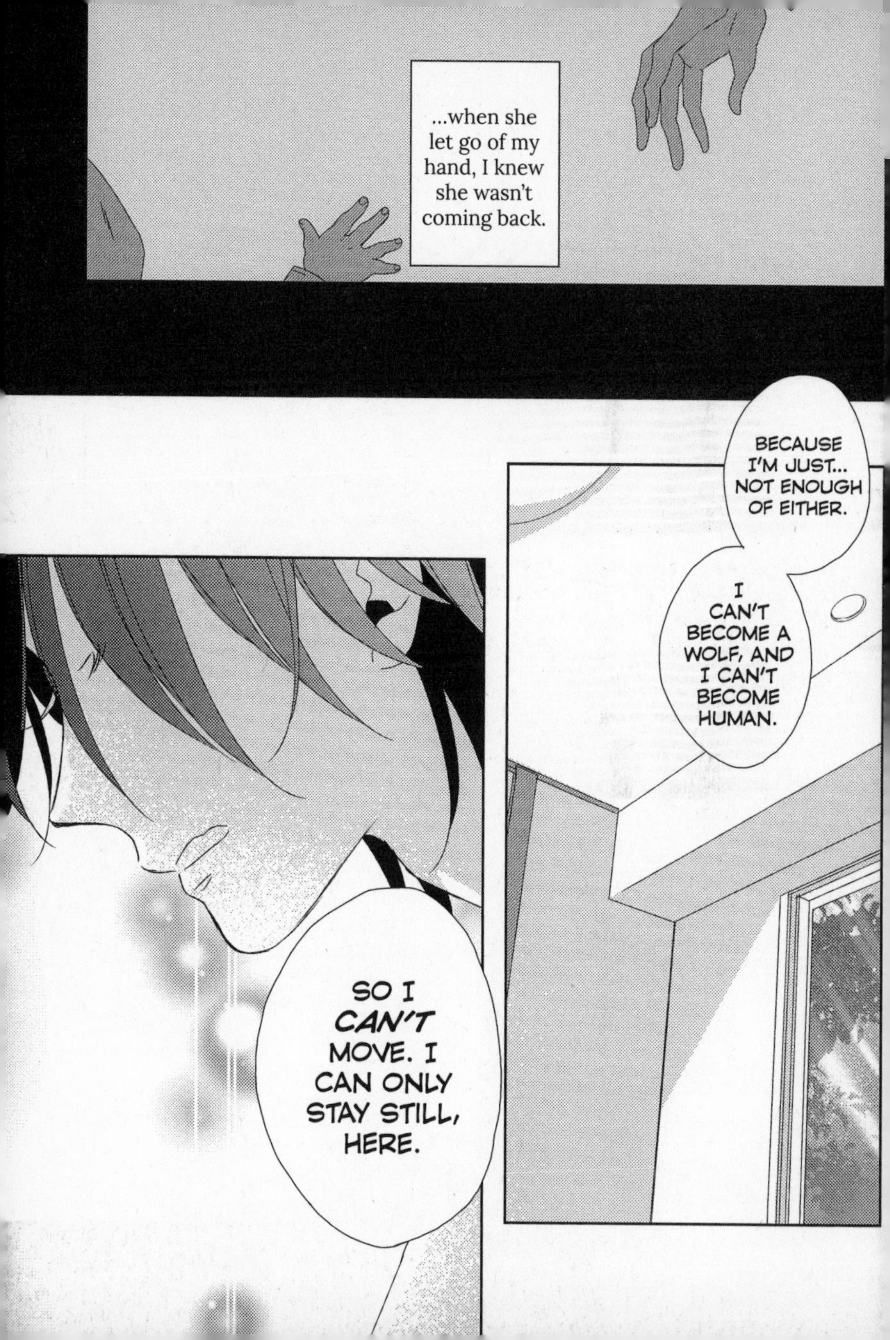
...when she let go of my hand, I knew she wasn't coming back.
BECAUSE I'M JUST... NOT ENOUGH OF EITHER.
I CAN'T BECOME A WOLF, AND I CAN'T BECOME HUMAN.
SO I *CAN'T* MOVE. I CAN ONLY STAY STILL, HERE.

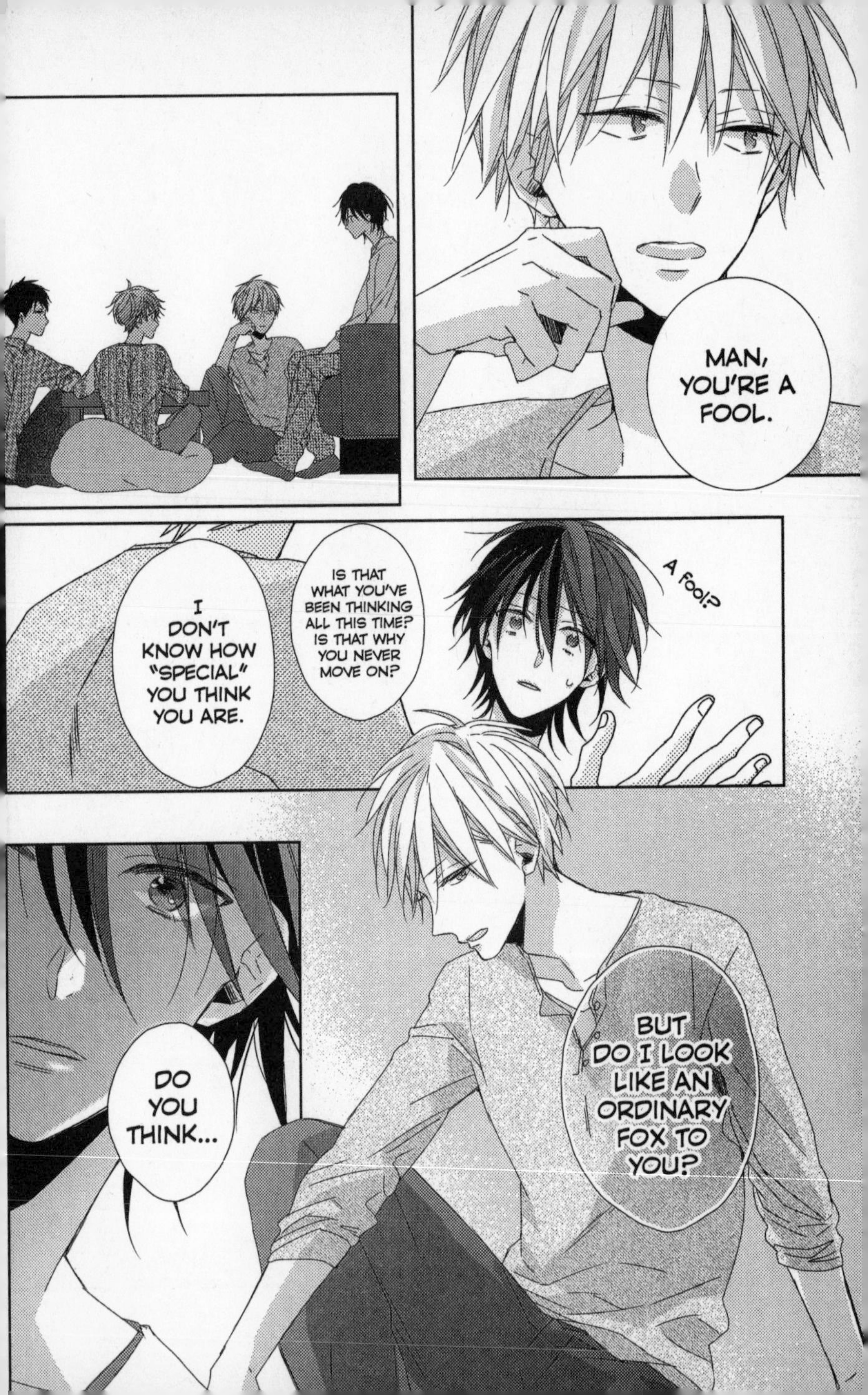
MAN, YOU'RE A FOOL.
A FOOL?
IS THAT WHAT YOU'VE BEEN THINKING ALL THIS TIME? IS THAT WHY YOU NEVER MOVE ON?
I DON'T KNOW HOW "SPECIAL" YOU THINK YOU ARE.
BUT DO I LOOK LIKE AN ORDINARY FOX TO YOU?
DO YOU THINK...

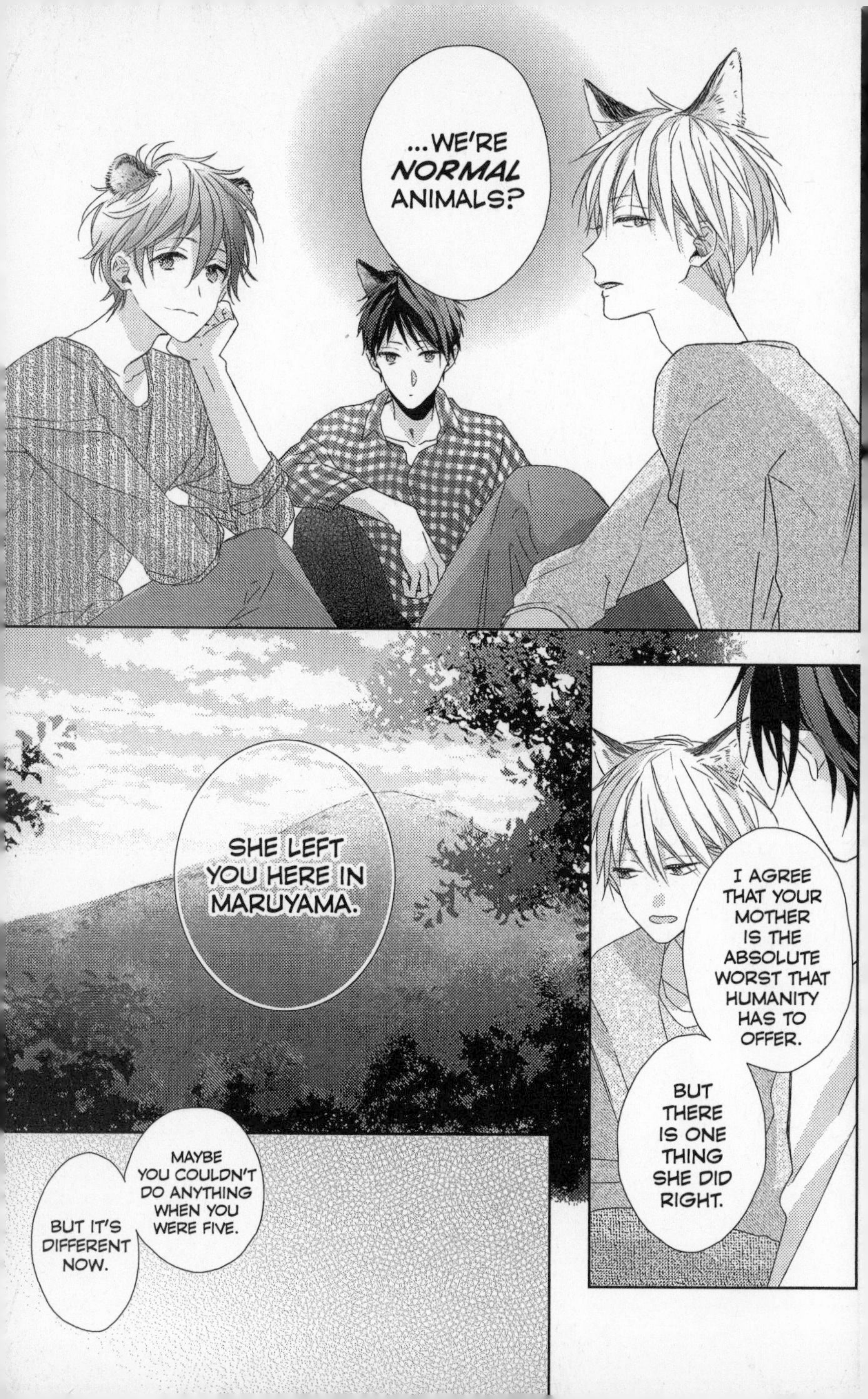
...WE'RE NORMAL ANIMALS?
I AGREE THAT YOUR MOTHER IS THE ABSOLUTE WORST THAT HUMANITY HAS TO OFFER.
BUT THERE IS ONE THING SHE DID RIGHT.
SHE LEFT YOU HERE IN MARUYAMA.
MAYBE YOU COULDN'T DO ANYTHING WHEN YOU WERE FIVE.
BUT IT'S DIFFERENT NOW.

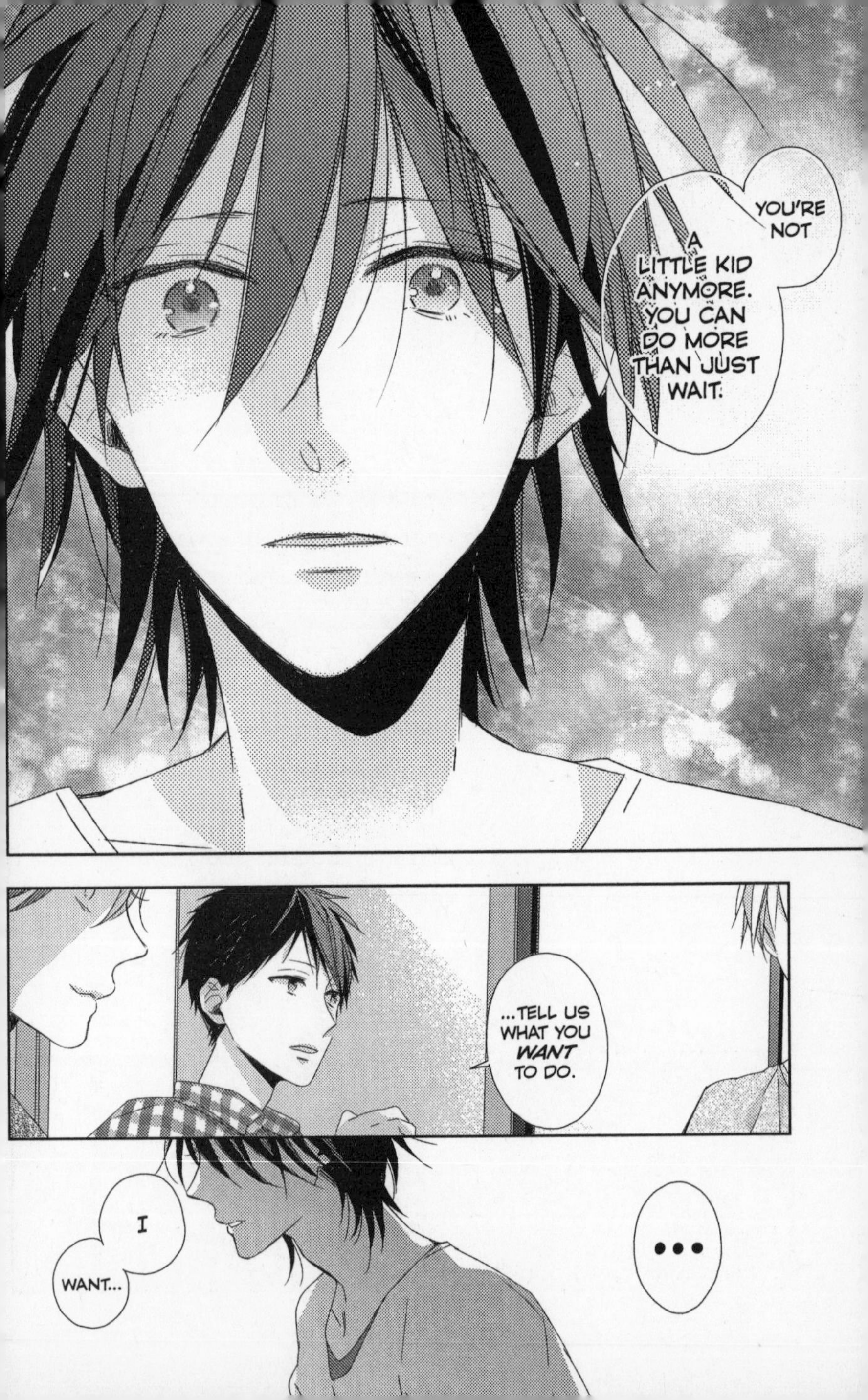
YOU'RE NOT A LITTLE KID ANYMORE. YOU CAN DO MORE THAN JUST WAIT.
...TELL US WHAT YOU *WANT* TO DO.
...
I WANT...

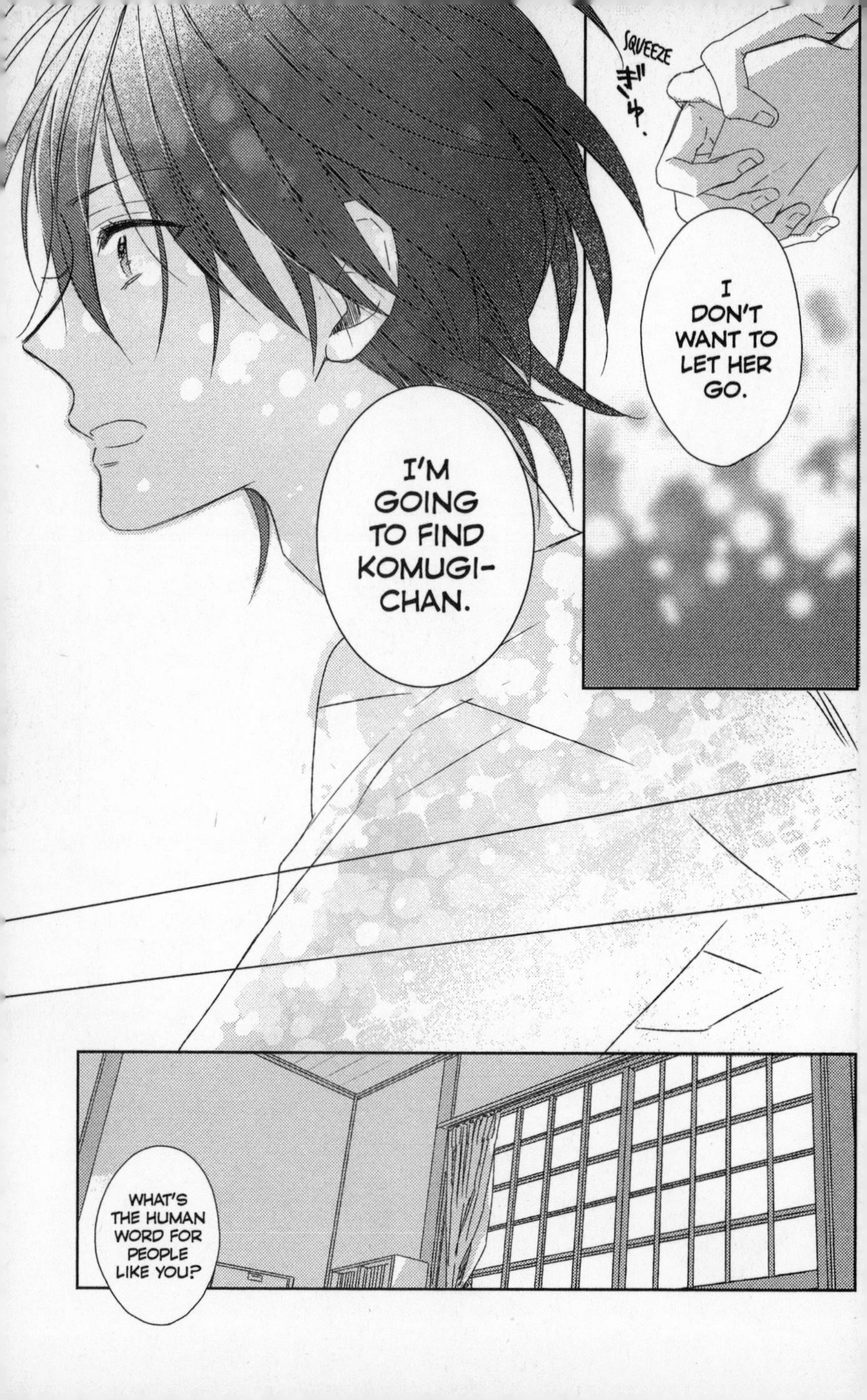
SQUEEZE
ぎゅ.
I DON'T WANT TO LET HER GO.
I'M GOING TO FIND KOMUGI-CHAN.
WHAT'S THE HUMAN WORD FOR PEOPLE LIKE YOU?

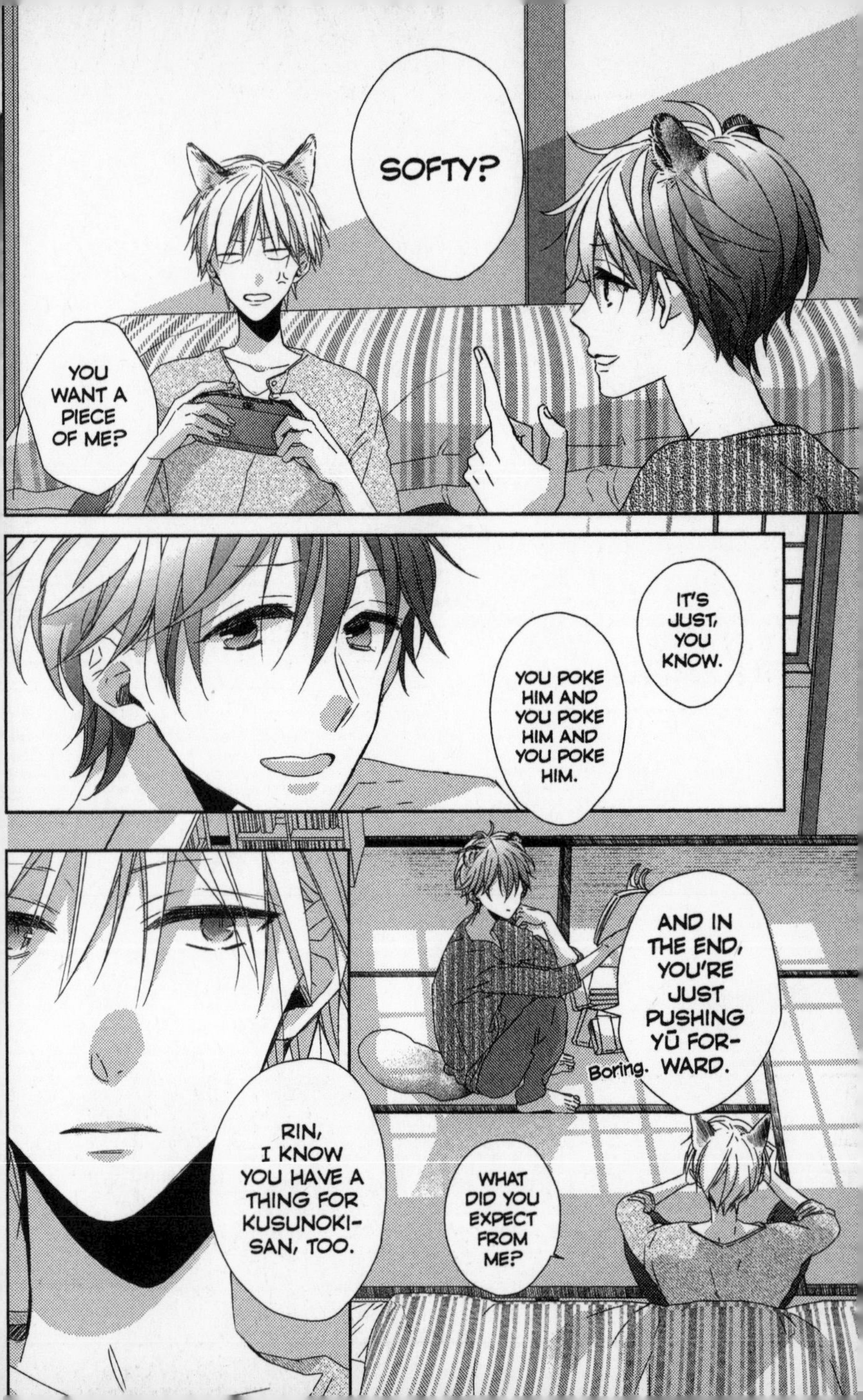
SOFTY?
YOU WANT A PIECE OF ME?
IT'S JUST, YOU KNOW.
YOU POKE HIM AND YOU POKE HIM AND YOU POKE HIM.
AND IN THE END, YOU'RE JUST PUSHING YŪ FOR-WARD.
Boring.
WHAT DID YOU EXPECT FROM ME?
RIN, I KNOW YOU HAVE A THING FOR KUSUNOKI-SAN, TOO.

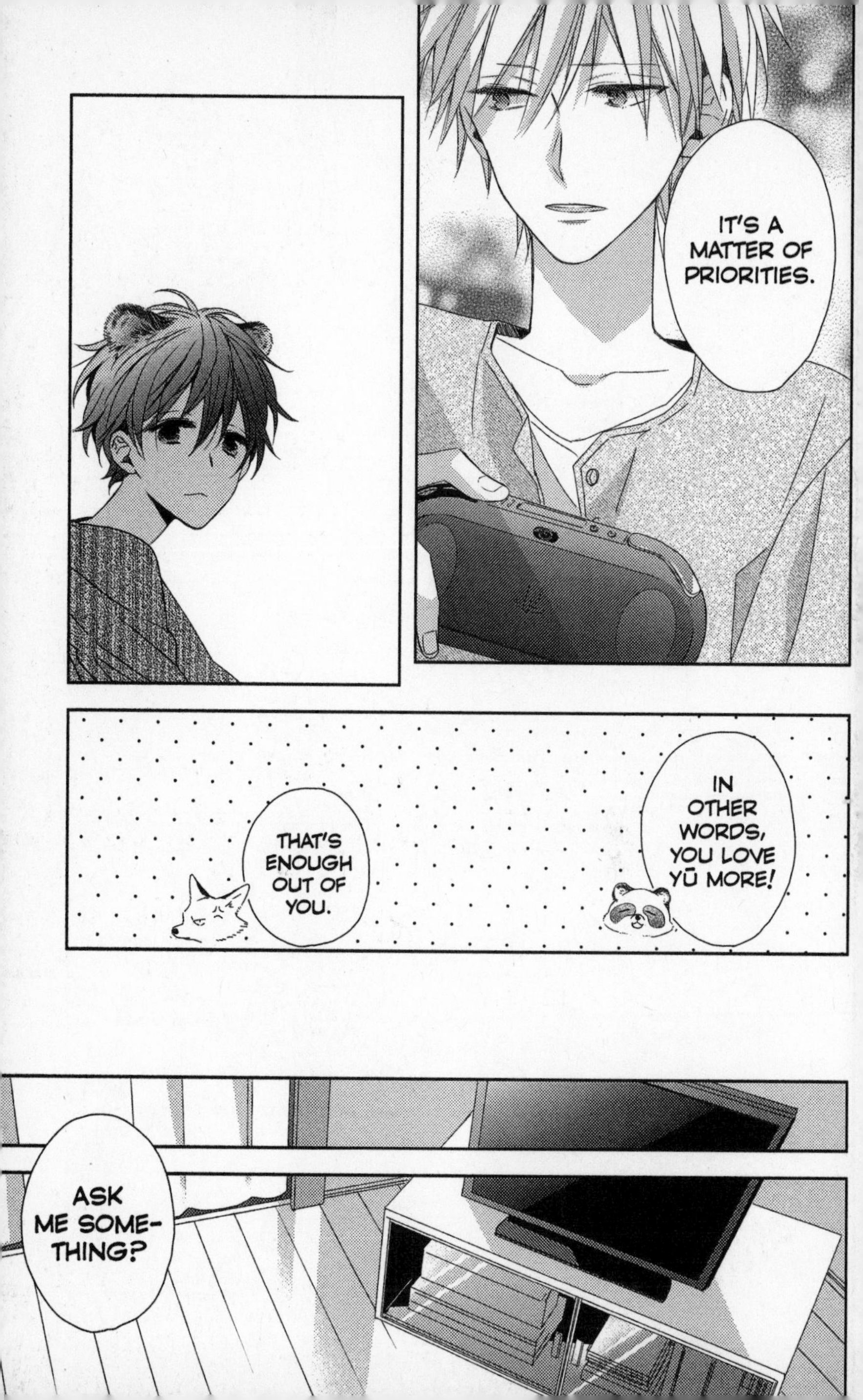
IT'S A MATTER OF PRIORITIES.
IN OTHER WORDS, YOU LOVE YŪ MORE!
THAT'S ENOUGH OUT OF YOU.
ASK ME SOME-THING?

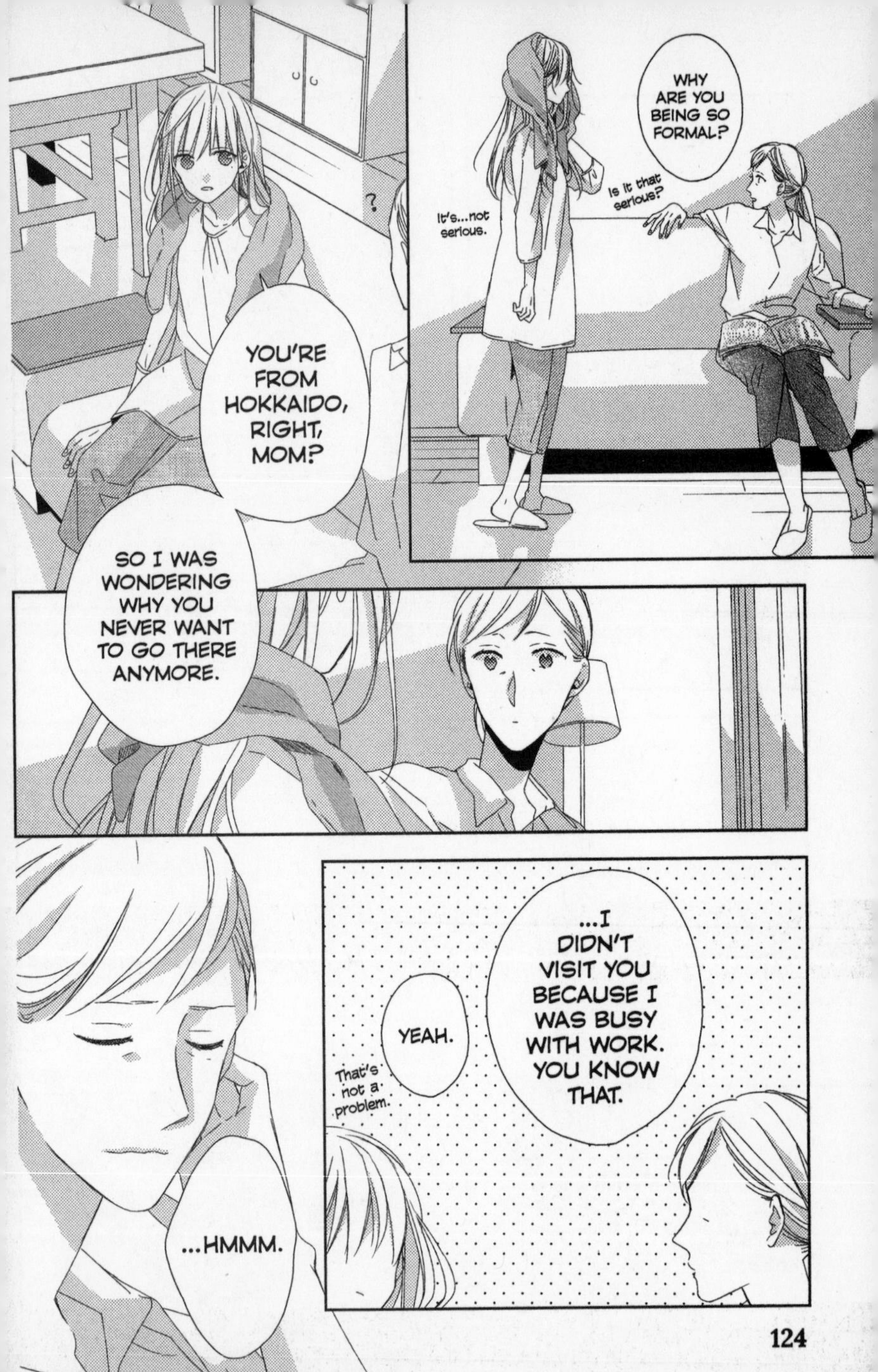
WHY ARE YOU BEING SO FORMAL?
Is it that serious?
It's...not serious.
YOU'RE FROM HOKKAIDO, RIGHT, MOM?
SO I WAS WONDERING WHY YOU NEVER WANT TO GO THERE ANYMORE.
...I DIDN'T VISIT YOU BECAUSE I WAS BUSY WITH WORK. YOU KNOW THAT.
YEAH.
That's not a problem.
...HMMM.

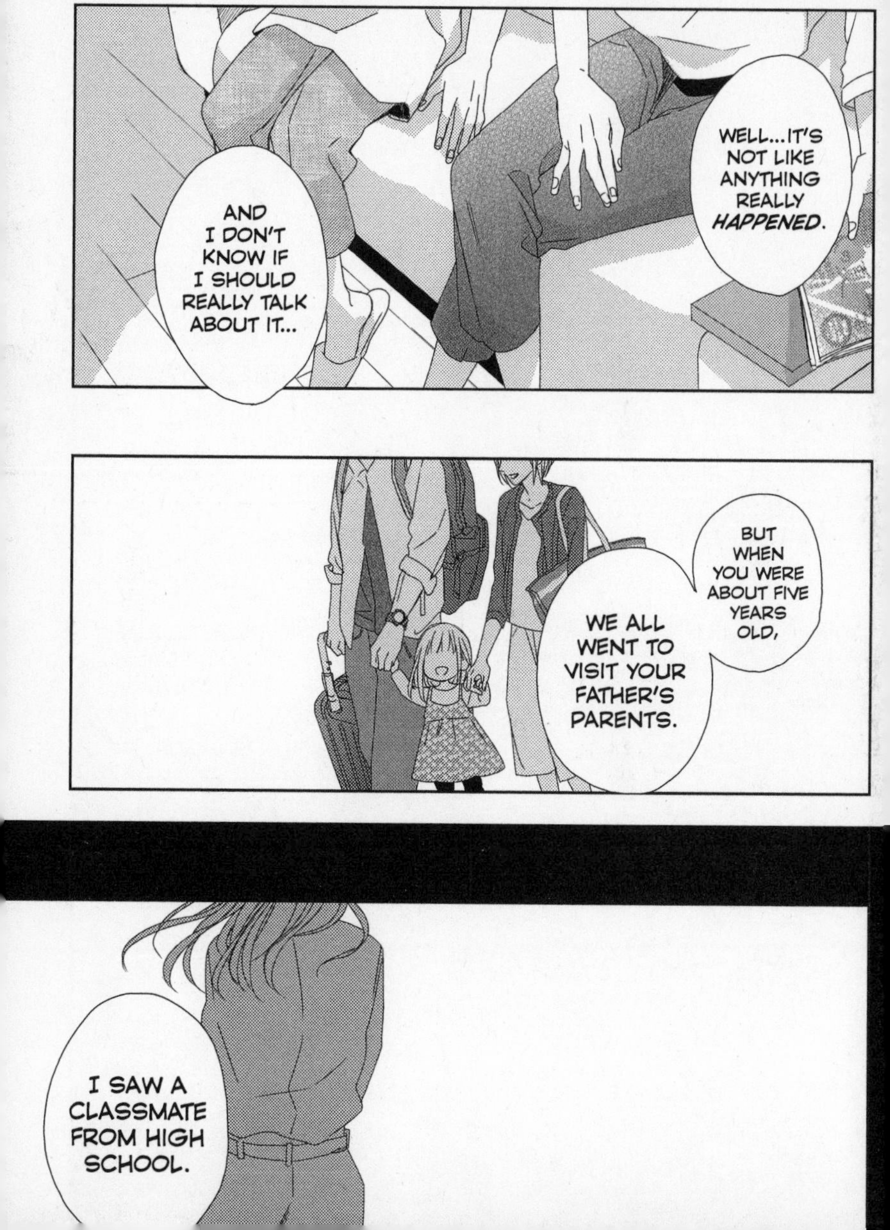
WELL...IT'S NOT LIKE ANYTHING REALLY *HAPPENED*.
AND I DON'T KNOW IF I SHOULD REALLY TALK ABOUT IT...
BUT WHEN YOU WERE ABOUT FIVE YEARS OLD,
WE ALL WENT TO VISIT YOUR FATHER'S PARENTS.
I SAW A CLASSMATE FROM HIGH SCHOOL.

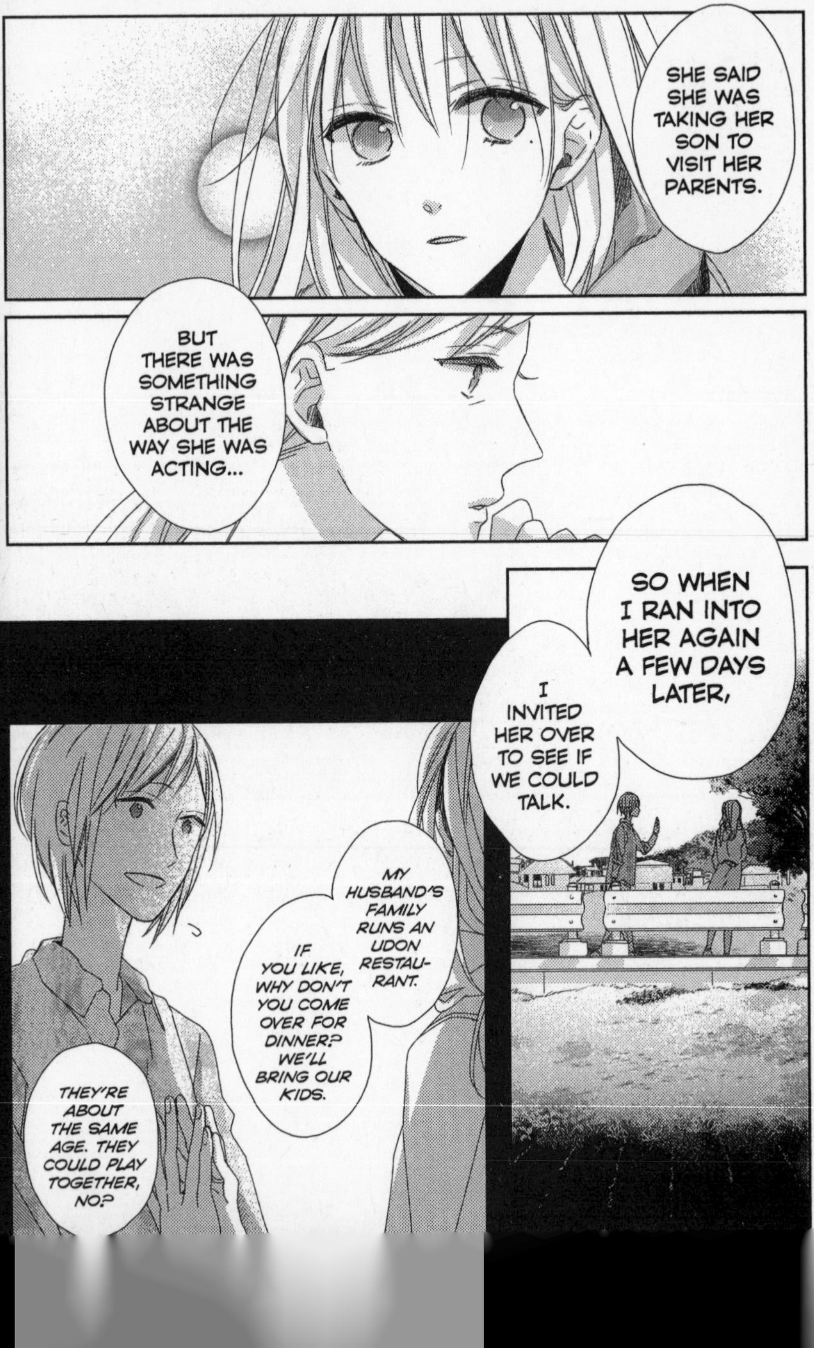
SHE SAID SHE WAS TAKING HER SON TO VISIT HER PARENTS.
BUT THERE WAS SOMETHING STRANGE ABOUT THE WAY SHE WAS ACTING...
SO WHEN I RAN INTO HER AGAIN A FEW DAYS LATER,
I INVITED HER OVER TO SEE IF WE COULD TALK.
MY HUSBAND'S FAMILY RUNS AN UDON RESTAU- RANT.
IF YOU LIKE, WHY DON'T YOU COME OVER FOR DINNER? WE'LL BRING OUR KIDS.
THEY'RE ABOUT THE SAME AGE. THEY COULD PLAY TOGETHER, NO?

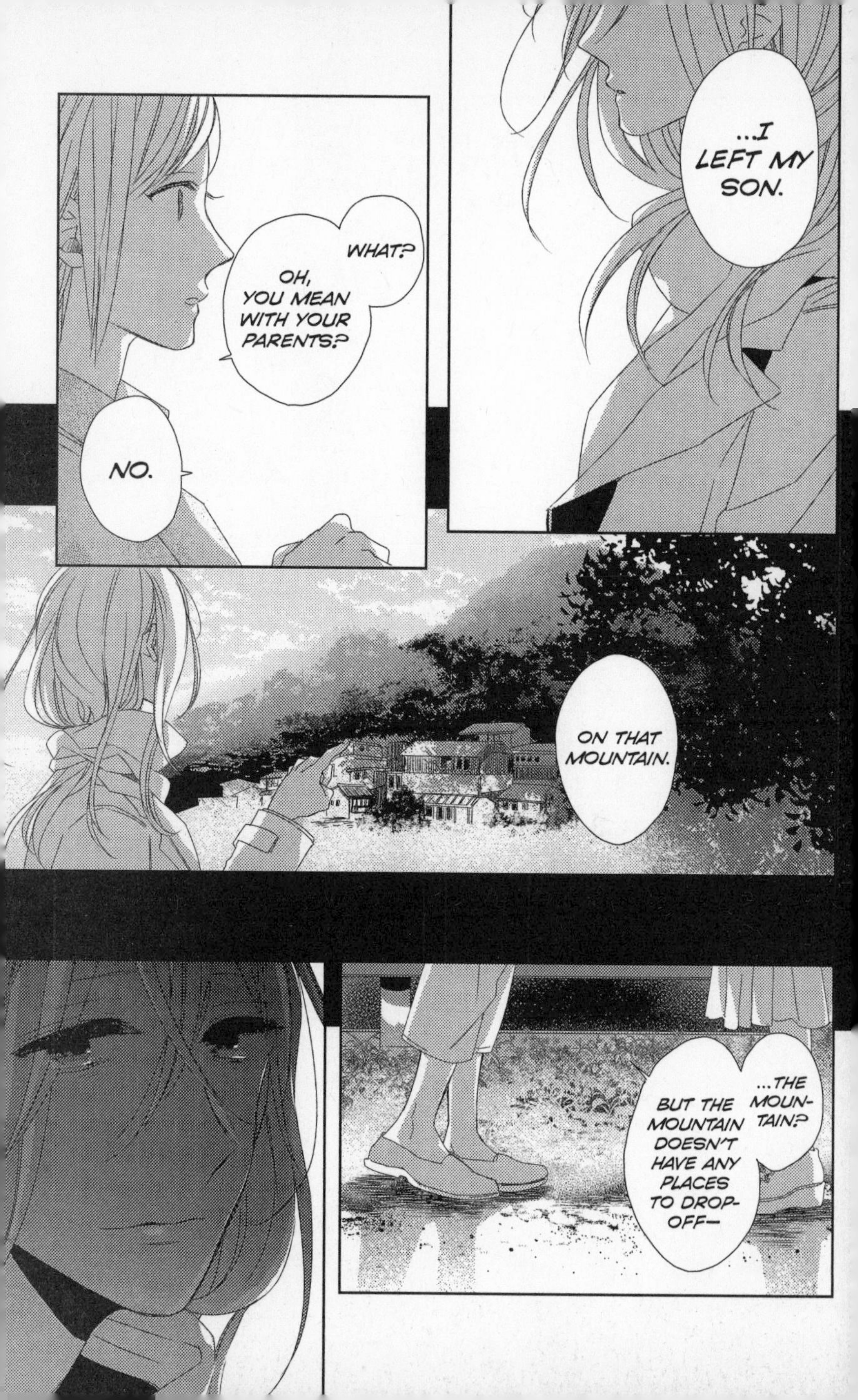
...I LEFT MY SON.
WHAT? OH, YOU MEAN WITH YOUR PARENTS?
NO.
ON THAT MOUNTAIN.
...THE MOUN-TAIN?
BUT THE MOUNTAIN DOESN'T HAVE ANY PLACES TO DROP-OFF—

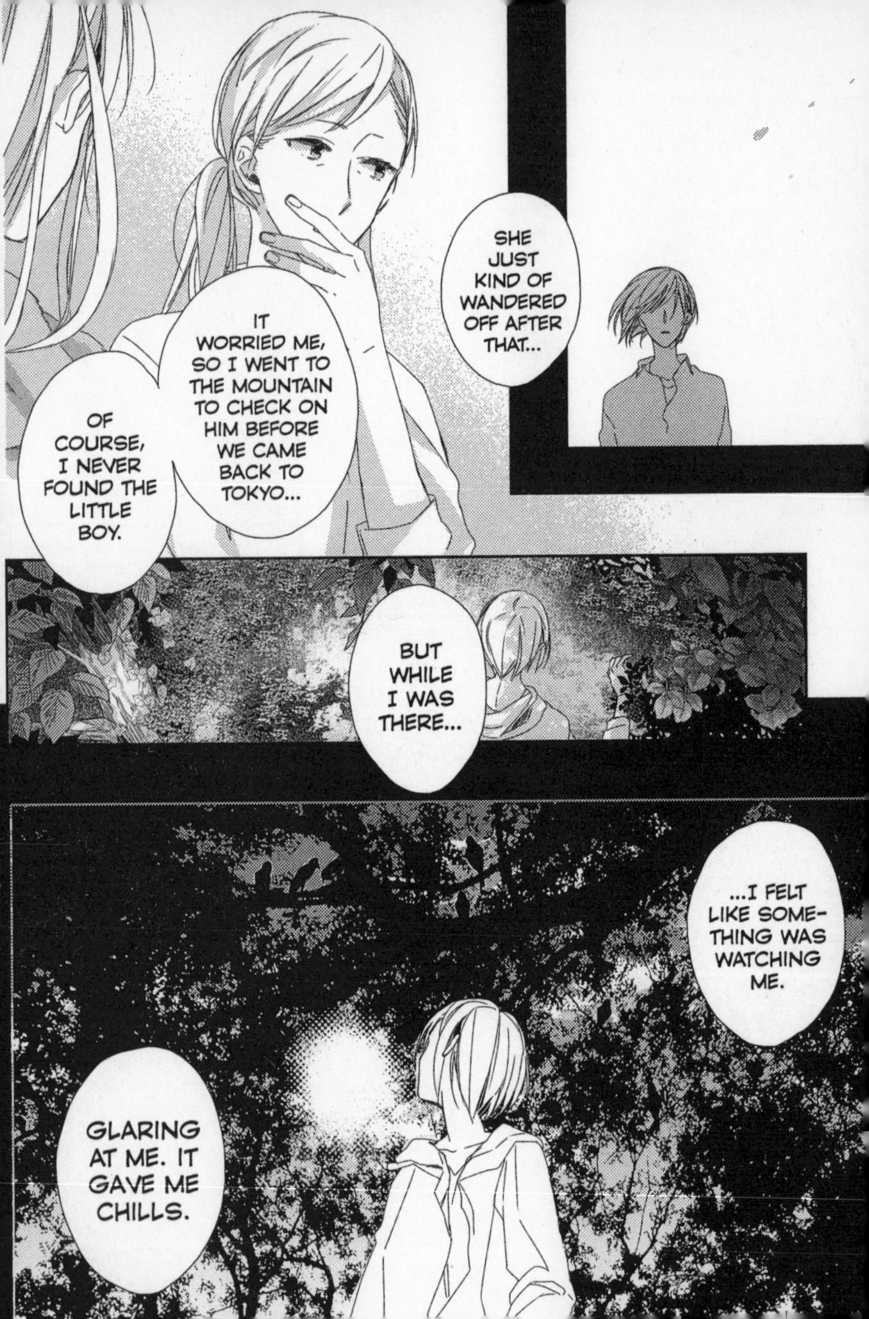
SHE JUST KIND OF WANDERED OFF AFTER THAT...
IT WORRIED ME, SO I WENT TO THE MOUNTAIN TO CHECK ON HIM BEFORE WE CAME BACK TO TOKYO...
OF COURSE, I NEVER FOUND THE LITTLE BOY.
BUT WHILE I WAS THERE...
...I FELT LIKE SOMETHING WAS WATCHING ME.
GLARING AT ME. IT GAVE ME CHILLS.

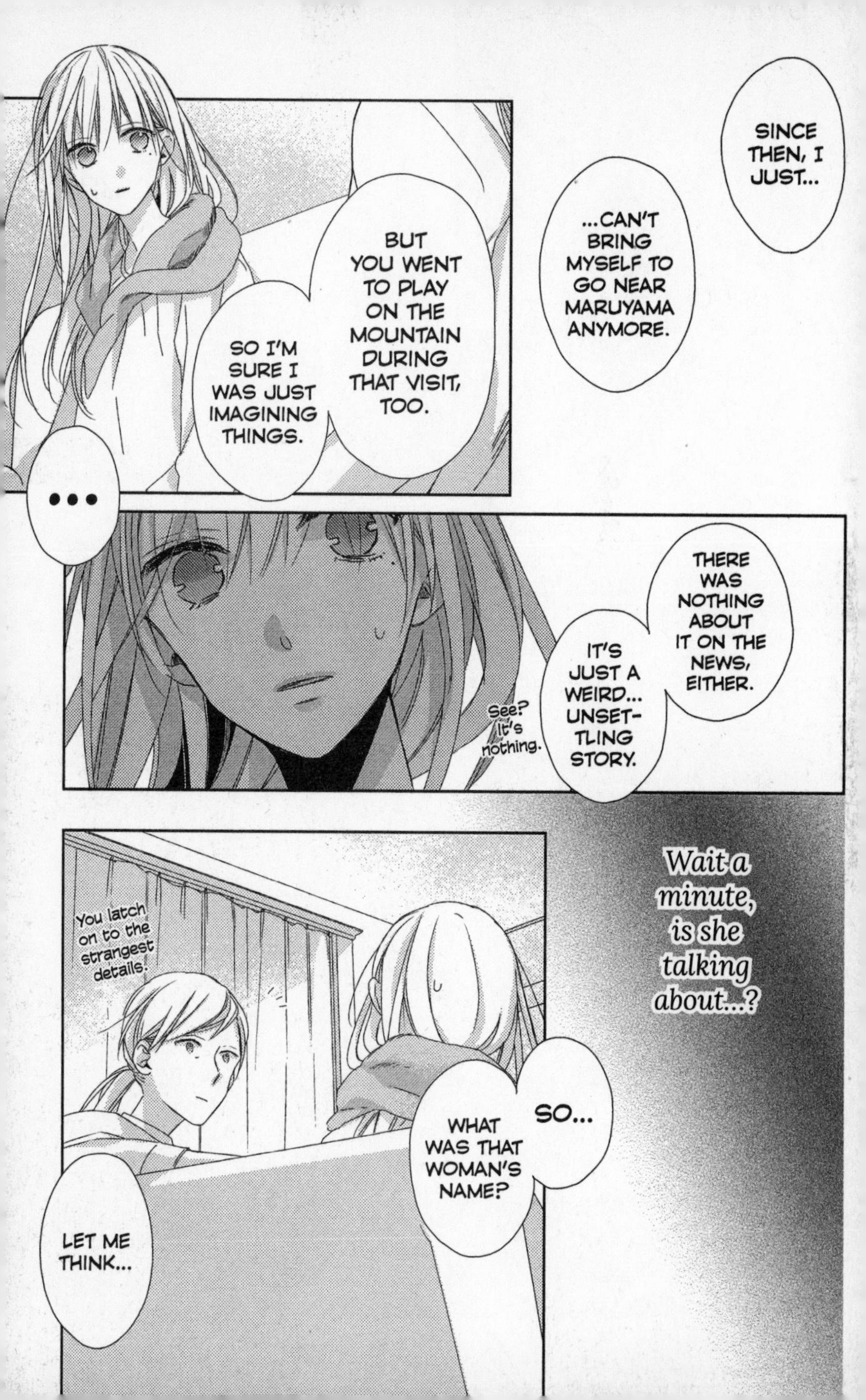
SINCE THEN, I JUST...
...CAN'T BRING MYSELF TO GO NEAR MARUYAMA ANYMORE.
BUT YOU WENT TO PLAY ON THE MOUNTAIN DURING THAT VISIT, TOO.
SO I'M SURE I WAS JUST IMAGINING THINGS.
...
THERE WAS NOTHING ABOUT IT ON THE NEWS, EITHER.
IT'S JUST A WEIRD... UNSET-TLING STORY.
See? It's nothing.
Wait a minute, is she talking about...?
SO...
WHAT WAS THAT WOMAN'S NAME?
You latch on to the strangest details.
LET ME THINK...

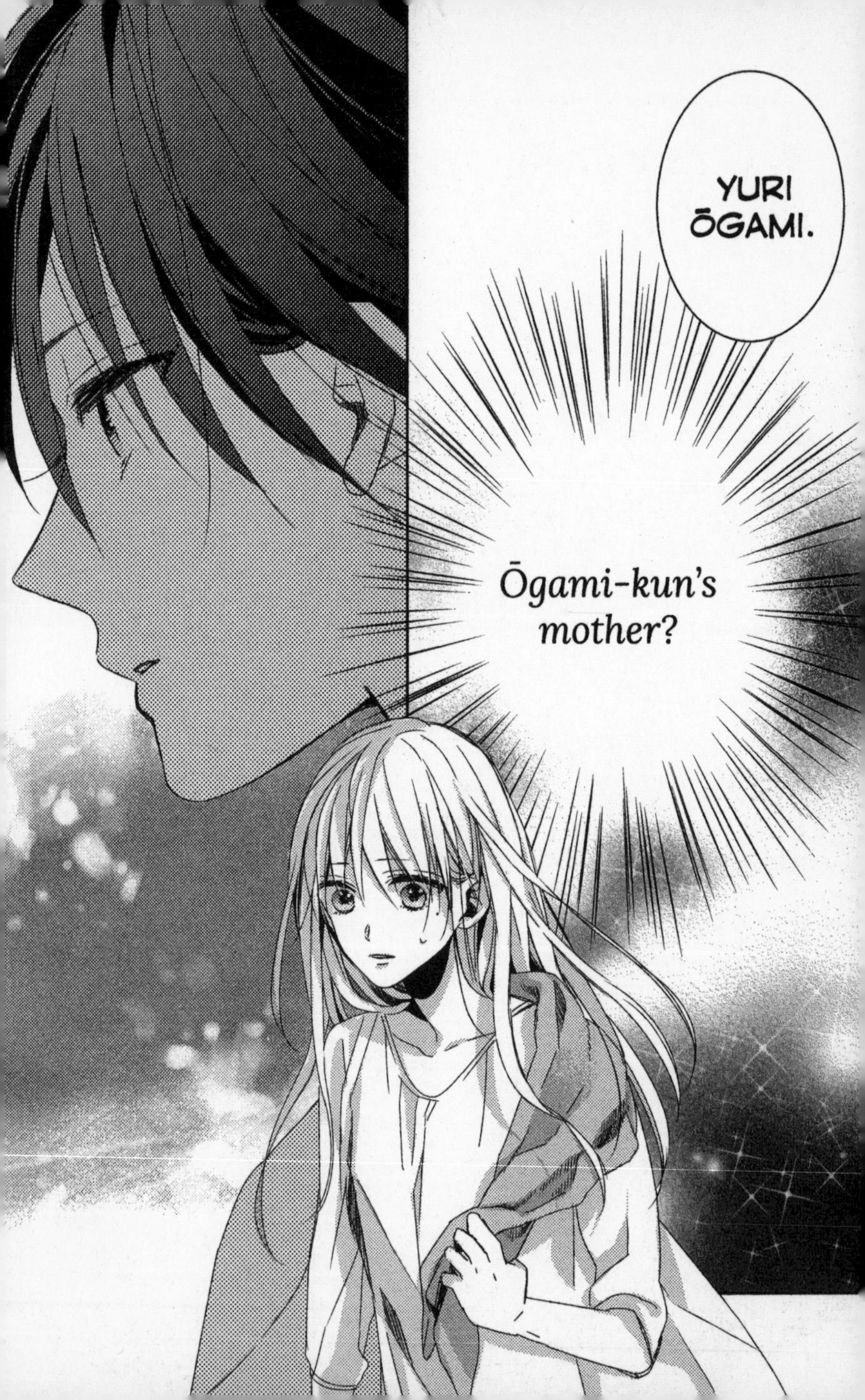
YURI ŌGAMI.
Ōgami-kun's mother?

# Chapter 13

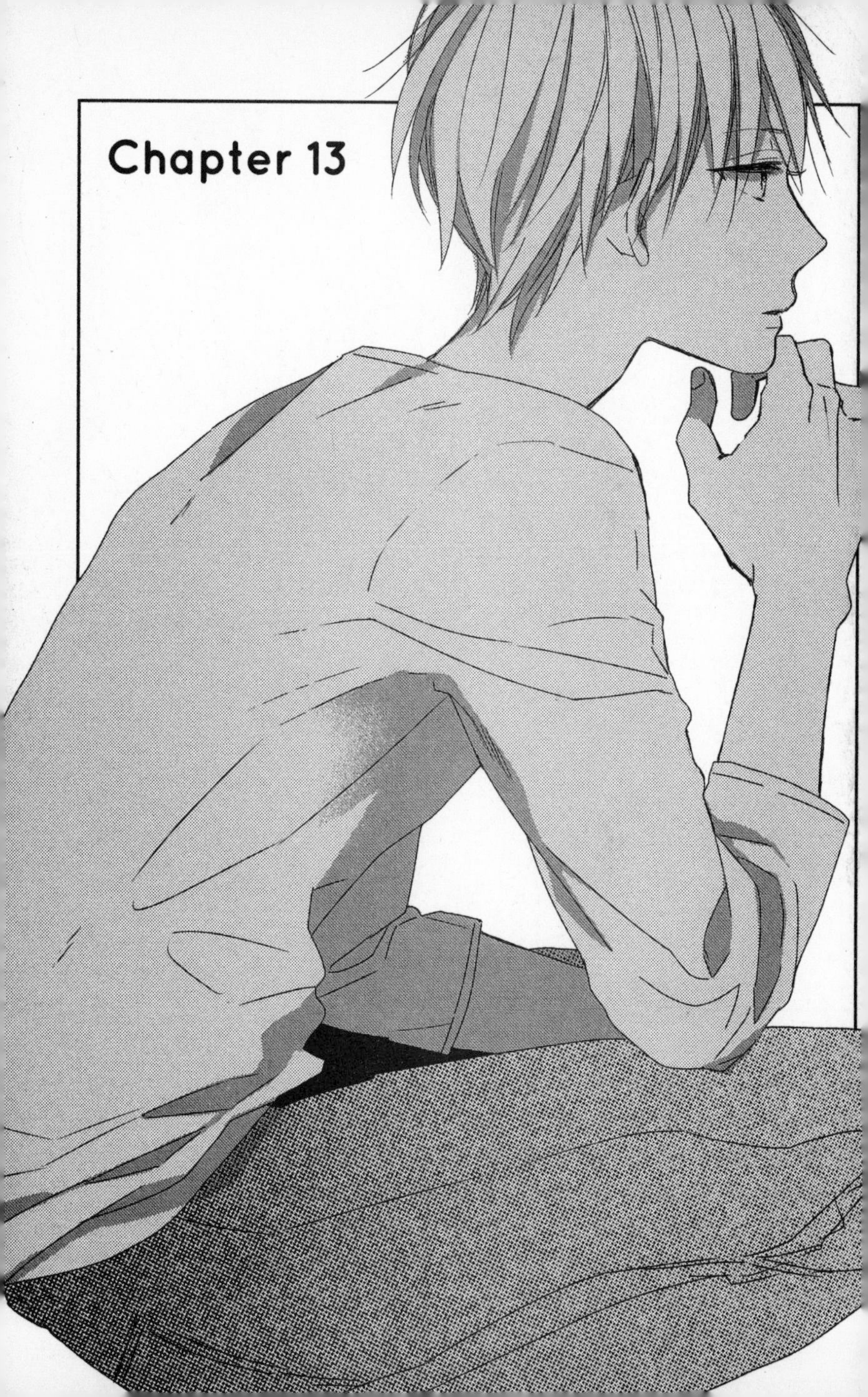

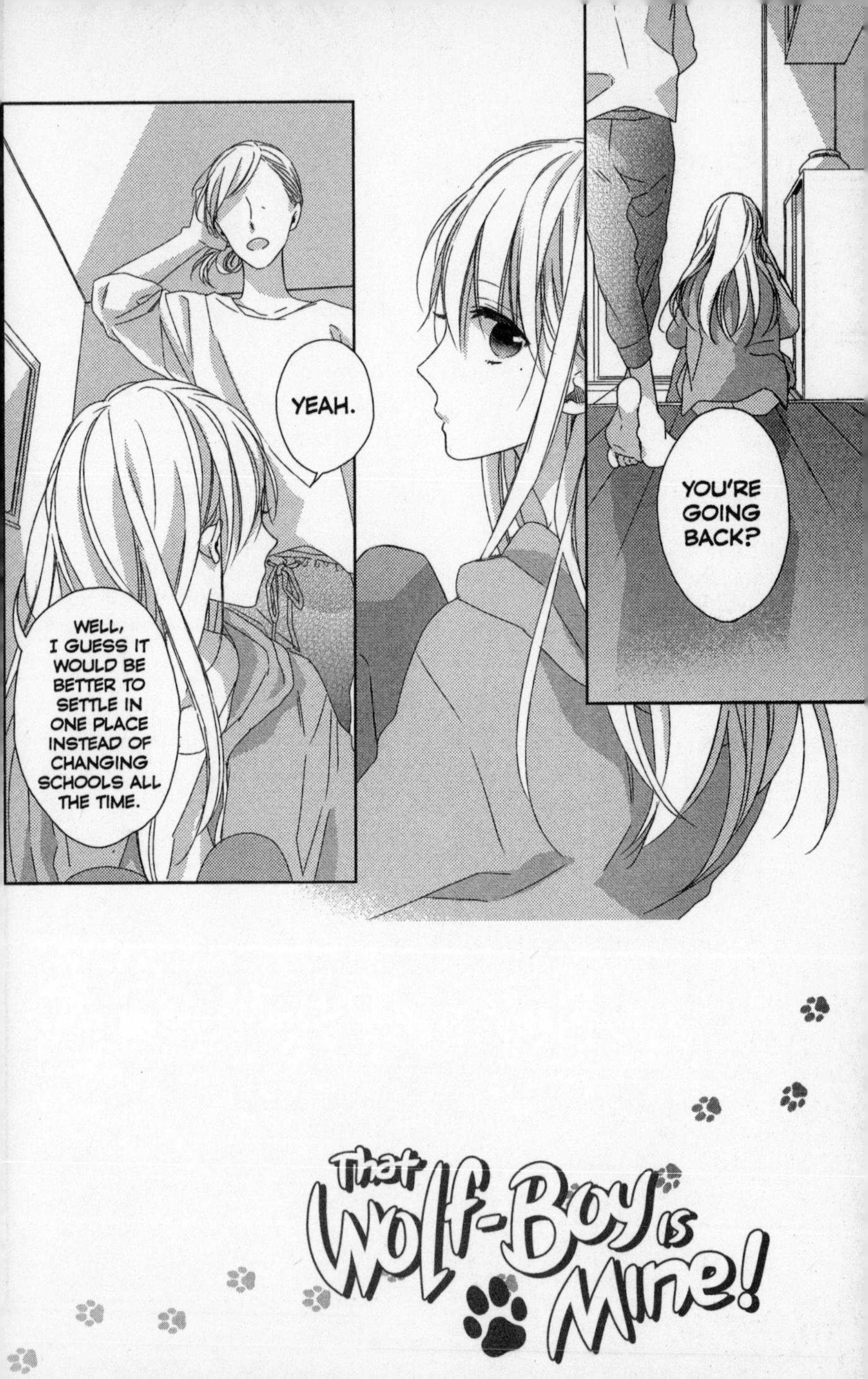
YOU'RE GOING BACK?
YEAH.
WELL, I GUESS IT WOULD BE BETTER TO SETTLE IN ONE PLACE INSTEAD OF CHANGING SCHOOLS ALL THE TIME.

That Wolf-Boy is Mine!

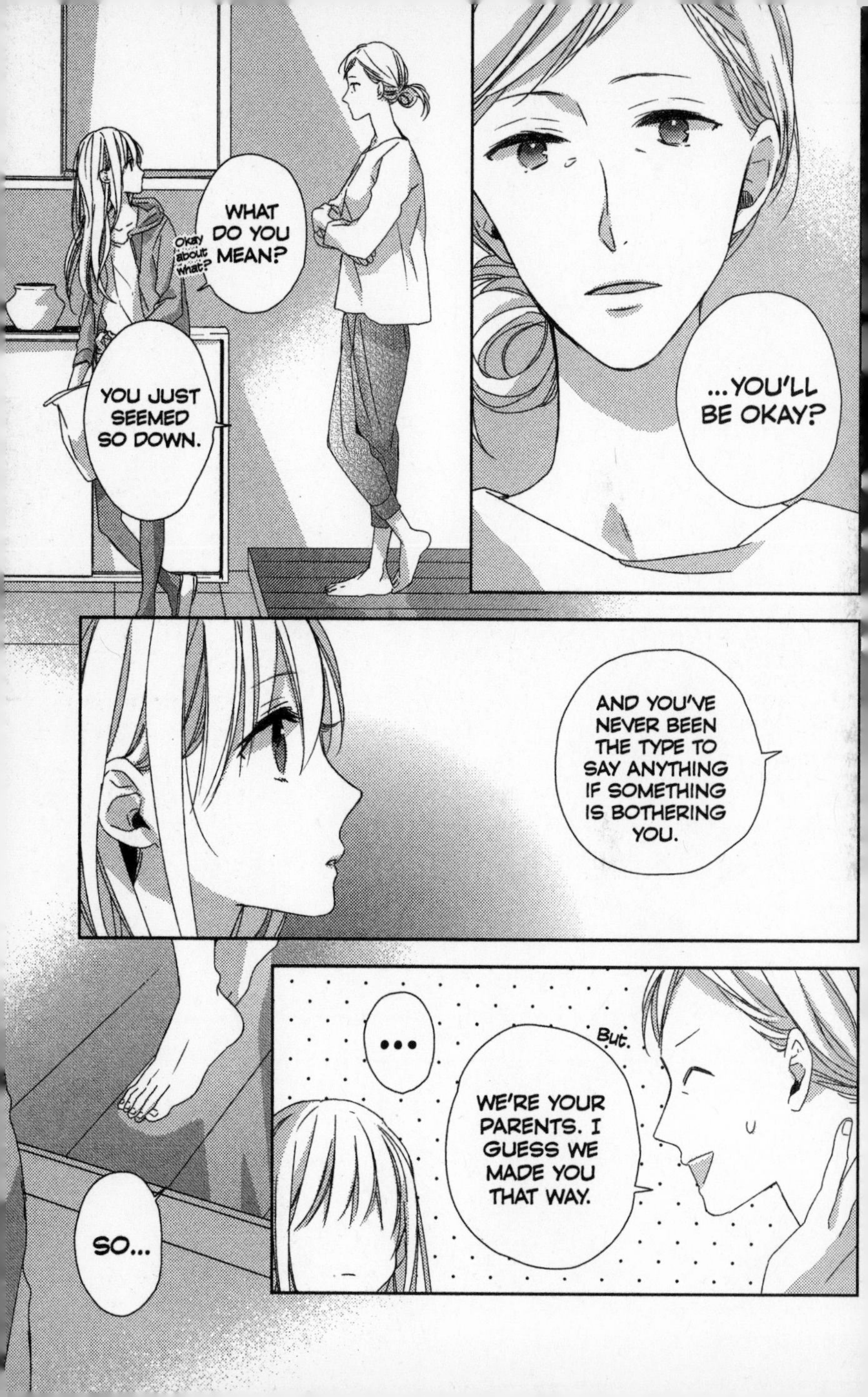
...YOU'LL BE OKAY?
WHAT DO YOU MEAN?
Okay about what?
YOU JUST SEEMED SO DOWN.
AND YOU'VE NEVER BEEN THE TYPE TO SAY ANYTHING IF SOMETHING IS BOTHERING YOU.
But.
WE'RE YOUR PARENTS. I GUESS WE MADE YOU THAT WAY.
...
SO...

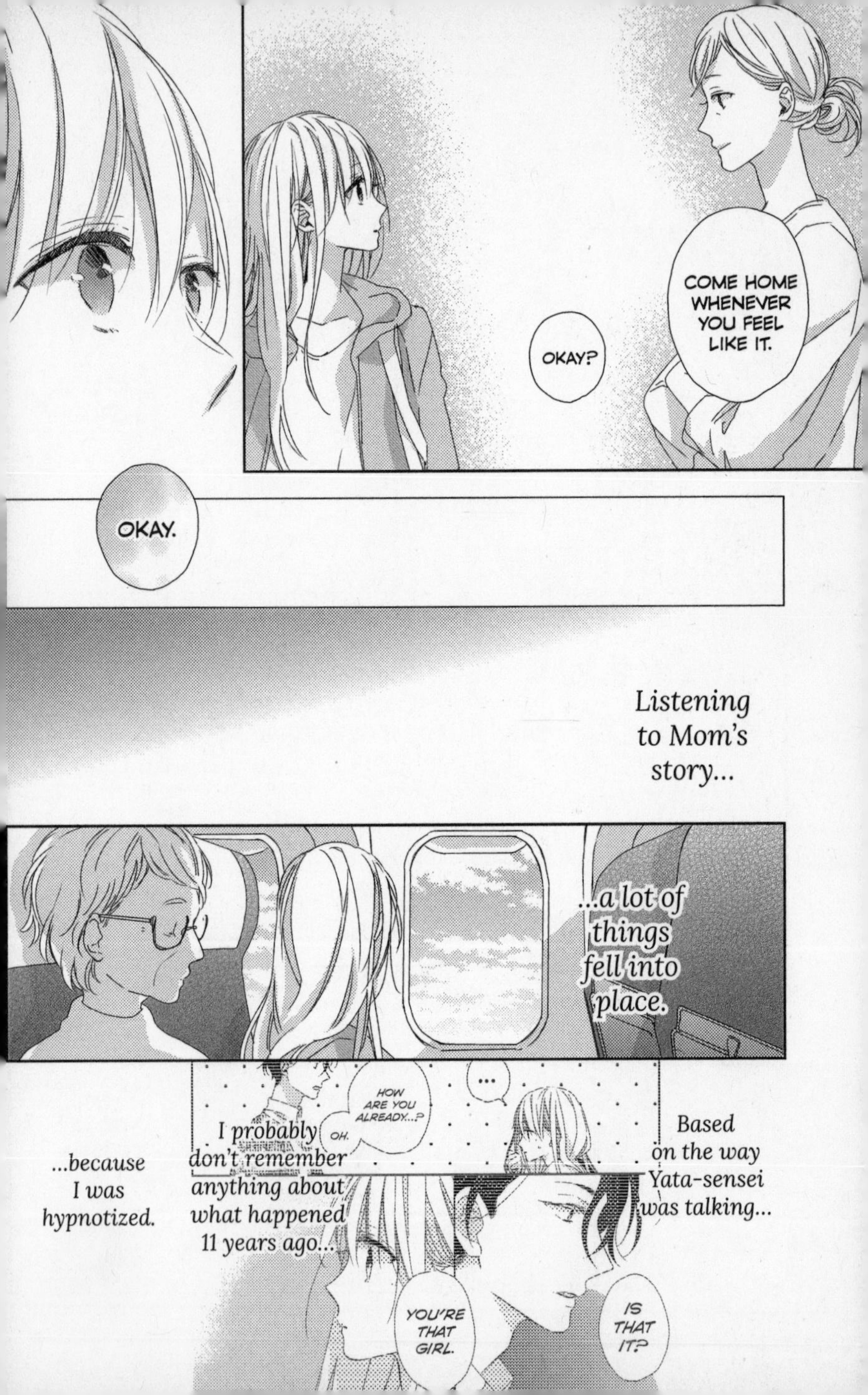
COME HOME WHENEVER YOU FEEL LIKE IT.
OKAY?
OKAY.
Listening to Mom's story...
...a lot of things fell into place.
Based on the way Yata-sensei was talking...
...
HOW ARE YOU ALREADY...?
OH.
I probably don't remember anything about what happened 11 years ago...
...because I was hypnotized.
IS THAT IT?
YOU'RE THAT GIRL.

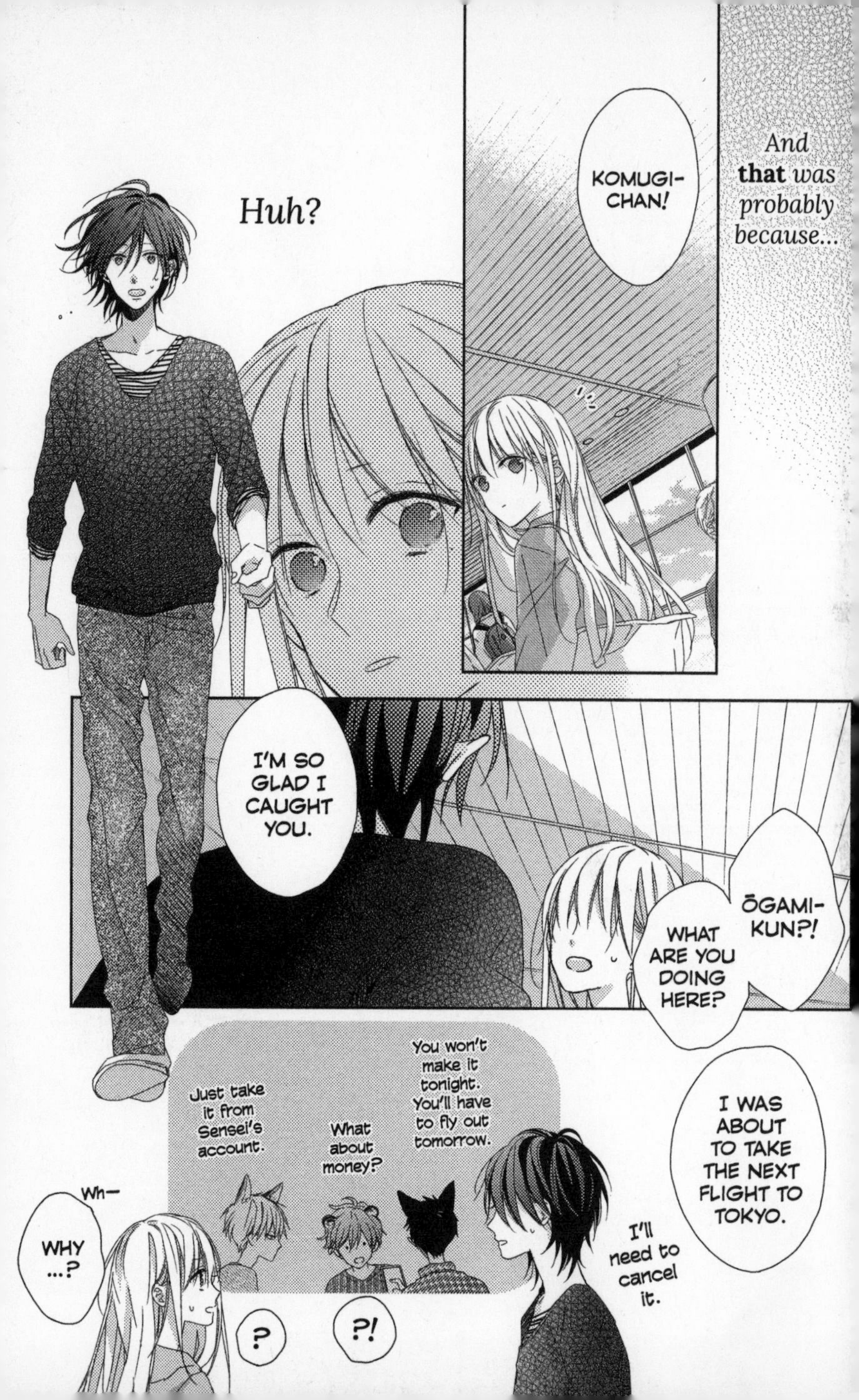
And **that** was probably because...
KOMUGI-CHAN!
Huh?
ŌGAMI-KUN?!
WHAT ARE YOU DOING HERE?
I'M SO GLAD I CAUGHT YOU.
I WAS ABOUT TO TAKE THE NEXT FLIGHT TO TOKYO.
I'll need to cancel it.
You won't make it tonight. You'll have to fly out tomorrow.
What about money?
Just take it from Sensei's account.
?!
?
Wh—
WHY ...?

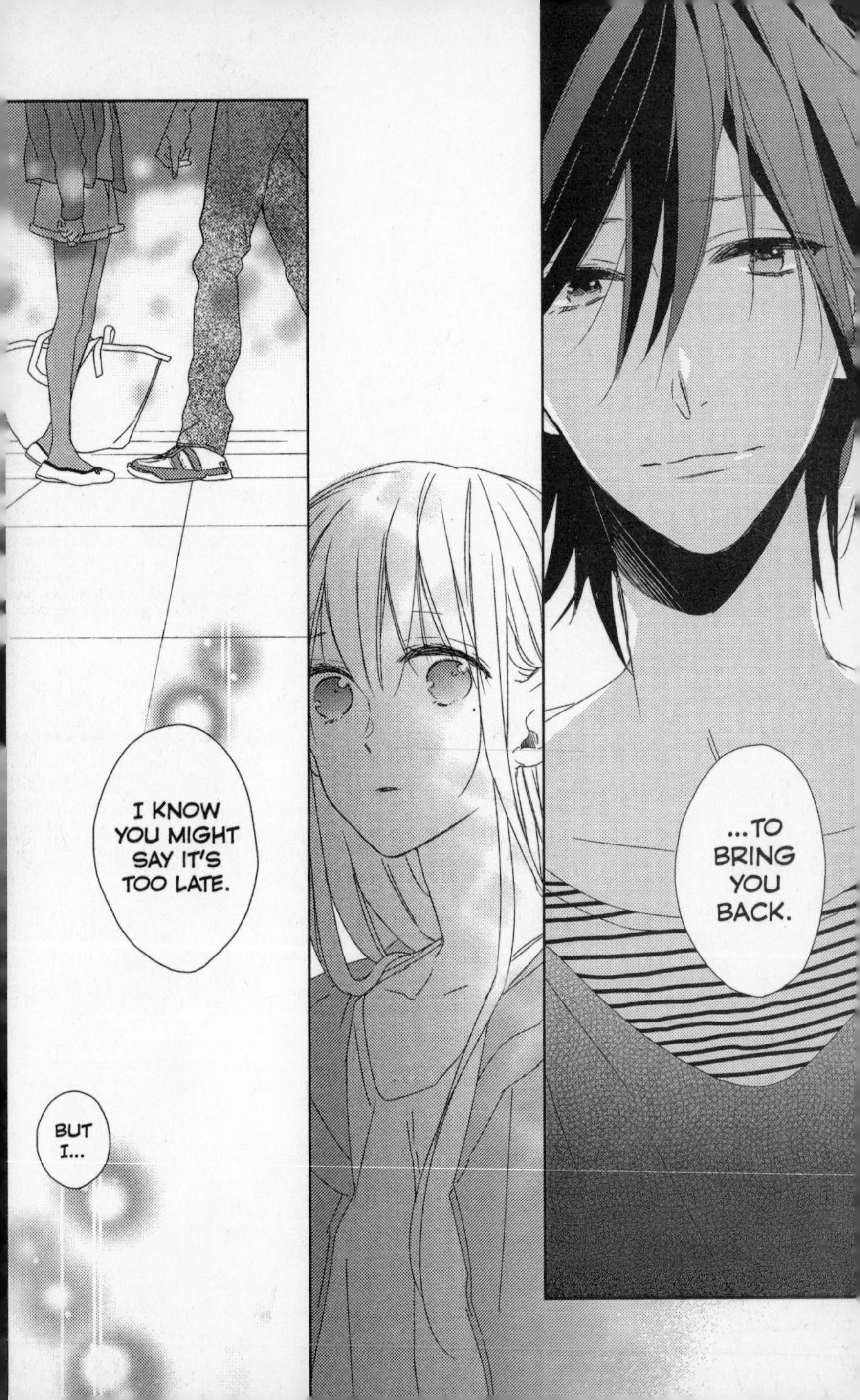
...TO BRING YOU BACK.
I KNOW YOU MIGHT SAY IT'S TOO LATE.
BUT I...

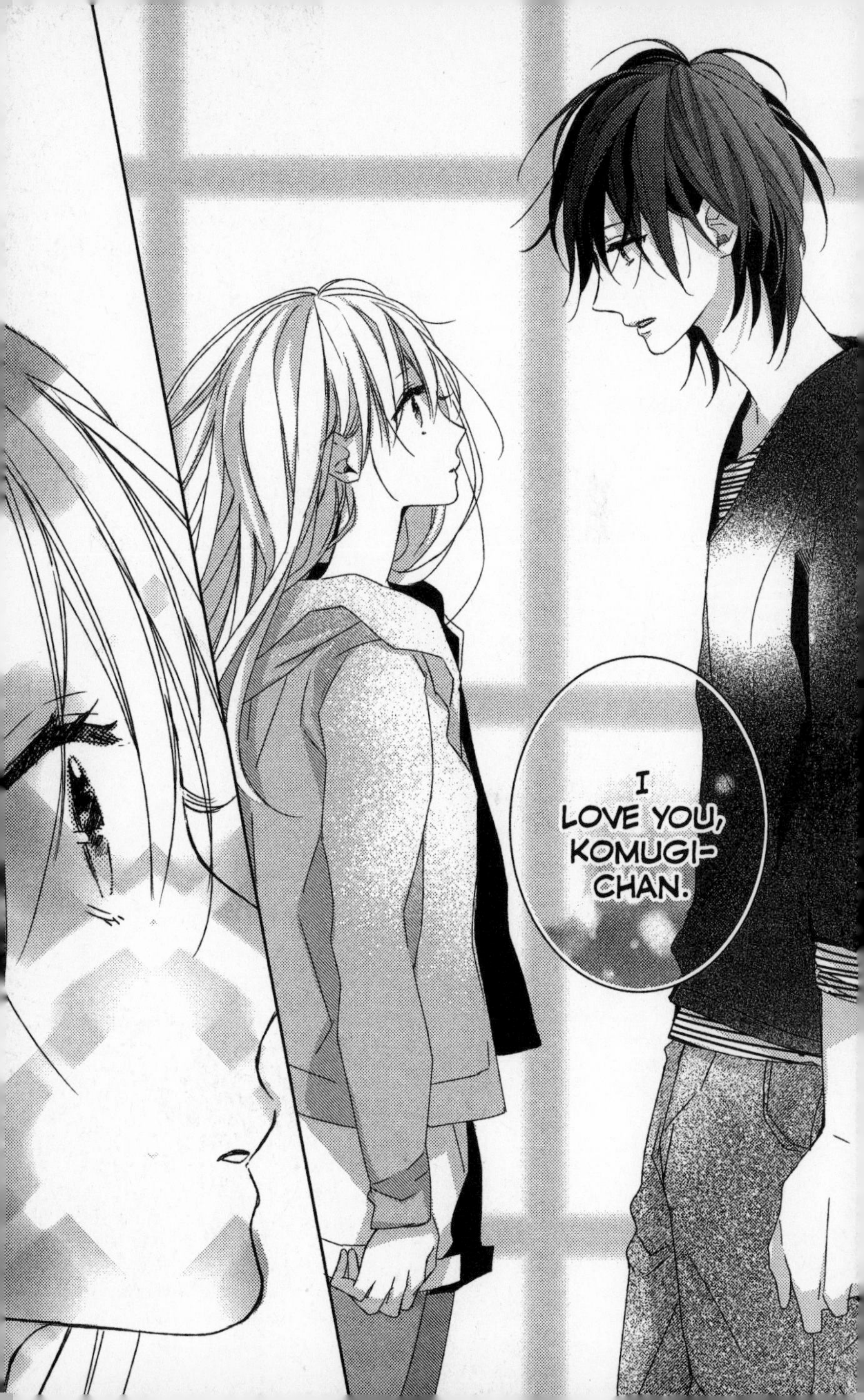
I LOVE YOU, KOMUGI-CHAN.

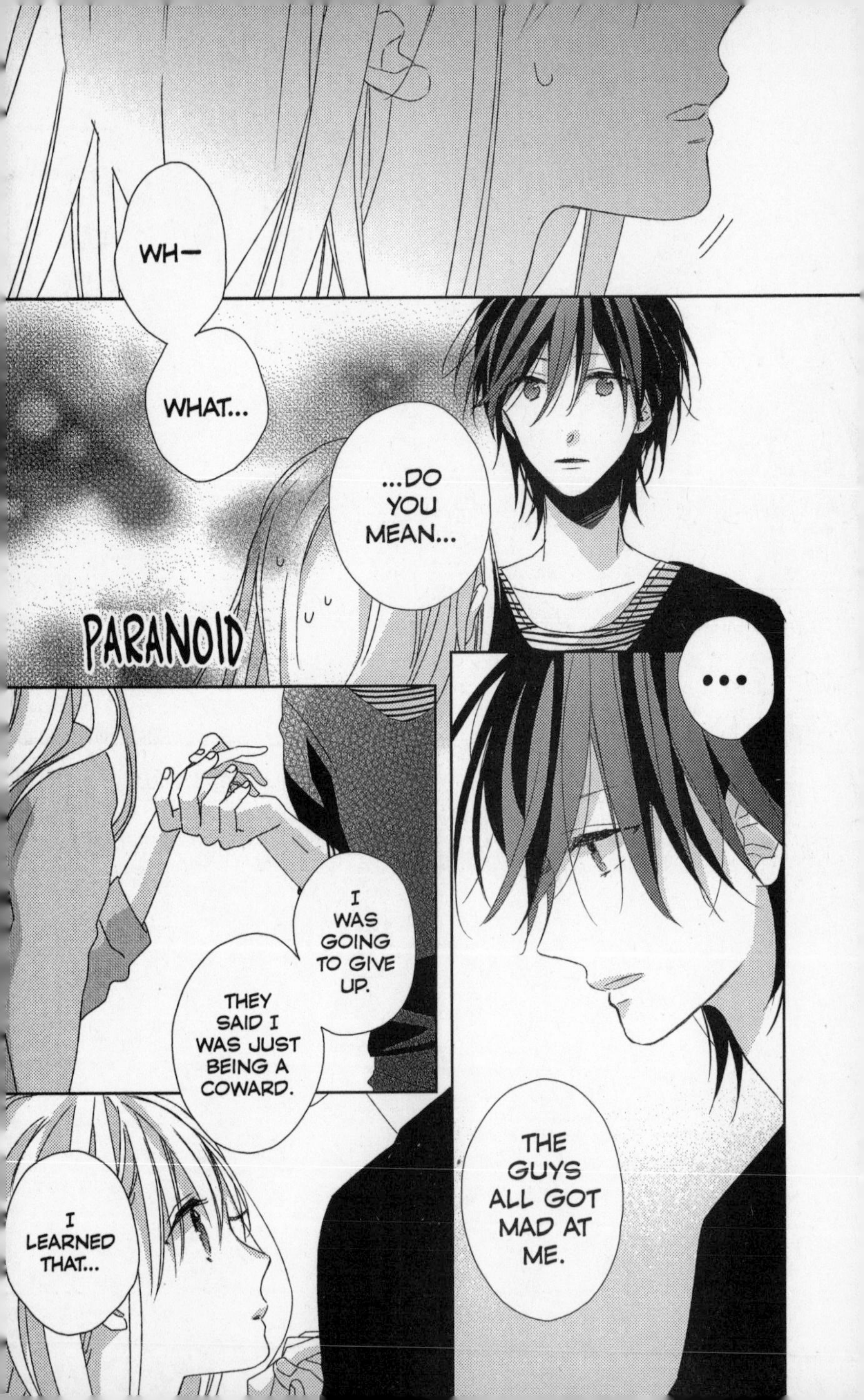
WH—
WHAT...
...DO YOU MEAN...
PARANOID
...
THE GUYS ALL GOT MAD AT ME.
I WAS GOING TO GIVE UP.
THEY SAID I WAS JUST BEING A COWARD.
I LEARNED THAT...

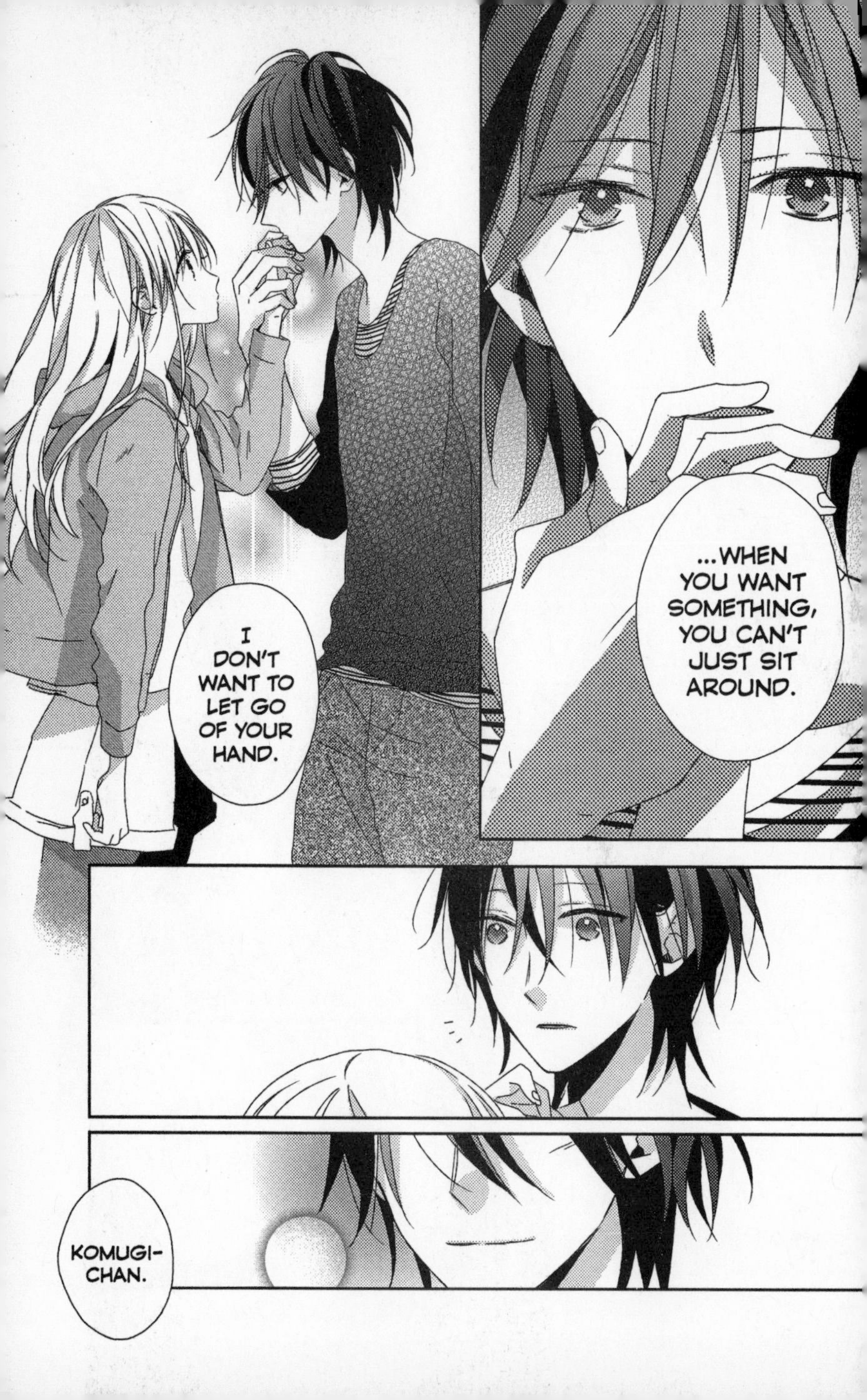
...WHEN YOU WANT SOMETHING, YOU CAN'T JUST SIT AROUND.
I DON'T WANT TO LET GO OF YOUR HAND.
KOMUGI-CHAN.

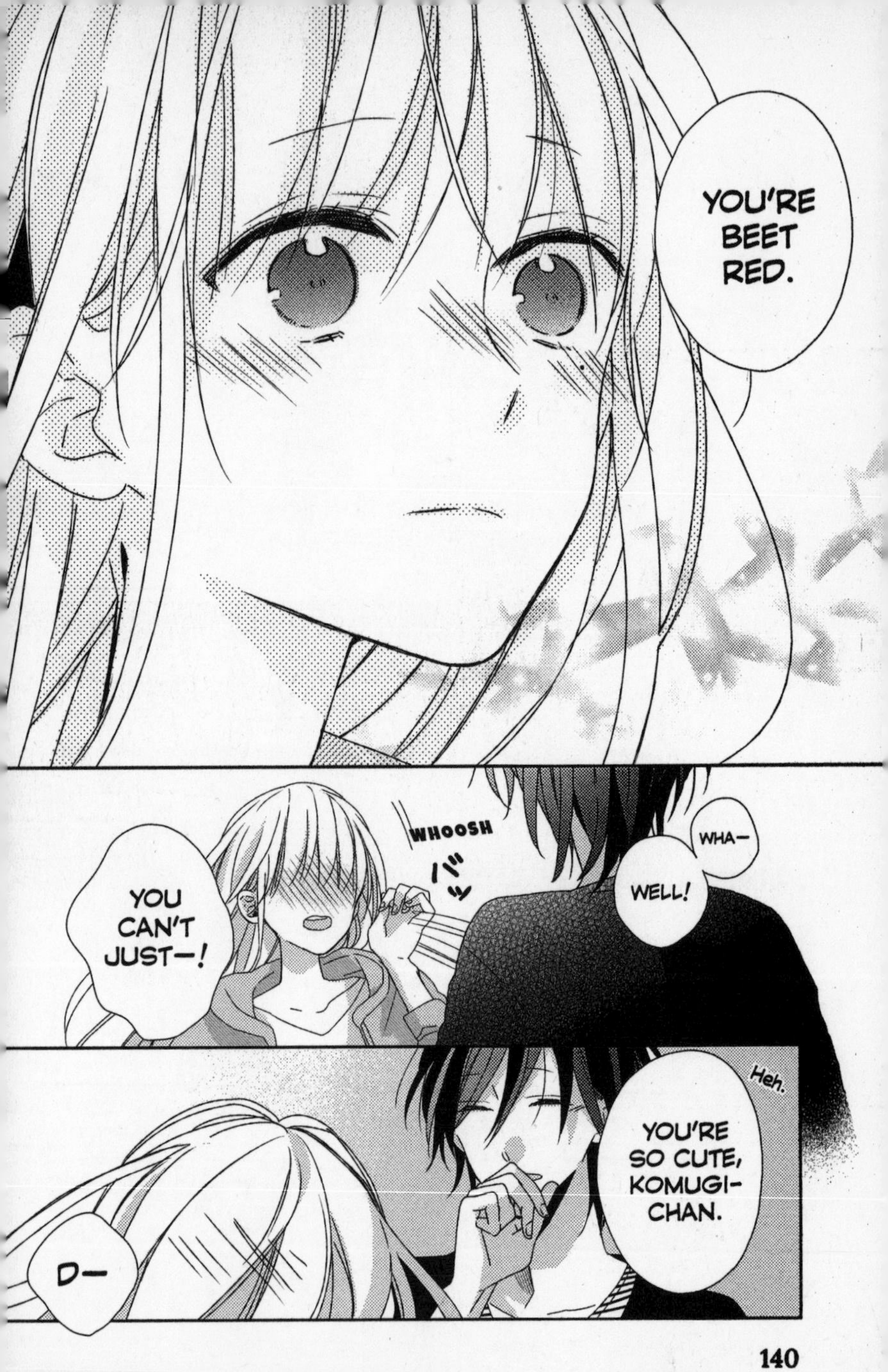
YOU'RE BEET RED.
WHA—
WELL!
WHOOSH
バッ
YOU CAN'T JUST—!
Heh.
YOU'RE SO CUTE, KOMUGI-CHAN.
D—

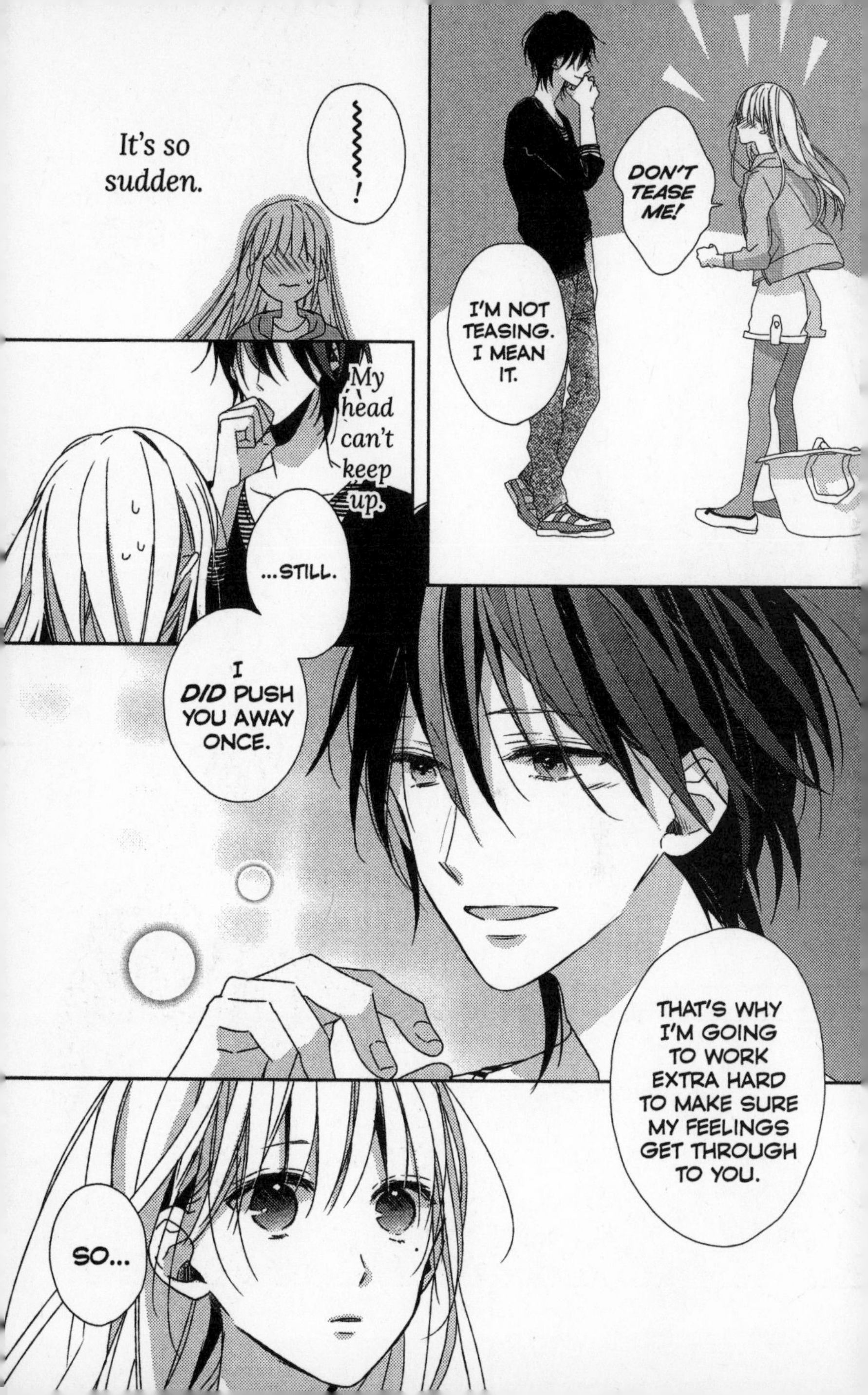
DON'T TEASE ME!
I'M NOT TEASING. I MEAN IT.
It's so sudden.
My head can't keep up.
...STILL.
I DID PUSH YOU AWAY ONCE.
THAT'S WHY I'M GOING TO WORK EXTRA HARD TO MAKE SURE MY FEELINGS GET THROUGH TO YOU.
SO...

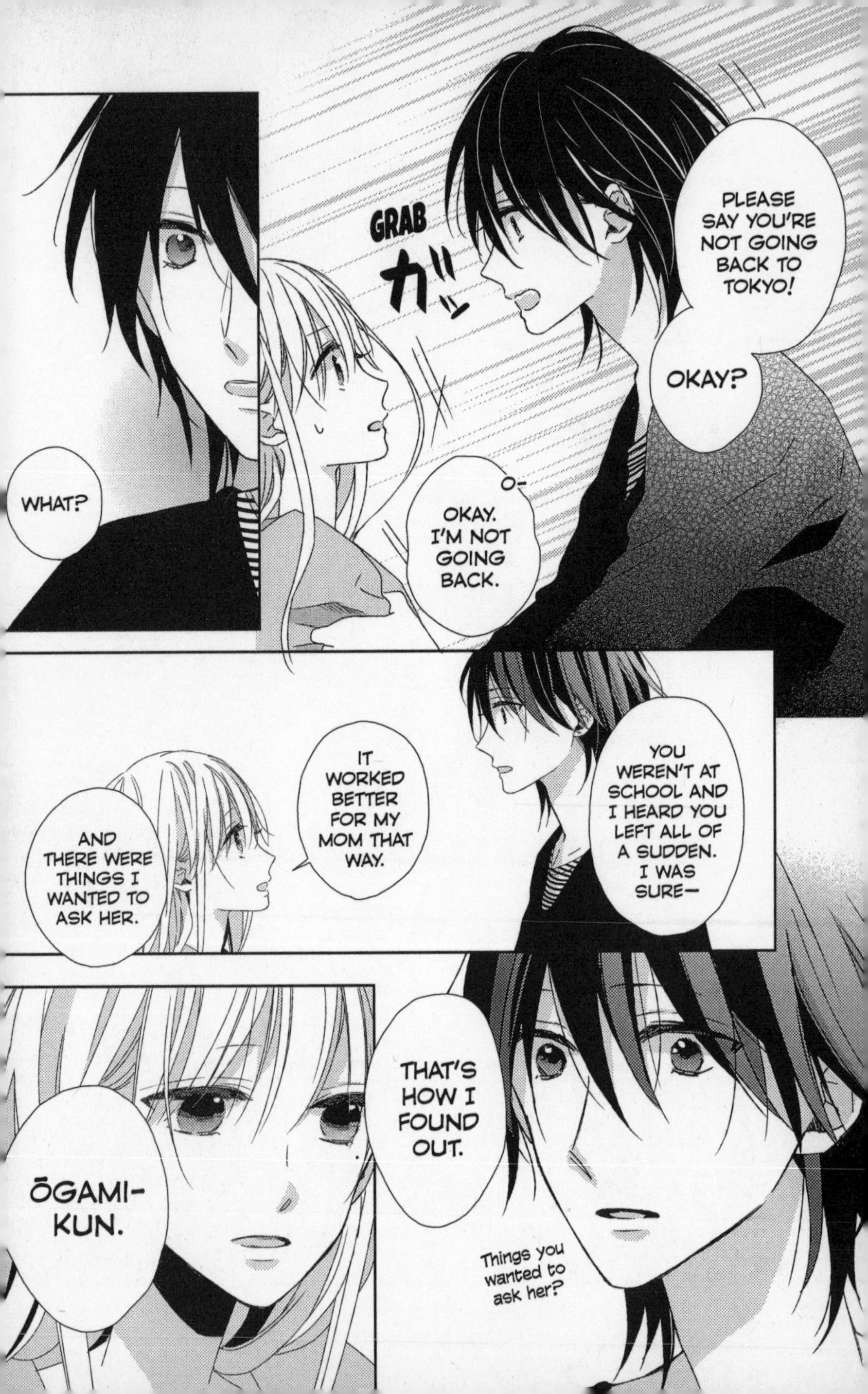
PLEASE SAY YOU'RE NOT GOING BACK TO TOKYO!
OKAY?
GRAB
ガッ
O-
OKAY. I'M NOT GOING BACK.
WHAT?
YOU WEREN'T AT SCHOOL AND I HEARD YOU LEFT ALL OF A SUDDEN. I WAS SURE—
IT WORKED BETTER FOR MY MOM THAT WAY.
AND THERE WERE THINGS I WANTED TO ASK HER.
THAT'S HOW I FOUND OUT.
Things you wanted to ask her?
ŌGAMI-KUN.

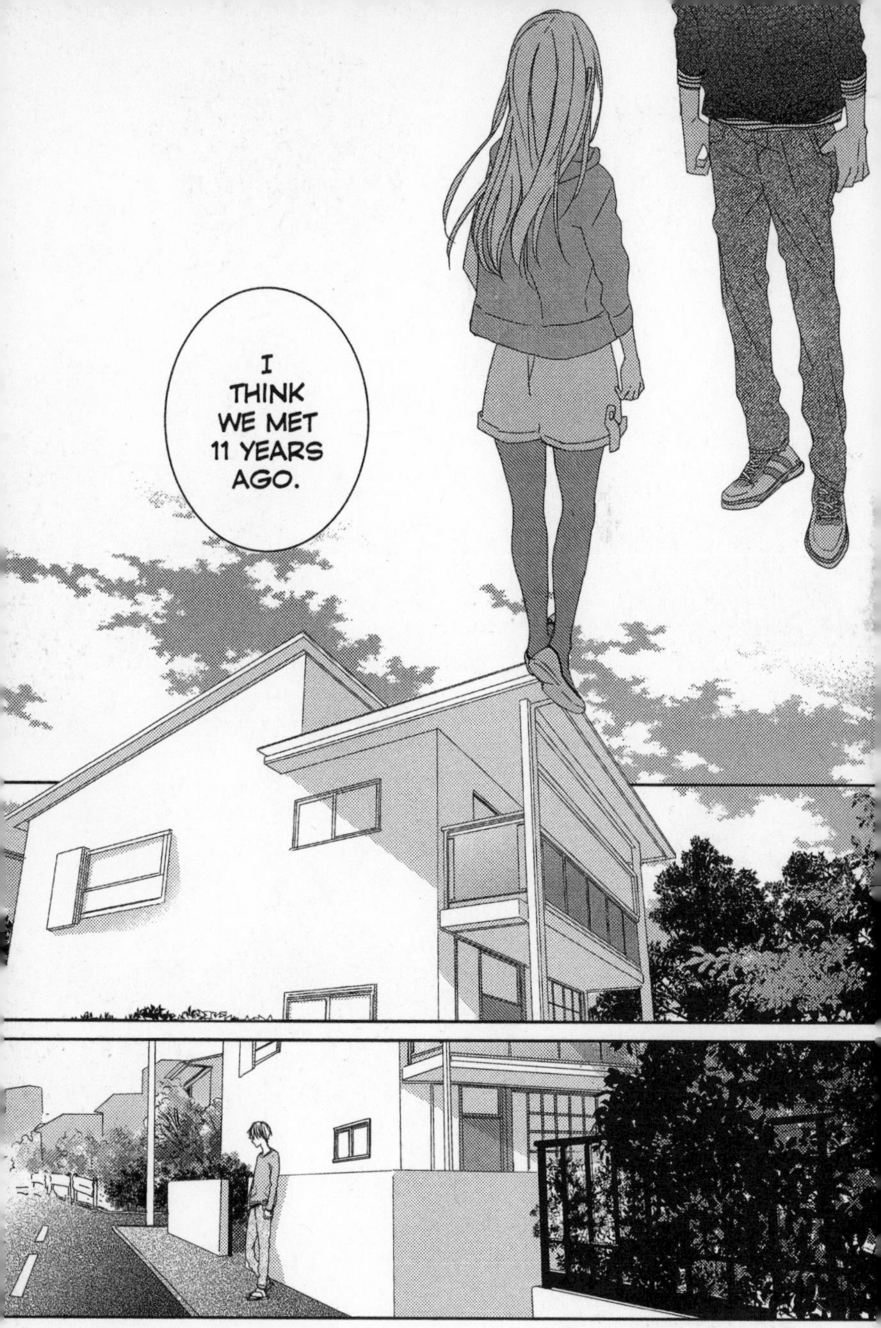
I THINK WE MET 11 YEARS AGO.

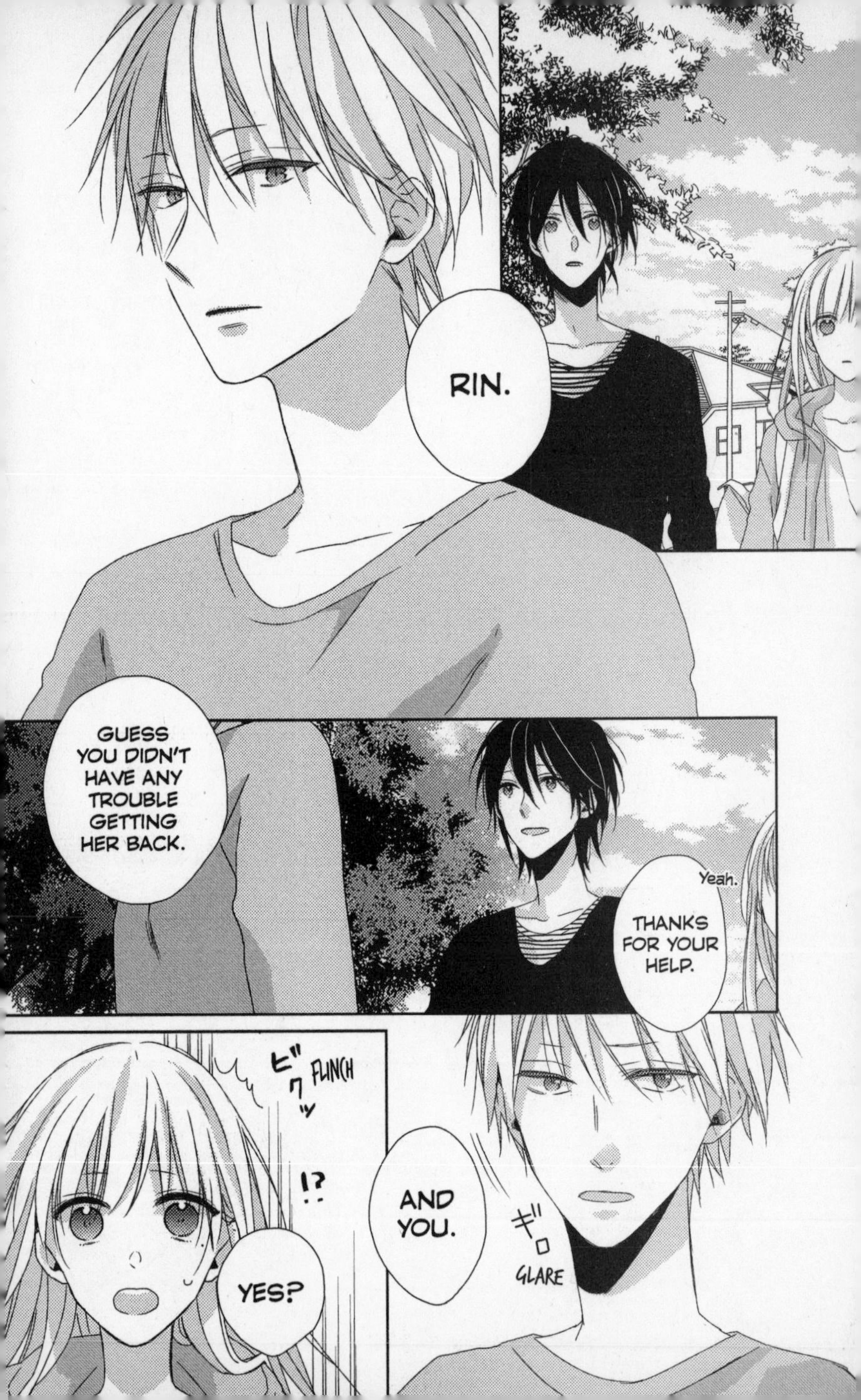
RIN.
GUESS YOU DIDN'T HAVE ANY TROUBLE GETTING HER BACK.
Yeah.
THANKS FOR YOUR HELP.
AND YOU.
ギロ
GLARE
ビクッ
FLINCH
!?
YES?

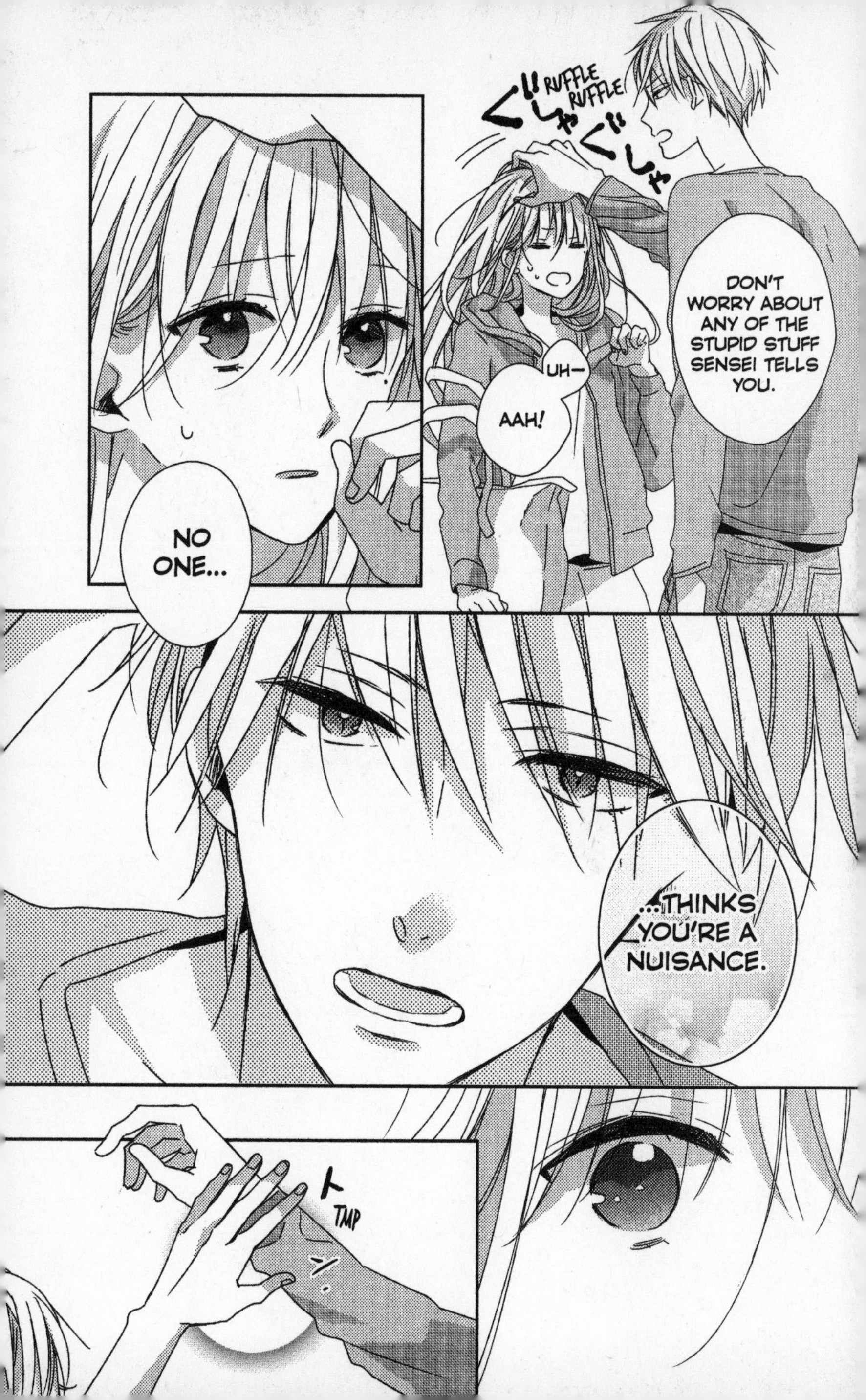
ぐしゃぐしゃ
RUFFLE RUFFLE
DON'T WORRY ABOUT ANY OF THE STUPID STUFF SENSEI TELLS YOU.
UH— AAH!
NO ONE...
...THINKS YOU'RE A NUISANCE.
ト
TMP

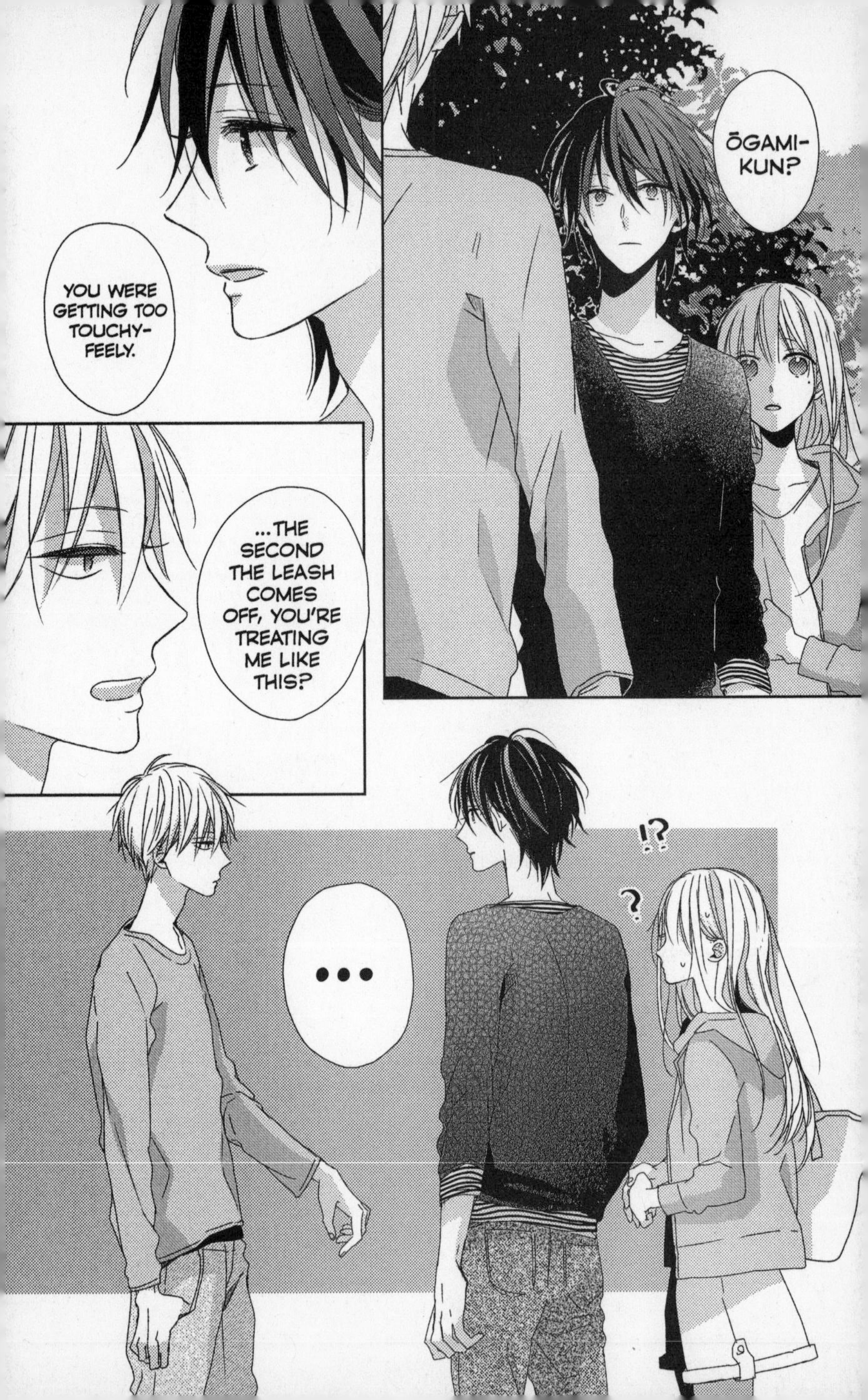
ŌGAMI-KUN?
YOU WERE GETTING TOO TOUCHY-FEELY.
...THE SECOND THE LEASH COMES OFF, YOU'RE TREATING ME LIKE THIS?
!?
?
•••

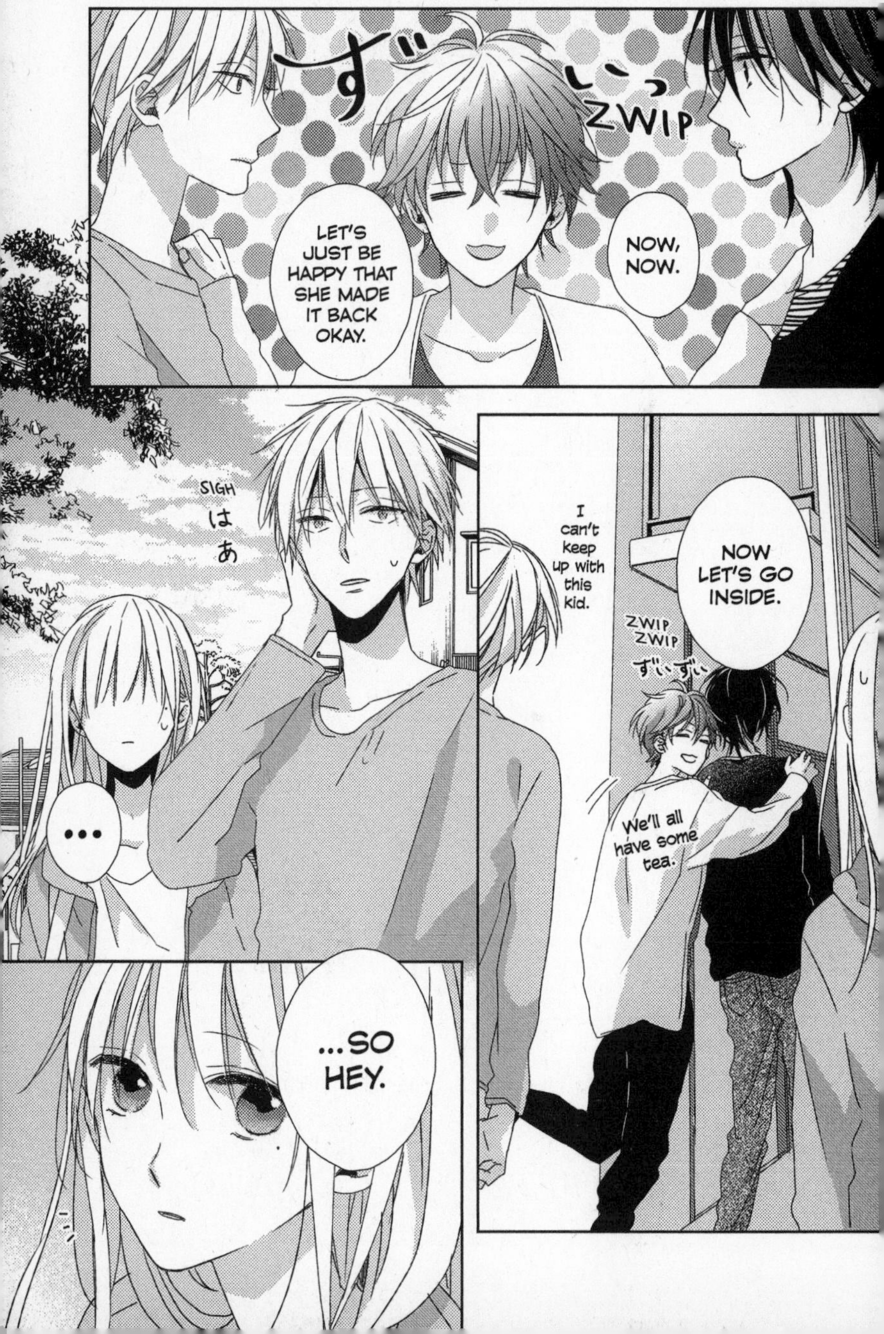

ずいっ
ZWIP
NOW, NOW.
LET'S JUST BE HAPPY THAT SHE MADE IT BACK OKAY.
NOW LET'S GO INSIDE.
I can't keep up with this kid.
ZWIP ZWIP
ずいずい
We'll all have some tea.
SIGH
はあ
...
...SO HEY.

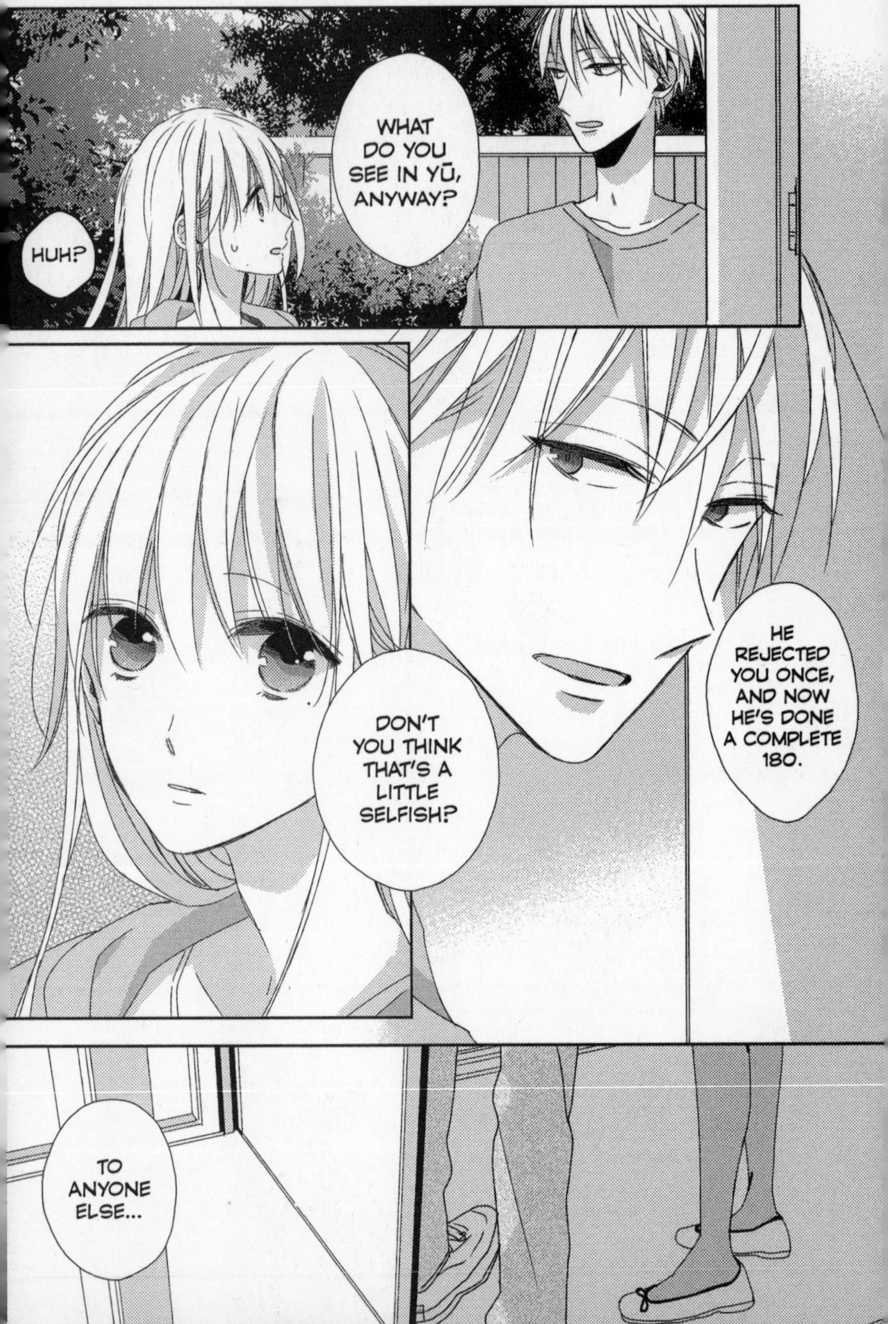
WHAT DO YOU SEE IN YŪ, ANYWAY?
HUH?
HE REJECTED YOU ONCE, AND NOW HE'S DONE A COMPLETE 180.
DON'T YOU THINK THAT'S A LITTLE SELFISH?
TO ANYONE ELSE...

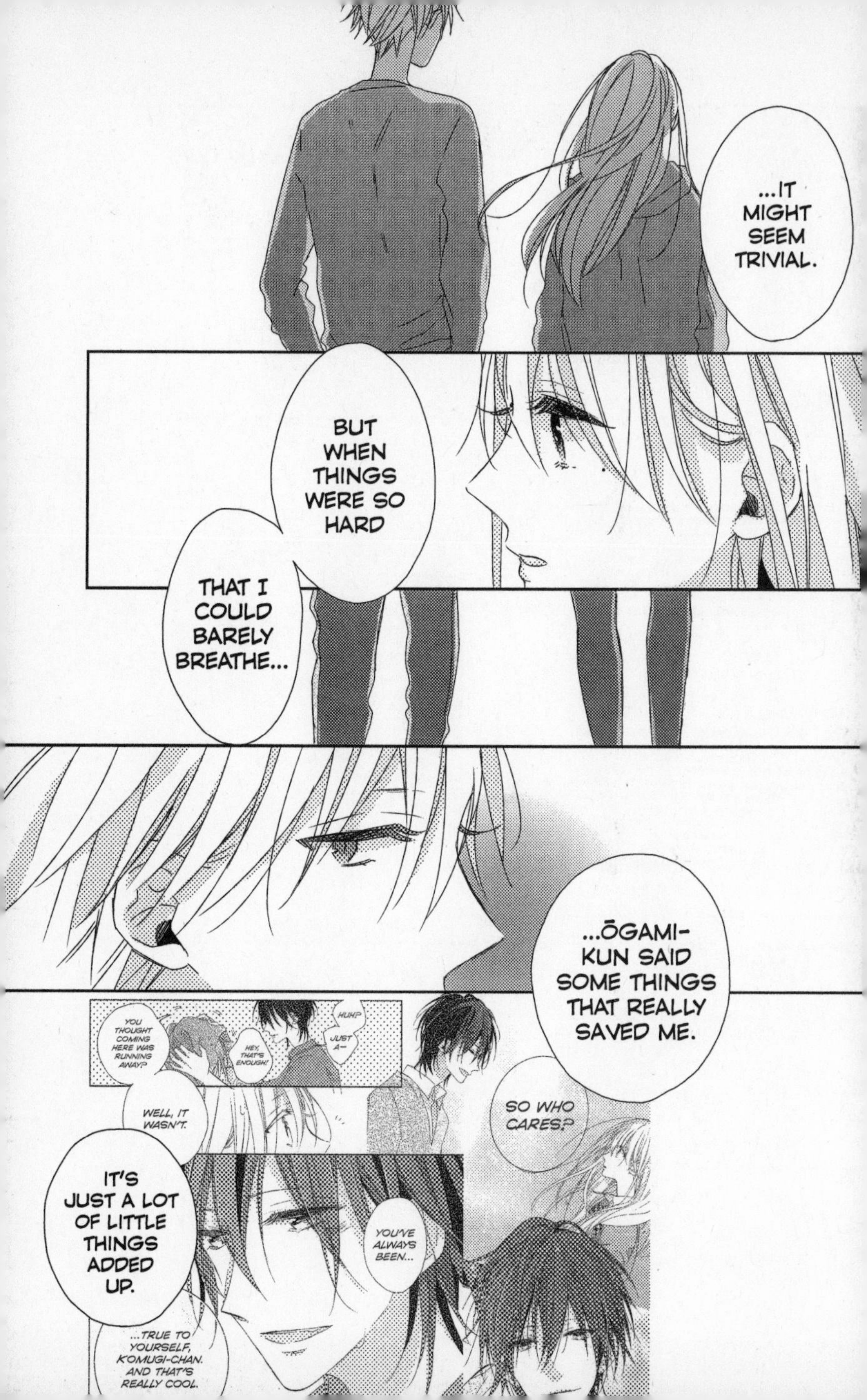
...IT MIGHT SEEM TRIVIAL.
BUT WHEN THINGS WERE SO HARD
THAT I COULD BARELY BREATHE...
...ŌGAMI-KUN SAID SOME THINGS THAT REALLY SAVED ME.
HUH? JUST A—
HEY, THAT'S ENOUGH!
YOU THOUGHT COMING HERE WAS RUNNING AWAY?
WELL, IT WASN'T.
SO WHO CARES?
YOU'VE ALWAYS BEEN...
...TRUE TO YOURSELF, KOMUGI-CHAN. AND THAT'S REALLY COOL.
IT'S JUST A LOT OF LITTLE THINGS ADDED UP.

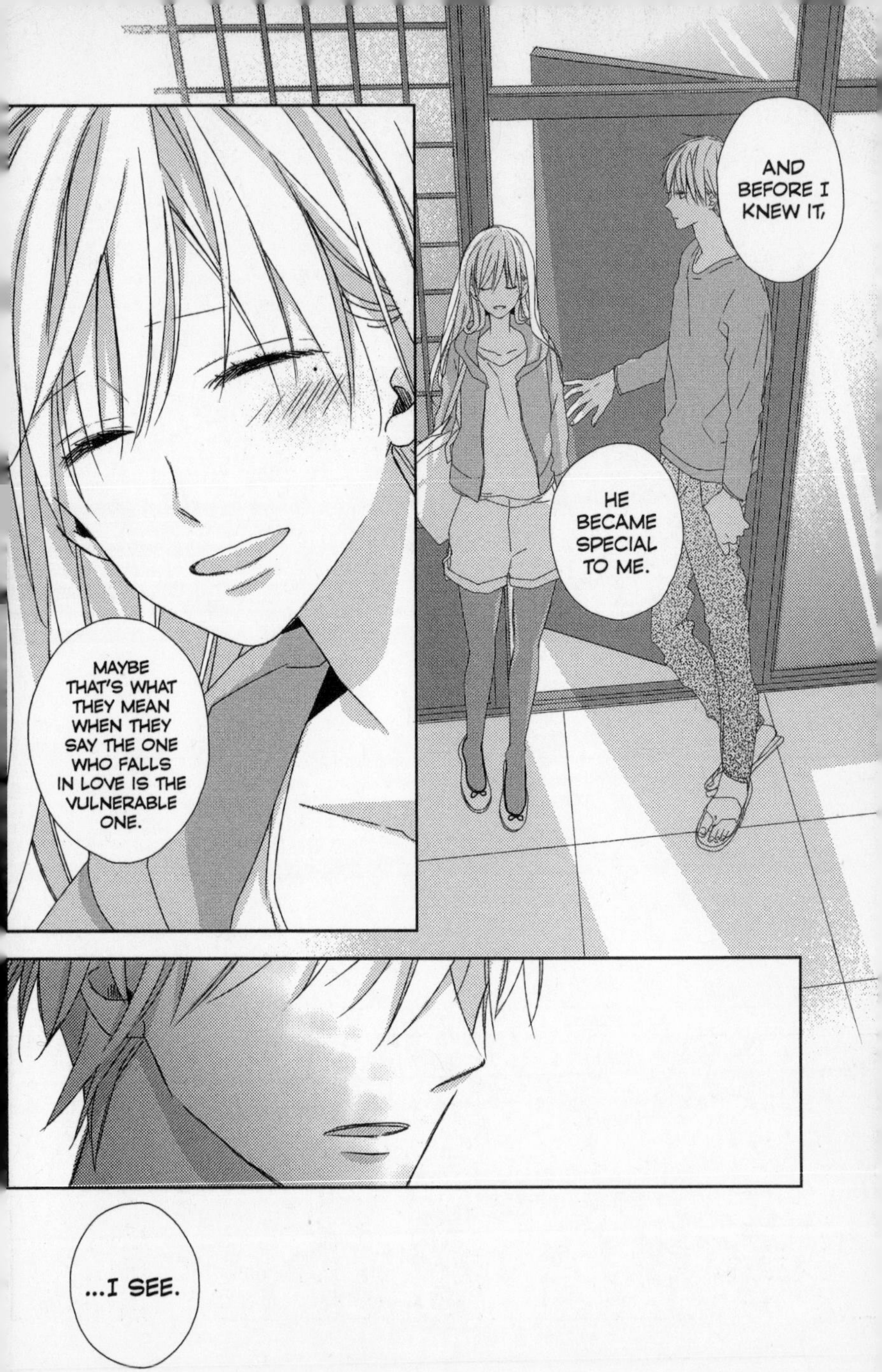
AND BEFORE I KNEW IT,
HE BECAME SPECIAL TO ME.
MAYBE THAT'S WHAT THEY MEAN WHEN THEY SAY THE ONE WHO FALLS IN LOVE IS THE VULNERABLE ONE.
...I SEE.

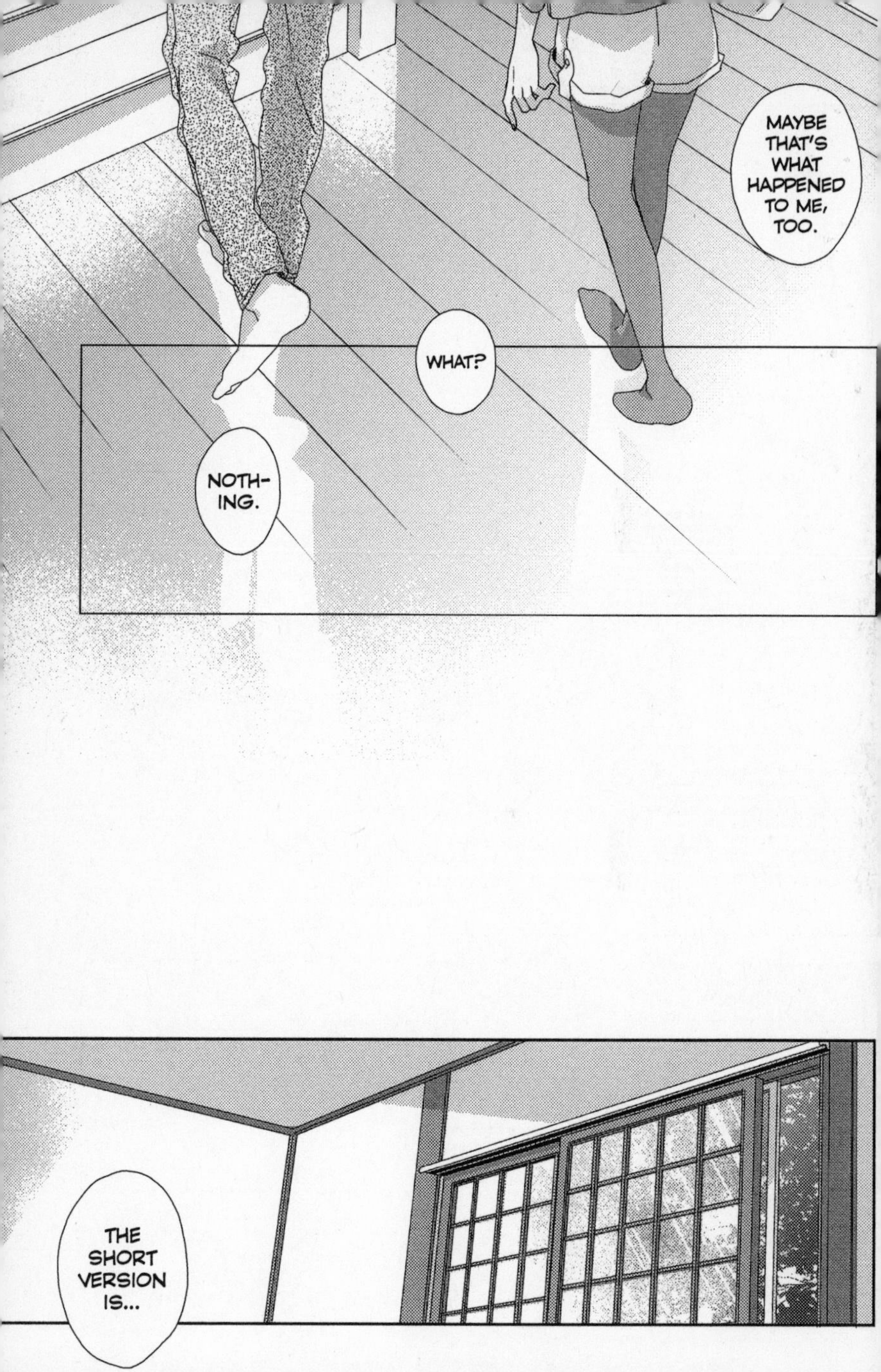
MAYBE THAT'S WHAT HAPPENED TO ME, TOO.
WHAT?
NOTH-ING.
THE SHORT VERSION IS...

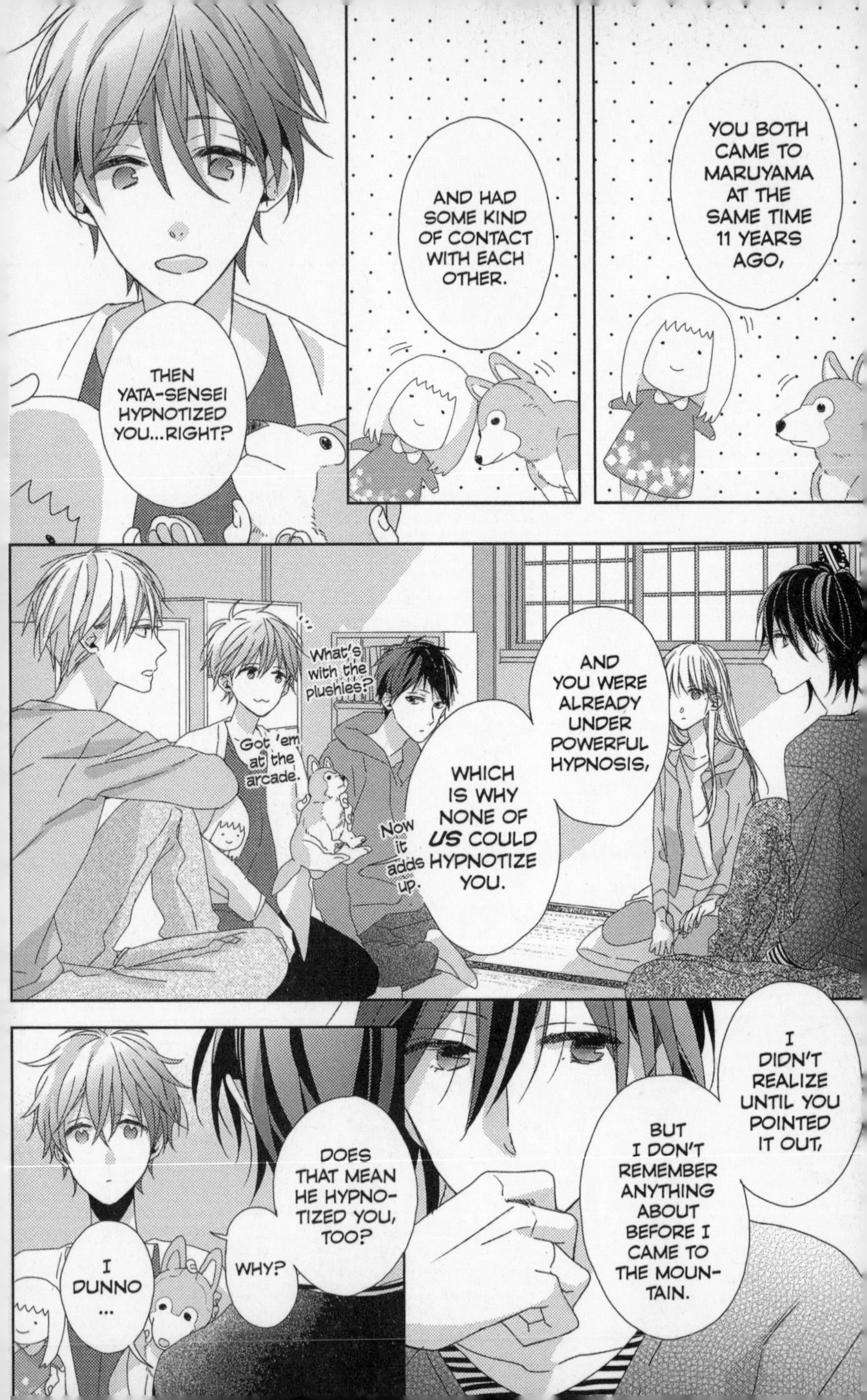
YOU BOTH CAME TO MARUYAMA AT THE SAME TIME 11 YEARS AGO,
AND HAD SOME KIND OF CONTACT WITH EACH OTHER.
THEN YATA-SENSEI HYPNOTIZED YOU...RIGHT?
AND YOU WERE ALREADY UNDER POWERFUL HYPNOSIS,
WHICH IS WHY NONE OF *US* COULD HYPNOTIZE YOU.
What's with the plushies?
Got 'em at the arcade.
Now it adds up.
I DIDN'T REALIZE UNTIL YOU POINTED IT OUT,
BUT I DON'T REMEMBER ANYTHING ABOUT BEFORE I CAME TO THE MOUNTAIN.
DOES THAT MEAN HE HYPNOTIZED YOU, TOO?
WHY?
I DUNNO...

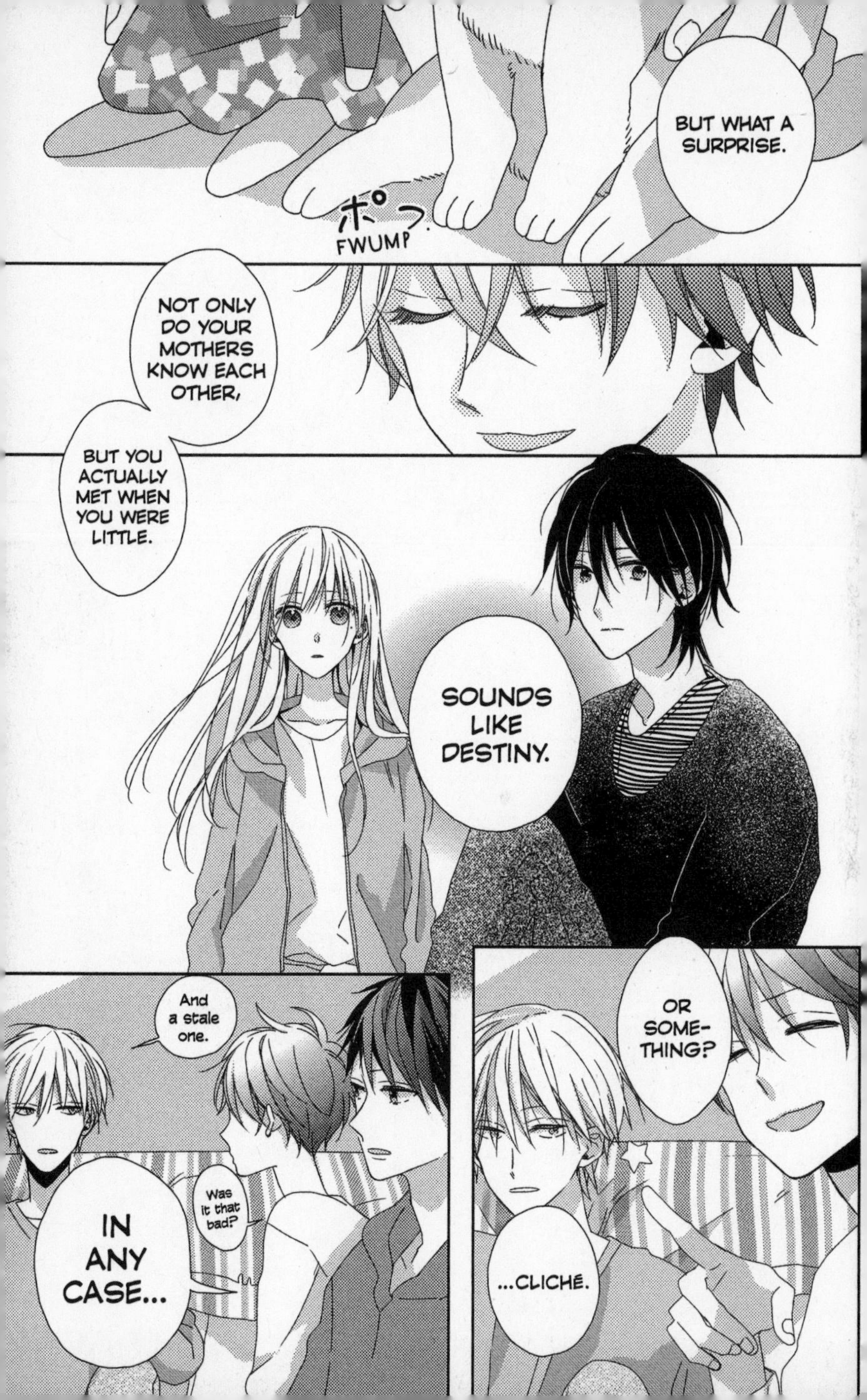
BUT WHAT A SURPRISE.
ポっ
FWUMP
NOT ONLY DO YOUR MOTHERS KNOW EACH OTHER,
BUT YOU ACTUALLY MET WHEN YOU WERE LITTLE.
SOUNDS LIKE DESTINY.
OR SOME-THING?
...CLICHE.
And a stale one.
Was it that bad?
IN ANY CASE...

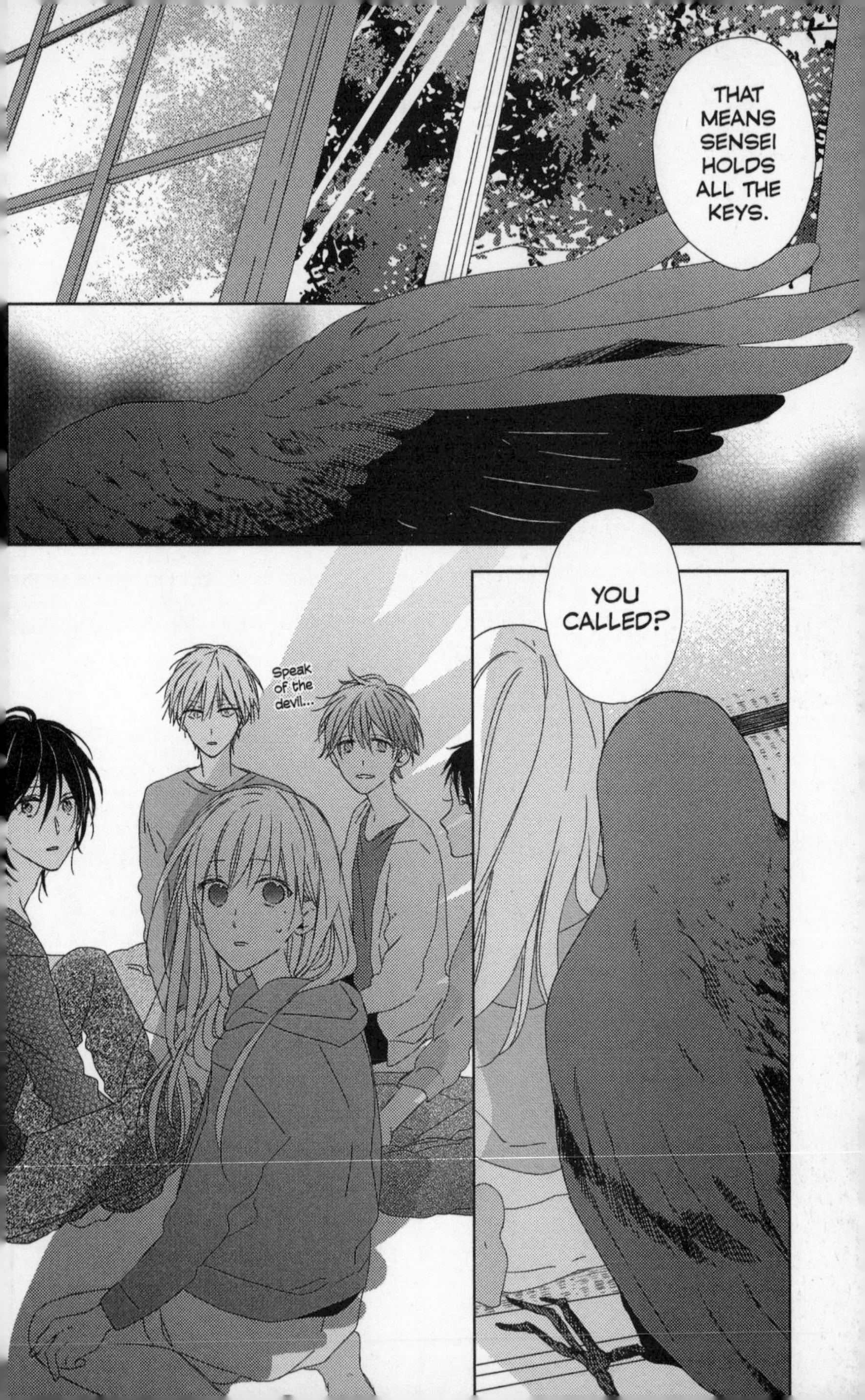
THAT MEANS SENSEI HOLDS ALL THE KEYS.
YOU CALLED?
Speak of the devil...

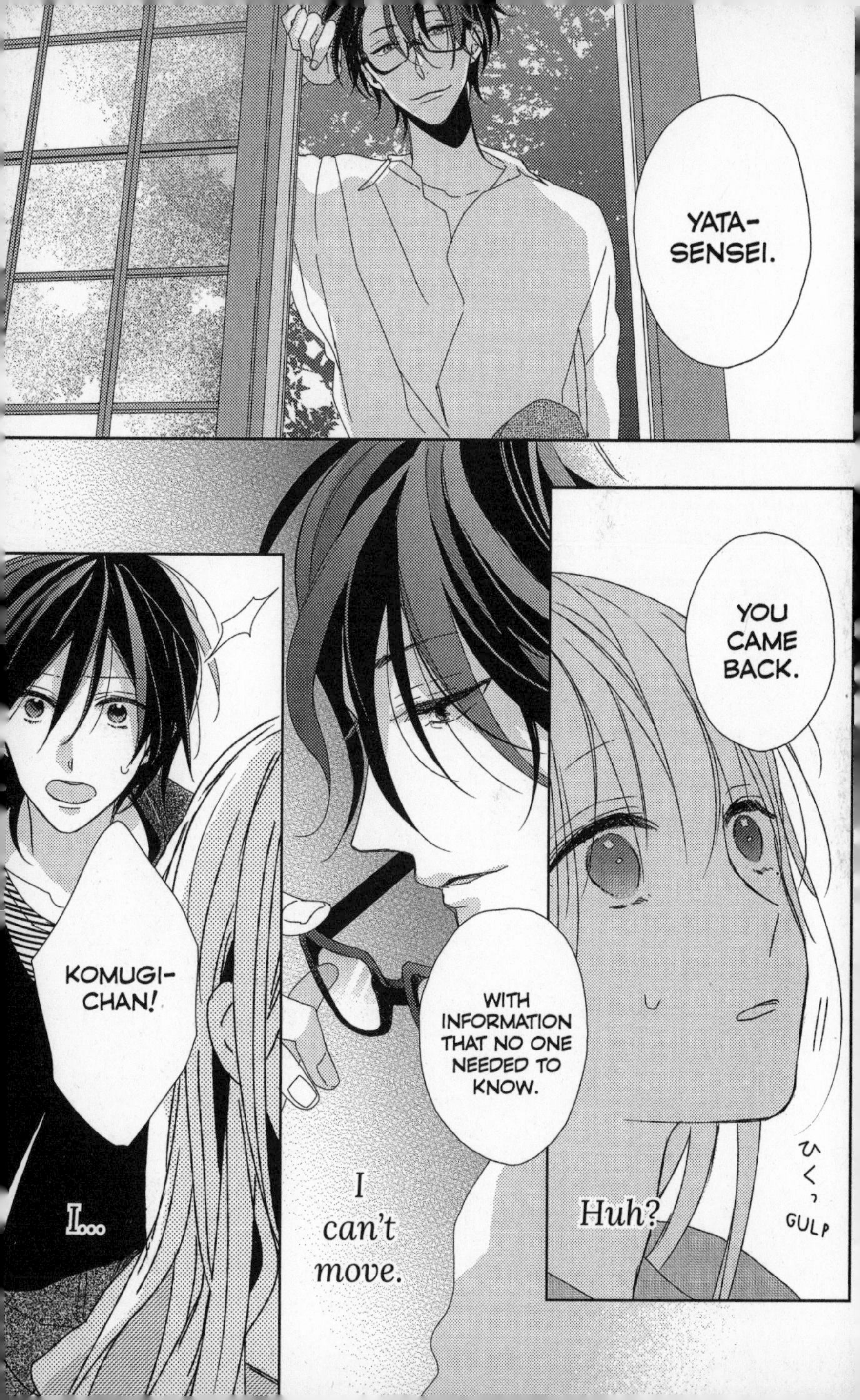
YATA-SENSEI.
YOU CAME BACK.
ひくっ
GULP
Huh?
WITH INFORMATION THAT NO ONE NEEDED TO KNOW.
I can't move.
KOMUGI-CHAN!
I...

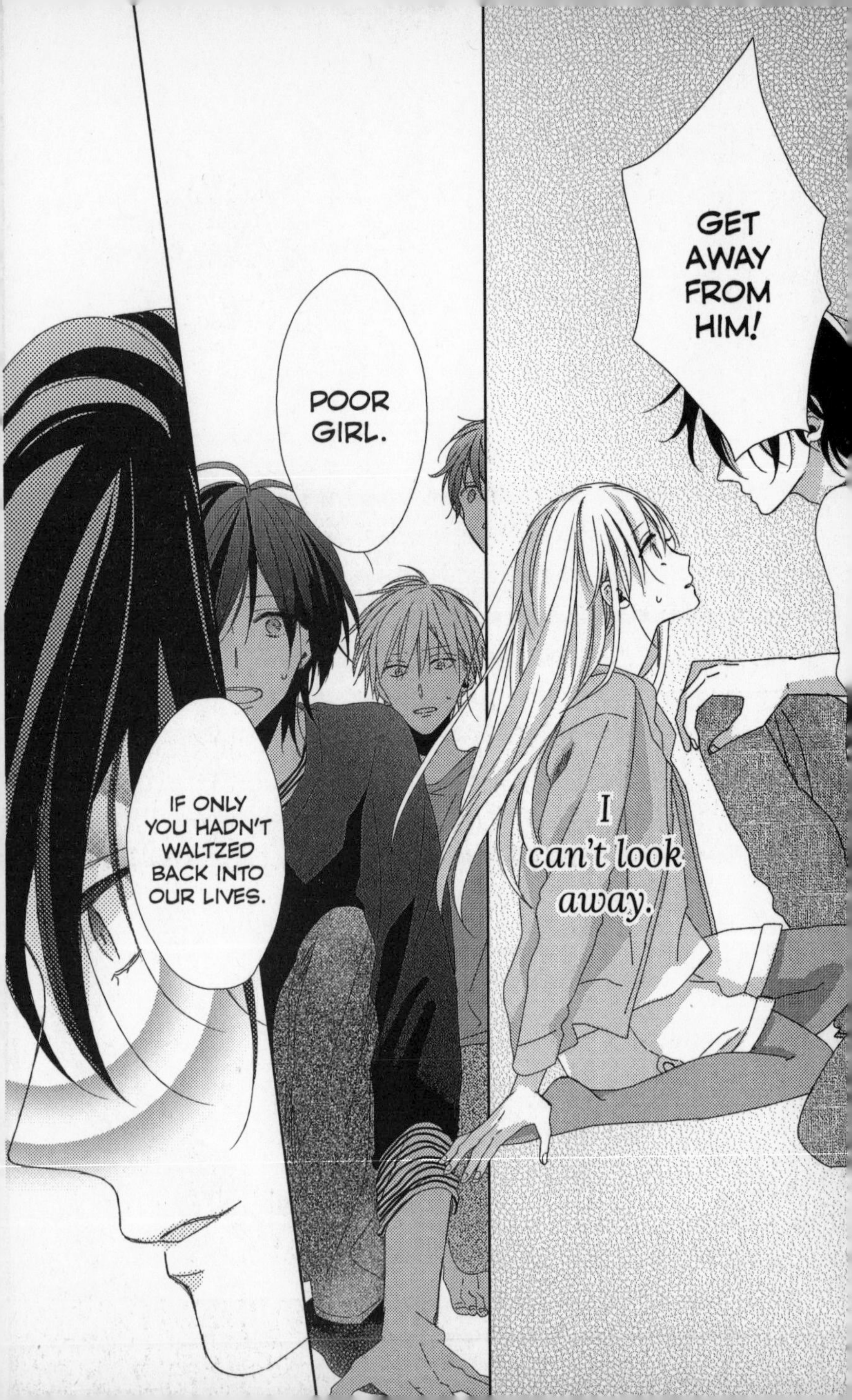
GET AWAY FROM HIM!
I can't look away.
POOR GIRL.
IF ONLY YOU HADN'T WALTZED BACK INTO OUR LIVES.

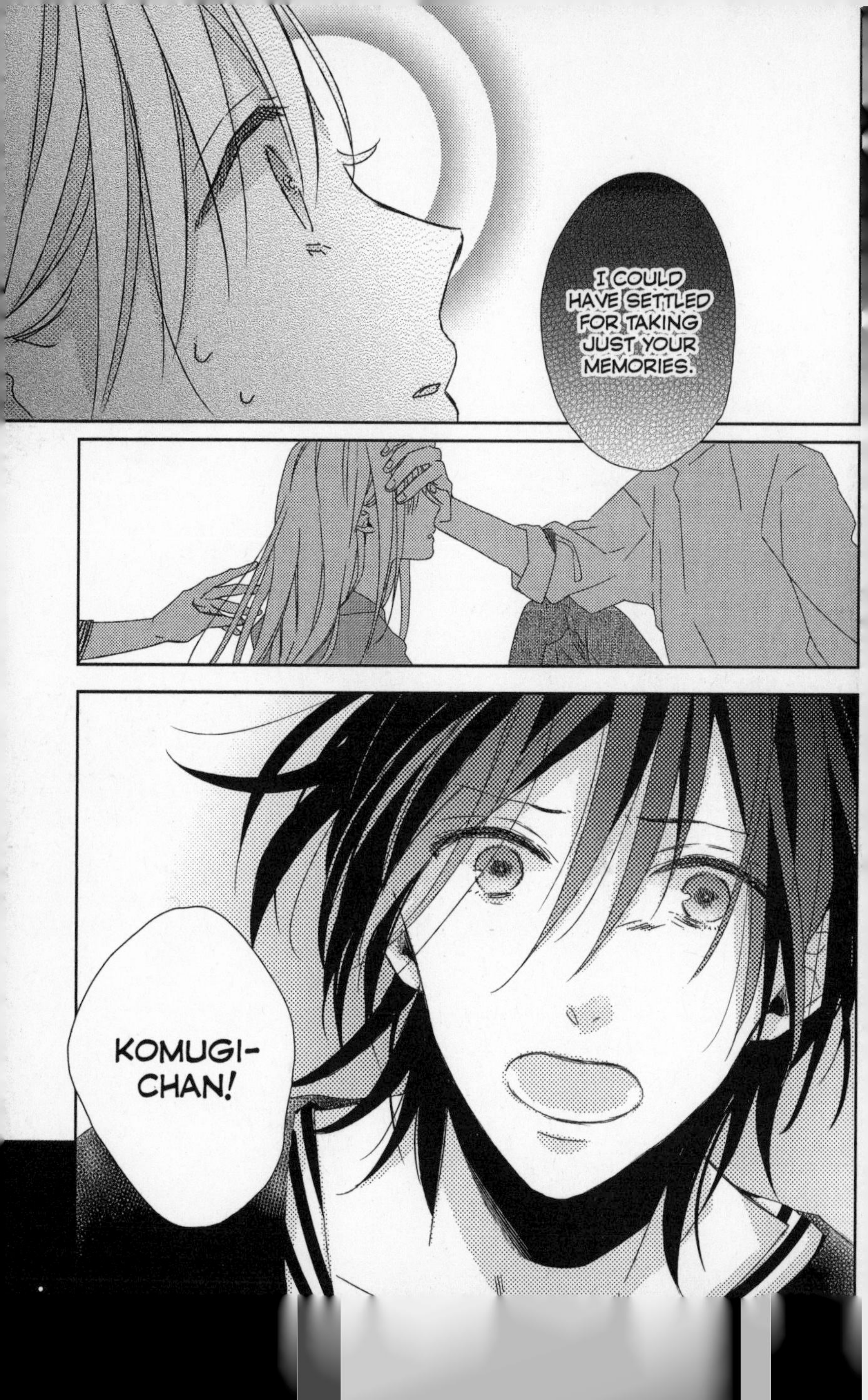
I COULD HAVE SETTLED FOR TAKING JUST YOUR MEMORIES.
KOMUGI-CHAN!

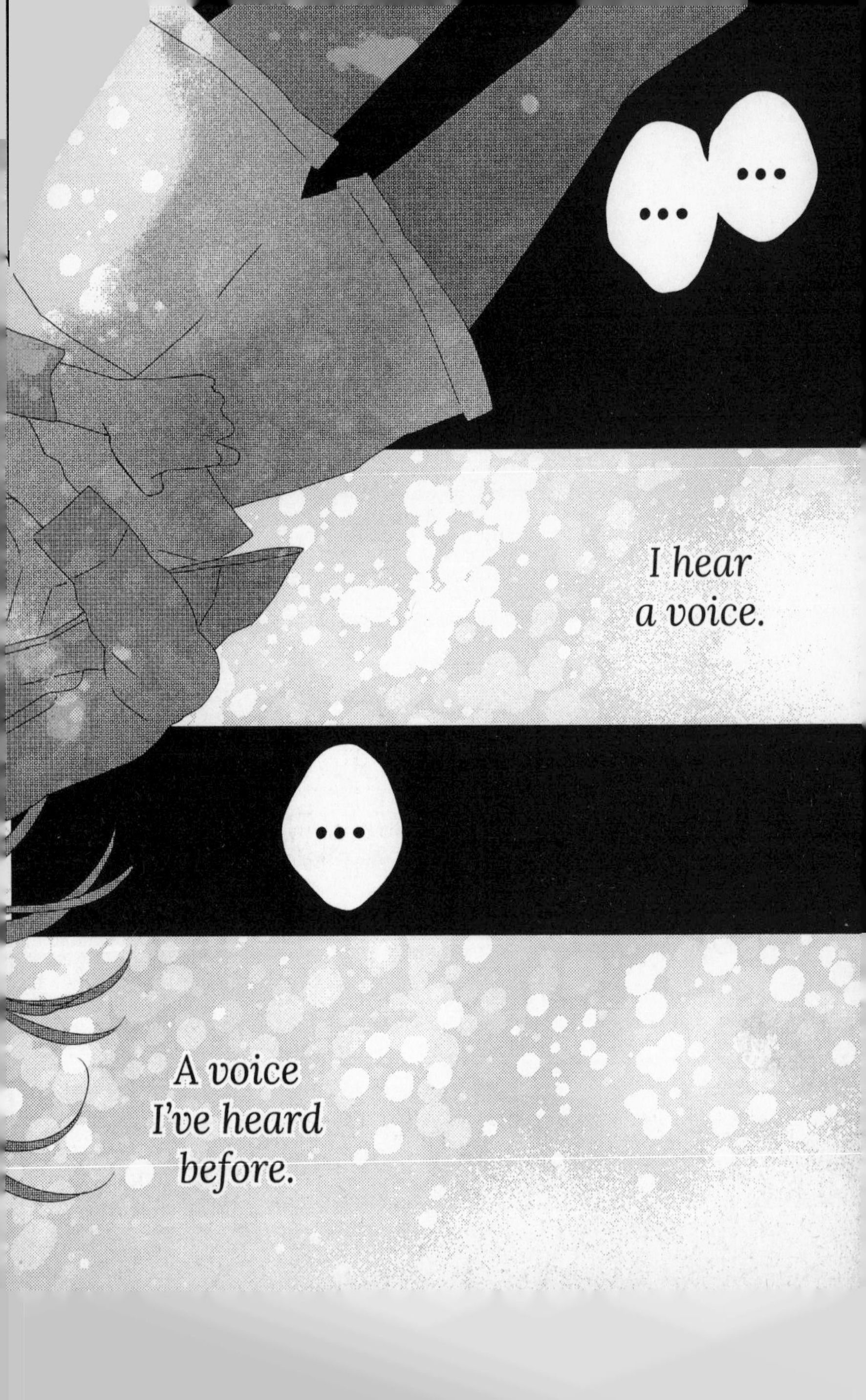
...
...
I hear a voice.
...
A voice I've heard before.

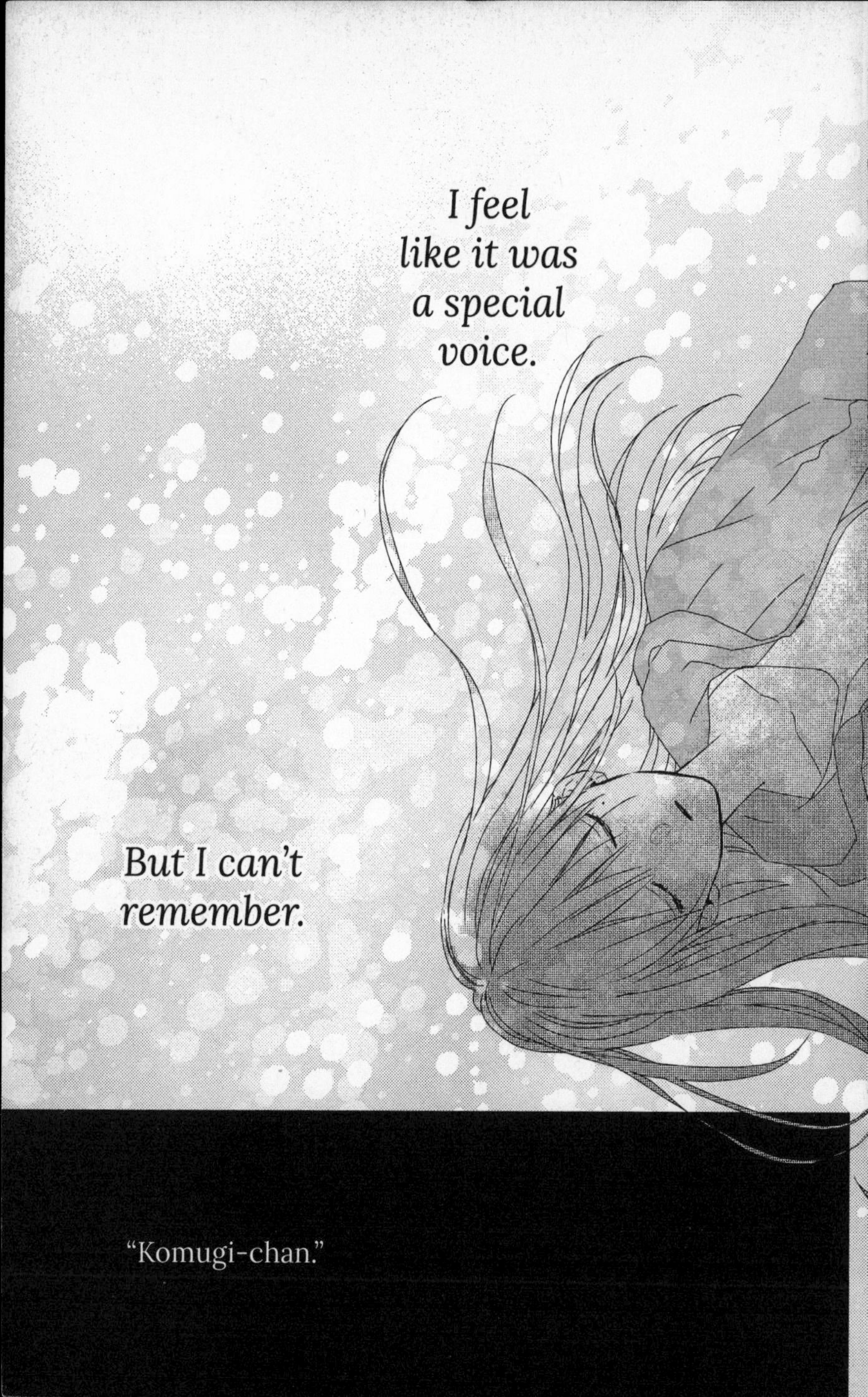
I feel like it was a special voice.
But I can't remember.
"Komugi-chan."

Someone's
calling my
name.

But who...?

To be continued in Volume 4

That Wolf-Boy is Mine!

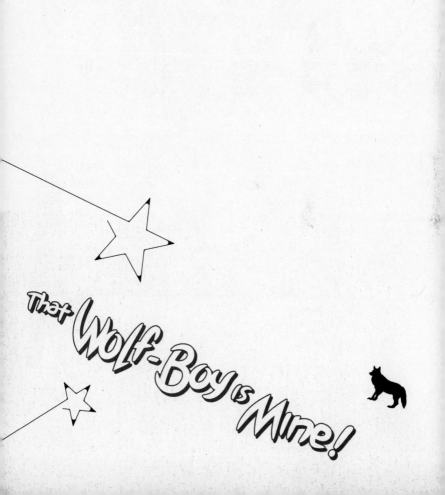

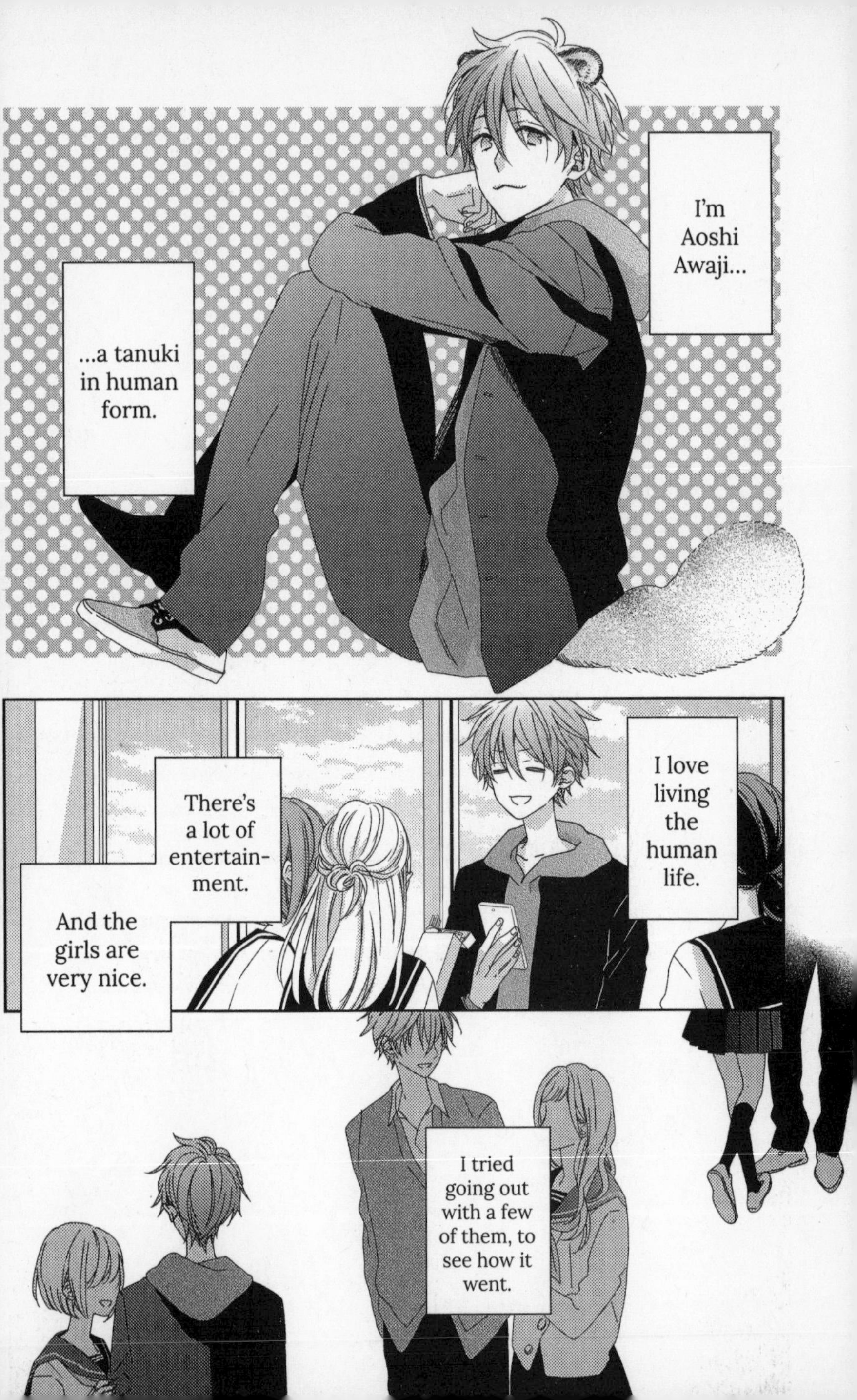
I'm Aoshi Awaji...
...a tanuki in human form.
I love living the human life.
There's a lot of entertain-ment.
And the girls are very nice.
I tried going out with a few of them, to see how it went.

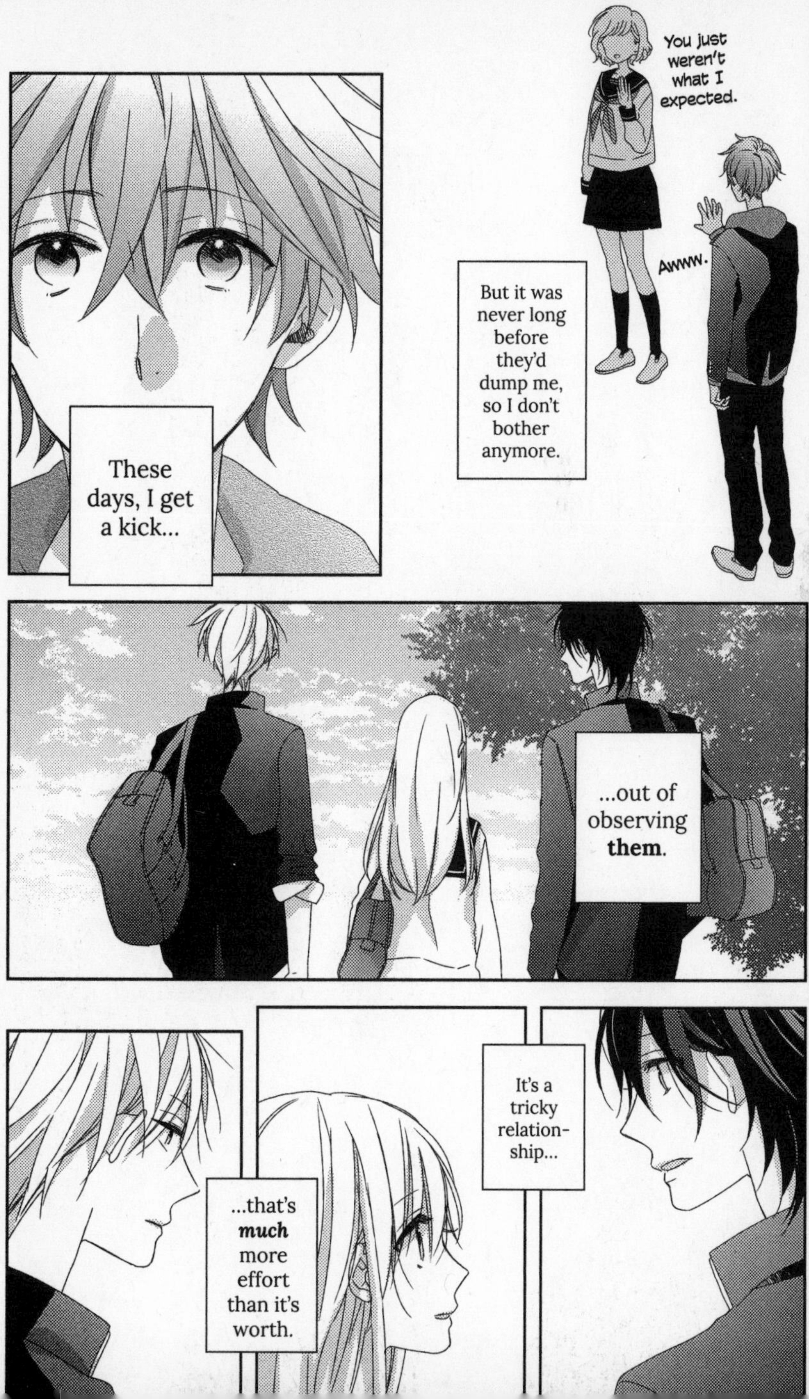
You just weren't what I expected.
Awww.
But it was never long before they'd dump me, so I don't bother anymore.
These days, I get a kick...
...out of observing **them**.
It's a tricky relationship...
...that's ***much*** more effort than it's worth.

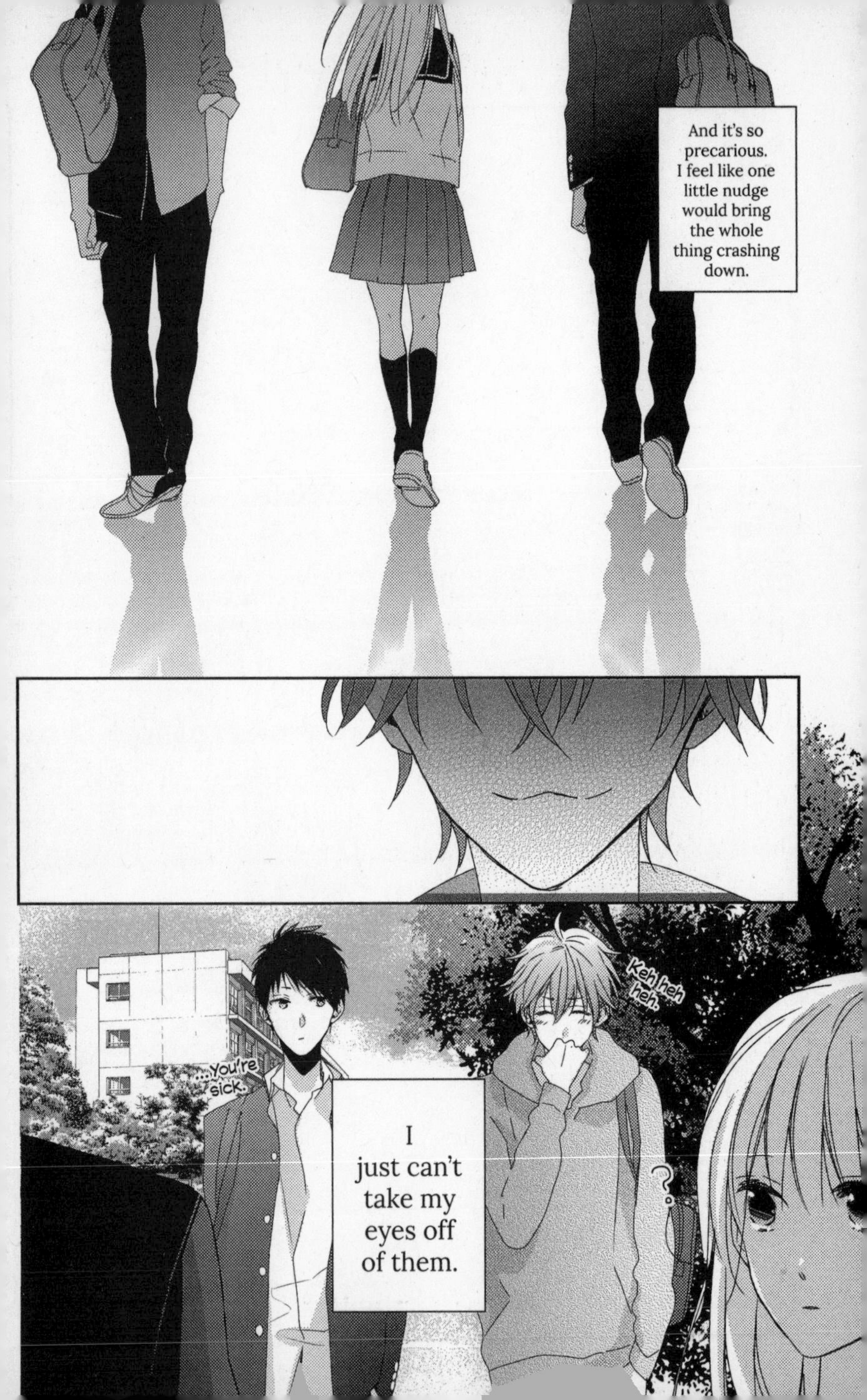
And it's so precarious. I feel like one little nudge would bring the whole thing crashing down.
Keh heh heh.
...You're sick.
?
I just can't take my eyes off of them.

# Afterword

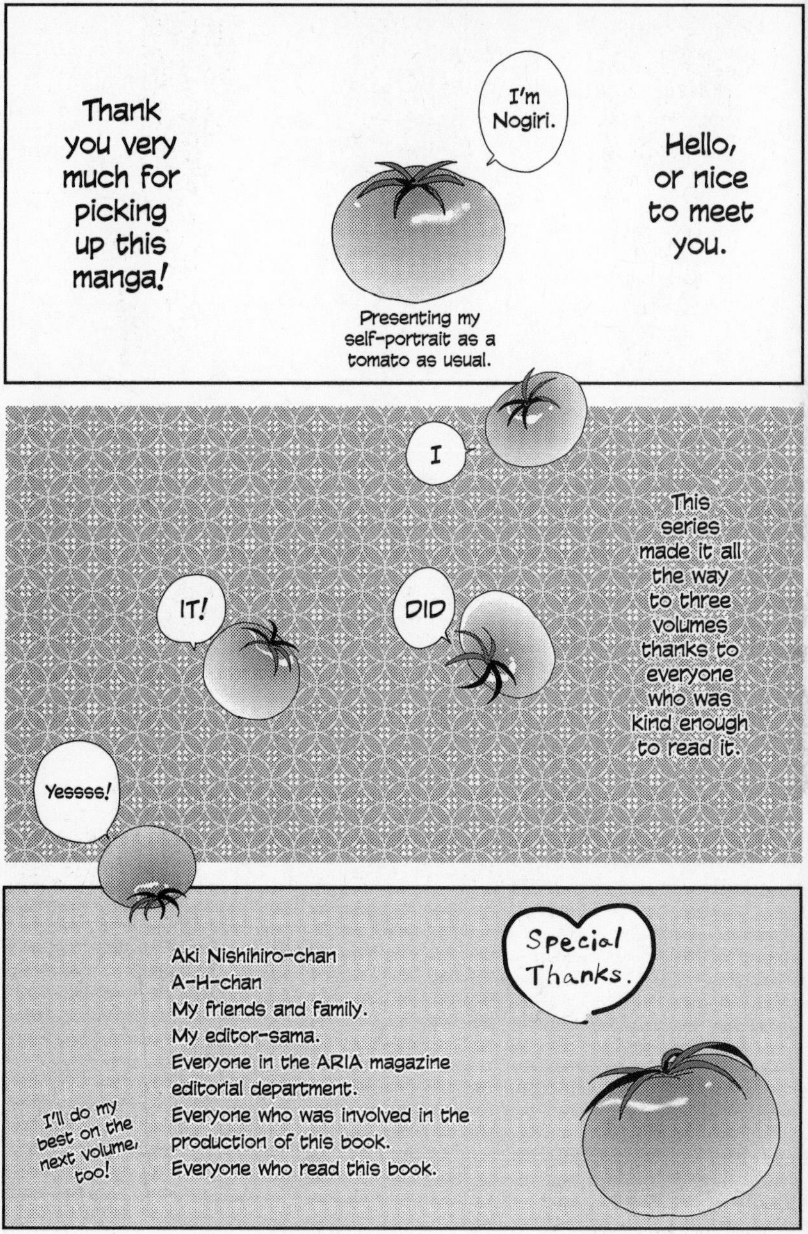
Hello, or nice to meet you.
I'm Nogiri.
Thank you very much for picking up this manga!
Presenting my self-portrait as a tomato as usual.
This series made it all the way to three volumes thanks to everyone who was kind enough to read it.
I
DID
IT!
Yessss!
Special Thanks.
Aki Nishihiro-chan
A-H-chan
My friends and family.
My editor-sama.
Everyone in the ARIA magazine editorial department.
Everyone who was involved in the production of this book.
Everyone who read this book.
I'll do my best on the next volume, too!

# Translation Notes

**Sneaky little tanuki,** page 63
It might be interesting to note that in the Japanese text, Komugi only calls Aoshi a tanuki, which, as we all know, is what he is. But according to Japanese traditions, tanuki are known for being sneaky and deceptive, so it's not uncommon to call a human with those traits a "tanuki."

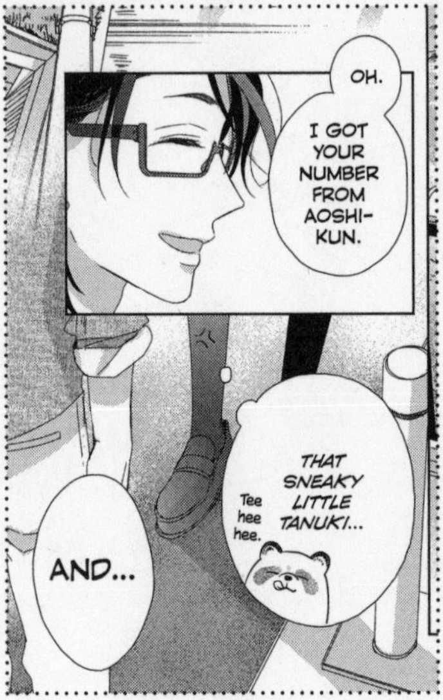
OH.
I GOT YOUR NUMBER FROM AOSHI-KUN.
THAT SNEAKY LITTLE TANUKI...
Tee hee hee.
AND...

**Day duty,** page 79
In Japanese schools, the students in each class take turns with certain clerical responsibilities, such as keeping the class diary and preparing materials for certain classes.

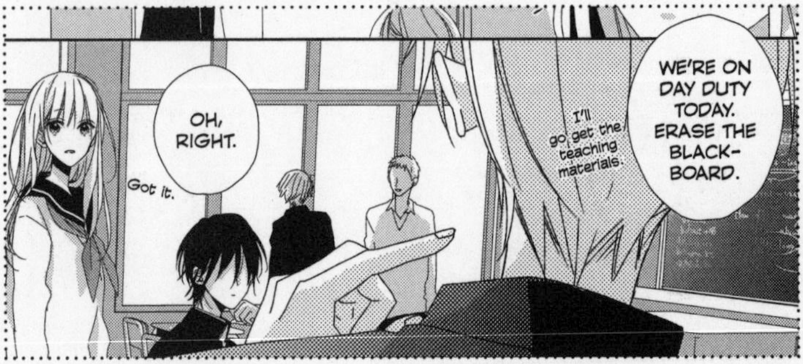
WE'RE ON DAY DUTY TODAY. ERASE THE BLACK-BOARD.
I'll go get the teaching materials.
OH, RIGHT.
Got it.

**Manjū,** page 103
A *manjū* is Japanese for any type of Asian bun, savory or sweet. Here, the grandparents are talking about a Japanese confection with a doughy outside, filled with something sweet. A common and traditional filling is *anko*, a sweet red bean paste.

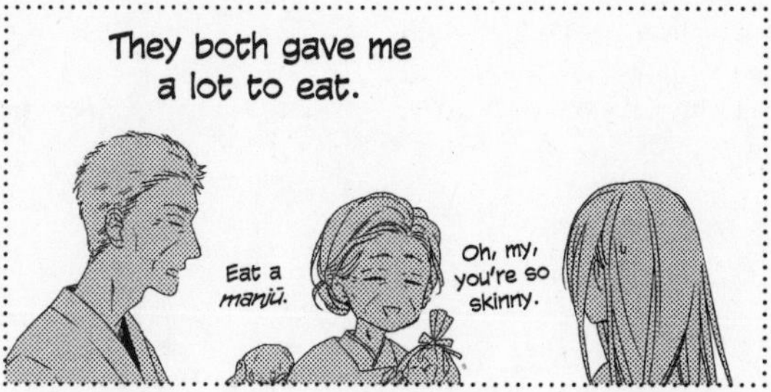
They both gave me a lot to eat.
Oh, my, you're so skinny.
Eat a *manjū*.

**I left my son,** page 127
In the original Japanese, this statement doesn't sound quite as heartless. She uses the word *azukeru*, which means "to leave **in the care of [someone]**," indicating that she didn't just abandon him in the woods; she expected that he would be taken care of somehow, or at least that's the impression she wanted to give.

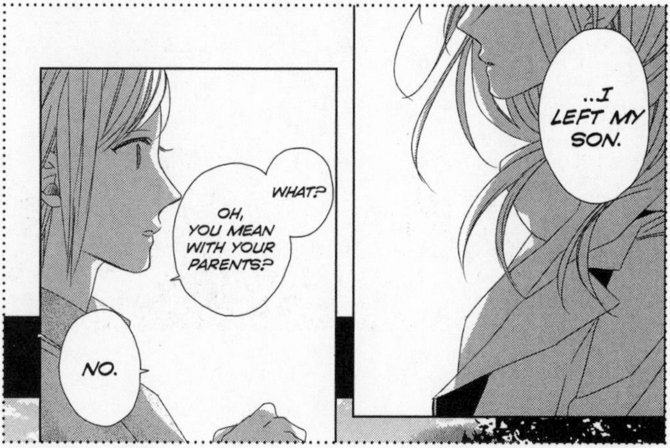
...I LEFT MY SON.
WHAT? OH, YOU MEAN WITH YOUR PARENTS?
NO.

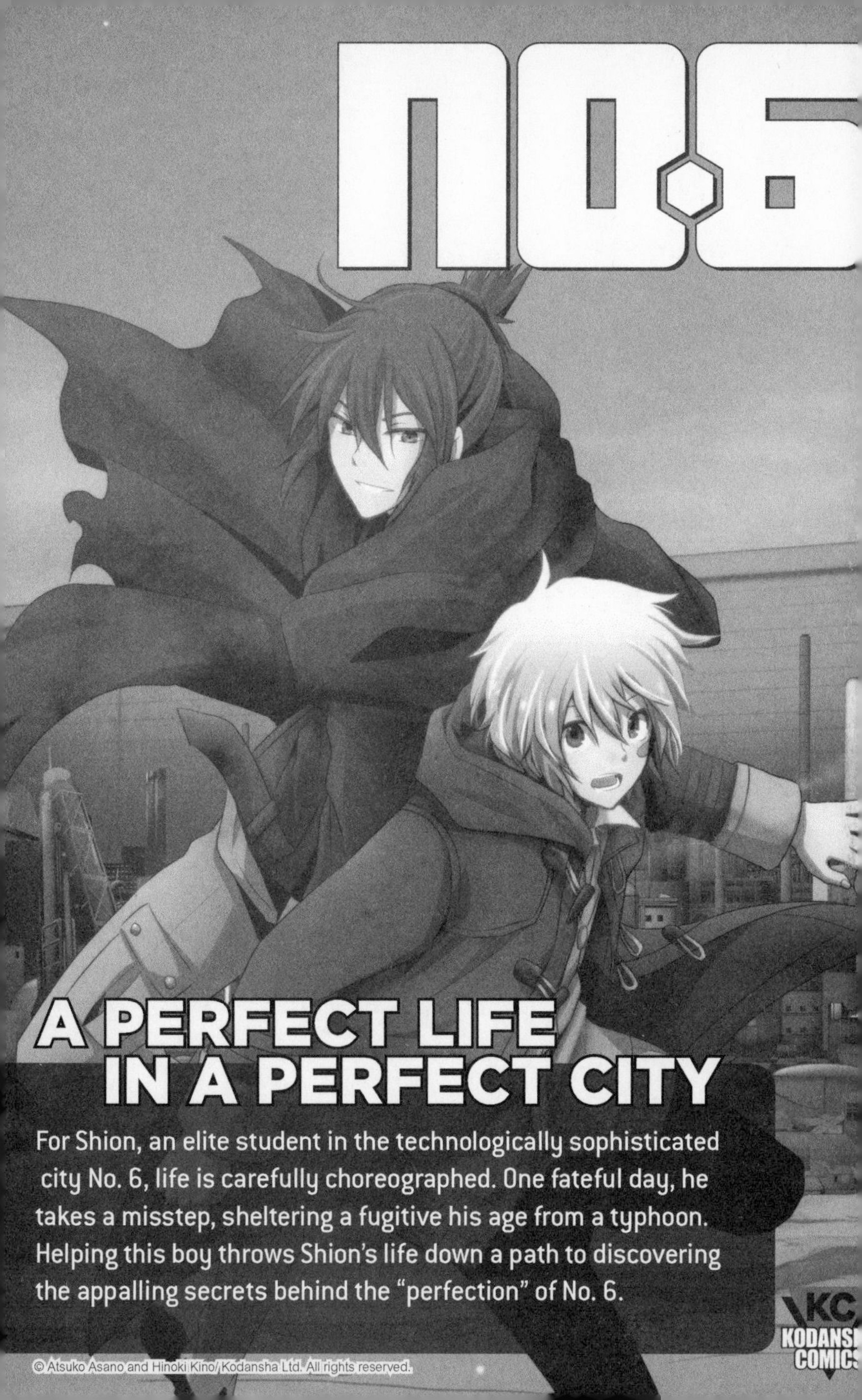
NO.6
A PERFECT LIFE IN A PERFECT CITY
For Shion, an elite student in the technologically sophisticated city No. 6, life is carefully choreographed. One fateful day, he takes a misstep, sheltering a fugitive his age from a typhoon. Helping this boy throws Shion's life down a path to discovering the appalling secrets behind the "perfection" of No. 6.
KC KODANSHA COMICS
© Atsuko Asano and Hinoki Kino/ Kodansha Ltd. All rights reserved.

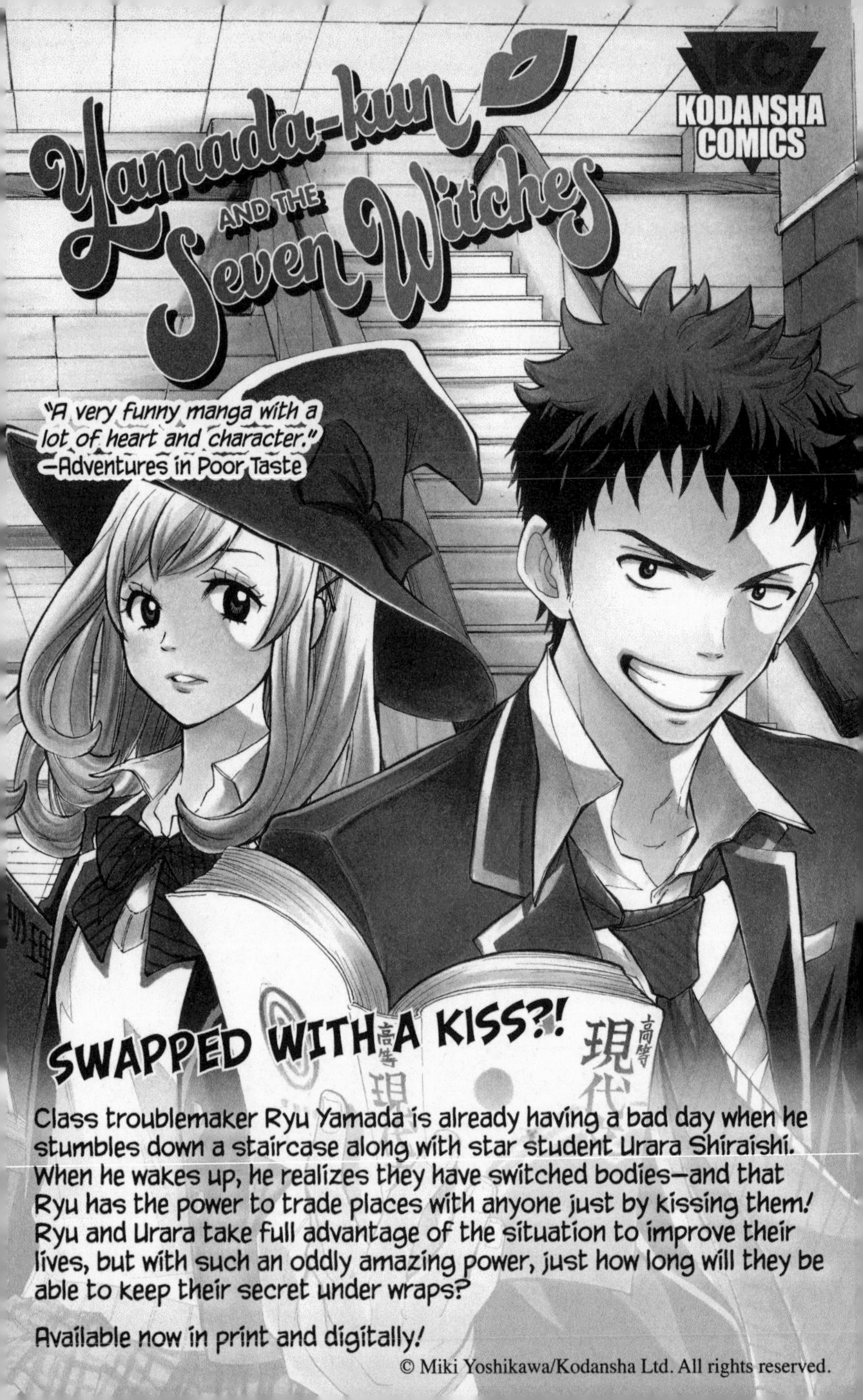
Yamada-kun AND THE Seven Witches
KODANSHA COMICS
"A very funny manga with a lot of heart and character." —Adventures in Poor Taste
SWAPPED WITH A KISS?!
Class troublemaker Ryu Yamada is already having a bad day when he stumbles down a staircase along with star student Urara Shiraishi. When he wakes up, he realizes they have switched bodies—and that Ryu has the power to trade places with anyone just by kissing them! Ryu and Urara take full advantage of the situation to improve their lives, but with such an oddly amazing power, just how long will they be able to keep their secret under wraps?
Available now in print and digitally!
© Miki Yoshikawa/Kodansha Ltd. All rights reserved.

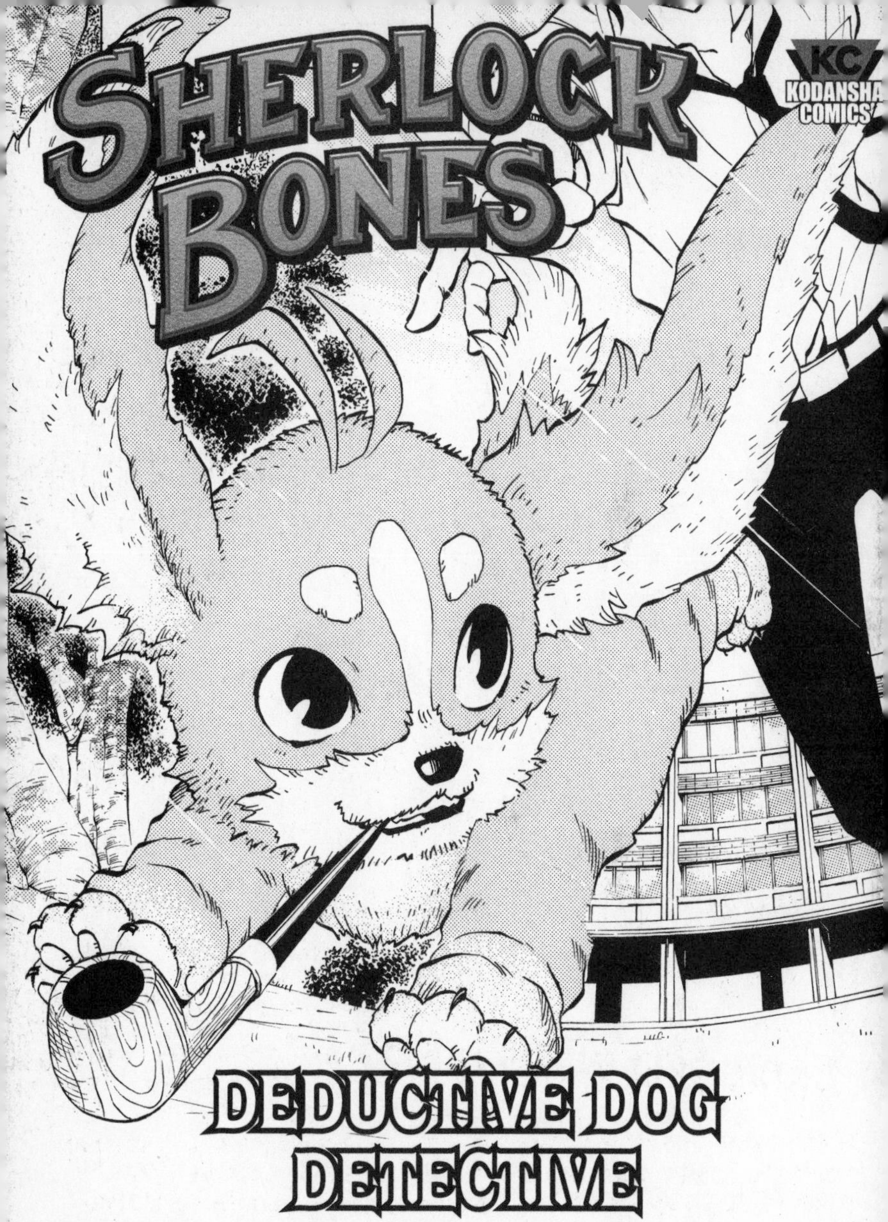
KC
KODANSHA COMICS
SHERLOCK BONES
DEDUCTIVE DOG DETECTIVE

When Takeru adopts a new pet, he's in for a surprise—the dog is none other than the reincarnation of Sherlock Holmes. With no one else able to communicate with Holmes, Takeru is roped into becoming Sherdog's assistant, John Watson. Using his sleuthing skills, Holmes uncovers clues to solve the trickiest crimes.

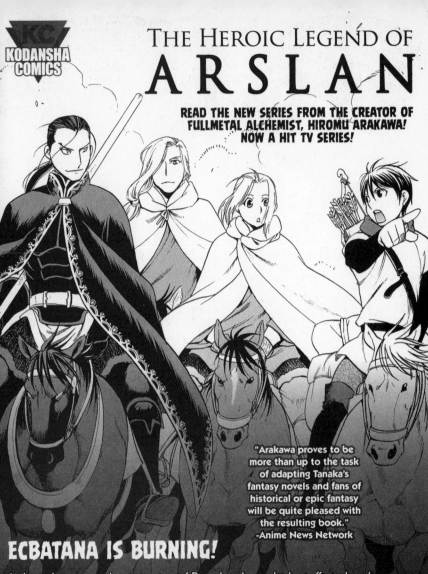

**Praise for the anime:**

"The show provides a pleasant window on the highs and lows of young love with two young people who are first-timers at the real thing."

-The Fandom Post

"Always it is smarter, more poetic, more touching, just plain better than you think it is going to be."

-Anime News Network

**Mei Tachibana has no friends — and says she doesn't need them!**

But everything changes when she accidentally roundhouse kicks the most popular boy in school! However, Yamato Kurosawa isn't angry in the slightest— in fact, he thinks his ordinary life could use an unusual girl like Mei. But winning Mei's trust will be a tough task. How long will she refuse to say, "I love you"?

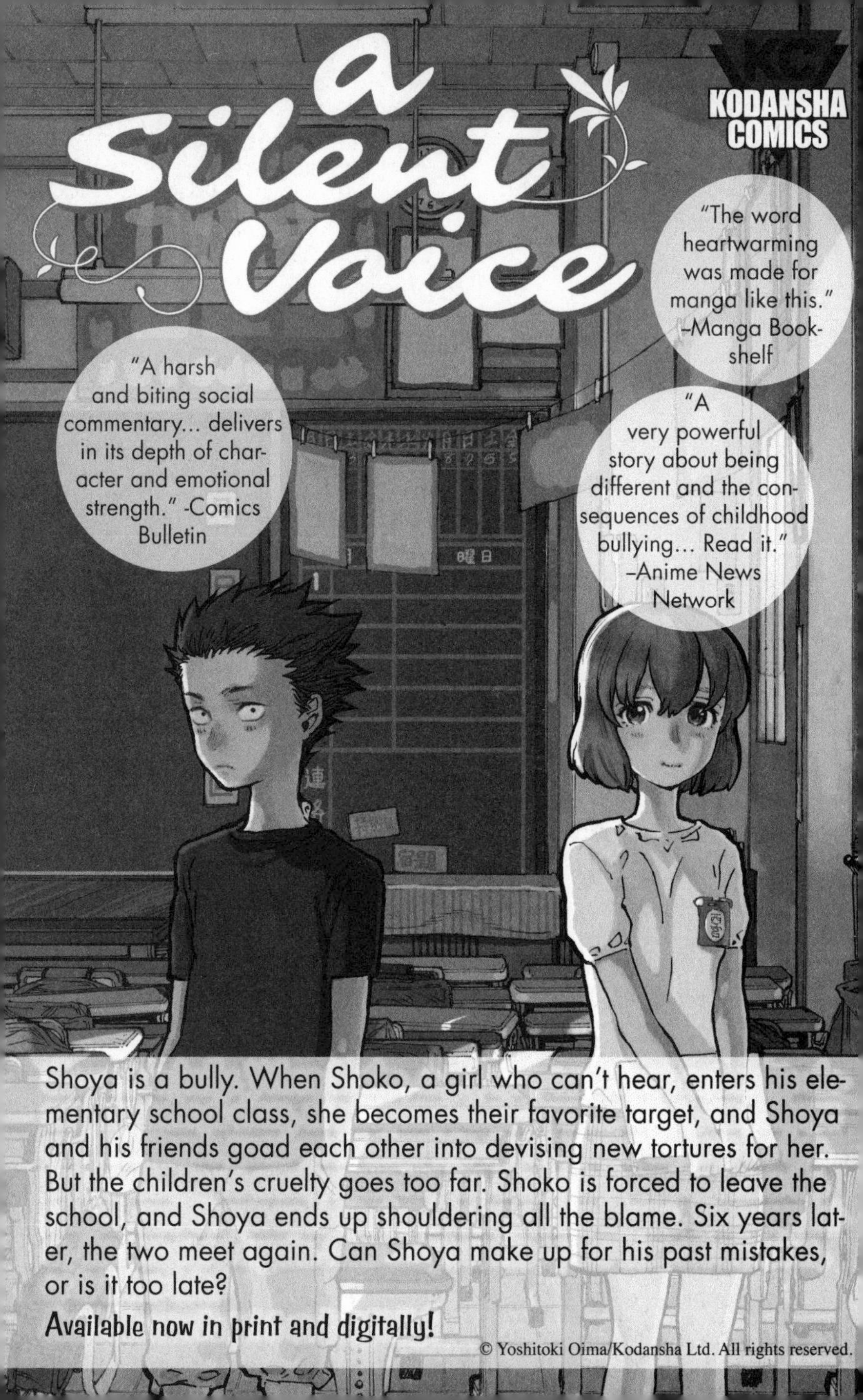
a Silent Voice
KODANSHA COMICS
"The word heartwarming was made for manga like this." –Manga Bookshelf
"A harsh and biting social commentary... delivers in its depth of character and emotional strength." -Comics Bulletin
"A very powerful story about being different and the consequences of childhood bullying… Read it." –Anime News Network
Shoya is a bully. When Shoko, a girl who can't hear, enters his elementary school class, she becomes their favorite target, and Shoya and his friends goad each other into devising new tortures for her. But the children's cruelty goes too far. Shoko is forced to leave the school, and Shoya ends up shouldering all the blame. Six years later, the two meet again. Can Shoya make up for his past mistakes, or is it too late?
Available now in print and digitally!
© Yoshitoki Oima/Kodansha Ltd. All rights reserved.

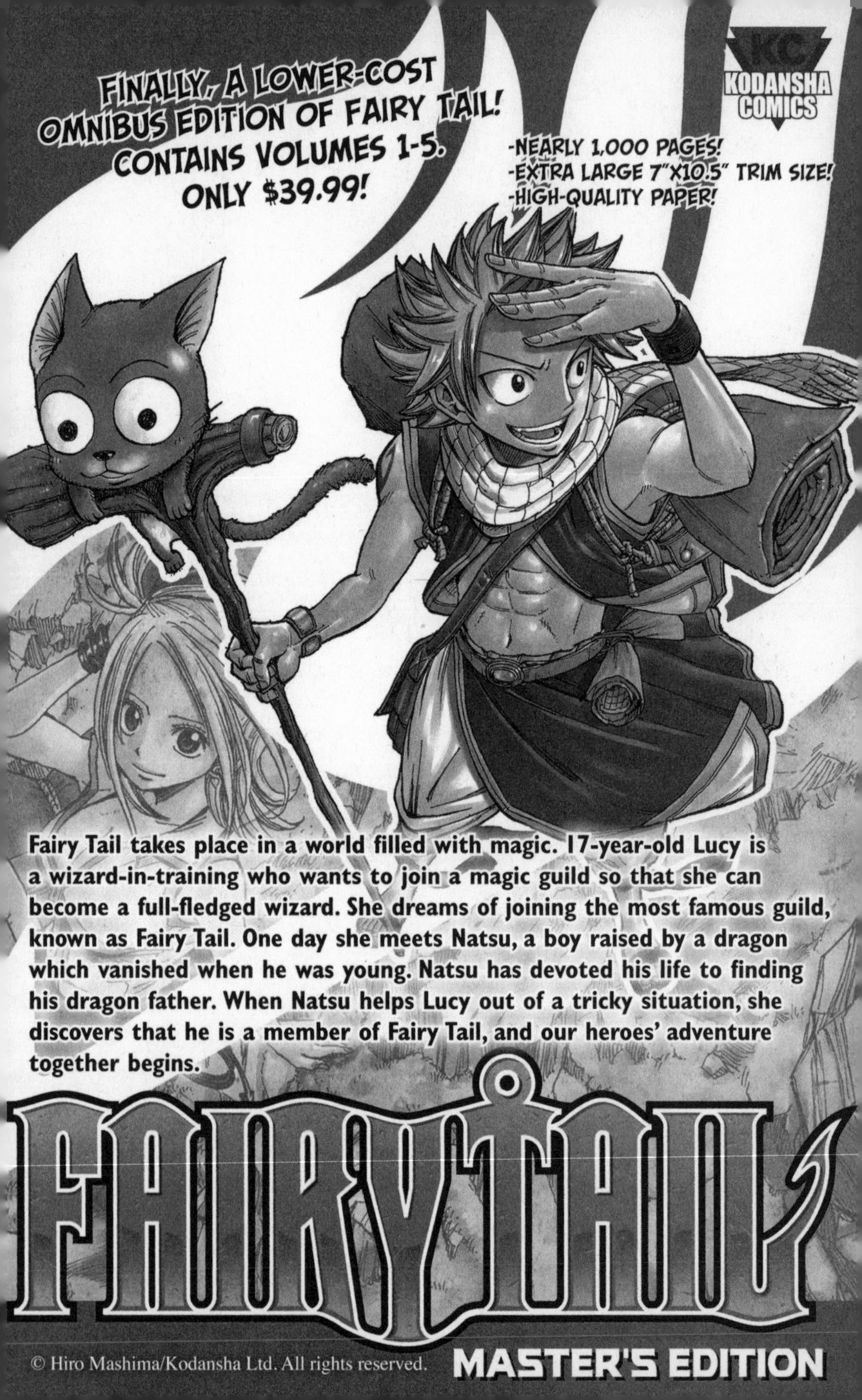
KC KODANSHA COMICS
FINALLY, A LOWER-COST OMNIBUS EDITION OF FAIRY TAIL! CONTAINS VOLUMES 1-5. ONLY $39.99!
-NEARLY 1,000 PAGES!
-EXTRA LARGE 7"X10.5" TRIM SIZE!
-HIGH-QUALITY PAPER!
Fairy Tail takes place in a world filled with magic. 17-year-old Lucy is a wizard-in-training who wants to join a magic guild so that she can become a full-fledged wizard. She dreams of joining the most famous guild, known as Fairy Tail. One day she meets Natsu, a boy raised by a dragon which vanished when he was young. Natsu has devoted his life to finding his dragon father. When Natsu helps Lucy out of a tricky situation, she discovers that he is a member of Fairy Tail, and our heroes' adventure together begins.
FAIRY TAIL
© Hiro Mashima/Kodansha Ltd. All rights reserved.
MASTER'S EDITION

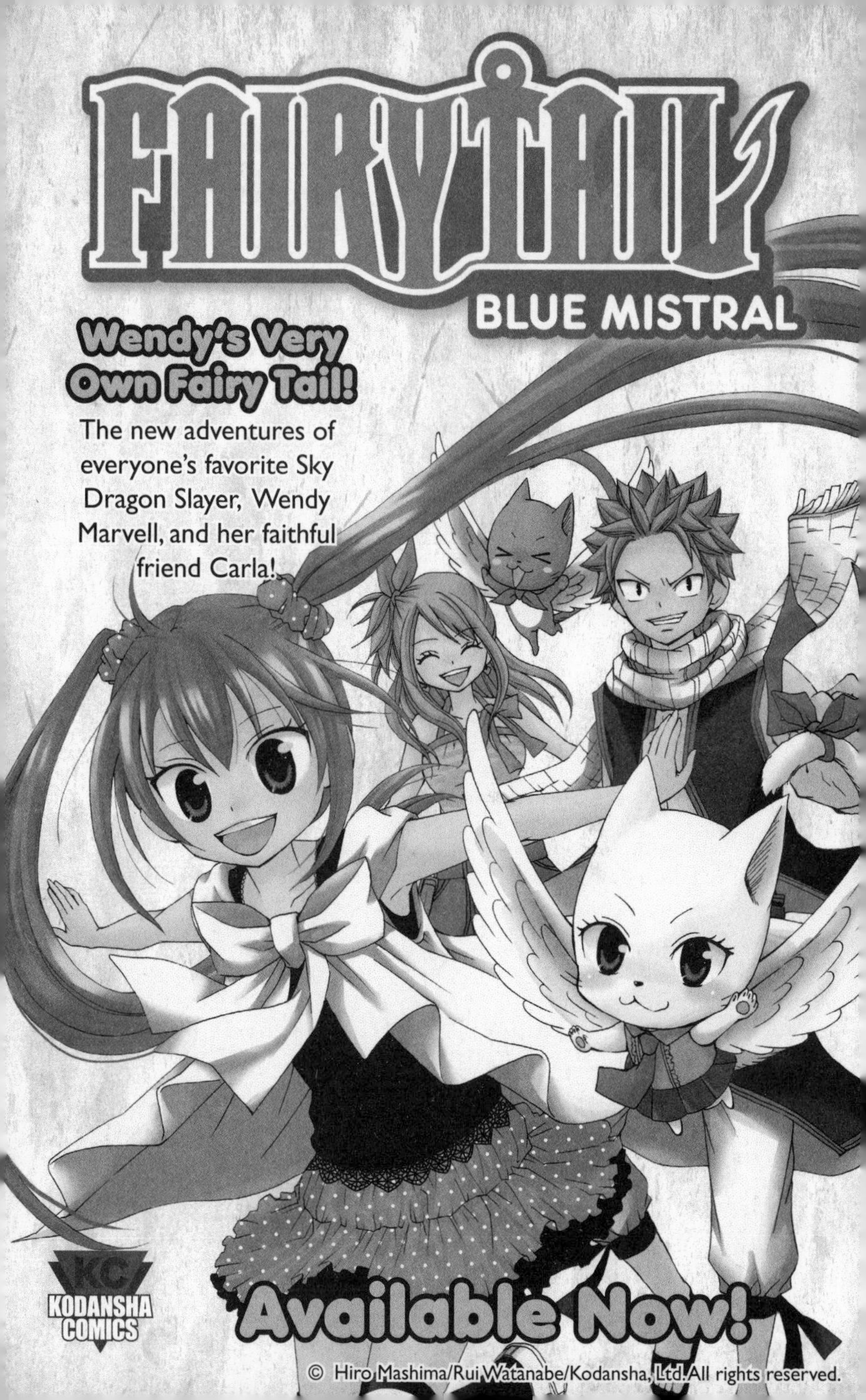
FAIRY TAIL
BLUE MISTRAL
Wendy's Very Own Fairy Tail!
The new adventures of everyone's favorite Sky Dragon Slayer, Wendy Marvell, and her faithful friend Carla!
KC
KODANSHA COMICS
Available Now!
© Hiro Mashima/Rui Watanabe/Kodansha, Ltd. All rights reserved.

*That Wolf-Boy is Mine!* volume 3 is a work of fiction. Names, characters, places, and incidents are the products of the author's imagination or are used fictitiously. Any resemblance to actual events, locales, or persons, living or dead, is entirely coincidental.

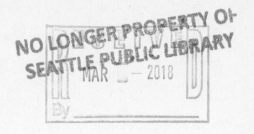

A Kodansha Comics Trade Paperback Original


Published in the United States by Kodansha Comics, an imprint of Kodansha USA Publishing, LLC, New York.

Publication rights for this English edition arranged through Kodansha Ltd, Tokyo.

ISBN 978-1-63236-375-6

Printed in the United States of America.

www.kodanshacomics.com

9 8 7 6 5 4 3 2 1
Translation: Alethea and Athena Nibley
Lettering: Sara Linsley
Editing: Haruko Hashimoto
Kodansha Comics edition cover design by Phil Balsman